THE EMPERORS OF CHOCOLAT

JOËL GLENN BRENNER

The Emperors of Chocolate

Inside the Secret World of

HERSHEY AND MARS

RANDOM HOUSE NEW YORK

Portions of this work were originally published
in different form in *The Washington Post*.

Grateful acknowledgment is made to Alfred A. Knopf, Inc., and David
Higham Associates for permission to reprint excerpts from *Charlie
and the Chocolate Factory* by Roald Dahl. Copyright © 1964 and
renewed 1992 by Roald Dahl. Rights in the British Commonwealth
are controlled by David Higham Associates. Reprinted by permission
of Alfred A. Knopf, Inc., and David Higham Associates.

Acknowledgments of illustration sources appear on page 349.

Library of Congress Cataloging-in-Publication Data

Brenner, Joël Glenn.
The emperors of chocolate: inside the secret world
of Hershey and Mars / Joël Glenn Brenner.
p.   cm.
Includes bibliographical references and index.
ISBN 0-679-42190-4
1. Hershey Foods Corporation—History.   2. Mars, Incorporated—
History.   3. Chocolate industry—United States—History.   4. Candy
industry—United States—History.   5. Chocolate candy—United
States—Marketing—History.   6. Competition—United States—Case
studies.   7. Hershey, Milton Snavely, 1857–1945.   8. Mars, Forrest.
I. Title.
HD9200.U54H473   1999
338.7′664153′0973—dc21   98-21610

Random House website address: www.atrandom.com

Printed in the United States of America on acid-free paper

5 6 7 8 9

BOOK DESIGN BY BARBARA M. BACHMAN

FOR MARSHALL, MY SWEET

*A*ND IT WASN'T simply an ordinary enormous chocolate factory, either. It was the largest and most famous in the whole world! . . . And what a tremendous, marvelous place it was! It had huge iron gates leading in to it, and a high wall surrounding it, and smoke belching from its chimneys, and strange whizzing sounds coming from deep inside it. And outside the walls, for half a mile around in every direction, the air was scented with the heavy rich smell of melting chocolate!

Twice a day, on his way to and from school, little Charlie Bucket had to walk right past the gates of the factory. And every time he went by, he would begin to walk very, very slowly, and he would hold his nose high in the air and take long deep sniffs of the gorgeous chocolatey smell all around him.

Oh, how he loved that smell!

And oh, how he wished he could go inside the factory and see what it was like!

—ROALD DAHL,
Charlie and the Chocolate Factory

Author's Note

This book began in the summer of 1989 with a routine assignment from my editors at *The Washington Post*. The task: to write a feature story about Mars, Inc., detailing the company's response to Hershey's emergence as the nation's No. 1 candy maker. I knew nothing about the huge candy company located just outside the nation's capital. I hadn't realized Mars was a family-owned business, nor was I aware of its obsessive, secretive nature. The files on Mars in the *Post* library were as thin as candy wrappers. The patriarch of the company, Forrest Mars, Sr. (sometimes called the Howard Hughes of Candy), had granted only one press interview in his lifetime, and that was to a trade journal back in 1966. The only other contact with the media had been in 1981, when Mars invited *Washington Post* reporter Thomas W. Lippman to its M&M plant in Hackettstown, New Jersey. In an interview with Mars executive Howard L. Walker, Lippman learned a few of the fascinating secrets that had made Mars one of the most successful companies in the world.

Mars had agreed to talk with Lippman in response to a barrage of criticism launched at the company after it increased candy bar prices. Hershey Foods Corp., Mars's chief competitor, had called the price increase "unjustified," and *Forbes* magazine had attacked the "brazen" price increase as the act of a "greedy monopolist." And so the company lifted its veil of secrecy ever so slightly, in a rare attempt to justify its actions to the public. As Mars made clear, however, the interview with Lippman would be a onetime exception to the company's closed-door policy.

Thus, when I set out to learn about Mars, it was no surprise that my initial phone calls went unreturned. When I asked to speak with a company representative, the receptionist at Mars headquarters in McLean, Virginia, politely responded, "I'm sorry, we don't do that."

It took more than a year of cajoling and persuading to convince Mars officials to cooperate with me. The first break came when a source I discovered in Lippman's notes gave me the direct phone number to Mars's corporate counsel, Ed Stegemann, saying if I wanted to get to the Mars family, Stegemann was the gatekeeper. Stegemann and I had dozens of brief phone conversations. In each, he made the same basic point: *We don't talk to the press, so why do you keep calling me?* Stegemann's "cooperation" went only so far as directing me to the public relations firm of Parker/Vogelsinger, which occasionally consulted for Mars.

My lunch with Barbara Parker and Sue Vogelsinger, in the fall of 1989, was a strange experience. For more than two hours, they interviewed me, asking the kinds of questions I would normally ask of them: Where was I born? Where did I go to school? Why had I become a journalist? What was my motive in pursuing the Mars story? What, they wanted to know, was I really after?

I told them I would not write a story without Mars's cooperation— that is, I would not rely solely on the tales and rumors told by competitors and ex-employees. But I also told them I wasn't going to go away. During the months that followed, we played a game of chicken: Stegemann, Parker and Vogelsinger waited to see whether I would write my story without their help—or better yet, give up; I waited for them to realize that it was in Mars's best interest to talk to me.

Meanwhile, I called each of them, every week, to repeat my request and once again state my case. As I told Stegemann, "If you like the story, you can send out reprints and reject all future inquiries on the grounds that 'the story has already been done.' If you hate it, you can say, 'We cooperated once, and look what it got us.' "

It was January 1990 when Stegemann called my office and invited me to Mars's headquarters for lunch. Over sandwiches from the deli—which Mars associates facetiously refer to as the "executive dining room"—I reiterated my desire to write a fair, accurate and thorough account of the Mars business. My importuning echoed the desires of many Mars executives, who believed the company had long been treated unfairly by the press and thought Mars should break its silence to correct the myths and misconceptions that had always gone unchallenged. At Stegemann's urging, the company's co-presidents, John Mars and Forrest Mars, Jr., eventually came to agree.

Over the next two years, I was given full access to the company's operations around the world. I interviewed more than 150 people intimately involved with the company, from newly hired associates in

Prague to company scientists in England and thirty-year veterans in McLean. I toured dozens of offices and factories in the United States, England, France, Germany, Denmark, Norway, the Netherlands and Czechoslovakia. I was given access to the Mars family's personal archives and the company library, and allowed to interview—for the first time ever—John and Forrest Jr., who run the company today.

I found a world as peculiar as that depicted in the Roald Dahl fantasy *Charlie and the Chocolate Factory.* The company bears the indelible mark of its patriarch, Forrest Mars, Sr., whose idiosyncratic management philosophy has helped Mars become one of the most productive and profitable privately owned companies in the world. The resulting story in *The Washington Post Magazine* attracted national attention and won several awards. It also outraged the Mars family, who promptly closed their doors to me and haven't spoken to a reporter since.

But this was just the beginning of what I discovered on my journey into America's candy companies. In my reporting on Mars, I discovered a fact that puzzled and intrigued me. It seemed that Mars's best-selling candy, M&M's, had actually been developed in a cooperative venture between Mars and its archrival, Hershey. No one at Mars provided any details, except to say that one of the *M*s in M&M stood for R. Bruce Murrie, the son of Hershey's longtime president. I knew that somewhere in the tangled relationship between Mars and Hershey lay the true story of both companies, and I knew that it would take a book to tell the remarkable tale of America's great chocolate empires.

I spent much of the next two years in Hershey, Pennsylvania, trying to learn as much about Milton Hershey's legacy as I had about Forrest Mars's. Although Hershey stock is publicly traded, the company is almost as secretive as Mars. In fact, John Long, Hershey's director of corporate communications, cited the competition with its privately held nemesis as the primary reason for Hershey's furtiveness. "They don't talk a lot about their business," said Long. "Why should we?"

Hershey refused to permit interviews with current personnel, apart from a one-hour interview with CEO Kenneth Wolfe. All other questions were directed to former CEO Richard Zimmerman and to the Hershey Community Archives, administered by Pamela Whitenack—an employee not of Hershey Foods but of the M.S. Hershey Foundation. The history of Hershey detailed here is based largely on Whitenack's archival collection and on my own interviews with more than fifty former Hershey employees. Dozens of others still associated with the company also agreed to talk, providing their identities were kept confidential.

Of course, there is an industry beyond the two behemoths, and I also visited many smaller competitors, from Ferrara Pan Candy Co. and Tootsie Roll Industries, Inc., to Henry Heide Candies, Inc., and Brooklyn's JoMart Candies. I talked to food brokers and cocoa merchants and chocolate historians, and gained a new perspective by doing several freelance assignments for the PR firm that represented the National Confectioners Association. I interviewed nutritionists and botanists, food chemists and famous chefs, and even attended "chocolate school," an annual two-week seminar at the University of Wisconsin, where industry workers learn the science behind chocolate and candy manufacturing. I heard stories of industrial spies and paranoid executives, legends about the mystical powers of chocolate and tales of corporate competitiveness that put the cola wars to shame. It was a story as rich and compelling as chocolate itself.

But as I researched, it was not the business strategies or product innovations or hidden secrets that kept my attention; it was the extraordinary characters behind the candy bars we take for granted. Milton Hershey, it turned out, was every bit as captivating a personality as Forrest Mars, Sr. Both men were driven by fantastical dreams: Mars by dreams of empire, and Hershey by dreams of utopia. Hershey wanted to create not just a company but an industrial paradise, and after making an immense fortune he promptly gave it all away. Few realize that the Mars family is one of the wealthiest in the world, but even fewer know that Hershey profits support the world's richest orphanage.

These two emperors of chocolate stand for something important in American business history: innovation and imagination and individuality. They built empires from dreams, and those empires continue to beguile and enchant us, and make our mouths water.

CONTENTS

THE EMPERORS OF CHOCOLATE

HERSHEY AND MARS BOTH SUPPLIED U.S. TROOPS WITH CANDY DURING WORLD WAR II, TRUMPETING THEIR EFFORTS IN PROMOTIONS ON THE HOME FRONT.

MARS, INC., FACTORY OUTSIDE AMSTERDAM, JULY 31, 1990, JUST BEFORE MIDNIGHT

*T*HEO LEENDERS HADN'T moved from his desk all day. He just sat there, stiff and silent, his eyes riveted to the sleek black telephone in front of him as if his gaze could convince it to ring. He thought the phone call would have surely come through by now. After all, three days had passed since he left his first message for Omar Sharir,[1] the twenty-seven-year-old manager of Mars's Middle East operations. Sharir, a marketing man and fresh recruit Leenders had sent to the region only six weeks earlier, was supposed to be living at the SAS Hotel in Kuwait City while looking for permanent housing and becoming familiar with the sales territory. But no one at the SAS had seen him for days.

Leenders had left a half-dozen messages with the hotel operator and had even sent the SAS manager to check Sharir's room, but nothing seemed out of place. Nevertheless, Leenders was worried. Sharir was green and arrogant. Born in Egypt, he spoke fluent Arabic though he had lived most of his life in London. Leenders knew Sharir was a savvy sales-man, but he wasn't sure the freshman was ready for a big assignment like Kuwait, where he was to oversee and expand the company's Persian Gulf business. Forrest Mars, Sr., the now-retired patriarch of the Mars empire, seeded this territory in the late 1960s, hiring locals to distribute M&M's, Snickers bars and Uncle Ben's rice to Arab shopkeepers. Now, some twenty years after the Old Man sold his first chocolate bar in the desert, the gulf region accounted for more than $40 million in sales annually,[2] with Kuwait and Saudi Arabia the leading markets.

Sharir's job was to keep it that way.

His first priority: to convince Kuwaiti merchants to devote precious store space to a new candy bar display, specially designed by Mars engi-neers. The new display case looked like any ordinary shelf unit, but it was refrigerated, allowing merchants to prominently display Mars chocolates in the heat of the day while the competition's candy stayed buried in the freezer in the back of the store—a distinct advantage for Mars. Sharir was supposed to persuade shopkeepers to make room for the new units by proving that sales of Mars products would be more profitable than sales of chips or sundries, which already crowded the shelves. Sharir was expected to report on his progress daily, but he hadn't called Leenders in Amsterdam since the previous week.

Now, at 2 A.M. local time, Leenders was giving up hope. If Sharir didn't reach him by late morning, he would have to call Mars headquar-ters in McLean, Virginia, and report the young man's disappearance. The thought made him cringe, like he'd eaten a piece of sour candy.

NEXT DAY, MCLEAN HEADQUARTERS,
JUST OUTSIDE WASHINGTON, D.C.

Edward J. Stegemann was worried and everybody knew it. The finesse and poise that were typical of the well-dressed corporate attorney had vanished in a frenzy of scowling and pacing and barking.

"Damn it," he yelled across the open office, his remark aimed at no one in particular and, at the same time, at everyone in the room. "Shit."

For three weeks now, Stegemann had closely monitored the growing political crisis in the Persian Gulf. On July 17, when Iraqi president

Saddam Hussein gave his "Revolution Day" speech, a rousing oratory peppered with attacks on neighboring Kuwait, Stegemann received a personal translation of Hussein's fiery prose from the intelligence unit at Mars Electronics, a division of the company that, among other things, gathers information on political activities around the world that might affect Mars operations. While Hussein's verbal assault piqued Stegemann's interest, he wasn't deeply disturbed by it; Hussein was known to be a hotheaded fanatic, and Stegemann, like most of the world, had regarded the speech as bluster.

It wasn't until July 24—when two Iraqi armored divisions massed on the Kuwait border—that Stegemann became concerned enough to telephone friends at the State Department to get the inside track on the Iraqi dictator's intentions. Stegemann reminded his contacts—men he knew from his previous career as a U.S. intelligence agent[3]—that Mars had a rapidly expanding business in the Persian Gulf. The company, he said, would do whatever was necessary to protect its investment in the region, which included two full-time Mars executives, a state-of-the-art distribution warehouse in the free port of Jebel Dhanna in the United Arab Emirates and an extensive network of local candy brokers who distributed Mars products in six gulf states.

If trouble was brewing, he told his State Department sources, he needed to know.

But Stegemann's contacts had informed him, just as the government had informed the media, that there was no cause for concern. The Iraqi president promised he would never attack Kuwait, and on July 25, Hussein had personally told the U.S. ambassador to Iraq that the border tanks were meant only to intimidate.

Based on these assurances, Stegemann had advised the owners and CEOs of Mars, Inc.—John Mars and his older brother, Forrest Mars, Jr.—to proceed with business as usual. The brothers did not order Mars personnel to leave the gulf region; just the opposite, additional Mars managers were flying to Saudi Arabia from London right now for a regularly scheduled meeting on marketing strategy for the coming fall season. The team would arrive in Riyadh, the capital of Saudi Arabia, in a matter of hours, just after Stegemann received word from Leenders that Sharir was missing.

"Christ," Stegemann moaned into the telephone as he listened to Leenders's report. "This is just great."

"I'll keep trying to reach him," Leenders assured the corporate counsel in McLean. "I'll send a distributor to look for him."

"You do that," Stegemann barked. "Now!"

But less than twenty-four hours after Stegemann ordered the search for Sharir, Saddam Hussein did the unthinkable, sending his troops to invade Kuwait. Without hesitation, the United Nations Security Council and President George Bush denounced the invasion and demanded the immediate, unconditional withdrawal of Iraqi forces. The United States froze Iraqi and Kuwaiti assets and banned all trade and financial relations with Hussein. On August 3, Iraq said it would withdraw troops from Kuwait within two days, but when the deadline came, hundreds of Westerners were detained in Kuwait City or taken to Baghdad instead. No one knew if Sharir was among them.

"We phoned and phoned, and he never returned our calls," Leenders said. "Finally, SAS International told us he was gone. He had left the hotel. We said, 'Bloody hell, where is he?' That was the hotel where all the internationals were staying . . . but he wasn't there."

Leenders called the Egyptian secret police, hoping they might help in the search as Sharir was an Egyptian citizen. He also sent telegrams directly to Baghdad demanding Iraq release all international citizens from Kuwait, which on August 8 was "annexed" by its Iraqi invaders. Leenders pleaded with the British Embassy, the American Embassy and the Egyptian Embassy for news of his missing colleague. But for four weeks, there was no word. Not a message or a rumor. Nothing.

Mike Davies couldn't imagine what had happened to Sharir, but he didn't have much time to think about it. What began for him as a regularly scheduled marketing meeting in Riyadh had turned into a nightmarish effort to save Mars's Middle East operations from collapse. All channels leading into the gulf had been blocked by the U.S. Navy; communication with anyone in Kuwait was impossible for those not in the military; journalists from around the world were swarming around the King James Hotel, where Davies and the other Mars managers were staying, making it impossible for the Mars executives to send even a simple fax to McLean because the machines were so jammed. It was a circus that threatened the entire business.

If Mars couldn't get its products into the region and distribute them as usual, the record-breaking sales year that Davies had envisioned would be lost. What's more, the company's relationships with local shopkeepers and candy brokers, carefully cultivated over decades, could be severely damaged. That would make it impossible for Davies to expand Mars sales in the future. And that could ultimately cost Davies his job.

"Saudi was fifty percent of the business; Kuwait was twenty-five percent," Davies recalled. "We had to turn the whole thing into an opportunity or else."

As Iraqi troops prepared for a showdown, marching closer and closer to the Saudi border, Davies and the rest of the London team hurriedly set up a crisis management center in a conference room of the King James. The posh, European-style hotel was quickly becoming a headquarters for every major media outlet in the world, including CNN, which was mesmerizing America with its frontline, twenty-four-hour coverage of the events unfolding in the gulf.

But the men from Mars were oblivious to all of this; their mission, as spelled out by headquarters, was to protect the Mars franchise—to sell Mars bars, Milky Ways, Starburst Fruit Chews and Uncle Ben's rice to anyone who could possibly use the products during the standoff.

In just a few days, Davies and his team plotted a new marketing campaign aimed at increasing Mars sales throughout the region. They code-named the operation "SuperSavers," and Davies personally traveled to Bahrain, Qatar and the UAE to launch the program.

"We told the trade [distributors and shopkeepers], 'We know times are tough, the future is uncertain, but our products are the market leaders in their category.

" 'You know that if you buy our products you can sell them quickly— you don't have to tie up your money in inventory you can't sell. . . . We, as a company, are prepared to stick by you. We are here for the duration, and we won't abandon you in this time of crisis.' "

Other than the pitch, the program was basic: special rebates, coupons and price breaks to merchants. For example, a 10 percent discount on the invoice price of Uncle Ben's or a free case of candy bars for every ten cases purchased.

As sales orders rolled in, Davies next turned his attention to the military, where the big bucks were at stake.

Mars products were necessary foodstuffs, critical in a time of war, he told the U.S. Army Command Center, which was overseeing the flow of hundreds of warships, aircraft carriers, supply barges and troop carriers to the gulf. Candy bars might seem secondary to B-1 bombers and Black Hawk helicopters, but, Davies told the generals, "Snickers bars are just as necessary as weaponry." After all, none of the countries participating in Operation Desert Shield, as the initial maneuvers came to be known, had time to establish supply lines before sending troops to the region. Mars was the only company to operate an air-conditioned distribution warehouse and control an enormous fleet of refrigerated supply trucks, a boon to the troops who were being scattered throughout the 400,000 square miles of Saudi Desert.

Overnight, Mars received permission to continue shipping its products, and as President Bush drew a line in the sand and authorized the first call-up of military reserves in more than two decades, Mars began loading candy bars, instant rice and ice cream onto barges headed for Jebel Dhanna.

"We were supplying both the U.S. and the British military, and the Saudis," said Davies. "We were one of the only companies—if not *the* only company—where the U.S. military came and actually inspected our warehousing facilities and checked it all out and qualified us as an authorized supplier."

But, for Mars, the real war had only just begun.

It was Hershey Foods Corp.—not Mars—that held the prestigious reputation for serving as the U.S. military's chief candy maker. Although Mars worked closely with the U.S. Army in the early 1940s, placing M&M's in C rations during World War II, Hershey's relationship with the Pentagon extended back more than eighty years.

The maker of America's best-known candy bar—and Mars's archenemy—first supplied candy to U.S. soldiers in 1914 at the outbreak of World War I. After the war was over, the company's chemists and food technologists continued to work closely with the U.S. quartermaster general to develop high-energy chocolate rations that could sustain the GIs when they had nothing else to eat. The result was the famous Field Ration D, a nutrition-packed "subsistence" chocolate made from a thick paste of chocolate liquor, sugar, oat flour, powdered milk and vitamins. Although the bar tasted nothing like a typical Hershey bar, it could withstand temperatures of up to 120 degrees Fahrenheit and contained 600 calories in a single serving. The bar was the first to be sealed in cellophane to keep it fresh; it was protected from heat and humidity by a brown cardboard box coated with wax. The entire package could be immersed in water for an hour and remain unspoiled, just as government regulations required.[4]

In 1942, when the United States entered the war against Germany and Japan, the military ordered Hershey to commence full-scale production of the new ration bar, and for the next four years the Hershey plant operated around the clock, seven days a week, churning out half a million Ration D bars per shift. At the time, the factory was considered the most modern chocolate manufacturing facility in the nation. The plant was so efficient it supplied nearly every candy company in the country—including Mars—with chocolate to manufacture candy bars.

"When you ate Snickers or M&M's in those days, you were eating Hershey's chocolate," boasts Hershey archivist Pamela Whitenack. "It might have been a Mars candy bar, but it was *our* chocolate that made it taste so good."

By Hershey's estimate, the 1.5-million-square-foot plant provided more than 75 percent of the nation's eating chocolate. The factory was the only one in the United States equipped with continuous cocoa bean roasters, industrial-sized mixers, automatic molding machines, wrapping machines and partly automated packaging equipment. None of this machinery, however, helped much when it came to producing the Ration D, as any old-timer in Hershey will tell you.

"It was like clay when we got it from the mixing room," remembers Leonard Hoffman, who worked on the production line. "You had to shovel it into huge bread dough mixers and cool it down, then it became more like putty.

"God knows what all was in that bar—I happened to find out the hard way how nourishing it was. When I was cooling it, I would reach into the mixer and make a little ball about the size of a marble and put it in my mouth. Funny, I was never hungry—used to take my lunch home with me every day."

Philomena Castelli, one of hundreds of women who kept the Hershey plant running during the war, recalls the physical strength required to keep the line running smoothly: "That bar could kill you if you weren't careful. It got stuck to the molds and the rest of the machinery, and you had to go in there with your hands and dig it out. But we did it because we knew the GIs needed chocolate. They needed Hershey to win the war."

Castelli and others of her generation still talk of the day in 1942 when the quartermaster general himself came to Hershey to present the company with the military's highest award for civilian contributions to victory. Every Hershey worker received a pin commemorating the award. Castelli still wears hers, a tiny gold-toned *E* for Excellence.

By the time the war was over, Hershey had earned four more military citations and had supplied more than one billion rations to U.S. soldiers—a feat that turned Hershey into a household name. From 1945 on, the Hershey brand was synonymous with chocolate to the U.S. consumer. Purchasing a Hershey bar became as patriotic as reciting the Pledge of Allegiance. The candy was as American as baseball, as popular as the Fourth of July.

Of course, Hershey products had gained national attention even before the war. With much fanfare, Hershey bars were carried to the Antarctic in 1928 and again in 1932 by adventurer Admiral Richard Byrd, who subsisted on the candy as he led the first expeditions through the frozen tundra. But it was WWII that made Hershey famous around the world—and that established the company as the military's chief candy supplier, a position Hershey was ill-prepared to give up.

So, as the battleships *Wisconsin* and *Missouri* steamed toward the Persian Gulf in the fall of 1990, Hershey chairman and CEO Richard A. Zimmerman ordered his chemists to determine whether full-scale production of a new ration bar would be possible. Code-named, appropriately, the Desert Bar, the new candy was to be Hershey's contribution to troop morale, a familiar taste of home amid the scorching Saudi dunes.

The Desert Bar, Hershey declared, was a tremendous advance over the Ration D, which had served the military through the 1970s. It tasted just like an original Hershey bar but could withstand temperatures up to 140 degrees Fahrenheit. Instead of liquefying in the heat, the Desert Bar turned soft and fudgy, a breakthrough in chocolate technology that took decades of intense research to perfect.

Zimmerman boasted that except for egg whites—which were used to help alter the melting point of the chocolate—the Desert Bar contained the same ingredients as a piece of ordinary candy. "That's why you cannot notice a real difference in the taste," he explained. But he refused to say anything more about how the bar actually withstood the heat.

"That is our secret," he told the Associated Press. "It's a special technology that we simply cannot share."

$\mathcal{N}$ot that it is difficult to produce a non-melting chocolate; Hershey had solved that riddle long ago by simply replacing the cocoa butter in the Ration D with a fat that could withstand extremely high temperatures. The problem was that the substitute fats always made the chocolate taste terrible, like eating a mixture of wax and chalk.

Chemically speaking, what makes chocolate so unique and irresistible is that its melting point is slightly below body temperature. Hold a chocolate bar in the palm of your hand and it becomes a gooey mess. But place it on your tongue, and instantly, you're overwhelmed with mouthwatering delight. That's because the cocoa butter dissolves first and distributes the rest of the chocolate ingredients over the taste buds in quick succession, starting with the sugar. Remove the cocoa butter and the entire eating experience is altered.

The puzzle for Hershey and the rest of the industry was how to preserve the quality of real chocolate while still protecting the candy from the devastating effects of the sun. The payoff for such a discovery was potentially enormous, since some 30 percent of the Earth is plagued by high temperatures year-round, and at any given time, one-quarter of the rest is sweltering in summer heat.

Before the advent of air-conditioning, chocolate manufacturers could not even conceive of selling chocolate bars in climates such as these. When temperatures climbed above 78 degrees Fahrenheit, the melting point of cocoa butter, Hershey, Mars, Nestlé and others simply shut their doors and halted production until the return of cooler weather. Selling candy in the Saudi Desert was completely out of the question. When Willis Carrier invented the dehumidifying system that made modern air-conditioning possible, he forever changed the way chocolatiers did business, opening up markets around the globe. But even he couldn't solve all of the manufacturers' problems. Every year, tens of millions of dollars in chocolate products are ruined because of electrical outages, coolant failures and penny-pinching shopkeepers who refuse to keep their cooling systems running through the night. In the Third World, where air-conditioning is rare, chocolate is as scarce as ever.

But if a manufacturer could overcome these barriers, billions of dollars in new candy bar sales would be there for the taking. Hershey and other chocolate makers salivated at the thought.

During the 1980s, the industry poured millions of dollars into cocoa butter research. Chocolate manufacturers endlessly tested new fat compounds and fiddled with new fat combinations. They studied how fats delivered the flavors in a chocolate bar and experimented with hundreds of different methods of altering the melting point of the cocoa butter itself. Many scientists believed the answer was hidden inside the cocoa bean, the source of cocoa butter and the intense liquid chocolate "liquor." Still others were devoted to the theory that some outside component, a fake fat or some other ingredient, was required to solve the riddle.

In 1987, the first breakthrough came, not from a chocolate manufacturer, but from a small research firm in Morris Plains, New Jersey, called Food-Tek, Inc.[5] The company's president, Gil Finkel, was a pioneer of chewy cookies and strudel, and he had been working on a nonmelting chocolate recipe for almost a decade. His patent was the first to involve technology that rearranged the molecular structure of the cocoa butter to make it more stable. But critics complained that Finkel's chocolate still tasted like paraffin, and although he managed to license the invention to firms in Japan, Europe and the United States, the only result was a minor product in Southeast Asia.

The following year, scientists at the Battelle Memorial Research Institute in Switzerland followed up Finkel's discovery with one of their own, announcing in May 1988 that seven years of research had culminated in "a chocolate that not only doesn't melt in your hand, it hardly melts anywhere else."[6]

A spokesman for the institute, which conducts research in commercial fields for itself and for a variety of clients, declared that the new chocolate tasted just like real milk chocolate and could withstand temperatures up to 100 degrees Fahrenheit.

"For the average consumer, the difference is not noticeable in the mouth," said Battelle's William McComis the day the discovery was made public. "Only a chocolate connoisseur might notice that it melts slower."[7]

Despite those claims, Hershey scientists publicly pooh-poohed Battelle's development, which involved rearranging the fat molecules in the cocoa butter to make it heat resistant. A spokesman for Hershey said of Battelle's discovery: "We've been checking out similar technology for years, and it just doesn't satisfy our concerns for quality."[8] Others in the industry, including Mars, also downplayed the announcement, saying Battelle's chocolate could never measure up to the real thing.

But privately, chocolate manufacturers around the globe were reeling from the news.

According to a former scientist at Battelle's U.S. headquarters in Columbus, Ohio, the day *The New York Times* ran a story about the discovery, the phones never stopped ringing.

"Everyone wanted a piece of it," said the scientist, who asked not to be identified for fear of being blacklisted by the industry. "The competition got very ugly."

As firms frantically negotiated to license Battelle's technology, a black market for information about the discovery quickly emerged.

"The rumors were flying," recalled the scientist. "How did we do this? What was the new twist? Did it really taste like chocolate? Everyone wanted to know.

"There were all kinds of stories floating around about how we had manufactured it, the chemicals we used, the processes we had perfected. I remember being cornered at a research convention in Geneva by guys from Mars and Hershey who were firing questions left and right. Somebody even showed me a Xeroxed report of what was supposed to be the secret to our discovery. I was blown away.

"Of course, none of it was true, but I think a lot of people spent an awful lot of time and money trying to chase down the rumors and duplicate our success."

Tension in the industry mounted as firms tried to figure out who had access to the technology and who did not. Some companies, like Nestlé, decided not to join the race, believing that heat-stable products were of limited value because no matter how "real" they tasted, they would never have the "mouthfeel" of an original chocolate bar.

But Hershey's management strongly disagreed. If the chocolate tasted good enough, they believed there was a solid market for it, especially in the southern half of the United States, where chocolate consumption has always lagged behind the rest of the nation. If nothing else, Hershey marketers thought, the product had potential for use in the military, a prospect that could prove extremely lucrative in the long run. So, secretly, a team of Hershey scientists joined with Battelle's researchers. By the fall of 1990, just as the buildup of troops in the Persian Gulf began, they were ready to test their creation.

As U.S. military troops gathered strength at the border with Kuwait, Hershey blitzkrieged the media back home with news of its breakthrough. In a not-so-subtle jab at Mars, Hershey's press releases, news conferences and radio announcements all hailed the company's triumph over the elements by "developing a candy bar that melts in your mouth, not in the sand." In December 1990, just before the ground war erupted, Hershey shipped 144,000 of the one-ounce milk-chocolate bars to the troops free of charge, making the evening news all across the country. In the following weeks, pictures of soldiers eating the candy bars showed up in *Life, People* and *Newsweek* magazines. Small-town newspapers even went so far as to include testimonials from soldiers who had tasted the bars in their "news from the war zone" columns.

"The media was just eating this up," remembers Lisbeth Echeandia, publisher of *Confectioner* magazine, a prominent industry journal. "To have a candy bar receive this much press attention was absolutely unheard of, a real coup."

By the time Hershey shipped another 750,000 bars to the gulf in February, the Desert Bar was being trumpeted on the home front as a real war hero, the perfect boost for the bored and homesick soldier.

On the front lines, however, it was an entirely different story.

From the port of Jebel Dhanna in the UAE, Mars was commanding the supply of candy to the gulf forces, with Davies and his salesmen going to extremes to protect the company's distribution lines.

While businesses worldwide were pulling their executives out of the region, Davies and a handful of other Mars workers "volunteered"—in typical Mars fashion—to remain in the gulf throughout the conflict. (They were never specifically required to make this sacrifice; the corporate culture simply left them little choice.)

Explained Davies: "We wanted to ensure that our products cleared the ports and got distributed throughout the region. We felt that the only way to do that was to stick around." Or get fired.

Apparently, Omar Sharir agreed. Although his colleagues at Mars feared they would never again hear from the company's Kuwait representative, five weeks after disappearing from Kuwait City Sharir surfaced in Jordan, a bit shaken but in good health. The young businessman told Davies he had decided to escape as soon as he heard that Iraqi troops had assembled at the border. For more than a week, he hid in a basement in Kuwait City. After Iraqi troops overran the country, he disguised himself as an Arab bedouin and traveled 350 miles to Baghdad, straight into enemy territory, so as not to arouse suspicion. Armed with his Egyptian passport, he then made his way to Jordan, where he stayed with a childhood friend until it was safe to travel to Riyadh and rejoin the Mars team.

The result of efforts like Sharir's were clear. On Thanksgiving Day 1990, frozen Snickers bars nestled against the turkey and reconstituted mashed potatoes on every U.S. soldier's plate. Mars products were available at every military Post Exchange, while Hershey products were nowhere to be found.[9]

"I know Hershey made a big song and dance about their desert product, and I've actually seen one and tasted one and had a look at it," said Davies. "But I had everyone searching Saudi Arabia for it, and we never found one."

Quietly, Mars had actually been supplying the troops with its own heat-resistant products—M&M's and Galaxy Block Chocolate—which were being manufactured in Mars factories in Australia and England. Although Mars's formula for these chocolates differed slightly from Hershey's, the products were based on the same technology developed by Battelle.

"The troops loved 'em," said Davies. "They were eating our heat-resistant M&M's faster than we could ship 'em."

Eventually, news of the competing products reached Hershey, Pennsylvania, where CEO Richard Zimmerman was working frantically to secure business from the military. In a last-ditch effort to earn the Pentagon's loyalty, Zimmerman decided in the summer of 1991 to switch combat zones: On Memorial Day weekend, Hershey rolled out the Desert Bar to the American public, seizing on the patriotic zeal that had overcome the country. Cases of Desert Bars flooded the nation's supermarkets and drugstores, where Americans eager to support the troops snatched them up.

"It was a novelty," noted Echeandia. "Everybody wanted to test it to see if it would melt. It got Hershey a lot of notice, although it never became a really big seller."

But while Hershey was clearly winning the PR war at home, it was Mars that had captured the attention of the U.S. brass. When the Pentagon called for bids on a contract for 6.9 million non-melting chocolate bars in August 1991, Mars won the business.

Just days after the contract was awarded, however, the U.S. General Accounting Office (GAO) suspended it. Hershey, it seemed, was not ready to surrender.

$\mathcal{A}$s Paul Lieberman read through the inches-thick file that had landed on his desk earlier that morning, it was all he could do to keep from laughing. As an attorney for the General Accounting Office—the independent agency established by Congress to investigate waste and fraud in government—Lieberman didn't find much humor in his job. But this one had him grinning.

The military contract he was being asked to review had been awarded ten days earlier to candy giant Mars, Inc., a company Lieberman knew very little about. He hadn't realized Mars was a local firm, headquartered just twenty minutes from his office near the U.S. Capitol, nor had he ever paid particular attention to the heated rivalry between Mars and Hershey. So he was more than a little amused by the voluminous protest filed that morning by three of Washington's highest-paid attorneys on behalf of Hershey and its Desert Bar.[10]

According to the filing, the Pentagon had hired Mars to produce heat-resistant chocolate bars for 18 cents apiece. The total cost of the contract was a mere $1.2 million—trivial by Pentagon standards and an amount that would normally stir little controversy.

"Usually, when we get these appeals, it's for the big money," explained Lieberman. "A contract of this size just isn't worth a big fight."

But Hershey executives felt differently. Outraged at losing the bid and certain Mars had cheated to win it, they accused Mars of making its chocolate bars with excessive amounts of lactose—a sugar found in milk that is permitted only in limited amounts under the Food and Drug Administration's standards for chocolate. Hershey claimed its heat-resistant candy bar met all FDA criteria; instead of extra lactose, Hershey used egg whites to stabilize the chocolate, an ingredient not specifically limited by federal standards.

Furthermore, Hershey stated, it had tested the product "believed to be the product being offered by Mars" and found that it melted at temperatures far below 140 degrees—the standard required by the military.[11]

"It couldn't stand up to the heat, and we knew it," said a researcher from Hershey. "We couldn't believe the Pentagon would let Mars get away with that."

According to Hershey's protest, Mars's bar also lacked the "mouth-feel" of a "real commercial chocolate bar." And, in summary, it was "woefully inferior" to Hershey's own product.[12]

"Bottom line, Hershey was accusing Mars of selling plastic, not chocolate," said Lieberman. "It was pretty harshly worded stuff."

*I*t didn't take long for all of Mars to get the news. The rumors had spread almost as fast as the production line at the M&M's factory could manufacture its brightly colored candies, which came tumbling off the conveyors at the rate of 12 million M&M's per hour. By the time Ed Stegemann arrived at his desk in McLean at 9 A.M., most everyone at Mars headquarters was talking angrily about Hershey's complaint. In the heated conversations taking place around the open office, even the way Mars employees spoke the name Hershey became an insult to the competition—it rolled off the tongue with an extra "sh," "Hershshey," like they were choking on it.

Everyone in the office believed that this time Hershey had gone too far. Competition between the two companies—which together control the lion's share of the $14-billion U.S. candy market[13]—was always fierce, even vicious on occasion. But now, the Mars workers agreed, Hershey had crossed the line to downright sleaze. Both companies had bid for the military contract fair and square, and Mars had won. But instead of accepting defeat graciously, Hershey was trying to steal the prize with false and malicious charges.

"This is outrageous," Stegemann fumed as he read through Hershey's protest, his face turning a deeper shade of red with each page. "Those lying SOBs."

Stegemann's frustration had been growing ever since Hershey's public relations department began working overtime to promote the Desert Bar. While the family-owned Mars company held fast to its long-standing policy of keeping its business activities quiet, Hershey had stolen headlines across the country with its version of the non-melting candy. Although hundreds of companies had fired up their production lines to help support the U.S. desert force of nearly half a million soldiers, Hershey's relentless PR ensured that on the home front, at least, the Desert Bar was the product mentioned most often—a fact that endlessly annoyed the workers at Mars.

By the time the war was over, it was Hershey—not Mars—that was the star of most newspaper articles on troop morale. And it was Hershey—not Mars—that the American public credited with supplying the soldiers with chocolate.

"We were over there working our asses off," said Stegemann, "and they were over here taking all the credit."[14]

Now, it was Mars's turn.

The normally elusive and media-shy attorney picked up the telephone and did what few Mars executives would dare: He dialed the business desk at *The Washington Post* and offered a seemingly candid twenty-minute interview on Mars's Pentagon contract.[15]

The next day, a small story appeared in the newspaper's financial pages giving Mars credit for beating Hershey in the race for the military's business. The story began: "Hershey Foods Corp. may have succeeded in selling its heat-resistant chocolate bars—better known as Desert Bars—to the public, but the Defense Department doesn't want them."

Stegemann never mentioned the pending dispute at the GAO.

$\mathscr{F}$or the next four months, the chocolate war continued to rage. At one point, Mars threatened to sue Hershey for defamation, according to one government source. Hershey, in turn, threatened to sue Mars for misrepresenting its products to the Pentagon. The war of words escalated until the GAO decided months later that the contract could not be overruled—whether Hershey's allegations were true or not—because the bidding process had been seriously flawed.

The Pentagon, it turned out, never tested Mars's chocolate to determine whether it met the contract's specifications. The initial call for bids, however, failed to require such tests, leaving Hershey without grounds for a GAO appeal.

"It was a mistake," Zimmerman said coldly. "A big mistake."[16]

Lieberman, who ultimately decided the dispute, agreed that the military handled the contract badly. But he still laughs when he thinks about the case, calling it one of the most bizarre and outlandish protests to reach his desk.

"The way Hershey was complaining, you'd have thought Mars was breaching national security by selling military secrets or something. But this contract was puny by Pentagon standards—and it was for chocolate, for goodness' sake. Chocolate.

"I mean, let me ask you: Whatever happened to Willy Wonka?"

Chapter Two

CANDY FROM STRANGERS

EACH YEAR, THE AVERAGE AMERICAN CONSUMES MORE THAN TWENTY-FIVE POUNDS OF CANDY, AND ADULTS ACTUALLY CONSUME MORE THAN CHILDREN.

ANDY. THE WORD itself is magic. A sweet invitation to childhood. To days of hide-and-seek and stickball and ABCs and sugarplums that dance like fairies in your head.

Never mind that you've never tasted a sugarplum. It's the fantasy that counts. That mystical, mesmerizing pull of licorice and lollipops, peppermints and chocolate drops. They beckon from the shelf like children from the playground, gentle reminders of a time when simply walking into a drugstore could make your mouth water.

Back then, a nickel bought a candy bar as big as a brick, and a penny filled a bag with suckers to spare. A piece of candy was more than just a treat; it was an experience. The sight of sour balls and jawbreakers, candy corn and gumdrops, and chocolate—mountains of chocolate—evoked such a sense of wonder that one could only stare at the counter daydreaming, certain of a faraway land where rivers flowed with cocoa and marshmallows hung from the trees.

Today, Tootsie Roll Industries, Inc., is the only company in America that continues to manufacture a penny-sized piece, although the midgees, or midget Tootsies, as they're called, can be purchased only in half-pound bags, retail price $1.39.

In the days when penny candy ruled the candy counter, you could tour the Tootsie Roll factory and the manufacturing centers of hundreds of other candy companies around the nation. Inside Tootsie's sprawling industrial compound, you could see mixers and grinders whip up mountains of chocolate-flavored taffy and extrude the sticky mass into a python-size Tootsie Roll. Next, gravity and machinery stretched out the giant roll, making it longer and longer and thinner and thinner, until the diameter shrank to just a quarter-inch and the roll was sliced into bite-sized pieces.

There were tours of the Hershey factory, too, where, as early as 1950, more than a million people a year gathered to see rivers of chocolate flow like waterfalls onto conveyor belts lined with cast-iron molds.[1] Inside each was stamped the name Hershey, which left its imprint on the chocolate bar so that when you threw away the wrapper, the name was still visible. In elementary school, it was thought customary to eat a Hershey Almond bar by biting the letter *H* first, and then the letter *Y*, and then the *E* and the *R,* leaving behind the *SHE*. No one knew why children nibbled the chocolate this way; they just did. Like playing hopscotch or kick ball or eating hotdogs, it was part of growing up in the U.S.A.

Sadly, most of the nation's candy factories are no longer open to outsiders. The Food and Drug Administration played its part with health regulations and concern for safety. But there was more to it than that: The candy industry—like so many others in the nation—has turned from its sweet beginnings into a bitter business.

Gone is the jolly bifocaled confectioner who delighted in watching children gobble down mouthfuls of sweets. In his place are two giant competitors, Mars and Hershey, which together control 75 percent of the candy rack.[2] In their candy kingdom, it's bar against bar—a chocolate slugfest.

Today's candy makers can't afford the openness of the old days. Manufacturers have to worry about marketing plans, production technology, advertising budgets, shelf space and takeovers. The result: Consumers in the nineties can get more information out of Dow Chemical Co. than they can out of Tootsie Roll, Hershey, Mars or any of the other 300 confectionery firms that make up America's $14-billion candy market.

Ever tried placing a telephone call to Mars, makers of Twix, Milky Way and the Snickers bar, which has ranked as the nation's favorite candy bar since the first polls were conducted in the 1970s? Calls to the company's Virginia headquarters elicit less information than calls to the Central Intelligence Agency, located just two miles away from the company's McLean office.

"Who is the president of Mars?" a caller asks.

"I'm sorry, I can't give out the names of our associates," a receptionist replies. Click.[3]

And Mars is not alone. The privately held company is squarely in the tradition of the rest of the industry, which remains dominated by family-owned firms. Many of these firms are into their third, fourth and fifth generations of ownership, unheard of in today's business world. They trace their roots back to a single founder, typically an immigrant with a family recipe and an affinity for sweets.

The story of how these firms developed and grew is one of the most fascinating in U.S. business. It is a tale of family dynasties, of entrepreneurial genius, of manufacturing brilliance and of marketing mishaps. It is also a history of America, as told through its sweet tooth.

Perhaps this story should have been shared long ago. But not in the candy business. Virtually all of the private firms in the industry, and even some of the publicly held ones, keep their operations to themselves, gladly sharing their products with the public but keeping everything else under wraps. As a result, candy has become one of the most secretive industries in the United States. Strange, really, considering there's nothing harmful in a Kit Kat or a Crunch bar, unless, of course, you're counting calories.

Nevertheless, it is impossible to get PEZ Candy, Inc., to reveal anything at all about the plastic gizmo that ejects candy bricks from the heads of Popeye, Goofy and Miss Piggy. The forty-two-year-old private company, based in Orange, Connecticut, has become a part of American pop culture, but it will reveal nothing about its business, not even who owns it. There is no spokesperson for the company, no printed information about its products and no interviews with its personnel, including President Scott McWhinnie, a Harvard-trained MBA who is as tight-lipped as they come. Oddly, inquiries to the company are sometimes directed to PEZ collectors, who, in the absence of information about PEZ, have formed their own network to share PEZ folklore.

Even Hershey, which has publicly traded stock and is required by law to share information with shareholders and potential investors, is as uncommunicative as possible. And the company, which currently ranks ahead of Mars in the U.S. market, isn't shy to admit it.

"Just because we're publicly held doesn't mean we have to talk openly about what we do," said Richard Zimmerman, who stepped down as Hershey's chairman and CEO in 1993. "Our competition is largely private, and that gives them the advantage. They don't have to say anything about their business, so why should we?"

Because of this attitude, few people outside the candy industry are aware of the intense competition among Hershey and Mars and other candy makers, although the chocolate wars have been raging since the early 1960s, when Forrest Mars, Sr., vowed to beat Hershey at its own game. It's always Coke and Pepsi that are cited by the media and the public as *the* example of industry rivalry. The press follows the cola wars as though Coke and Pepsi were players in the World Series.

In 1991, the year of the Persian Gulf crisis, *The Wall Street Journal* published no less than thirty articles on the Coke and Pepsi one-upmanship. But not a single word was written on the raging battle over the non-melting chocolate bar. Joseph Viviano, president of Hershey Chocolate, finds that a bit humorous. "We're just as bad as Coke and Pepsi—probably worse," he said. "It's just that we don't talk about it, so nobody pays any attention."

For all of the furious competition between the candy titans, both Mars and Hershey intentionally downplay the struggle because they realize it could hurt their wholesome images. They kept the Desert Bar dispute out of the press, and to this day the two companies are uncomfortable talking about the GAO appeal.[4]

"That's water under the bridge," Zimmerman said of the GAO protest. "I don't really think we need to go into that"—a common refrain in candy land.

When Hershey held a press conference in 1993 to introduce one of its newest products, Hershey's Hugs, the company led an extremely abbreviated tour of the new $50-million processing plant where Hugs were being made. The press was allowed to watch as the white- and milk-chocolate Hugs rolled off the line, but no one was permitted to see how the candies were actually being manufactured. White plastic sheets surrounded the machinery to block the view.

To learn more about Hugs, I pushed for an interview with one of the candy's creators. But Dennis Eshleman was not free to speak about how Hugs are made, repeating: "We just don't need to get into that." And the answers he did provide were closely monitored by a Hershey press officer who never left his side.

Ultimately, a worker at the plant—under condition of anonymity— shared some of the secrets to Hugs. He understood the public's appetite for such sweet details, but even he feared that by sharing the mystery, he risked losing his job.

In fact, most of the people interviewed for this book asked that their identities be protected. Most blamed their caution on strict corporate policies that forbid them from speaking to outsiders about their work, but others attributed their desire to remain anonymous to the intense competition in the industry.

"It's a real battle zone out there," said a Hershey marketing executive. "No one wants to be blamed for sharing secrets with the competition. If anyone found out I was talking to you, they'd call me a leak and want me canned. I know that sounds extreme, but in this business, you can't be too careful."

Hershey management agreed to cooperate with the writing of this book on a limited basis only. Officially, all questions were channeled through former chairman and CEO Richard Zimmerman. If Zimmerman was unable to answer, the company's press officers occasionally stepped in, but repeated requests to interview other Hershey managers were denied.[5]

Even Hershey's archivist, Pam Whitenack, whose job it is to keep the record of Milton Hershey's legacy and share it with outsiders, was reminded by Hershey Foods management not to share any confidences. (Although Whitenack is not employed by the candy company, her employer, the M. S. Hershey Foundation, is owned by the trust that holds the controlling interest in Hershey Foods.) Whitenack said Hershey Foods was extremely nervous about having a journalist rummaging through the archival collection—a collection over which the company has no direct control—and cautioned her repeatedly to be careful of what she disclosed.

"They can't tell me what to do," she said one afternoon in frustration. "This is my job, this is what the Trust pays me for, but [Hershey Foods] can't understand that."

On several occasions while working with Whitenack, I watched her own requests for information get inexplicably lost or delayed, although none of the requests seemed particularly sensitive, like the time she asked for background on the company's early advertising campaigns. Trying to explain the hypersensitivity to such topics, she said: "[Hershey Foods is] so obsessed with their image and with the fact that Mars is so private, they just get paranoid. . . . Everything is treated like a secret over there. Everything."

Because its stock is traded on the New York Stock Exchange, Hershey is forced to disclose information deemed material to its stock price, like its quarterly financial performance, its changes in management, fluctuations in ingredient costs or other matters likely to affect an investor's decision to buy Hershey shares. But outside of that, the company is mum.

"Trying to get an interview with Hershey is almost as bad as trying to get one with Mars," said Caroline Mayer, reporter for *The Washington Post*. "They're one of the toughest companies in the food business."

Likewise, the industry is perfectly happy to share data on candy consumption, on the effects of candy on health and nutrition and on the general history of the business, but it is eerily silent when it comes to the fate of individual companies.

Ask the National Confectioners Association (NCA) whether chocolate causes acne, and it will produce dozens of studies showing no correlation between the teenage nightmare and the eating of a Nestlé's Crunch. But ask about the heated competition between Hershey and Mars, and it's strictly no comment.

"I'm simply not allowed to discuss it," said NCA spokesman William Sheehan,[6] a hint of apology in his voice. "Individual companies are strictly off-limits."

Richard O'Connell, who for thirty years ran the NCA and the Chocolate Manufacturers Association, defends such furtiveness this way: "Do you have any idea how hard it is to come up with something new in the candy business? I don't blame the industry for being paranoid; there's a lot at stake."[7]

With Hershey and Mars firmly in control of the majority of the market, and the other 300-odd candy firms groping to find or keep their niche, it's "very tough to succeed," said O'Connell. To increase profits, firms must do one of two things: increase their market share or become more efficient than the competition, neither of which is easy.

The industry averages about 150 new products each year,[8] yet only a handful of those become popular enough to stay on the shelf. Moreover, most of the so-called new candies are merely variations on age-old themes.

"There's only so much you can do with chocolate, peanuts and caramel—if you get my drift," O'Connell said. "Besides, Americans are so nostalgic about their candy bars, it's almost impossible to get them to try something new."

Mars and Hershey—the Candy Kings, as they're known to insiders—can readily attest to that. Take Mars's Bounty bar, for example. In 1988, Hershey turned the candy world upside down when it unexpectedly acquired the U.S. division of Peter Paul/Cadbury, maker of Mounds, Almond Joy and York Peppermint Patties. To compete with Hershey's new muscle, Mars introduced the Bounty bar in 1989, a chocolate-covered coconut bar reminiscent of Mounds. But Bounty failed after just two years, even though every blind taste test Mars conducted showed consumers preferred it 2 to 1 over the competition.[9]

"In the minds of Americans, coconut bars mean just one thing: a Mounds or Almond Joy," said Lisbeth Echeandia of *Confectioner* magazine. "Mars just couldn't get past that nostalgia."

Ironically, Forrest Mars, Sr., patriarch of the Mars family empire, stole his idea for the Bounty bar in the early 1950s from Peter Paul Candies.[10] He introduced his version of the bar in the United Kingdom and Canada, where Peter Paul didn't operate. Bounty quickly became a major brand, and today, Canadians will tell you Bounty is their favorite coconut bar. They've never heard of Mounds.

It wasn't that Forrest Mars, Sr., was a rogue or a thief; he was just, well, efficient. Given the finite number of available ingredients, the limited understanding of science and manufacturing and the relatively narrow range of consumers' candy preferences, it made perfect business sense to borrow hot-selling products from the competition, alter them slightly and resell them as one's own. It was in this manner that the global candy industry developed over the years, and that it continues to develop today.

Take Hershey's Skor bar, for example. The chocolate-covered toffee bar was introduced in 1982 to compete head-on with the Heath bar. But the original recipe for Skor was actually copied from Heath in the early 1900s by a Norwegian candy maker, Freia Marabou A.S. When the

Heath company refused to give Hershey the rights to manufacture its bar, Hershey turned to Marabou and purchased the recipe for Skor, bringing the product full circle.[11]

And Heath is just one of hundreds of examples. Britain's favorite candy bar—the Mars bar—is, in fact, a slightly sweeter version of the American Milky Way. America's Starburst Fruit Chews are Britain's Opal Fruits. The Kit Kat bar in the United States came from the Kit Kat bar in Europe. The list goes on and on. Generally, the key to candy success over the years has not been in confecting sumptuous new treats, but in getting the product to market before the competition.

Anyone who developed a truly new candy, making history in the process, almost always did it by accident.

Peanut brittle, for example, was invented in 1890 by a New England housewife, who, when making a peanut taffy in her kitchen, mistakenly added baking soda instead of cream of tartar to the syrup bubbling on the stove. Caramel was created in the Midwest by a curious confectioner who added milk to his butterscotch recipe in an effort to improve the flavor. The more milk he added, the softer and creamier the butterscotch became, until suddenly, he had invented a whole new confection.[12]

It didn't take long for accidents like these to be copied by competitors, and although today's confectioners act in a somewhat more gentlemanly manner—typically purchasing the rights to manufacture each other's candies—copying is still common. It's just kept quiet.

"It happens every now and again," said O'Connell, a sheepish grin creeping across his face. "Of course, I can't tell you who's been involved, but I've heard stories."

Ever wonder why candy trends seem to come and go all at the same time? In the mid-1980s it was gummies. In the 1990s, it's anything sour. A valid explanation, of course, is that popular candies quickly attract followers. But that doesn't explain how thirty different companies all introduced gummy worms, gummy bears, gummy fish and gummy snakes in the same year. Or why blue became the hot candy color virtually overnight, with hundreds of companies introducing blue foods at the 1992 national candy trade show in Washington, D.C.

"It is a little odd," admits Sheehan of the NCA. "But, really, I think it's just coincidence. The trends are just obvious to everyone in the business."

Still, Hershey and other candy companies say they can't be too cautious. After all, it's not as if they can patent a new candy bar. They must protect themselves from outsiders—and from their own employees. It is for this reason that no one in the industry will openly discuss new products—even those that have already hit the shelves, for fear they might spill a tasty trade secret. Marketing plans are handled with similar care: Disseminated to only a handful of people, they are treated like top-secret Defense Department documents. Hershey's plans are marked "Strictly Confidential" in bold red ink, and they're shredded almost as soon as they're printed to avoid potential leaks.[13]

Recipes, too, are closely guarded. Tucked inside alarmed safes, they are shared only on a need-to-know basis. That way, workers on the manufacturing line can never reveal exactly how the candies are made. In fact, the manufacturing process itself is the most prized secret of all.

"Anyone can read the ingredients on a Hershey bar," explains Hershey's Richard Zimmerman. "But to actually make a Hershey bar, you have to know a lot more than that." Like how the milk is processed to give the bar its distinct flavor. And which varieties of cocoa beans are used to develop the right chocolate liquor. And how long Hershey mixes and blends its chocolate to create that familiar consistency. Those are the real candy mysteries. And you can bet Hershey will do everything in its power to keep them mysterious.

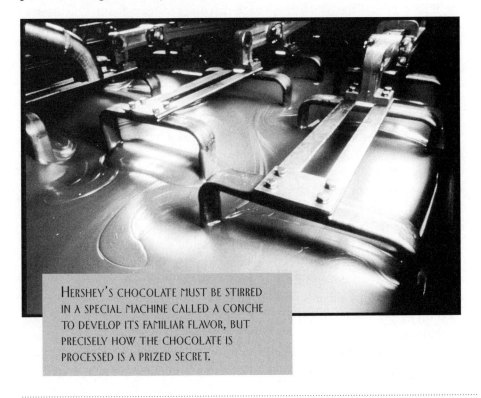

HERSHEY'S CHOCOLATE MUST BE STIRRED IN A SPECIAL MACHINE CALLED A CONCHE TO DEVELOP ITS FAMILIAR FLAVOR, BUT PRECISELY HOW THE CHOCOLATE IS PROCESSED IS A PRIZED SECRET.

Mars, too, goes to great lengths to keep its manufacturing processes under cover. The company designs all of its own candy-making machinery, and it keeps its factories humming with its own squadron of engineers. Only a handful of outsiders have ever been allowed inside Mars's industrial candy land, and those who have must sign confidentiality agreements stating they will never share what they saw.

If Mars needs outside contractors to fix a particular problem, it insists on blindfolding the alien workers and escorting them through the plant to the area in question. Once the problem is resolved, the contractors are blindfolded again and politely removed from the premises.[14]

The smaller candy companies are just as discreet, although for somewhat different reasons. More than half of them are family-controlled, single-product operations. They don't set candy prices, like Mars and Hershey, and they don't control large amounts of shelf space, like Mars and Hershey. Nor are they nearly as efficient.

The only thing that keeps these companies afloat is their niche—some unique product or nostalgic recipe that is so special it can draw candy-craving consumers out of their beds in the middle of the night in search of an all-night convenience store.

That's how Rita Martin, a truck-driving redhead from Oklahoma, explains her affection for Valomilk, a gooey, marshmallow-filled chocolate cup made in Merriam, Kansas, by a man named Russell Sifers.

Martin once spent an entire Saturday cruising around Kansas, stopping at QuickTrip after QuickTrip, in search of as many boxes of Valomilk as she could find.

"I didn't even bother to turn off my truck. I just hopped out, bought what they had, and threw it in the back," she said in a letter to the candy's maker.

Sifers gets stacks of fan mail from Valomilk lovers around the country. One man wrote of using a box of the stuff to propose to his girlfriend; a woman told of breaking up family squabbles by offering Valomilk all around. Sifers knows his product will never give Hershey or Mars a run for the money, but he's got his worshippers and says that's all he needs.[15]

But in the face of ever-greater competition from the big boys, and the mounting costs of doing business, that may no longer be enough. Hundreds of candy firms like Sifers's have gone out of business or been gobbled up by the competition in recent years. And the trend shows no sign of abating.

"We've lost an entire generation of candy products in just the last two decades," laments Ray Broekel, an industry historian and self-described candy bar guru. "It's terribly upsetting to watch them vanish so quickly. It gives me the shivers."

As each product disappears, it takes a piece of American culture with it. The Whiz bar, Pecan Pete, the Astro-Nut, Starbar and Smile-a-While are only a few of yesterday's favorites that are now just memories, and more follow every year.[16]

Ellen Gordon, president of Tootsie Roll Industries, states as fact that her company would have disappeared long ago had she and her husband, company chairman Melvin Gordon, not owned the majority of Tootsie Roll's voting stock.

"We've worked hard to keep suitors away," Gordon explains. "We want Tootsie to remain independent. Hopefully, our children, or the employees working in the company, will be able to run it someday."[17]

To that end, the Gordons recently have gone on a buying spree of their own, acquiring Warner-Lambert's chocolate and caramel division in 1993, which includes brand names like Junior Mints, Sugar Daddy, Charleston Chew! and Sugar Babies. In 1991, Tootsie acquired the Charms Co., America's largest lollipop manufacturer and maker of the Charms Blow Pop.

These acquisitions helped place Tootsie among the largest candy firms in the business, a position the Gordons hope will keep them from becoming prey for a bigger competitor. But just in case this strategy isn't enough, the couple continues to spread the word that Tootsie is not for sale.

The sincerity of this message can be seen on Wall Street, where Tootsie's stock is all but ignored by investors. Only two analysts even track the company's performance, despite Tootsie's impressive history of earnings and dividend increases. Wall Street traders blame Tootsie for the brush-off, saying the firm makes little effort to talk about its operations.

"The company is extremely reticent," says Elliott Schlang, an analyst with Tucker Anthony, Inc., in Cleveland. "They do not give any guidance on current operating conditions. Therefore, the stock is covered [by analysts] on a very limited basis."

Ellen Gordon is unapologetic. "We're busy making Tootsie Rolls," she says. "We haven't spent a great deal of time with the investment community. And why should we? It would only call attention to our business, and we're not interested in that."

Lisbeth Echeandia estimates that at the current rate of consolidation, fewer than 150 candy companies will be operating by the year 2010, down from 6,000 firms at the industry's peak in 1945.[18] The families responsible for such venerable products as the Heath bar, the Clark bar, 5th Avenue, Oh Henry!, PayDay, Zagnut, Milk Duds and Mary Jane have all sold out and left the business in recent decades. Now these candies are being manufactured by the industry's top ten players, a trend that Echeandia says will continue.

"The writing has been on the wall since the 1940s, when Mars and Hershey blew everybody else out of the water. Since then, the big guys have kept getting bigger and the little guys have kept getting smaller," she observes.

Did you know that there is only one U.S. company left that makes mid-priced gift-boxed chocolates? In 1993, Russell Stover Candies, Inc., bought out its last competitor, Whitman Chocolates, for $35 million. Confectioner Stephen F. Whitman founded Whitman's in 1842 when he set up shop near Philadelphia's shipyard and began buying exotic candies from sailors. The company began marketing its trademark Whitman's Sampler in 1912.

Russell Stover Candies of Kansas City, Missouri, was already the largest player in the gift-box market before the takeover. When Louis L. Ward, the businessman who built Russell Stover, died in 1996, he left a fortune estimated at $500 million.

If you've never heard of Ward, you're not alone. Like the rest of the players in the industry, he closely guarded his privacy and refused to discuss his business. He objected to being put on lists of richest Americans. "I think that sort of thing is wrong in America," he told *The Kansas City Star* in 1983. "I feel that lists such as this don't serve any worthwhile purpose." Today, his company is being run by his two sons, Thomas and Scott, who are just as protective of the firm. They don't publish the company's financial results and release only the most basic information about their business. Analysts estimate Russell Stover has fifty retail stores, five factories and 6,000 employees—although no one knows for sure.

So far, antitrust regulations have failed to stop giants like Russell Stover from acquiring other candy firms. The same year Stover acquired Whitman's, the E. J. Brach Corp. acquired its biggest competitor, Brock Candy Co., leaving only a single maker of traditional individually wrapped candies like Starlight mints. Hershey, too, has bought nearly a dozen popular brands since the mid-1980s. In one of its more recent acquisitions (December 1996), Hershey shocked the industry by purchasing one of its largest remaining competitors, Leaf North America, maker of such classic candies as Good & Plenty, Jolly Rancher, Whoppers, Milk Duds, Heath and PayDay. This $440-million acquisition followed closely on the heels of Hershey's purchase of one of the oldest candy companies in America, Henry Heide, Inc., maker of Jujyfruits and Wunderbeans. Hershey paid $12.5 million for the New Jersey–based company, which the Heide family had owned and operated for more than 125 years—since 1869. And while Mars is more reluctant to acquire outside companies, that hasn't stopped it from expanding. In fact, Echeandia and others predict the two rivals will eventually control more than 90 percent of the industry.

Why? It all boils down to this basic fact: Whoever controls the most shelf space wins.

How many times have you walked into a supermarket with a grocery list in hand that read: "Buy Reese's Peanut Butter Cups." Never. But how many times have you driven through a gas station, intending only to fill your gas tank, and wound up buying M&M's, too? And just when was the last time you walked up to a vending machine, stared at all the brightly colored wrappers inside and *didn't* end up buying a candy bar?

As any candy manufacturer can tell you, no one ever *plans* to buy a Snickers or a Clark bar. It just happens. One minute, you're standing in line at the supermarket, your bread, milk and eggs arranged neatly in your basket. Then, the line stalls as the customer in front of you slowly unloads a cart full of food. You're bored and you're restless, and you look around, and suddenly, right there beside you—a Butterfinger. The yellow-orange wrapper catches your eye, and before you've even had a chance to think about it, the candy bar is resting comfortably right beside your milk—which is skim, of course.

It happens to everyone. It happens to me almost every time I go to the store. Candy makers count on this phenomenon for 90 percent of their business. The other 10 percent, they calculate, results from planned purchases, like when you buy a bag of miniatures for Halloween, or when your boyfriend says he's sorry with a box of chocolate.

This obviously creates a dilemma for the candy manufacturer. How can he know when you'll get a craving for nougat? It's not like aspirin, which everyone, at some point, needs to purchase. Candy is not a necessity. It's a treat. A delight. A frivolous indulgence. To some, it's an obsession—but it's not *necessary*. You can live your entire life without ever savoring a Hershey's Kiss, rolling it around on your tongue as it melts, anticipating the moment when it dissolves. The only way to ensure consumers buy Hershey's Kisses is to put the candies where they can't be avoided—in the drugstore, the supermarket, the convenience mart, the gas station, the office lounge, the cafeteria and every rest stop from New York to L.A. If they see it, they will buy it. That's the candy makers' mantra.

Hershey, which stole the candy crown from Mars in 1988 with its purchase of Peter Paul, has more power than any other company in America to get its products in front of consumers. Mars, which has been struggling ever since to regain the throne, commands almost as much authority. Together, they account for eight of the ten top-selling candy bars in the country—and it's been that way for more than thirty years.[19] M&M's alone generate more revenue than Camel cigarettes or Maxwell House coffee.[20] Reese's Peanut Butter Cups, the nation's No. 3 brand (owned by Hershey), outsells such well-known products as Advil and Ivory Soap.[21]

Hard to believe they all began with the same handful of ingredients— a copper kettle, a bag of sugar . . . and a dream.

Chapter Three

THE PLANET
MARS

A Mars office looks like no
other corporate office:
A spartan, no-nonsense
environment without
privacy, perks or pretension.

*A*T 6:30 A.M., sharp, John Mars pulls his Jeep station wagon into the small, empty parking lot at 6885 Elm Street in McLean, Virginia. He parks toward the rear of the unadorned, unmarked two-story brick building. Except for the Hardee's serving breakfast next door, the neighborhood is quiet.

Today, as usual, John is wearing a blue shirt, striped tie, dark slacks and thick-soled shoes that lost their polish long ago. At fifty-eight, he slouches as he walks. His eyes never leave the pavement as he hurries toward the back entrance of the nondescript and unassuming headquarters.

To anyone who might have seen him that bright crisp morning, there was nothing to suggest he was anything but another careworn businessman—shabby leather briefcase in hand and pocket protector protruding from his button-down cotton oxford shirt. Certainly, there was nothing to hint that this graying figure with the slight paunch, so unremarkable in appearance, is the leader of one of the most successful companies in the world. Which is just how John Mars prefers it.

The chief executive of Mars, Inc., who runs the company with his older brother, Forrest Jr., is obsessed with anonymity. All details of his personal life are a carefully guarded secret. He is loath to appear in public, resisting requests even to address his own workers at closed company gatherings. He has not been photographed since college, when he posed for his Yale yearbook, and, according to those who work closely with him, he is apt to wear disguises when conducting business with corporate outsiders. Although he spends 80 percent of his time visiting Mars operations worldwide, his travel plans are strictly classified. Ed Stegemann is one of the few trusted confidants informed of his whereabouts, and even Stegemann doesn't always know where to locate John Mars, because he often changes his schedule at the last minute to avoid would-be followers. He has never signed a hotel registry and owns nothing in his own name. He shuns the media, and except for one brief interview that he granted me in 1991, he has never talked with the press.

While such furtiveness appears extreme, it is not entirely without reason; after all, *Fortune* magazine has ranked the Mars family as the third richest in the world.[1] Stegemann says he has found strangers lurking outside the McLean building. Furthermore, he adds: "Their name is Mars. Try hiding that from outsiders!"

But the mystery that surrounds the candy giant is about more than taking precautions. It is a reflection of the Mars family's personal style—a quirky, eccentric, nonconformist approach that pervades every aspect of the business.

Founded by John Mars's grandfather in 1922, and owned and operated by the Mars family ever since, the company is the largest candy manufacturer in the world. With sales of roughly $20 billion a year and interests stretching from Helsinki to Hong Kong, Mars is bigger than such corporate giants as RJR Nabisco, McDonald's and Kellogg. And though archrival Hershey Foods outsells Mars in America, Mars is actually four times the size of Hershey on a global basis.[2]

In the United States, Mars controls more than one-third of the candy aisle. In Europe, Mars brands are just as popular. In fact, Britain, not the United States, ranks as the company's leading market.

And Mars is much more than just candy. With its seventy divisions and 28,000 employees, Mars manufactures the premium ice cream treat DoveBar; the pretzel snack Combos; the nation's leading rice, Uncle Ben's; and scores of other products around the world. In Australia, Mars is the largest manufacturer of spices and sauces. In Italy, the company distributes fresh pasta and pizza. On a global basis, Mars sells almost as much pet food as it does candy and snacks. With brand names like Whiskas, Sheba and Pedigree, Mars registered sales of more than $7.5 billion in 1996.[3] Only Nestlé S.A., which markets the Friskies brand, comes close.

But while Mars's universe of products is among the world's best known, the company behind the brands is not. And that, too, is the way John Mars prefers it.

Mars spends an estimated $400 million a year to advertise its products across America,[4] but since its founding, the company itself has operated inside a fortress of silence. This impenetrable shroud has bred a host of popular myths about Mars and its owners, who have found themselves splashed across the pages of the tabloids ("Wacky, Wealthy Man from Mars lives like a hermit—& rules with an iron fist," screams a headline in the *National Enquirer*) and likened to the cloak-and-dagger agents of the CIA who work just down the street. The business press portrays the family similarly, calling Mars the "black hole of the packaged goods universe"[5] and dubbing Forrest Mars, Sr., the "Howard Hughes of the candy world."[6] *Nutty, bizarre, strange*—these are words commonly used to describe Mars and its owners, much to the company's chagrin.

Frustrated by the negative press and determined to combat these persistent misconceptions, Stegemann and other top executives began pushing the family to open their world to the press—just as I contacted Mars for an interview. It took a full year however, before the family finally agreed. In an extraordinary break with its eighty-year-old policy of keeping the business under wraps, Mars invited me to tour the company's operations worldwide and interview everyone, from the factory workers to the sales managers to the company's executive officers.

Over the course of two years, I traveled with Mars personnel across the United States and Europe, visiting offices and manufacturing facilities from Houston to Amsterdam. I watched as Mars made its first attempt to open up the markets of the former Soviet Union—where Snickers today is the No. 1 selling candy bar. I visited the company's European headquarters in the industrial town of Slough, just outside London, where Forrest Mars, Sr., laid the foundation for today's Mars empire. And I toured the city of Prague with new Mars recruits as they planned their first advertising assault on the city. In all, I interviewed more than 150 past and present Mars employees. When *The Washington Post,* then my employer, published the inside account of how the mysterious planet Mars operates, local radio personalities responded by giving Mars its most positive press in decades. Hundreds of people who read the story called the McLean office to inquire about jobs. Nevertheless, the family viewed the publicity harshly. According to Stegemann, the brothers were furious over my explicit descriptions of them, especially my detailed account of how John Mars arrives at the office each morning.

"That was a violation of their privacy—a threat to their lives," said Stegemann. But the brothers were reacting to more than that.

"They're just not used to being judged by outsiders," said Barbara Parker, a public relations consultant hired by Mars to help handle my inquiries. "I don't think it mattered what the article said—they weren't going to like it. Nobody is allowed to judge them, especially not the press."

The day the story appeared, John Mars fired Parker and her partner, Sue Vogelsinger, saying he never wanted to see them at Mars headquarters again.[7] To ensure that the photographs used in the story would never be reprinted, the company also paid *The Washington Post*'s freelance photographer $20,000 for the rights to the pictures.[8] And ever since, the company has refused all requests for interviews, including my own.[9]

In explaining Mars's new position, Ed Stegemann sent a letter: "Somebody once said that public relations at Mars was a classic oxymoron—I suspect that's true," he wrote. "You can't have an effective public relations department without people being devoted to it. We just use our people for the main purposes of business and only rarely are we able to divert into the peripheral areas. Please do not think it is a lack of interest, it is more a lack of people and time."

Despite this rebuff, many workers have continued to speak under condition of anonymity, saying the brothers were mistaken to bury their heads in the sand. "They have come to the conclusion that any publicity is bad publicity," said former executive Hans Fiuczynski, who retired in 1992 from the company's candy division. "I don't think they'll ever open themselves up to scrutiny again; they don't see any benefit to it."

Paranoid, insecure, neurotic? Maybe, but the Mars family sincerely believes that publicity is a distraction from their central goal, which is making the best products on the market.

The ability to be secretive "is one of the finest benefits of having a private company," said Forrest Jr. "Privacy at times today seems a relic of the nonmedia past, but it is a legal right—morally and ethically proper and even desirable—and a key to healthy, normal living," he told a group of business majors at Duke University. It "allows us to do the very best we can, the very best we know how, and to do so without being concerned with self-aggrandizement."

The Mars family can't understand why this attitude should elicit so much comment and criticism, and that outsiders should view their insistence on privacy as strange—though neither John nor his brother has ever worried much about other people's opinions.

Owning the company gives them the right to be as different as they please.

The McLean building is pitch-black inside as John Mars unlocks the basement door and takes the stairs to the second floor. There, he flicks on the lights and does what few CEOs in America would even dream of doing: He pulls his time card—marked J. F. Mars—and punches in.

Behold the universe of Mars, Inc., where all employees are called "associates" and everyone, from the president on down, is paid a 10 percent bonus for arriving on time. There are no perks here—no corporate office suites, no company cars, no reserved parking spaces, no executive washrooms. There are no private offices, either. John makes his way through a sea of black metal desks—the kind schoolteachers might use—and plastic chairs in varying colors from orange to beige. Four glass-enclosed conference rooms provide the only sense of privacy; a smattering of potted plants and some company-related pictures are the only decor. This is the nerve center of a multinational, multibillion-dollar empire, but it looks more like a back office.

John and Forrest Jr. share the role of chief executive, dividing responsibilities along lines of interest. They sit in a back corner of the huge room with their sister, Jacqueline, who serves as the corporate vice president. They share one secretary among them.

It is not the kind of life one might imagine for a family whose net worth, according to *Forbes* magazine, is more than $13 billion.[10] But then, there is much about the Mars family and its corporation that is surprising:

• *Status* is a dirty word at Mars. Everyone works side by side, regardless of rank, without separate offices. No one has a personal secretary, everyone makes his own photocopies and everyone handles his own telephone calls. Those who travel fly coach, never first class.

• Bureaucracy is anathema. Writing memos is against corporate policy, and everyone, including the family, works on a first-name basis. Meetings take place only "as needed," and elaborate presentations are deemed a waste of time. Corporate headquarters in McLean employs just fifty-one people, including John, Forrest Jr. and Jackie.

• Paychecks are tied directly to the company's performance. If profits explode, associates can earn bonuses equal to five, ten, even fifteen weeks' salary. But if profits shrink, so does an associate's income.

• Cleanliness is an obsession. On any given day, the company boasts, the acceptable level of bacteria on a Mars factory floor is less than the average level in a household sink. Conveyor belts gleam, pipes shine and fixtures that may be a decade old appear brand-new. The slightest suspicion of contamination is enough to halt production for hours.

• Quality is a compulsion. Perfection in tiny details like the *M* on an M&M or the squiggle on top of a chocolate bar is painstakingly pursued. Millions of M&M's are rejected for sale every day because their *M*s missed the mark or their shells didn't glow like headlights. A pinhole in a single Snickers is cause to destroy an entire production run.

For those who believe that an $18-billion multinational corporation is fated to drown in a quagmire of mid-level managers, executive perks, meetings and memoranda, the accomplishments of Mars may be a little hard to believe. But then, conventional wisdom melts in the hands of the Mars family, which has always followed its own recipe for success.

In many ways, this unconventional, patriarchal style is the firm's greatest strength. But it may be its greatest weakness as well.

At Mars, it is virtually impossible to tell where the family ends and the company begins. No product goes to market, no major decision is made without the Marses' approval. The company's obsessions are the family's obsessions; its idiosyncrasies are their idiosyncrasies; its dreams are their dreams; its mistakes are theirs also.

The brothers' unique approach—which is predicated on their father's ideals—has forced Mars to turn down many promising acquisitions because of the potential for culture clash. Buying a business would mean assimilating hundreds of new employees into Mars's no-frills, hard-driven environment. No easy task, the company admits.

"Obviously, our corporate culture is not for everyone," said John Mars. "But it's what keeps us alive."

The cost of such an attitude is dear. On July 22, 1988, the brothers watched passively as Hershey acquired the U.S. candy division of British giant Cadbury Schweppes, stealing Mars's U.S. lead for the first time since Forrest Sr. took control of his father's Chicago candy operation in 1966.

The family acknowledged that Mars rejected the same opportunity, leaving the door wide open for Hershey. But, they insist, the Mars culture left them little choice.

"We don't buy and sell businesses," said John. "We build."

But the building, too, is carried out strictly in accordance with the family's beliefs.

"You want to know why Mars doesn't make any products with peanut butter?" asks Alfred Poe, former marketing director of the candy division. "It's because the family doesn't eat peanut butter. They don't like it." (John, Forrest Jr. and Jackie did not eat peanut butter and jelly sandwiches growing up; they were raised in England, where peanut butter is despised.) In the early 1990s, Poe succeeded in convincing Mars to give peanut butter a try—but his PB Max candy bar didn't last long. Launched in 1990, the Mars brothers yanked it from the market just two years later, even though it had reached sales of $50 million, an impressive performance by most companies' standards.[11] Mars continues to manufacture peanut butter M&M's, the only other peanut butter product in its repertoire. But even that candy languished for ten years on the drawing board before the Mars brothers gave permission for its launch, and marketing executives say the brothers continue to be hyper-critical of its performance.

On the other hand, Poe continues: "You want to know why they're so hung up on hazelnuts? Because they eat hazelnuts! It doesn't matter if Americans like peanut butter and despise hazelnuts. They're going to do what they're going to do."[12]

Dozens of hazelnut-based products have been tested in the Mars kitchens over the years, and according to one food chemist in Hackettstown, the Mars brothers believe Toffifay—a hazelnut candy manufactured by Germany's Storck GMBH—is one of the best in the business, even though Toffifay sales have never topped $50 million.

Ed Stegemann scoffs at the notion that Mars is run by the family's whims. "Sure, [the brothers] have the final say on business decisions, but that doesn't mean they control every little part of the business. They're open to ideas—you just have to prove your case. . . . It is *their* money."

But as any student of industry knows, mixing family and business can produce a dangerous brew—so dangerous that fourth-, fifth- and sixth-generation family firms are virtually nonexistent. There is no long-term model for this way of achieving success.

"At Mars, if your last name doesn't begin with an *M*, there's only so far you're going to go," said former top executive Claude Eliette-Hermann. "Everybody who works there knows that. It's a real limitation to the business."

Eliette-Hermann, who ran the company's pet food operations for twenty-five years and is still highly regarded by Mars, left the company for just that reason. "I had gone as far as I could go," he explains, from his new post as president of Chanel S.A. in Paris.[13]

"Everything at Mars is about power," said Poe. "Every discussion ends with, I'm the owner, so I'm the boss. There's no room for anybody else."

In the end, say these executives, the brothers are not competing with the rest of the candy industry, but with their family legacy.

John and Forrest Jr. work ten-hour days, seven days a week, even though they could well afford to laze about on a Caribbean island. Instead, the brothers spend their lives traveling, inspecting Mars plants worldwide and directly overseeing each division.

Executives say the brothers manage the business far more closely than their father ever did. "He was a strategist," said David Brown, who worked with Forrest Sr. for more than thirty years. "They are hands-on with a vengeance."

The results of their hard work can be seen in the numbers. Since the brothers took control of the company in 1973, Mars has grown from sales of $800 million to nearly $20 billion.[14] In less than twenty years, they have expanded the business around the globe, to Moscow and Beijing, Cairo and Sydney. They have added new divisions, including Mars Money Systems, the largest maker of electronic coin changers in the world, and Mars Electronics, which oversees the company's intelligence-gathering operations and worldwide communications. No longer content to make just candy, they have broadened Mars into ice cream, snacks, drinks and frozen foods.

John Mars, an industrial engineer, has spearheaded the company's efforts toward automation, developing better manufacturing techniques and vastly improving the company's efficiency. Forrest Jr. and Jackie have focused on the products themselves, striving to make brands like Uncle Ben's and M&M's recognizable around the world.

According to friends, the three rarely take vacations and almost always clock in before dawn. But ask them why they do it and they cannot answer.

"I had to do something, didn't I?" John Mars asks rhetorically as he tries to explain why he has devoted his life to the family business. "I mean, in my day, if you wanted to earn a living, you had to get a job. There was no discussion—none of this 'I'm going to live off my parents' that kids have nowadays. You'd be locked out of the house if that's the way you wanted it.

"This job was as good as any, I suppose," he concludes, his face blank, his tone matter-of-fact.

On most days, John and his brother are oblivious to the fact that the business they're so focused on is the business of candy—of selling treats, fun, laughter and solace to children and adults. Mars could be the manufacturer of ball bearings and tire irons; it makes no difference to John and Forrest Jr. They are in the candy business because their father was in the candy business, and his father before him.

As if to remind the Mars siblings of this heritage, a grand, imposing portrait of Forrest Sr., along with a painting of Frank Mars, the company's founder, decorate the entryway in McLean. Forrest appears to have been in his late sixties when the portrait was rendered. He is nearly bald, with a large hook nose and closely set dark eyes. His thin, pursed lips give him a disapproving look.

It's an expression his sons must have seen often as they were growing up.

For the Marses, childhood was one long lesson in frugality. Their father was so dedicated to building his business that in the early days, he refused to spend money on his wife or his children. When Forrest Mars first set up shop outside London in 1933, Audrey Mars's father had to come and rescue his daughter and her newborn son from the cold, tiny flat that Forrest had rented. Audrey stayed in the United States with her parents, taking care of Forrest Jr., until her husband consented to rent a bigger home.

Still, Forrest Mars was never one for luxury. Audrey managed the household without help, and John, Forrest Jr. and Jackie were forced to work for everything they got. There were no allowances, no fancy cars, no extravagant clothes. "Forrest Mars didn't want to raise a bunch of playboys," explains Stegemann. "He wanted them to do something with their lives, to be productive."

According to the attorney, John and his brother have no concept of their riches. "Deep down, they believe they are poor," Stegemann says. And by all accounts, they live normal, everyday lives.

John and his wife, Adrienne, have lived in the same house in the northern Virginia suburbs for twenty-two years. Their two-story colonial is subdued compared with other upper-middle-class homes nearby. There is no in-ground pool, no private tennis court. With its cedar shakes and wood siding, the house sports a weathered look. On occasion, John says, the roof leaks.

In the spring, Adrienne can be seen on the front lawn, clearing the weeds from beneath the bushes or planting new bulbs in the flower garden. If John's home, he'll cut the grass.

Although Forrest Jr. recently purchased a $1-million condo in an upscale suburban high-rise, there is little else about his life that hints at the extent of his wealth. He doesn't belong to a country club; he's not a stylish dresser. His 1980 Mercedes was a gift from his mother.

"It's as though they don't believe they deserve any better," said a close family friend. "They pride themselves on being average, middle-class Americans."

Although Mars earns profits of hundreds of millions of dollars each year, the brothers seldom draw dividends from the company, living on salaries that are said to be about $1 million per year (less than one-quarter the average compensation for a Fortune 500 CEO). The family's modest compensation is mirrored in the way they run the business, demanding an after-tax return on sales of just 3 percent. More than this, the Marses believe, would be unfair to consumers. (Most publicly owned companies aim for returns of about 7 percent.)

But fairness isn't the only factor motivating Mars's fiscal policy.

"Why should the family take a huge profit out of the company and have to pay taxes on it?" explains Stegemann. "Why not just leave

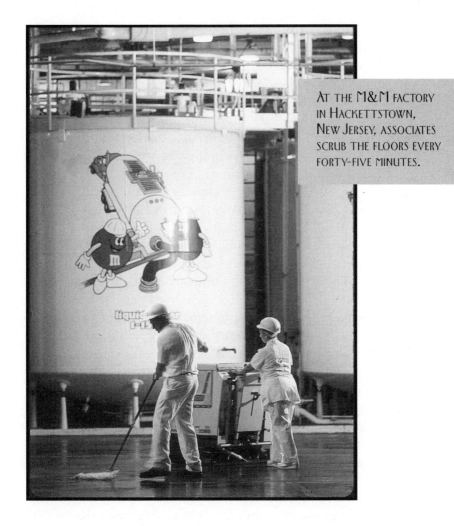

the money where it is and reinvest it in the business? They don't *need* the money for anything. The best way to use it is to expand and build the company."

The result of this policy is best seen inside the plants, which are state of the art from top to bottom and are considered by competitors to be the most efficient in the industry.

Mars operates more than forty factories, including fifteen in the United States. Virtually all make use of the family's secret recipes twenty-four hours a day, seven days a week, at speeds few can imagine: In Chicago, at the company's oldest plant, Fun Size Milky Way bars roll off the line at the rate of 5,520 bars per minute. In a year, the plant can produce enough bars to circle the globe—twice. In Waco, Texas, where Skittles are manufactured, Mars makes enough of the colorful fruit-flavored bits each year to leave a trail every inch to the moon.

The company's drive for efficiency has bred one of the most effective workforces in business. Mars produces more candy per employee than any other company in the industry. In 1990, for example, Mars's revenue averaged out to $429,000 per associate. At Hershey, that figure was $228,000. To attract the best people to its team, Mars pays its workers the highest salaries in the business. A worker on the factory line can earn more than $60,000 a year, including overtime and bonuses, while an executive vice president makes more than half a million dollars annually.

"There's just no place like it," said Ginger Macklin, who retired from her job as a schoolteacher in 1987 and now manufactures Starburst Fruit Chews for Mars. "There isn't another company in America that would treat me this well."

It might seem as if these accomplishments—providing thousands of high-paying jobs, making the finest-quality products and earning millions upon millions in profits—would bring a sense of pride and satisfaction to the company's owners. But not to the Marses, who find little contentment in what they do.

John Mars never dreamed of being Willy Wonka—he's never even read the Roald Dahl story *Charlie and the Chocolate Factory,* in which the mythical Wonka searches for an heir to his magical candy kingdom. The Mars siblings never asked to inherit their father's company; that responsibility was thrust upon them by birth, and it haunts them to this day.

That may sound ridiculous to anyone who has never been shackled by the responsibility of a family-owned firm. Who wouldn't want to run the world's biggest candy factory? you ask yourself. Who wouldn't want to lord over rivers of chocolate? Make a little girl smile? Just remember this: When John, Forrest Jr. and Jackie Mars were children, they never got to eat a single M&M. Their father said the brightly colored candies just couldn't be spared.

He needed every last one.

Chapter Four

MELTS IN YOUR MOUTH

MARS CHANGES THE MIX OF
M&M COLORS TO KEEP IN
SYNC WITH CONSUMER
TASTES. THE CURRENT MIX?
THIRTY PERCENT BROWN,
20 PERCENT RED AND
YELLOW, AND 10 PERCENT
ORANGE, BLUE AND GREEN.

WHAT IS IT about M&M's? The sugar-coated pellets aglow in the colors of childhood. The edible white *M*s that appear magically stamped, centered and perfect. The sumptuous treasure of milk chocolate hidden inside each and every one.

Maybe it's the shell, smooth and shiny like a jewel, as festive as a party. You pop them into your mouth—not too many at once—and let them roll slowly over your tongue and in-and-out-and-around your cheeks. Eventually, the outer layer of candy begins to soften, but before it dissolves away completely, you let your teeth close in, crushing the shells into sweet, splintery pieces.

You want to savor the moment, to let your jaw relax and relish the sensation of the smooth creamy chocolate against the hard, crunchy candy. But you can't. The thought of the next mouthful is too powerful. Quickly, you swallow; and then, without thinking, you reach for more.

It's no accident. Really. The scientists at Mars call this grazing—the unconscious act of grabbing for your second, third or fifteenth serving—and they've gone to great lengths to make sure that it happens.

Explains Allan Gibbons, one of hundreds of chemists working on Mars research and development: "The chocolate in the M&M is what we call 'refreshing.' It's a less satiating sort of chocolate, so you can eat lots and lots of it."

In other words, because the chocolate isn't quite sweet enough to be fully satisfying, each swallow of M&M's leaves you with an insidious craving. How does Mars know it works? Simple.

"We test people in our offices," reports Gibbons. "We'd give them a bowl of M&M's every day—about a pound, I guess. And they'd have them on their desks and just be grazing away. We'd gauge how much they liked the product by how much they physically ate.

"We usually have one or two people whose results we have to eliminate, like this one guy who ate the whole bowl no matter what. But eventually, we can tell which recipe works best."

When Forrest Mars first introduced M&M's in 1940, he wasn't quite so scientific. His aim was to create a chocolate candy that wouldn't melt. The original idea, he said, came from the battlefields of Spain. While traveling through that country during the Spanish Civil War, Forrest saw soldiers eating chocolate lentils coated with sugary candy. Protected by the shell, the chocolate withstood the heat.

M&M's were Forrest Mars's first successful candy creation, after he left his father's candy business and struck out on his own. Today, the candy that "melts in your mouth, not in your hand," ranks as the world's most popular confection. M&M's are sold around the globe—in China, Russia, Turkey, France, Germany, Japan, England—generating revenue of more than $2 billion.

But except for sales figures, there are few facts about the brightly colored candies that are not in dispute—from how the candy originated, to who was responsible for its success, to what the two *M*s stand for.

There has long been a story—one the company cannot seem to dispel—that M&M's were introduced at the urging of the army, which wanted a snack for its fighting men during World War II. Another popular tale is that M&M's were invented for American bomber pilots, who needed a sweet, non-melting treat to munch during their long flights. But none of this is true, according to Mars.

Yet another story—that Forrest Mars stole the idea for M&M's from Rowntree & Co., a British manufacturer that introduced a similar product called Smarties in 1937—is also false, says the company. According to this legend, George Harris, head of Rowntree, was traveling along with Forrest when he made his great discovery. The two entered into a gentleman's agreement, whereby Rowntree would market the product in Europe and Forrest would take it to the United States. Another version of the same tale has Forrest giving Rowntree the rights to manufacture his Mars bar in exchange for the rights to market a version of Smarties in America.

"That's absolute nonsense," insists Stegemann, Mars's trusted attorney. "It's true that Forrest went to Spain with a junior member of the Rowntree family, but it wasn't George Harris and there was no agreement."

There was another agreement, however, that Mars reluctantly acknowledges. This one, with Hershey.

Ask a factory worker at Mars what the *M* stands for, and the answer is always the same: "Mars, of course."

And the second *M*?

"That stands for Mars, too," they say. " 'A name so nice, Forrest used it twice'—didn't you know?"

The truth is, the second *M* stands for Murrie—as in R. Bruce Murrie, the son of William Murrie, longtime president of the Hershey Chocolate Co. and Milton Hershey's dearest friend.

R. Bruce Murrie was originally Forrest Mars's partner in the M&M business. (Although you'd never learn he had anything to do with it by talking with employees at Mars.) In fact, as the residents of Hershey, Pennsylvania, will tell you, M&M's Chocolate Candies probably wouldn't exist if it weren't for Murrie and Hershey.

"M&M stands for *Murrie* and Mars," corrects Howard Phillippy, retired engineer for the Hershey Chocolate Co. "What seems now very unusual, actually helping your competitors to the extreme, is, well . . . at that time, it was common."

Phillippy, who helped design the equipment used to manufacture the Hershey's Kiss, said he remembers modifying Hershey machines for the first M&M plant in Newark, New Jersey, "because Murrie was [president of the chocolate company] at the time and his son was one of the *M*s of M&M."

Richard Bacastow, who also worked for Hershey when M&M's were introduced, said he thinks it's ironic that people today blame Hershey for copying M&M's with its own product, Reese's Pieces.

"Hershey, during the war, sent all that technology and equipment to Mars [for M&M's], and they exploited the opportunity. We gave it away, really!"

Few people outside the industry are aware of this part of M&M's success. Understandably, neither company is quick to advertise it. But the truth is, the histories of these two industry rivals are closely intertwined. One could even argue that Mars would not have succeeded without Hershey, and vice versa.

To understand how these archenemies could once have been allies, we must go back to the very beginning, to the families that founded them. Only then can we understand the depths of their current rivalry. And only then can we appreciate how their competition has helped shape an industry.

HEY FELLOWS, LOOK WHAT MOTHER SENT ME...
AND DO I LOVE MILKY WAYS !

A MILKY WAY MUST AGE FOR AT LEAST TWO WEEKS TO DEVELOP ITS LIGHTER-THAN-AIR QUALITY. FRESH FROM THE PRODUCTION LINE, THE BAR HAS THE CONSISTENCY OF TAFFY.

ALTHOUGH THE HISTORY of Mars at times is sketchy, a messy blend of fact and myth, at least one thing is certain: Not long after the company's founder, Frank Mars, was born on September 24, 1883, he contracted polio. It was the virus that dictated the course of his career.

The disease left Frank permanently crippled, unable to walk or stand without a cane. As a young boy, he wore orthotic braces and was almost entirely dependent on his mother. He couldn't stand well enough to dress himself, couldn't navigate stairs, couldn't walk long distances. Instead of stickball and street hockey, Frank's days were filled with aromas from the family kitchen, where he spent most of his time perched on a stool watching his mother cook. Frank's father was a gristmill operator, first in Pennsylvania and later in St. Paul, Minnesota, where the family moved while Frank was still young. His mother made good use of the sacks of flour his father often brought home instead of paychecks, churning out breads, pies, cookies, cakes and, occasionally, candy. Frank was fascinated by all of it. Watching simple ingredients like flour, eggs and water transform into dumplings, pancakes and fritters was, to Frank, like watching a rainbow stream across the horizon: Out of sunlight and water came magic.

Candy, of course, was Frank's favorite. It was fun to beat divinity, pull taffy and shape fondant. Fun, too, to lick the spoon. But it was the process that fascinated him most. Fudge required the exactitude of a surgeon. Caramel, the patience of a nurse. He learned quickly that candy-making is a critical science, unstable and apt to fail. The dos and don'ts of making candy read like warnings on a child's chemistry set.

First, the weather. It does make a difference, with cooked candies especially. A dry, cool, clear day is best; moisture in the air will keep the candy from hardening. Second, ingredients must be measured precisely. Substitutions cannot be made, and recipes should never be doubled or halved but followed to the letter. Candies *do not* take to improvisation. Third, the temperature. Ingredients must be boiled to 230 degrees Fahrenheit to form a thread, but should never exceed 270 degrees or the sugar crystals will turn brittle and crack. Never hurry the cooking *or* the cooling, and *never* stir the candy after the sugar has dissolved.

By the time Frank entered high school, he had mastered most of his mother's candy recipes and begun experimenting on his own. There is no indication, however, that any of these early experiments succeeded—which may explain his decision to earn a living by selling candies instead. Business records show that by 1902, Frank Mars was running a whole-sale candy firm outside Minneapolis, peddling sweets to small shopkeepers in and around the Twin Cities. That same year, he married Ethel G. Kissack, and their only son, Forrest, was born two years later.

When Frank entered the business at the turn of the century, the candy-making industry was in its infancy, with fewer than one hundred large-scale manufacturers in operation. Most of these firms were clustered in big cities in the Northeast and Midwest, like New York and Chicago, where cooler, drier temperatures dominated. But even these firms weren't producing the kind of treats that Americans associate with candy today. "Old-fashioned" favorites like Necco Wafers, Boston Baked Beans, Red Hots and Good & Plenty, didn't exist at the turn of the century. Neither did candy bars. Although Milton Hershey manufactured his first solid chocolate bar in 1895, it wasn't until after World War I that the bars gained popularity. Combination candy bars—which mixed chocolate with other ingredients—hit store shelves even later.

Much of what Frank Mars sold was penny candy. Spun from family recipes and passed down through generations, these candies were manufactured on a small scale mostly by women, like Frank's own mother, who cooked alone in their kitchens. Unwrapped and unbranded, these handmade treats were typically sold by retailers by the piece and bore generic names like lemon drops, peppermint sticks and licorice. Brokering these candies wasn't easy. It required a good amount of up-front cash to finance a sizable inventory and a large amount of travel, since candy supplies were erratic and customers were hard to find. Frank would often leave his family for weeks at a time, ever widening his search for a sale. But his travels rarely paid off. Candy is highly perishable, and more often than not, by the time Frank cut a deal, his goods were spoiled.

Life in the Mars household quickly turned desperate. Frank's business was nearing bankruptcy. Every penny had gone into the company and soon there was nothing left: no rent money, no food, few belongings. Terrified for herself and her son, Ethel Mars divorced her husband in the summer of 1910 on the grounds of nonsupport. She was awarded custody of six-year-old Forrest, and Frank was ordered to pay $20 a month in alimony. But the money never came.

Reluctantly, Ethel sent Forrest to live with her parents in North Brattleford, Canada, an isolated mining town in Saskatchewan. She remained in Minneapolis, taking a job as a sales clerk in a department store. She wrote Forrest often and forwarded money whenever she could, but the two rarely saw each other. Frank was absent altogether.

Soon after the divorce, he had remarried—to another Ethel, coincidentally—and moved west to Seattle. There, Frank decided to capitalize on his childhood fascination and try his hand at candy manufacturing. Once again, he poured all of his assets into the firm, but within a year, the company went under and creditors seized all of the couple's personal belongings, including their home—although Seattle candy makers claim Frank Mars never paid off all of his debt.

"He skipped town before anybody could catch him to settle up—it's legend around here," said Mark Haley of the Brown & Haley candy company, maker of a popular confection called Almond Roca and a competitor of Mars in those early days.

Frank's next stop was Tacoma, where in 1914, he failed for the third time. He blamed this latest bankruptcy on stiff competition, especially from Brown & Haley, and returned with his wife to Minnesota, where the territory was at least more familiar. With his last $400, he plunged into candy making once again, although this time it was a more modest affair.

Because of his credit history, no supplier in the Twin Cities would deal with him, so he couldn't buy ingredients in bulk. A handful of small candy makers agreed to sell him surplus sugar, corn syrup and extracts, but they demanded payment strictly in cash. To compensate for these limitations, Frank and Ethel lived in a sparse room above the kitchen he called his factory. Each day before dawn, he cooked a small, fresh batch of candies. Ethel took them with her on the trolley, selling them to passengers and shopkeepers along the route.

He named his company the Mar-O-Bar Co., after a gooey combination of caramel, nuts and chocolate he invented. But his best-seller was a butter cream concoction that had been popular on the West Coast, which he called Victorian Butter Creams. Woolworth and a dozen or so smaller retailers soon became steady customers, and by 1923, his business was a success.

But this is where the story gets sticky.

To hear Forrest Mars tell it, he is the one who turned Mar-O-Bars into millions.

In a videotape made for the family's personal archives, Forrest Mars says he gave his father the idea for the Milky Way, the nougat-centered candy bar that launched Mars into orbit.

"I had empire in my mind," Forrest declares in the only recorded account of the Mars company's beginnings. "Simple businesses, that's what you need, if you wish to go for the world."

Having grown up with his grandparents, Forrest knew little about his father. The two had not seen each other or corresponded since the divorce. His mother referred to Frank Mars as "that miserable failure," and she constantly carped at young Forrest to do better for himself. Forrest took the goading seriously.

Each day, he walked three miles to the nearest school, a one-room clapboard house that doubled as a church on Sundays, where he quickly established himself as a star pupil. His best subject was math. He could solve complicated equations instantaneously in his head, a skill that won him respect from his teacher and classmates. He delighted in games of skill—chess, cribbage and later bridge and poker. He took great pride in beating the adults around him, and in showing off his knowledge generally. He was always first to raise his hand in class; he read books far beyond his years; he collected trivia in every subject and would rattle off obscure facts at the slightest provocation.

Although most of his classmates never finished school—they were recruited early by the timber companies and coal mines—Forrest continued his education, encouraged by his mother. In 1922, he graduated Lethbridge High School in Alberta, Canada, and won a partial scholarship to the University of California at Berkeley, where he enrolled in the School of Mining. Forrest said he planned to become a mining engineer "with the idea of going back to Canada." But his entrepreneurial instincts soon overtook his schooling.

To pay his room and board, Forrest took a part-time job in the school cafeteria, scrubbing floors, washing dishes and hauling garbage. But he wound up, in his words, "the richest kid" on campus. By showing the chef how to reorganize the menus to utilize the meats Forrest could buy at steep discounts from wholesalers, Forrest earned an average of $100 a week in 1923—a fortune so vast he canceled most of his classes to concentrate on business. But when school closed for vacation, Forrest was out of work. So that summer, he joined a team of salesmen traveling the country hawking Camel cigarettes.

That's when he met his estranged father.

On the final night of the Camel tour, Forrest ordered his sales team to plaster the most famous street in Chicago—State Street—with Camel posters, because his boss told him to leave a trail showing the world he'd been there.

"We're going to go down there and put up our window bills on Cartier, on Marshall Field's, the whole main shopping district," Forrest instructed his men. "They'll *know* we've been in town."

The outrageous marketing ploy made headlines in every Chicago newspaper—and landed Forrest in jail. It was Frank Mars who bailed him out.

Although Forrest hadn't seen his father since he was six, he recognized Frank immediately. Short and thickset, with a prominent nose and disappearing chin, the two men looked a lot alike. Both wore glasses. Both had round fleshy cheeks and freckles. And strangely, they shared the same awkward rolling gait. Frank's was the result of polio and Forrest's the legacy of badly bowed legs, but anyone watching them would think the trait was hereditary.

Forrest had never seen a picture of his father, and the uncanny resemblance unnerved him. Since childhood he had identified with his mother's side of the family, and so he naturally assumed he took after her and her relatives. To see himself as the spitting image of Frank was an insult to his life's ambition; he didn't want to be anything like his father—and he certainly didn't want to look like him. Even more disturbing, Forrest quickly learned that Frank—"that miserable failure"—had found success in Minneapolis with his butter creams. He was now earning $60,000 a year and was living in a five-bedroom home outside the Twin Cities with his second wife and their daughter, Patricia. It was not a story that Forrest was prepared for.

Frank said nothing of his disappearance from Forrest's life. And perhaps afraid of the answers, Forrest, too, asked little about the past. Instead, the two men talked about business, the only neutral topic they had in common.

It was this conversation that changed the future of Frank's company, according to Forrest. He claims that while drinking chocolate malted milks at a nearby five-and-dime, he gave his father the idea for his first candy bar. It all started with a simple suggestion: "Why don't [you manufacture] something like Camel cigarettes?" Forrest asked Frank: "Why don't you make something that I can sell all over the United States?"

So far, Milton S. Hershey was the only candy maker selling products nationwide. The rest of the industry limited sales to local merchants, largely because their products didn't stay fresh long enough to be shipped any distance. Frank Mars's company was typical; more than 65 percent of his sales were in St. Paul and Minneapolis.

Forrest told his father: "You're making money, but we can't sell them anywhere outside of Minnesota. You've got problems even there."

Frank asked: "Well, what would you do?"

To which Forrest replied offhandedly: "Why don't you put this chocolate malted drink in a candy bar?"

"I was just saying anything that entered my head," Forrest explained later. "And I'll be damned if a short time afterwards, he has a candy bar. And it's a chocolate malted drink. He put some caramel on top of it, and some chocolate around it—not very good chocolate, he was buying cheap chocolate—but that damn thing sold. No advertising."

The new creation, dubbed the Milky Way, was strikingly different from its competitors. First, its solid chocolate coating kept the candy bar fresh. Second, because malt-flavored nougat—a whipped filling made of egg whites and corn syrup—was the bar's main ingredient, the Milky

Way was much bigger, tasted just as chocolatey, but cost much less to produce.

"People walked up to the candy counter and they'd see this flat little Hershey bar for a nickel and right next to it, a giant Milky Way. Guess which one they'd pick?" bragged Forrest.

In its first year on the market, 1924, the Milky Way brought in sales of nearly $800,000. The fluffy nougat quickly became Mars's hallmark, the centerpiece of all of Frank's candy creations.

That September, Forrest Mars returned to Berkeley, but he was no longer interested in mining.

"In the cafeteria, I was making more money—twice as much, three times as much money—as they're going to pay me as a mining engineer when I graduate," Forrest said. " . . . The hell with running some mines in the backwoods."

Inspired by his father's manufacturing success, and driven by his own competitive nature, he initially changed his major to metallurgy.

"I figured I'd mix some elements together and make some new metal or something," he said. "It didn't look too hard."

But then he heard about Irving Fisher, head of the department of economics at Yale University and one of America's leading economists. In a speech to Berkeley's undergraduates, Fisher railed against government intervention to increase employment. His ideas fascinated Forrest.

"I listened . . . and he's talking about something called inflation," Forrest recalled. "He's talking about money. . . . I don't really understand it but I went down to the dean and I said, 'I can't afford to wait. I've got to go to Yale to learn all about this money business.'"

In 1925, just before his junior year, Forrest transferred to Yale with the help of his father. He enrolled in the Sheffield Scientific School to study industrial engineering, hoping to learn all he could about commerce.

At Yale, Forrest paid close attention to his classes. But it wasn't long before he found himself another job—this time, selling neckties to his status-conscious classmates. The scheme rivaled his cafeteria gig, earning Forrest hundreds of dollars each semester, not to mention a lot of connections on campus. He sold neckties to the football players and glee club singers, to the fraternity boys and the secret societies. To make himself popular, he handed out free Camel cigarettes to all of his customers, a gesture that quickly endeared him to his classmates.

The necktie operation, like so many of Forrest's best business ideas, was the result of an unusually keen intuition. Perhaps it came from growing up poor, or from being forced to prove himself at a very young age. Whatever the reason, Forrest was a man surrounded by possibilities. Everywhere he looked, he saw an angle.

As he tells it, while shopping in Sulka & Co., a prestigious men's store, he came across a salesman tossing neckties into a large basket. It turned out the salesman was throwing the ties away, and that gave Forrest an idea: "Look, why can't I have them? I'll buy 'em and we'll sell them to Yale students . . . and when they get out of school, you'll have them all buying Sulka neckties."

Forrest paid 50 cents apiece for twenty neckties and sold them to his classmates for $2 each. When he ran out of inventory, he returned to the store for more, but Mr. Sulka raised the price to 75 cents. Not to be outdone, Forrest bought the ties and set up a kiosk in the student union, complete with carpeting, chairs and a mirror.

"And wouldn't you know, I got $2.50 for 'em," he boasted.

Although he lacked the good looks and high social standing that marked most of the Yale student body, he was popular on campus—especially with the faculty, who admired his drive and intelligence. And although some found him too arrogant and cocky, his business sense, self-assurance and seriousness earned him respect.

"I wanted to learn about money, about business," Forrest said of his Ivy League years. "I wasn't at Yale to be pampered, like some other boys."

Forrest told friends it enraged him to see sons of wealthy businesmen wasting time with girls, getting drunk and missing classes. His roommate, Pierre Holk, nephew of Pierre du Pont, agreed.

The two spent a lot of time together, dreaming up get-rich-quick schemes and talking about the future. Forrest pumped Pierre for all he knew about his uncle's business strategies and slowly came to learn how DuPont was structured and managed.

"Pierre taught me a lot about business," remembered Forrest. "He really got me thinking."

Forrest read every book he could find on du Pont, on Rockefeller, on Ford. But it wasn't the entrepreneurial ambitions of these men that impressed him; it was the nuts-and-bolts business principles each employed—their accounting practices, their manufacturing techniques, their internal organization. He absorbed himself in these nitty-gritty and seemingly mundane details, and by the time he graduated in 1928, he was ready to test all he had learned.

$\mathcal{F}$rank Mars's company, now called Mars, Inc., was moving to a swanky new plant on Chicago's west side. (A move Forrest claimed he encouraged.)

"I told my dad, 'The freight rate in Chicago is half that of Minneapolis . . . with this rate, we can really make some money.'

"So he begins to listen . . . and we start building in 1927."

Mars paid $45,000 for a large tract of land just north of Oak Park, a wealthy Chicago suburb. The site was known to golfers for over thirty years as the thirteenth, fourteenth and fifteenth holes of the Westward Ho golf course, but Frank turned it into a $500,000 showplace.

From the outside, the factory looked like a Spanish-style monastery, with stucco walls, red-tile coping, wrought-iron ornamentation, two-story arched windows and doorways, a beautiful cupola and a long canopy extending one hundred feet from the main entrance to the sidewalk. Absolutely nothing on the exterior hinted at the manufacturing activities inside. Mars wanted the structure to blend with the surrounding well-to-do neighborhood, and like the homes nearby, the Mars factory was bordered by broad, sloping lawns of brilliant green bent grass, beds of flowers, shrubs and towering trees.

"A casual passerby who didn't know what it was probably would think it was a fashionable club or some important institution—never a factory," wrote the *Chicago Tribune*. The newspaper called the plant "the most outstanding piece of industrial architecture in Chicago," and credited it with actually boosting home sales in the area.[1]

Inside, everything was cutting-edge. Designed by the engineering department of the Austin company—which built all of the automobile plants for Ford—the plant was sleek, modern, efficient and as automated as possible.

"We'd had one small enrober in Minneapolis," Forrest recalled, referring to the machine that coats the candy in chocolate. "But we had a whole line of 'em here. And we've got wrapping machines that'll wrap an uneven bar. We knew how to wrap a standard item, but how to wrap a bar that's not always quite the same shape? We learned that."

In 1929, Forrest said, the Chicago plant was cranking out as many as 20 million candy bars annually. His father wanted to broaden the company's product line, "but I told him to keep it simple," Forrest said.

In 1930, Frank Mars invented the Snickers bar—a peanut-flavored nougat bar topped with crunchy nuts and caramel, coated in chocolate. In 1932, he unveiled the 3 Musketeers, which took its name from its original design: three pieces of nougat candy—one chocolate, one vanilla and one strawberry. (When the price of strawberries rose, he dropped the design in favor of a single giant chocolate-flavored bar.)

The additions pushed Mars sales to more than $25 million in 1932, ranking Mars as the second-biggest candy maker in the country. Only Hershey was bigger. But there was no rivalry; in fact, Hershey and Mars were business partners.

"It was a different era," explains Richard Murrie, whose father was president of the Hershey Chocolate Co. until 1947. "Everybody knew everybody, everybody was friendly. My father was friends with Frank Mars. They admired and respected each other very much."

When Frank Mars was struggling in Minneapolis, it was Hershey, or more specifically, William Murrie, who helped him out.

The elder Murrie met Frank when he was trying to secure a steady flow of supplies for the Milky Way. He thought Frank's product might make it big, so when no other chocolate supplier would extend Mars credit, Murrie gave him an account. As Frank's company grew and became more successful, so did the relationship between Mars and Hershey.

When the two first joined forces, Hershey was selling just a small amount of chocolate coating to other food manufacturers. Nabisco, for example, bought Hershey chocolate flavoring for its Oreo cookies, as did other firms that couldn't afford to manufacture chocolate themselves. But company records show Hershey was considering closing down that business.

"It was so small, it was more expensive than lucrative," explained Earl Spangler,[2] former president of the chocolate company.

But then came Frank Mars.

"That's what really started it going," said Spangler. "Mars didn't buy coating from anybody else. Not Nestlé's, not Baker's, just Hershey's."

In 1921, Hershey recorded sales of just 8.3 million pounds of coating. By 1938, coating sales reached 8.4 million pounds *a month,* thanks in large part to Mars.[3] William Murrie saw Frank Mars not as a threat, but as one of his best customers. At the height of their relationship, coating sales accounted for one-quarter of Hershey's total chocolate output and 20 percent of Hershey's total sales, or about $7.5 million per year. Every week, as many as ten boxcars loaded with ten-pound blocks of solid chocolate left the Hershey railway station headed for Mars, Chicago.

So important was the Mars business that Hershey scientists developed a whole new line of special chocolate for each of Frank's inventions. The chocolate coating for the Snickers bar was milky and smooth, with just a hint of peanut, while the 3 Musketeers was extra sweet and chocolatey. The original Milky Way was enrobed with standard Hershey chocolate plus the slightest hint of malt.

For both companies, times were good. Frank Mars was tooling around Chicago in a $20,000 Duesenberg. His wife, Ethel, drove a sixteen-cylinder Cadillac. They built a vacation estate—a 100-foot-by-200-foot log mansion in Minocqua, Wisconsin, that Frank called his "fishing place." And they indulged a passion for horses, investing more than $2 million in a lavish Tennessee horse farm they named the Milky Way Stables. They owned an airplane, had servants in every quarters and plenty of money in the bank.

But Forrest Mars wasn't satisfied. "I wanted to conquer the whole goddamn world," he explained.

Unlike his father, who was permanently scarred from his early years in business, Forrest Mars had no fear of failure; it simply wasn't part of his makeup. He was constantly pushing Frank to expand the business. Everything had to be faster, cheaper, bigger, better.

Supposedly, Forrest was responsible for buying the company's raw materials, but he strutted around the Chicago plant as though he owned it, shouting orders at workers on the line and advising every manager from sales to accounting. He contradicted his father at every turn and argued obsessively with Frank about the future of the firm.

Soon, every worker in the plant was complaining about Forrest's know-it-all attitude and meddling nature. Frank Mars tried to ignore their criticisms; after all, Forrest was family, and now that they had reunited, he was desperate to make amends. But Forrest wasn't making it easy. He continued to question his father's judgment, and he demanded that Mars expand into Canada. Frank Mars didn't share his son's enthusiasm.

"My father says, 'We're making enough money. We have an airplane, we've got the fishing place, we got horses. Why do we need any more?'" recalled Forrest.

It's a question he himself would never ask.

"Why do I want to go on?" Forrest mused. "I want to go on because it's fun. I like building businesses. . . . I like the tension. I like the gamble. . . . The word *challenge* isn't too good a word for it. I think it's better to say the truth: I like the tension."

"It's like telling you I like to fish because I like that tug. It isn't how big the fish is that matters, it's that tug before you get it up. That's the most exciting time."

But Frank Mars wanted no part of it, and in the fall of 1932, he kicked Forrest out of the business.

"Things got bitter," remembered Forrest, "and I'm not proud of this. I told my dad to stick his business up his ass. If he didn't want to give me one-third [of the stock] right then, I said, 'I'm leaving.'

"He said leave, so I left."

Frank gave Forrest $50,000 and the foreign rights to the Milky Way, and Forrest set out to prove he could succeed alone, just as he always had before he came to Chicago. With his wife, Audrey, and his newborn son, Forrest Jr., he traveled to Europe to seek his own fortune, far from the shadow of his complacent father.

Fifteen months later, Frank Mars collapsed on the floor of the Chicago factory. He was rushed to the hospital with kidney failure and died a few weeks later. He was just fifty years old.

Forrest, his only son, was noticeably absent from his funeral.

*W*anting to rid himself entirely of Frank Mars's influence, Forrest started his first manufacturing concern in Paris, and it had nothing whatsoever to do with candy.

"I had a new way of keeping your shoes straight—shoe trees, you call 'em today," said Forrest. "It had this wire that hooked on the inside and a form that kept 'em straight. But I didn't know enough French to know how to sell the damned things."

Forrest tinkered with the idea of returning to confections, but first he wanted to become a candy maker himself.

"You can hire lawyers, you can hire accountants, you can hire advertising men or financial types," he reasoned. "But if you want to get rich, you gotta know how to make a product—and you aren't going to hire anybody to make a product for you to make you rich. They'll only make it for themselves."

Not surprisingly, given his competitive streak, Forrest was particularly interested in the one part of the candy business that his father didn't know: chocolate. So in early 1933 he traveled to Switzerland to study with the masters, working first at the factory of Jean Tobler, who in 1899 introduced an opulent line of chocolate bars, including his famous Toblerone, and next at the factory of Henri Nestlé, the chemist who invented milk chocolate in 1875 with a Swiss candy maker named Daniel Peter.[4]

"I was an hourly paid guy," remembered Forrest. "They didn't know who I was. I just told them I was an American, and the factory manager didn't care, all he cared was whether I knew anything about candy."

By posing as an ordinary factory worker, Forrest assured himself a first-class education in chocolate manufacture. But he wasn't the only candy maker to steal secrets this way. Stories abound of famous candy men sneaking inside factories by offering to work for the competition. While perfecting his recipe for milk chocolate, Milton Hershey supposedly toured several European factories, including a cheese factory in Switzerland, where he studied how the Swiss handled milk. (He was hoping to unlock the secret to blending milk and chocolate.)[5]

The Cadburys and Rowntrees sent so many moles to work in each other's factories that their spying became legendary, the basis of Roald Dahl's industry parody, *Charlie and the Chocolate Factory:*

> "You see, Charlie, not so very long ago there used to be thousands of people working in Mr. Willy Wonka's factory. Then one day, all of a sudden, Mr. Wonka had to ask every single one of them to leave, to go home, never to come back."
> "But why?" asked Charlie.
> "Because of spies."
> "Spies?"
> "Yes. All the other chocolate makers, you see, had begun to grow jealous of the wonderful candies that Mr. Wonka was making, and they started sending in spies to steal his secret recipes. The spies took jobs in the Wonka factory, pretending that they were ordinary workers, and while they were there, each one of them found out exactly how a certain special thing was made."

The practice became so rampant that candy makers in Europe—where most of the important industry innovations were taking place—began hiring detective agencies to investigate their employees. Sensitive manufacturing processes were designated off-limits to all but the most loyal workers. And businesses that dealt with candy makers were forced

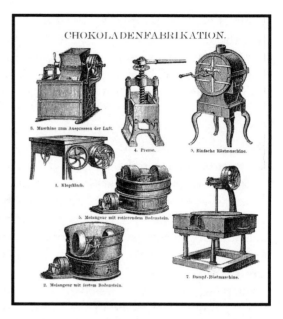

CHOKOLADENFABRIKATION.

3. Maschine zum Auspressen der Luft.

4. Presse.

6. Einfache Röstmaschine.

1. Klopftisch.

5. Melangeur mit rotierendem Bodenstein.

2. Melangeur mit festem Bodenstein.

7. Dampf-Röstmaschine.

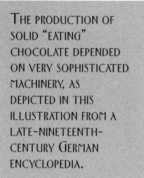

THE PRODUCTION OF SOLID "EATING" CHOCOLATE DEPENDED ON VERY SOPHISTICATED MACHINERY, AS DEPICTED IN THIS ILLUSTRATION FROM A LATE-NINETEENTH-CENTURY GERMAN ENCYCLOPEDIA.

to sign confidentiality agreements. But the precautions did little to stop the spying, which continues today.

"Mars's intelligence operations are infamous," said Jack Dowd, retired marketing executive for Hershey. "I know they tried to pump information out of suppliers and brokers and candy buyers—anybody they could. I wouldn't be a bit surprised if they infiltrated our ranks, although as far as I know, we never caught them at it."

None of the fifty candy companies I spoke with—including Mars and Hershey—acknowledged using such deceptive practices against their competitors. But at the same time, each firm complained that corporate espionage was a problem in the industry.

"I do know that industrial espionage has been used—used against us," said former Hershey CEO Richard Zimmerman. "And I do know that we worried quite a bit about having visitors in our plant . . . but visitors almost never saw the key areas, the critical areas. It was a very highly selective process of who got into those areas, and I'm sure that is still the case today."

George Greener, a former Mars executive, said he knows the company's European operations have been infiltrated by other European manufacturers, although he refused to name the perpetrators.

"It happens," he said. "Everybody knows it happens. The last guy who tried it was claiming to be a food technologist, which he was. But he was also being paid by another company to get a job at Mars and report on what we were doing." Greener said the ruse was discovered before the man was hired.

Forrest Mars never revealed his identity to his Swiss employers, but he defended this omission, saying: "They never asked."

At the time of his employment, the process of manufacturing chocolate was gradually shifting from improvisation to exact science as manufacturers experimented with various ways to render the essence from roasted cocoa beans. No two companies employed the same practices. In America, Milton Hershey was blending and smoothing his chocolate for a record ninety-six hours before allowing the candy to harden. In England, the chocolate was subjected to heat during mixing, which added a caramelized flavor to the finished product and shortened the mixing to about seventy-two hours. In Switzerland, manufacturers were adding condensed milk to the unsweetened chocolate to produce a creamier blend.

Each process produced its own unique chocolate flavor, and over time, these differences translated into distinct national tastes. The British, for example, prefer their milk chocolate very sweet and caramel-like, while Americans identify with the harsher, grittier flavor popularized by Hershey. German chocolate generally ranks as the richest because of its traditionally high fat content, while Italian chocolate is drier, more bittersweet. Swiss chocolate, considered the finest by connoisseurs, is characterized by a strong, aromatic, almost perfumey flavor, and the smoothest, silkiest texture.

Discerning such differences has become a trade all its own. Much like wine tasters, professional chocolate tasters train for years, fine-tuning their palettes to each nuance in the candy. Because the final product can be affected by hundreds of variables, it is the chocolate taster's job to keep the flavor "pure." At Mars, this is done in Elizabethtown, Pennsylvania, where the company's U.S. chocolate is produced. Every day at 3 P.M., a panel of tasters is called in to test each batch at each stage of production.[6] Seated at a kitchen table, they sample the chocolate from the last twenty-four hours and report their findings on an elaborate checklist that covers texture, color, flavor and meltability. The job is not as exciting as it sounds, however. Swallowing is not allowed, and the chocolate they test has not yet been sweetened. (The sugar would mask any off flavors.) Besides, it's very difficult work; chocolate is one of nature's most complex flavors. So numerous are its properties that chemists have been unable to synthesize it despite decades of research.

"Chocolate is Mother Nature's best-kept secret," says Maurice Jeffery, a manufacturing consultant. "We still haven't unlocked all of its mysteries, and reproducing it is out of the question."

Explains one chemist in McCormick & Co.'s flavor division: "If you're a mountain climber, you want to climb Mount Everest. If you're a flavor chemist, you want to make the perfect chocolate."

Flavorists have mastered sour apple, piña colada, vanilla and pistachio, but their chocolate doesn't even come close. That's because chocolate contains more than 1,200 different chemical components, about six times as many as lemon or strawberry, which are a cinch to make in the lab. Chemicals known as "top notes" or "volatiles" contribute to chocolate's aroma; "background" notes give chocolate its bitterness and aftertaste; and cocoa butter—which isn't even in a flavorist's repertoire—provides chocolate's meltability and mouthfeel.

None of the 1,200 chemicals in chocolate is dominant, like the vanillin in vanilla or the menthol in mint that give them their distinctive flavors. Instead, chocolate is a complex combination of hundreds of chemicals that give off rosy notes, honey notes, leafy notes, nutty notes, bitter notes and even sweaty notes. While they all work together in real chocolate, they're impossible to harmonize in synthesized form. For example, one chocolate chemical, trimethylamine, emits a strong note of spoiled fish, which overpowers every other chemical in the test tube. Real chocolate, however, wouldn't taste the same without it.

Further limiting the chemists' efforts, only 20 percent of the chemicals known to occur naturally in chocolate have been approved by the U.S. government for use in foods. So when flavorists discovered a dash of a cyanide-based chemical in chocolate, there was nothing they could do; federal standards prohibited them from reproducing it for consumers.

The complexities and mysteries surrounding chocolate were not lost on Forrest Mars. He carefully observed the various methods of production and took detailed notes on the results.

"I'd see how much sugar they put in, the kind of milk they used," he remembered. "I'd watch some guys heat their conches [the machines that mix the chocolate] and other guys cold conche.

"Some would run the same mixture through a battery of refiners, while another guy might run it through just once. Mr. Hershey, why he used to slap that stuff, mixed it for days. The Swiss, they were a little more scientific."

In 1933, when Forrest had learned all he could, he headed for England to launch his own confectionery. "At least there I could speak the language," he explained. But the beginning wasn't easy. The British market was saturated with sweets from local manufacturers like Rowntree & Co. and Cadbury Brothers Ltd., which together controlled nearly 100 percent of solid-chocolate sales. These were mammoth-sized corporations employing tens of thousands of workers and producing millions of pounds of chocolate each year. The Cadbury Dairy Milk bar was the Hershey bar of Britain, although it was sweeter and creamier and came in "tablets" a half inch thick.

By the time Forrest Mars showed up, Cadbury was already manufacturing chocolate in Ireland, Australia and South Africa. The Cadbury family owned one of London's largest newspapers and its members were involved in Parliament, the military and local government. Rowntree also owned a London newspaper, and its influence was just as widespread. The company was considered Britain's most savvy marketer, with promotions that included coupons, full-page advertisements and billboards. Like Cadbury, Rowntree boasted vast operations abroad, in Ireland, Australia and Canada. Its staples included Black Magic chocolates, Kit Kat and Aero bars.

Forrest Mars was an outsider. And against such giant competitors, his $50,000 seemed useless. He scrapped his plans to open a Chicago-sized factory and, like his father before him, set up a tiny kitchen in a small industrial town about thirty miles north of London called Slough. He and Audrey and little Forrest Jr. lived in a one-room cold-water flat behind the "factory," and Forrest went to work creating an Anglicized version of the Milky Way, which he egotistically dubbed the Mars bar.

In the Mars tradition, he devoted everything he had to the product, leaving little for his family. The situation became so bleak that Audrey wrote to her parents in America, complaining that the heat in the apartment never worked and that there was very little food. When Forrest refused to remedy the situation, she and Forrest Jr. returned to America to live with her parents.

Forrest was never ashamed of this. It was simply a matter of business—what was required at the time.

"My father-in-law took them back to America to feed them," he stated matter-of-factly. "So, they went home."

Meanwhile, Forrest bought some secondhand manufacturing equipment from Baker Perkins Ltd., a well-known supplier, and he secured malted milk from a man who had occasionally helped his father. He also lined up an account with Cadbury to purchase chocolate, knowing it would be years before he could afford to manufacture his own. On the August bank holiday of 1933—with four employees working in an ice-cold room barely bigger than a clerk's office—he produced his first candy bars. He traveled to London to sell them himself, and within a few months, he had established a small following.

Once again, it was the nougat that made the difference. Forrest altered the fluffy filling slightly, adding more sugar and a little less malt to satisfy British tastes, and he covered it in even sweeter caramel. When surrounded by the beloved flavor of Cadbury's, the Mars bar captured all that the British adored about chocolate. It was sweet and creamy and rich, and it was bigger than any other bar on the market. Sales soon took off, and Forrest began furiously expanding his tiny factory to keep up with demand.

But all was not perfect. Forrest wanted to expand his offerings beyond Mars bars, but every other candy he tried was a failure. A bar called So Big, the biggest candy bar ever introduced, was a disaster, remembered Forrest, "because nobody could eat that much candy at once," and the leftovers quickly melted in your pocket. Forrest also experimented with a pineapple version of the Mars bar, inspired by a drop in the price of the tropical fruit, but that bar also flopped. In 1937, he gambled by trading cocoa commodities—a big mistake. "I lost my shirt," he reluctantly admitted.

But he defended these early mistakes by saying, "I'm not a candy maker. I'm empire-minded." And it is in the factory in Slough that he developed the austere principles that still guide the Mars empire today.

For running the business according to his strictures, Forrest paid his managers three and four times what other companies offered. In return, he demanded complete devotion, asking employees to work with him twelve and fourteen hours a day. To ensure that everyone pulled his weight, salaries, including his own, were tied to corporate performance.

He lectured on quality with the zeal and regularity of a Sunday preacher. An improperly wrapped candy bar or a pinhole in the chocolate coating sent him into a dither. He would hurl boxes of poorly wrapped chocolate across a room and would terrorize the factory floor if he noticed Mars bars without enough caramel.

His longtime financial officer, David Brown, praised his cunning business sense and his absolute dedication to the product. But in recalling how he came to be Forrest's chief accountant in the early days at Slough, Brown remembered only one thing: fear.

"Few people wanted to go work for him directly," said Brown, who spent thirty-seven years as one of Forrest's top lieutenants but wouldn't dare consider the man his friend. He described his dealings with Forrest as amicable, "as long as you had a strong duck's back—if you could take a certain amount of tantrums. . . . He could be cruel and demanding—you just had to know how to shake it off."

What he lacked in charm, he made up for in determination. Forrest was a risk taker with an uncanny ability to sense potential. "He was always prepared to consider outlandish ideas," said Brown. In 1934, not long after the Mars bar proved a success, Forrest purchased a small British company called Chappel Bros., which was canning meat by-products for dogs. Throughout Europe, dogs and cats were eating table scraps. No one had even considered an alternative. But Forrest saw possibilities. He believed he could convince pet owners that Chappie's canned food was more nutritious, and it wasn't long before Britain and the rest of Europe bought the idea. With no competition, Petfoods Ltd. soon dominated the market. Within five years, Forrest had increased sales fivefold, to £100,000. Chappie became the cornerstone of Mars, Inc.'s, pet food empire, which today accounts for nearly half of the company's total sales.

This is what Forrest loved, building businesses. Not managing them. He left the managing to others and spent his time tinkering with new products, new manufacturing techniques, new ways to improve quality and efficiency. Those who worked for him described him as a dictator. But he was much more than that. He was an explorer, a conqueror. He wanted everything made cheaper and faster than the competition. To do that, he brought the wisdom of outside industries into his businesses. He studied the production of steel to learn how to conduct a product through his plant without touching it. He studied the manufacture of cement to better understand how to mix his own ingredients. He borrowed DuPont's planning system and patterned his management structure after T. G. Rose's *Higher Control in Management,* a British book that emphasizes flat, simple organization. He routinely rebuilt the standard candy manufacturing equipment, making it less wasteful and easier to operate. And he was never satisfied.

"Wherever he could, he applied the principles of economics, mathematics and science," remembers Charles W. Kaufman, a business professor who worked for Forrest as a consultant in the 1960s. "He was way ahead of everybody else in the industry. They were just candy makers. He was an entrepreneur."

To ensure his workers arrived promptly, Forrest installed a time clock and offered an additional bonus to those who were never late. He also instituted a complicated system of checks and balances to ensure the quality of his candy. All workers on the factory floor were authorized to halt production if they noticed something wrong, and they were berated by Forrest if they didn't do just that.

"Forrest would rant and rave about how *we* represented the customer inside the factory," said Mark Cross, who worked at Slough in those early days. "He was fanatical about quality and was constantly inspecting everything himself. He was on you like a mosquito if he suspected you weren't doing your job right."

Today, business gurus loudly espouse the merits of such practices. Total Quality Management, Worker Empowerment and Total Responsibility—these are modern business buzzwords. But what they really mean is, be like Forrest Mars—give workers a sense of ownership in the final product; reward employees for their performance; encourage workers to make decisions for themselves; focus on quality, quality, quality. Such popular new products as General Motors's Saturn have been built on these so-called innovative ideas.

To be fair, no one outside of Mars knew that Forrest was preaching these practices in the 1930s. And to some degree, neither did Forrest. He had no fancy label for his management style, no carefully ordered theory for his approach. He didn't read about it in some comprehensive manual. His philosophies grew naturally out of his exacting personality and his study of the businesses around him. Those who worked closely with Forrest said he couldn't have run his company any other way.

"It was in his blood," said Duke Vance, one of Forrest's top managers. "He never once thought of doing it differently."

By 1939, Mars Ltd. was ranked as Britain's third-largest candy manufacturer. Forrest had opened a factory in Brussels and had started selling his Mars bars across Europe. But soon after steering his company to success, Forrest had to leave the country.

To help raise money for World War II, the British government had imposed a special tax on all resident foreigners. Forrest later claimed that members of the Rowntree and Cadbury families who were active in Parliament had pushed for the tax to run him out of town, although he could never prove it.[7]

"They wanted to shut me down," he said. "And the war gave them the perfect opportunity." Of course, Forrest had no intention of paying the tax, but he refused to close his business. Instead, he left it in the hands of Collin Pratt, his top British manager, and returned to America.

Although his father had long since died, the Mars factory in Chicago was being run by his stepmother and her family, and there was no room for Forrest. He had other plans, anyway. With the war spreading across Europe, he thought that the candy-coated chocolates he had seen during his travels in Spain might be in demand. So he headed for Hershey to work out a deal.

M.S. HERSHEY
DEALER IN

MACHINERY HALL
LENGTH 1402 FEET WIDTH 360 FEET

FINE CONFECTIONERY, FRUITS, NUTS, &c.

o. 935 SPRING GARDEN STREET,   PHILADELPHIA.

MILTON HERSHEY OPENED HIS FIRST
CANDY SHOP AT AGE NINETEEN. IT
WENT UNDER AFTER SIX YEARS—
THE FIRST OF SEVERAL FAILURES.

ITTING IN AN old and frayed easy chair, smoking a
Corona-Corona cigar and playing solitaire, Milton Hershey looked
more like a lonely, half-forgotten grandfather than a millionaire
industrialist who had introduced the world to the nickel chocolate
bar. It had become his habit to sit there, playing cards or Chinese
checkers, listening to the war news on the cabinet radio that was the
only other piece of furniture in the room. When he couldn't sleep,
which was often, he would prop himself up in the chair, an afghan

gathered around his legs, listening to the commentators until the soft light of the morning sky reminded him of the new day.

At eighty-five, he rarely left this room anymore. Except for visits to Atlantic City, where, he said, the seaside air invigorated him, he preferred the familiar comfort of his two-room suite in High Point Mansion, located in the center of the town of Hershey, Pennsylvania. The mansion, which he built for his wife, Kitty, in 1908, no longer belonged to him. He had given it away in 1930, to be used as a clubhouse for the newly organized Hershey Country Club. But he kept two rooms on the second floor for himself and, now that he was no longer traveling the world, he conducted most of his business from the tiny sitting room, which doubled as dining room and boardroom.

Although no longer involved in the business firsthand, he gathered executives in his suite each day to lunch with him and report on operations. He never said much at these meetings, just listened and nodded. But then, Hershey was never a man of words. Lacking any formal education, he preferred to let others do the talking, interrupting only when he didn't understand or when he disagreed. The only person he was known to have real conversations with was William Murrie, his closest friend and the president of the chocolate company since 1908. The two of them would often sit for hours playing cards, smoking cigars and reminiscing.

Their conversations were modest ones, absent ego or pontification. They enjoyed poking fun at each other, and gave as much credit to others for their successes as to themselves. One of their favorite stories, which they frequently shared with whoever happened to be listening, was of the first time they met—in a billiard hall in Lancaster, Pennsylvania. At the time, Murrie was a "drummer," a traveling salesman for a confectionery wholesale firm out of Pittsburgh. A wisecracker and teller of tall tales, he regaled Hershey with stories of his past—his days as a semi-pro baseball player, a telegrapher for the Western Maryland Railroad, a railroad scab in Chicago. Hershey admired Murrie's gregarious, charming nature—so completely opposite his own—and when Murrie bragged that he could sell more candy than Hershey could manufacture, Hershey took him up on his boast.

The year was 1895, and Hershey, who had already made a vast fortune selling caramels, had only just begun manufacturing chocolate. A wholesale price list of his earliest chocolate creations contained more than one hundred different items. There were Chocolate Cigars and Chocolate Cigarettes, Chocolate Blossoms, Sweet Peas, Chrysanthemums, Chocolate Bicycles, Lady Fingers, Vassar Gems and Princess Wafers. A coating of lampblack turned a light chocolate dark, and a fancy ribbon turned any item into a De Luxe. Murrie took the line on the road, and within a year, he had sold more chocolate than the plant could produce, just as he had promised. The feat so impressed Hershey that he invited Murrie to stay in Lancaster and named him general manager, and later president, of the Hershey Chocolate Co. For the next fifty years, Murrie remained Milton Hershey's right-hand man and trusted confidant.

The two men were not at all alike. At six foot four, Murrie was a fiendishly handsome Scotsman, with a thick head of red hair that the years had slowly turned Santa Claus white. His broad shoulders and flashy smile gave him a Hollywood appearance, which he used unabashedly to woo customers and close deals. Were it not for his stately manner and strict Catholic observance, he could easily have been mistaken for a more unsavory, snake-oil type—for he had that ability to steal you blind before you knew you'd been robbed. Next to Murrie, Hershey seemed almost demure. Soft-spoken, with gentle aqua-blue eyes, he was stocky and a good head shorter than Murrie. His most distinguished features: a thick, dark mustache and heavy eyebrows that combined to give him a touch of old-world elegance.

Hershey liked to start things: to invent new candies, build new businesses, lay out towns and factories. To him, planning and creating were the excitement. Murrie was just the opposite. He was a doer, a mover and shaker who lived to bring ideas to fruition. It was Murrie who actually oversaw the day-to-day operations of the chocolate plant; Murrie who handled the sales, the marketing, the logistics and the distribution. Over time, his behind-the-scenes role earned him the nickname "the Inventor's Implementor." It seemed whatever product Hershey could invent, Murrie could make a success.

The two men were practically inseparable, especially after each was widowed. They shared the same desk, dined together daily and stayed up late most nights playing cards. In their younger days, they played snooker and eight ball in Hershey's billiard room—games that would go on and on since neither was willing to lose his wager. But they kept their competition to the pool room; outside of it, they were a team, building up the business until Hershey became a household name.

This was Murrie's proudest achievement. Although never directly taking credit, he loved to boast how the business had grown from sales of half a million dollars. He would tell his salesmen at every chance how he'd outsold the production run in his very first year, and he urged them all to do the same. Not that selling Hershey chocolate was so hard anymore; the nickel bar, introduced in 1900, had become an American icon. Before Hershey entered the business, chocolate was a luxury available only to the rich. Three manufacturers were producing chocolate candies in the United States in the late 1800s: Walter Baker in New England, and Etienne Guittard and Domingo Ghirardelli in California. (Surprisingly enough, all three are still in business.) None of these companies produced on a large enough scale to make chocolate affordable, however; and none had yet learned the secret of manufacturing milk chocolate.

It was Milton Hershey who revolutionized the industry. He was the first to make milk chocolate in America. And by manufacturing candy bars the way Henry Ford made automobiles, Hershey brought milk chocolate to the masses. His technical innovations and populist vision made him a multimillionaire, but unlike the other great industrialists of his time—Gould or Carnegie, Morgan or Hearst—Hershey never reveled in this particular accomplishment. It was not at all what he was about.

Milton Snavely Hershey was born in 1857 in a crossroads hamlet in central Pennsylvania called Hockersville. This was farm country—cows and corn as far as the eye could see—and home to the Plain People who had emigrated from Switzerland and Germany in the early 1700s to escape religious persecution. Hershey's parents, Fanny and Henry, were Mennonites, an Anabaptist sect similar to the Amish who dressed in distinctly somber fashion, rejected secular education and, almost without exception, were farmers who led purposefully simple lives devoted to God and the land.

Milton's mother was the daughter of a Mennonite minister and a devoted follower. Dressed always in traditional garb—a severe, tightly fitted gray dress, white prayer cap and black bonnet—she was a sternly religious woman who preached frugality and piety and feared extravagance. The only mystery in her life was how she married Henry Hershey, who, although born to a Mennonite family, had nothing in common with his ancestors.

Henry read *The New York Times* and Shakespeare; he was enamored of science and politics. The black loamy fields of his family's homestead held little interest for his vivid imagination, which was filled with romantic schemings and grandiose dreams. Instead of farming, he wanted to become an inventor, an explorer or an entrepreneur. When oil was discovered in western Pennsylvania in 1860, Henry mortgaged his family's farm to cash in on the boom—but within a year, the money was gone and the family had returned to Hockersville.

His future ventures were no more profitable. He tried his hand at writing but couldn't get his outlandish stories published. Next, there was the "farm" at Nine Points, forty-four acres of steep, rocky knolls on the outskirts of Lancaster. Agriculturally, the parcel was a disaster, but Henry didn't mind—that was part of the adventure. He built a seven-foot dam on the property, creating a pond he filled with trout and goldfish. He sank a shaft in his northernmost field, looking for ore that wasn't there. He planted berry bushes, fruit trees, shrubs and something that looked like alfalfa, which he called ornamental grass. He named this eclectic undertaking the Trout Brook Fruit and Nursery Farm, and though the ambitious experiment never earned any money, he called it his greatest triumph—much to his wife's dismay.

Fanny despised Henry's ill-conceived pursuits. She considered his ambitions frivolous and wanton—the work of the devil—and implored him to return to farming and the Mennonite ways. If nothing else, she insisted he support his family, which, in addition to Milton, now included a daughter named Serena. But Henry wanted nothing to do with "the gray-minded people who cannot rejoice," as he described them. He continued to revel in the secular: drawing up blueprints for a perpetual motion machine, experimenting with canning vegetables, conjuring up far-fetched inventions. In all, he tried some seventeen different enterprises during his lifetime; not one earned him a living.

Throughout the 1860s, the Hershey family was almost always broke and constantly on the move. Neighbors remember seeing Milton going about the streets barefoot, selling berries door-to-door. Others remember the Hersheys driving together in a wagon, peddling brooms and butter. For Milton and Serena, it was an unhappy childhood, made harsher by the hostility that pervaded Henry and Fanny's marriage.

The two fought over everything, including Milton's future. Henry wanted his son educated. Fanny did not. As a result of this tug-of-war, Milton attended seven different types of schools, from freethinking to puritan, over an eight-year period. In the end, he was barely literate, having received the equivalent of only a fourth-grade education. His father tried to remedy the situation by apprenticing him to a printer in 1871, but his hopes were well beyond the fourteen-year-old Milton, who was fired within three months. And it only got worse.

MILTON'S FATHER, HENRY HERSHEY, AS HE APPEARED IN 1898.

Ever since Milton's four-year-old sister had died of scarlet fever in 1867, Fanny had blamed Henry for her daughter's death. She taunted him, threatened him and eventually threw him out. She wouldn't file for divorce; that was against her Mennonite ways. But she made sure Henry kept his distance.

Milton never took sides in his parents' feuds. He hated his father's exile, but he said nothing—not even when his mother began using Henry's failures to lecture him about the evils that come from pipe dreams. Fanny wanted to teach her son the value of hard labor, thrift and realism. She didn't want Milton to spend his time with intellectual pursuits; she wanted him to make something, to work or farm, in the tradition of his ancestors. Because of his father, Milton never learned the farming skills so prized among the Mennonites; but, like most children, he adored sweets and was vaguely interested in making candy. That was respectable enough for Fanny, who apprenticed him to Joseph R. Royer, a well-known confectioner.

At Royer's Ice Cream Parlor and Garden, one of Lancaster's most popular businesses, tradition and experiment ruled without the benefit of science. Royer was a craftsman, and his apprentices learned by doing. Hershey learned to feel the "crack" of the candy, to sense that critical moment for removing a batch from the kettle. He displayed a natural flair for experimentation, perhaps from watching his father, and slowly came to understand the intimate relationship between timing, temperature and taste. Neither here nor anywhere else did Milton Hershey learn science or chemistry. In later years, researchers in the Hershey labs noticed that Milton had no concept whatsoever of a chemical reaction. You just kept adding ingredients until the mixture tasted right, and the question "Does it work?" covered everything he wanted to know.

At age nineteen, after four years at Royer's, Milton set out on his own and established a taffy business in Philadelphia. With only $150 borrowed from his mother's relatives, it was a struggle to produce on a scale large enough to make money. But eventually, the Philadelphia shop grew to nine employees, including Fanny. Hershey sold fruit and nuts and ice cream in addition to candy, and he was on his way to building a solid reputation; then in 1880, Henry Hershey blew in—a hurricane of hope, speculation and disaster.

Hearing of his son's fledgling success, Henry saw an opportunity for redemption. "If you want to make money," he told his son, "you have got to do things in a big way."

Henry presented Milton with his own recipe for "medicated candies," and suggested they broaden the business to capture a share of the lucrative cough drop market. He also designed a new display cabinet to showcase his sweets, and he convinced Milton to begin manufacturing them. An advertisement in the *Confectioners' Journal,* in December 1880, pictures Milton S. Hershey's candy cabinets, "patent applied for," and suggests the lucky purchaser would double his candy sales in no time.

But Milton and his father didn't have enough capital to conduct an extensive sales campaign, and the gamble with the cabinets brought a new financial crisis every month. Creditors grew impatient, and Milton borrowed from relatives to make ends meet. He moved into smaller quarters but still could not cover his expenses. His mother and her sister, Martha, who had lent him money, warned him that his father was irresponsible, scatterbrained, a loser—and said it was dangerous for Milton to be associated with him. Henry would have to leave, they said, or Milton would lose their financial support.

Milton agreed, of course, that Henry's ideas were ruinous, but he loved and respected both of his parents and could not choose between them. Exhausted from trying to save the now-failing business, and unable to cope with his parents' conflicting demands, Milton fell seriously ill in what was later described as a complete mental breakdown. Bedridden for weeks, he recovered only after Henry proposed this solution: He would sell Milton his half share of the celebrated cabinet business for $350. The newspapers had reported silver out west, Henry told Milton, and if he could just raise enough money to stake his own mining claim, he would gladly move on.

But the damage had already been done, and six months later the Philadelphia shop went under. Ashamed and dejected—and owing his mother's family a considerable sum—Milton decided to leave Pennsylvania and join his father out west. Although Henry had written letters describing untold wealth and excitement in Denver, when Milton arrived he found little suited to his talents. He tried his hand at mining until, eventually, he found work with a local confectioner. It turned out to be his first break.

To give caramels their chewy consistency, every other confectioner in America was using paraffin—the waxy, white hydrocarbon mixture used in candles. But trial and error had taught a Denver candy maker, whom Milton never identified by name, that whole milk would yield the same satisfying chew. And the milk-based caramels tasted better and stayed fresh for an indefinite period.

After learning the confectioner's secret, Milton headed to Chicago, in the company of his father. Although the evidence is somewhat unclear, it appears they went into business together, making caramels and cough drops. But the partnership didn't last long. Henry's ideas were still too high-flying for Milton, and in 1883 they again parted ways. Milton headed to New York, where he took a job with a candy manufacturer during the day. In the evenings he made caramels to sell for himself. Eventually, he saved enough money to open his own shop on Sixth Avenue, between Forty-second and Forty-third streets. But Henry soon followed Milton to New York, and once again, following his father's advice, Milton grew the business quickly—too quickly, as it turned out.

When he moved to larger quarters, he was forced to pay two rents and could barely keep up with his bills. His caramel sales were slow, and he went heavily into cough drops, hoping for a faster turnover. In the end the entire business collapsed, and Milton hired himself out as a manual laborer just to get enough money to return to Lancaster.

By now, Milton's failures had so soured his mother's relatives that they regarded him as just another black sheep. Upon his arrival in town, none of his family offered to take him in. His mother and Aunt Martha eventually agreed to help him start a new business, provided Henry stayed far away. This time, Milton agreed.

With two copper kettles, a marble slab, mixing paddles, molasses and a couple hundred pounds of sugar salvaged from his New York enterprise, Milton, his mother and her sister started again. Milton made caramels, which the two women wrapped by hand in tissue paper. When each batch had been cooled, cut and wrapped, Milton peddled it around town. His recipe was extremely popular, and within a few months he managed to buy a pushcart to sell farther afield. But he didn't have enough money to really expand the business, and his family refused to loan him any more. He tried the local banks but had no luck.

Then, one afternoon in 1887, an Englishman visiting Lancaster took a fancy to his caramels. He offered to introduce Milton's Crystal "A" candies to London if they could be produced in sufficient quantity to make it worthwhile. Here was the chance of a lifetime, but it called for more and larger kettles, a bigger staff and extra rooms—and all that was needed immediately. What happened next would make anyone believe in the American Dream.

Hershey went into the Lancaster National Bank and asked a banker named Frank H. Brenneman for a loan of $700. Hershey said his aunt would endorse the note; she had a small house assessed at about $1,500, and he got the loan for ninety days. With the money in hand, Hershey rushed to fulfill his new contract. But when the note came due, Hershey had not yet completed production and he had to tell Brenneman he couldn't pay. He begged the banker to visit his business and determine for himself whether the note should be renewed. Brenneman was impressed with Hershey's drive and sincerity, but he didn't know what to do, especially when Hershey said that, in addition to the renewal, he needed another $1,000 to fill his London order.

On a hunch, and against bank policy, Brenneman decided to take the risk and lend him the money. Unable to present his bosses with the note, he put it in his own name to avoid any questions. His good deed proved to be the turning point in Milton Hershey's career. Less than ten days before the new note came due, Hershey was paid by his London contact and rushed to the bank to retire his obligation. From that point forward, expansion drove his business.

Milton grew his Lancaster Caramel Co. block by block, until it covered 450,000 square feet. When that wasn't enough, he bought a

factory in nearby Mount Joy and opened a retail store on Canal Street in New York City. He purchased a third factory in Chicago and a fourth in Reading.

By 1890, thirty-three-year-old Milton Hershey was wealthier than he had ever dreamed. He bought his mother the house of her choice in Lancaster, and he began traveling the world. His trips to Europe lasted weeks, sometimes months. He toured museums, walked the streets, visited shops and endlessly priced goods. He surrounded himself with fine things—furniture, art, horses—all the trappings of a real gentleman, until nothing of his simple Mennonite background remained.

In 1891, he bought himself a large handsome brick house with wide porches and a sweeping front lawn. He filled it with his exotic collections, which included tropical birds, paintings from Mexico and Egypt and sculptures from Italy. He also joined the Lancaster Coaching Club and raced about the countryside driving his own carriage.

Despite her obvious disapproval, Fanny Hershey said nothing of her son's lifestyle. And Milton never openly judged his mother, not even when she listed herself as a widow in the Lancaster directory. In fact, the only outward discord in their relationship came in 1898, when Milton married Catharine Sweeney, the daughter of an Irish immigrant iron-worker. Sweeney was only twenty-six and Milton past forty when they wed in a private ceremony in the rectory of New York's St. Patrick's Cathedral. Fanny, who had come to assume that her son would always be a bachelor, was extremely jealous of his new young bride.

Kitty was everything Fanny was not: a beautiful Irish Catholic girl with an engaging smile, voluminous auburn curls and enormous blue eyes. She dressed in the latest fashions; enjoyed entertaining, the arts and the theater; and was eager to accompany Milton in his travels, which were taking up more and more of his time. To say Fanny disapproved of Milton's wife is being polite. She barely spoke to Kitty, except to ask her, as she unpacked her trousseau, whether she was "ever on the stage." It was an insult Kitty never forgot.

Following the marriage, Milton's life changed dramatically. He left the business in the hands of his top managers, preferring to spend his time with Kitty. They redecorated the house in Lancaster, painting it bright yellow in contrast to the drab Amish hues that smothered the rest of the town, and began playing host to Pennsylvania's most substantial citizens. Dinner parties at the Hershey home were stately affairs, with

FOR MILTON, BUSINESS HELD FAR LESS FASCINATION THAN THE WONDERS HE SAW ON HIS TRAVELS.

exotic menus taken from the Hersheys' trips abroad and lavish desserts of caramels and chocolate.

When they weren't entertaining, the Hersheys traveled. Milton wanted to show his new bride all he had learned about the world. They visited museums and great castles, Stonehenge and the Pyramids. Often gone for months at a time, they toured extensively through Europe, the Orient and South America, taking in tourist attractions and collecting antiques. No matter where they were, Milton saw to it that Kitty had a bouquet of fresh flowers at her bedside every morning—just one of the dozens of ways he doted on her. The habit eventually led to the establishment of the Hershey Gardens in Hershey, Pennsylvania, renowned today for its hundreds of varieties of roses.

Kitty, in turn, worshipped Milton completely. She supported him, encouraged him and doted on him like a nursemaid, calling him "my little Dutchman." She never told him what to do, never questioned his judgment and always treated him with the respect due a gentleman. But while it seemed Milton had at last found himself a loving family, he was still like the poor boy peering into the window of the corner candy store, wanting the one thing in life he could not have: his parents' reconciliation.

The year before he married Kitty, Milton had restored his family's name in the town of Hockersville by purchasing the old Hershey homestead, where his father had been raised. He then rebuilt the barn, repaired the living quarters, hired some farm hands and invited Henry and Fanny to live there.

Having never made it on his own, Henry was only too happy to oblige. Rumors spread that he had worked alternately as a preacher, a miner, a painter, a carpenter and had even lived as a hobo in the seedy Bowery in New York City. But when he showed up in Hockersville, Henry looked much the same as when he'd left: silk hat, cane and Prince Albert jacket, albeit a bit dusty and worn.

Milton invited Fanny to rejoin her husband—begged her, in fact. But she refused, conceding only to resume the marital status of "Mrs. Henry Hershey" and stop calling herself a widow.

It was a meager triumph for Milton. As a boy, he naively assumed he could fix his parents' marriage by making his own life a success. At forty-one, he was still holding on to that childish belief.

MILTON AND HIS
BELOVED WIFE,
KITTY, IN
1910.

OTHING ABOUT BUSINESS excited Milton Her-
shey. He hated accounting and finance. Statistics mystified him. Cash
flow, logistics, distribution, sales—he wanted no part of it. The only
business concept Milton Hershey understood was product, but even
that was getting tedious. Like his father, he liked to experiment, to
invent, to try things that had never been done before. By 1900, the
Lancaster Caramel Co. had grown beyond experimentation. The
company ranked as the nation's leading caramel manufacturer, with
more than $1 million in annual sales. It employed more than 1,500
workers in four factories, producing hundreds of varieties of caramels
sold around the world. This was no corner candy store, the likes of
which still dominated the industry. The Lancaster Caramel Co. was a

major corporation, with a board of trustees, a national sales force and twenty full-time bookkeepers.

Milton did his best to pretend that nothing had changed since the days when he, his mother and his Aunt Martha worked side by side in Philadelphia. Whenever he wasn't traveling with Kitty, he could be found among the workers in the Lancaster plant, his sleeves rolled up, buried elbow-deep in cooked caramel. He still loved to trifle with recipes. He would hold court on the manufacturing floor, adding a little of this and a dash of that to a fresh batch of candy until he had created something new. A contest to name the virgin confection would follow, with employees shouting out suggestions—the more exotic the better. Then he would begin class, teaching everyone how to knead the sticky mass of fresh caramel until it became smooth and springy, ready for molding. He would walk amid the bubbling copper cauldrons, tasting and testing each batch of syrup to be sure it was consistent with the last, showing his workers how to boil the syrup properly and how to fix a mistake. This was the part of the business he treasured; the rest of it he ignored.

It never mattered to him whether a new product would sell; it was the experiment that counted. Nor did it matter whether his plants operated efficiently (which they did not—given the vast number of products that Hershey insisted they produce). Profit, too, was of little concern. "I have more money than I know what to do with," he would often say. And he meant it. Although he and Kitty shared one of the most elegant houses in Lancaster, it was nothing compared to the château-style mansions flaunted by other millionaires. In many respects, the Hersheys remained quite plain. Milton treated Kitty to the best and most fashionable clothes, but he kept his own wardrobe basic, shunning the flashy suits and cuff links worn by other men of his status. They never bought a vacation home or kept a livery, as was the convention of the upper class.

It wasn't that Hershey was stingy; he simply couldn't fathom a more extravagant lifestyle. But he always spent lavishly on ideas. He was fascinated by inventions and was constantly adding newfangled machinery to his plants. He learned about such innovations not from reading but through his travels. He visited halls of science, expositions and other factories. Everywhere he went, he looked for some twist, some novelty that might alter his business.

It was in this way that Milton Hershey first discovered chocolate. In the 1890s, most of America had never heard of chocolate. Hershey used cocoa powder to add a chocolatey flavor to some of his fanciest caramels, but the first time he saw real chocolate being manufactured was in 1893 at the Columbian Exposition in Chicago, the forerunner to the world's fair.

Milton loved these types of conventions. To him, it seemed the knowledge of mankind was on display. The wonders on exhibit in Chicago included the very first Ferris wheel and a dancer named Little Egypt, who introduced America to the hootchy-kootchy. But what interested Hershey most was a tiny display tucked among the exhibits of industrial machinery—the booth of J. M. Lehmann, a supplier of chocolate-making equipment from Dresden, Germany.

The smell of roasting cocoa beans wafting from Lehmann's rotating ovens, like the smell of fresh-baked brownies, enchanted Hershey. He watched in fascination as Lehmann hulled the roasted beans and ground them between granite rollers until they turned into the mouth-watering liquid known as "chocolate liquor." To this rich syrup he added sugar, vanilla and additional cocoa butter, mixing and churning the ingredients into a silky, viscous paste. Lehmann then poured the chocolate into plain square molds and let it harden, forming a bar.

Anyone who can remember the first time they tasted a Hershey bar can imagine how Milton Hershey felt when he bit into the delicacy, marveling at the flavor—so intoxicating, so intense and opulent, it penetrates the taste buds and heads straight for the brain.

On the spot, Hershey offered to buy Lehmann's entire display, which was shipped by rail to Lancaster after the exposition closed in 1893. The next year, the Hershey Chocolate Co. was born, in a back corner of the third floor of Hershey's caramel factory. To operate the new business, Hershey hired two chocolate makers from Walter Baker's chocolate mills in Massachusetts, along with several assistants and a local chemist. The manufacturing, crude by today's standards, was based on the time-tested process of roasting, hulling, grinding and pressing cocoa beans. Hershey made no attempt to manufacture milk chocolate, which requires a special expertise; instead, he focused on plain sweet chocolate that could be molded into hundreds of novelty shapes, following the European tradition.

He hired Murrie to sell his new candies, and to advertise them he bought a Riker Electric automobile, the first of its kind in Pennsylvania. Milton had seen the extraordinary contraption at the New York Automobile Show and insisted on purchasing the $2,000 floor model, equipped with electric lights, an electric bell and a top speed of nine miles per hour. Painted black with "Hershey's Cocoa" emblazoned on

MILTON HERSHEY'S RIKER ELECTRIC AUTOMOBILE WAS A MARVEL—THE FIRST HORSELESS CARRIAGE TO BE INTRODUCED TO LANCASTER.

each side, the car toured the state for the next year, selling chocolate to the crowds that invariably gathered to see it. Hershey also bought up billboards and took out newspaper advertisements, but he insisted that the best publicity of all was making a quality product.

To that end, he and Murrie began experimenting with ways to improve their chocolate creations. Hershey perfected a chocolate coating for his best-selling caramels, and he expanded his line to include unsweetened baking chocolate and cocoa. At the turn of the century, a wholesale price list of "Hershey's Fine Vanilla Chocolate Novelties and Fancy Packages" included no less than 114 different products. His finest candies were given French names, like Le Roi de Chocolat and Le Chat Noir. And he used the brightest ribbons and fanciest wrappings to distinguish his goods from those of the competition.

As time went on, Hershey focused himself more and more on this end of the business, for it appealed to him in a way that caramels no longer could. Success here depended upon innovation, experimentation and the mastering of new technologies. Although the chocolate industry was well established in Europe, it was in its infancy in America. Only a half-dozen companies owned chocolate-making equipment, and even fewer were producing quality products. Hershey was entering the business on the ground level, a prospect that reminded him of the old days and the thrill of enterprise.

But this newfound enthusiasm for business only partly explains Hershey's decision to give up caramels and focus on chocolate full-time. The truth is, outside of Kitty, Hershey's success had brought him little happiness. His parents continued to feud, and now they took turns competing for his affection, Fanny constantly reminding him of her role in his accomplishments and Henry egging him on to new and bigger business opportunities. Making matters worse, Kitty and Henry had sparked up a friendship, which served only to inflame Fanny's hatred of them both.

The constant tug-of-war grated on Milton like the two-ton granite rollers grinding out his candies. He tried to ignore the escalating tension, but, as before, found himself overwhelmed by his parents' conflicting demands. The only solution, he decided, was to get rid of the source of the friction: He would sell his caramel company to his chief competitor, and he and Kitty would leave Lancaster for good.

FANNY HELPED HER SON MAKE CANDY UNTIL THE DAY SHE DIED, WRAPPING KISSES BY HAND IN HER HOME ACROSS FROM THE FACTORY.

Radical as this sounded, the thought of selling the business was not entirely new to Milton. Earlier in the year, he had refused an offer to merge his firm with his closest rival, the American Caramel Co. The competition had answered his refusal with a handsome buyout proposal: $500,000 in cash and $500,000 in company stock in exchange for Hershey's caramel factories, trademarks, inventory and equipment. Initially, Hershey had ignored the proposal. But now he saw it differently: This was his opportunity to be free, to do as he wished with the rest of his life.

In March 1900, Hershey called his attorney and made arrangements to sell the business. Under terms of the agreement, he would retain the rights to his chocolate division but would agree not to enter the caramel business and compete against his old company. On August 10, 1900, he closed the deal, making headlines across the state. The *Philadelphia Tribune* blared in banner type: "Caramel Factory Sold: Milton S. Hershey Receives a Million Dollars for It." The *Lancaster New Era* wrote: "Hershey Sells Out to Rival; Move Stuns Industry." The *Lancaster Intelligencer* read: "Hershey Gives Up Empire for $1 Million."

No one, it seemed, could make sense of the deal. As far as any outsider could see, Milton Hershey was at the pinnacle of his career. He had a thriving business, plenty of money, a beautiful wife, a lovely home and the respect of everyone who knew him. At age forty-three, he was too young to retire, so what was he planning to do?

Several newspapers speculated that he sold the caramel division in order to devote himself entirely to chocolate—a story that has often been repeated in company literature and has generally been accepted by those who have studied Hershey's life. According to this version of history, Hershey knew from the moment he first tasted chocolate that it would be wildly popular. He supposedly shared this astute prediction with his cousin Frank Snavely, who was with him at the Chicago exposition. Snavely said that upon seeing Lehmann's machinery, Hershey dubbed caramels "a fad" and declared that chocolate would be in never-ending demand because "it is more than just a sweet, it is a food."

But to suggest that the Hershey story centers around this prophetic insight is to shortchange everything that Milton Hershey accomplished during the remainder of his life—accomplishments that go far beyond the nickel candy bar.

It's true that Hershey held on to the chocolate division, but he had no intention of actually managing it; that was up to Murrie. Nor did he intend to devote his life to developing it; he'd done that with caramels and the results were far from fulfilling. No, Hershey intended to retire and travel the world with Kitty. Two weeks after closing the deal with his rival, the Hersheys boarded a boat for Europe, the first stop on what was to be a lifelong cruise.

But they didn't get far in their journey before Hershey changed his mind. It wasn't chocolate that beckoned him to return, however. It was the voice of Henry Hershey still rumbling about in Milton's head—the voice of the dreamer who had seduced Milton, the child, with fantastical visions of Eden.

With the $1 million from his caramel operation, Hershey had the capital to invest in any dream he desired. He could no more squander the money on travel than Fanny Hershey could buy herself a new dress. But he wasn't about to reinvest that money in business; his vision was richer than that: Milton Hershey wanted nothing less than to build an industrial utopia, a real-life Chocolate Town, where anyone who wanted a job could have one, where children would grow up in celery-crisp air, where mortgages would dwindle in perpetual prosperity. Clear water and clear consciences. This was Hershey's vision of home *sweet* home.

How he settled upon this particular idea is a mystery; one can only speculate that he wanted to somehow make up for his own lacking childhood. He never explained his motivations, only his intentions: to build a model American community "where the things of modern progress all center in a town that has no poverty, no nuisances and no evil." This would be a place where leisure and education would be valued as much as hard work; where the houses would boast gardens, electricity and indoor plumbing; and where big-city amenities would be available to all, free of charge.

Upon hearing these plans, many of Hershey's friends and business associates called him a fool. "Mr. Hershey," said John McLain, who worked in the chocolate company office, "I read an article about George Pullman building a town so that every house had a lawn and an open backyard. He made loans to employees on the property. He built the town. And now the people are clamoring to have it annexed to Chicago."

"I don't see what they are going to annex mine to," said Hershey, "twelve miles from Lebanon, thirteen miles from Harrisburg, twenty miles from Lancaster."

"I hate to tell you this," replied McLain, "but the writer says, 'This man [Pullman], if he were a candidate for dog catcher in his own town, he would be defeated.'"

"I know we're taking chances," said Hershey. "But I won't be a candidate for dog catcher: I don't like dogs that much."

Hershey told his plans to William Blair, who had managed his caramel company for fifteen years.

"Don't you have an opinion?" asked Hershey.

"If you want my opinion."

"Of course, yes."

"My opinion would be that your friends should go into court and have a guardian appointed for you."

Even his wife, who had always kept her opinions to herself, wondered aloud if Milton "ought to go and have his head examined."

When asked how he expected to earn a profit on the venture, Hershey said simply: "I'm not out to make money. I have all that I need."

This would be no ordinary company town, like DuPont's Wilmington, Delaware; Deere & Co.'s Moline, Illinois, or any of the dozen other factory towns that were springing up around the country at the turn of the century. Hershey planned to build his business to support the town—not the other way around. His workers would be paid enough to live in a middle-class splendor of his own design, with swimming pools, ice-skating rinks, theaters, gymnasiums, sports arenas, public transportation and a public school system equipped to handle more than 1,500 students.

No expense would be spared, he said. No restrictions would be set.

In 1902, after scouring the East Coast for a suitable location for this ambitious vision, Hershey purchased 1,200 acres of undeveloped land in Dauphin County, just a mile from his birthplace. This was home to the Mennonites and Amish, devoted and dependable workers.

But more than that, this was the fertile valley known to locals as Pennsylvania dairy country—nothing but cows and pastures for miles around. Hershey knew that milk would eventually be his most important ingredient. As it was, his dark chocolate was still too strong and bitter for widespread appeal, and still too expensive. Hershey knew the solution lay in milk chocolate, which had a mellower flavor and lower cost. But perfecting a milk-chocolate recipe would turn out to be much harder than it sounded.

Chapter Eight

FROM BEAN TO BAR

MADAME DU BARRY, MISTRESS OF LOUIS XV, DRINKING HER CUP OF MORNING CHOCOLATE—THE HEIGHT OF FASHION AMONG EIGHTEENTH-CENTURY EUROPE'S ARISTOCRACY.

*N*O OTHER TASTE has the universal appeal of milk chocolate. In every culture to which it has been introduced it has become a favorite. Chocolate is accepted as readily in Malaysia and Mexico as it is in America—somewhat startling, considering the nations' divergent cuisines. But milk chocolate—like gold—possesses special, some say supernatural, powers. Few can resist the sumptuous combination of mellow, ivory milk and bold, alluring chocolate— together, they have captivated the world.

We savor milk chocolate, but we also take it for granted, knowing little of the centuries-long struggle to combine these two flavors. Few realize that milk and chocolate are natural enemies: Milk is 89 percent water, chocolate 80 percent fat (cocoa butter). And just as oil and water don't mix, so it is with milk and chocolate. Milk also contains a lot of butter fat, which has a tendency to turn chocolate rancid. And its molecular structure doesn't match well with chocolate's, resulting in a product that tends to be lumpy instead of creamy smooth. For these reasons, milk chocolate is a surprisingly recent invention. For centuries, it eluded the efforts of monks, doctors, chemists and chefs. By the time milk chocolate was mastered, inventors had already unlocked the secrets of the submarine (1775), the electric streetcar (1834), the telegraph (1837), the camera (1839) and the machine gun (1861).

For most of human history what was called chocolate was actually a beverage made from coarsely ground cocoa beans and spices—a bitter, heavy precursor to today's hot cocoa. Although no one knows how humans struck upon the process of making the drink, archaeological evidence reveals that the ancient peoples of Mesoamerica were enjoying it as early as 1000 B.C. By the time of Christ, cacao tree cultivation had reached the Aztec civilization in Mexico, where chocolate was believed to be divinely inspired—a gift from the god Quetzalcoatl, who brought the seeds of the cacao tree from the Garden of Life and gave them to Man. When the great Swedish botanist Linnaeus formally named the cacao tree, he paid homage to its divine roots, calling it *Theobroma cacao,* "the food of the gods." The Aztecs considered the cacao tree and its special seeds as valuable as gold and silver. They offered cocoa beans to their deities, paid them to their rulers in tribute and used them as money. In Aztec society, only the royalty was allowed to consume chocolate—a tradition that would continue in Europe.

To prepare the prized beverage they called *chocolatl,* the Aztecs used only old, worn beans—those no longer fit for currency. The beans were sun-dried and roasted in earthen pots, and their shells were removed. The kernels, or nibs, were then ground over a fire box on a stone called a "metate." Various ingredients were added to this paste—including chili pepper, vanilla, ground maize and the plant achiote (for a bloodred color). The mixture was patted into little cakes and placed on banana leaves to cool and harden. To make chocolatl, the cakes were broken into pieces, dropped in water and the liquid was whipped to a thick, foamy consistency.

Christopher Columbus was the first European to be introduced to this exotic potion. On his fourth voyage to the New World, in 1502, he tasted chocolatl and returned to Spain with some of the dark, almond-shaped beans. But it remained for the Spanish explorer Hernán Cortés to grasp the enormous potential of the cocoa bean. In 1519, during his first visit to Mexico, Cortés was invited by the Aztec ruler Montezuma to drink the royal beverage from a golden goblet. The luxury and mystique surrounding the beverage intrigued him, and he wrote to his king, Charles I of Spain, that chocolate "builds up resistance and fights fatigue. A cup of this precious drink permits a man to walk for a whole day without food." Before returning home, Cortés established a cacao plantation in Mexico. He recorded the Aztec recipe for chocolatl and took the beans with him back to Spain.

The Spanish emperor was fascinated by the new flavor. He sweetened it with cane sugar, which was being imported from the Orient, and ordered the monks in their cloisters to protect the recipe and perfect it. For the next one hundred years, the Spanish clergy was responsible for roasting and grinding cocoa beans, and for keeping the drink a secret from the rest of Europe. Monasteries had often served as workshops for the creation of new foods, and in this tradition, they focused their efforts on improving the New World beverage. To counter the bitterness of chocolatl, the monks doctored it with new ingredients, adding anise, sugar, cinnamon, almonds, hazelnuts, powdered roses and orange water. The result: the first nonalcoholic stimulant beverage to be introduced to the continent. (Coffee did not reach Europe until 1615, and tea much later.)

Initially, most of Spain's cocoa beans were used for trade in the New World; only a few pounds were imported for the royal court and others wealthy enough to drink their money. Nevertheless, word of the beverage spread among the aristocracy and soon salons across Spain were serving guests chocolate. Everyone who tasted the drink was mad for it.

To understand its instant appeal, consider the European diet of the time—bread, porridge, cabbage, carrots and, for the rich, meat and game. As for beverages, the choices were wine, ale or water. There were no sweets, no extravagant desserts, no ice creams. In the early 1500s, sugar was just becoming widely available, as were spices from the Orient. But while these new ingredients were slowly expanding the European menu, chocolate was the most alluring, for it contained fat, in the form of cocoa butter. Served cold, thick enough to hold up a spoon, and swizzled to a froth with a molinet (a special stirrer), a cup of chocolate could satisfy for hours. Chocolate was sweet *and* satiating, a unique combination the aristocracy couldn't resist.

Over time, the aristocracy refined the drink, serving it hot in a "chocolate pot," an elegantly shaped carafe with a tiny hole in the lid for the stirrer. The pots, often crafted of gold vermeil and distinguished by their fancy molinets, became symbols of Spanish wealth and prosperity, and the drink itself became associated with excess, luxury and indulgence—connotations that have remained through the ages.

But chocolate was more than a status symbol; it was considered a font of potency, an elixir that could give one man the strength of ten. It could cure any ailment and stir undreamed-of physical prowess. In the words of the great German scientist Alexander von Humboldt, "The cocoa bean is a phenomenon, for nowhere else has nature concentrated such a wealth of valuable nourishment in so small a space."

Little by little, word of chocolate's extraordinary powers leaked out. In 1606, nearly a century after it was introduced to Spain, chocolate made its way to Italy via an aristocrat named Antonio Carletti, who introduced the fashion to the Italian upper class. In 1615, the Spanish court went public with the beverage when Anne of Austria married Louis XIII of France and the glamorous gift of Spanish chocolate was included in the bride's dowry.

From France, the drink crossed the channel to England, then to Denmark, Switzerland and Austria. By mid-century, the beverage was known throughout Europe. As it spread, its reputation grew, until it seemed chocolate could do just about anything. In 1662, Cardinal Brancaccio of Rome decreed that drinking chocolate would not spoil a fast, since it was a medicine good for virtually all human ills. Jean-Anthelme Brillat-Savarin, the gastronomic historian and philosopher, agreed with the church. Writing in 1825, he declared chocolate a panacea for mental stress and highly recommended it for the sick and the weak. Chocolate could allay "hectic heats," improve "consumptive complexions" and induce healing sweats. Physicians claimed chocolate was a complete food, a perfect thirst quencher and a reducer of fever.

Along with having these restorative powers, chocolate was praised as a potion for love, bringing relief to the broken-hearted and stirring amour in both men and women. Madame Du Barry is believed to have given it to all her suitors, and Casanova said he used it instead of champagne as an inducement to romance. Montezuma believed drinking chocolate made him virile. To this end, he drained a golden goblet full of the rich, brown liquid each time he entered his harem.

The provocative effects of chocolate were lauded in James Wadsworth's quatrain, contained in *A Curious History of the Nature and Quality of Chocolate*:

> *'Twill make Old women Young and Fresh;*
> *Create New Motions of the Flesh,*

And cause them long for you know what,
If they but taste of chocolate.

The connection between chocolate and romance seems almost universal. In the 1800s, physicians advised their lovelorn patients to eat a bit of chocolate to help calm their pinings. Today, chocolate is marketed as an essential step in seduction. Women are supposed to give in to men as they give in to chocolate. Chocolate is the hallmark of Valentine's Day; it can be bought molded in the shape of erotic body parts; in advertisements, it is often depicted as sexual. A recent television commercial for the Italian brand Baci shows a naked woman bathing in silver-wrapped chocolates. She blows kisses toward the man who bought them for her. The copy reads, "She knows, in Italian, Baci means kisses. And she also knows that with kisses, it's best to be generous."

The urban legend about the aphrodisiac effect of eating green M&M's is thus part of a long tradition ascribing amorous powers to chocolate. Pat D'Amato, spokeswoman for Mars's candy division, says the company has no idea how this rumor started. "We have no evidence to support that it is true or it's not true," she said with a smile.[1] Nevertheless, Mars recently launched an ad campaign capitalizing on the green M&M's sexy image. A voluptuous green candy with pouty lips and white go-go boots appears in an ad with comedian Dennis Miller. Miller asks "Green": "Is it true what they say about green M&M's?"

"What have you heard?" she replies with indignation. "That stupid rumor? That untruth? This is harassment and I don't have to take it, Miller."

We still speak of chocolate as if speaking of a drug. It is addicting, sinful, wickedly rich. We crave it, overdose on it and suffer from chocolate withdrawal. A "fix" of chocolate can relieve depression and calm anxiety. It provides strength and stamina—the perfect pick-me-up between meals.

Manufacturers capitalize on this lore. "A Snickers a day helps you work, rest and play." Or, as Godiva says, "If chocolate is your downfall, you might as well enjoy the trip." It's no accident that chocolate cake is called Devil's Food and that those who adore chocolate are called chocoholics.

So what's fact and what's fiction? Is chocolate addictive? Is it an aphrodisiac?

Like many foods, chocolate contains numerous mood-altering chemicals, such as phenylalanine, an amino acid that elevates mood and increases amiability, and magnesium, which helps the brain manufacture serotonin, a potent neurotransmitter linked to mood stability. Chocolate also contains caffeine, although a typical bar has far less than a cup of coffee.[2]

A substance closely related to caffeine, called theobromine, is also found in chocolate. It affects the nervous system, increasing alertness and concentration. For decades, Hershey operated a profitable sideline business extracting theobromine from discarded cocoa bean shells. The company sold the stimulant to Coca-Cola and other soft drink manufacturers, which used it to pep up their products. The extraction operation ceased in the 1950s after Coke found cheaper alternatives to the additive.

But of chocolate's psychoactive ingredients, the two most interesting are anandamide and phenylethylamine, chemicals found in the human brain that help arouse emotions and heighten bodily sensation. Anandamide is similar to the active ingredient in marijuana, tetrahydrocannabinol (THC), which may explain why people crave chocolate and why many people consume chocolate when they're depressed, says neuroscientist Daniele Piomelli, who discovered anandamide in chocolate in 1996.[3]

Phenylethylamine, called PEA, was discovered in chocolate in 1982. It, too, is associated with feelings of happiness and bliss. Win the lottery, get a promotion or fall in love, and your PEA level shoots up. But have a bad day, and your PEA level drops. In 1982, two New York psychopharmacologists, Donald Klein and Michael Liebowitz, suggested that people eat chocolate in order to boost their PEA, thereby experiencing the same euphoric feelings they have when they fall in love.[4]

But the link between chocolate, human emotion and these psychoactive drugs has never been scientifically proven. Although chocolate naturally contains PEA—about 1 milligram in a standard 1.4 ounce chocolate bar—so do many other foods, like smoked salami and cheddar cheese, which contain more PEA per serving than chocolate.[5] Researchers at the National Institute of Mental Health have also tested the effects of ingesting PEA by eating pounds of chocolate. They measured the PEA levels in their urine and found no change no matter how much chocolate they consumed. The same holds true for anandamide. Piomelli said that while chocolate contains anandamide, it may be difficult to eat enough chocolate to boost anandamide levels dramatically.

But there are connections between chocolate and mood. Observing lab animals, scientists at the Massachusetts Institute of Technology have found that certain cells of the hypothalamus portion of the brain send out pleasure signals in response to substances that are either sweet or fatty. They go mad with joy when the substance is both sweet AND fatty. Chocolate derives about 50 percent of its calories from sugar and about 50 percent from fat—a combination unequaled among foods.

"That unique mixture of fat and sugar is pure heaven to our brains," according to nutrition researcher Michael Levine. "Chemically speaking, chocolate really is the world's perfect food."[6]

Add the psychological associations—the fact that chocolate has been given as a reward since childhood and that it continues to signify love, appreciation and gratitude—and our experience of chocolate has an undeniable emotional component.

In every country where it is eaten, chocolate is the food craved most often.[7] Its appeal is particularly strong for premenopausal women. One of the largest studies on food preferences ever undertaken found that 97 percent of college-age women have specific food cravings; and they crave chocolate more than anything else. A 1996 study at the Monell Chemical Senses Center, a nonprofit research group in Philadelphia, found similar results. The study surveyed women between eighteen and thirty-five and found they craved high-fat sweets over entrées, 2 to 1. Mostly they craved chocolate in every form: candy, cake, cookies and ice cream.[8]

Drawing on this mix of lore and science, some nutritionists believe that women crave chocolate to make up for hormonal imbalances. According to their theories, women need chocolate because its sugar/fat composition releases serotonin and endorphins into the brain. These brain chemicals are lowest right before menstruation.

"Women *do* need chocolate as well as other foods high in starch, sugar and fat to stabilize moods, control weight, and revitalize well-being," writes nutritionist and author Debra Waterhouse in *Why Women Need Chocolate* (Hyperion, 1995). "Chocolate has the perfect combination of sugar and fat, plus a plethora of other ingredients that account for its unmatched biological and psychological experience."

Claims like these are nothing new. In 1660, a French nobleman said he used chocolate "to modify the vapors of his spleen and to fight against fits of anger and bad moods." Renowned English physician Henry Stubbe advised in 1662 that one ounce of chocolate was loaded with more fat and nourishment than a pound of meat—a claim Milton Hershey revived at the turn of the century. A physician in Amsterdam found chocolate had a soothing effect. "Chocolate is not only pleasant of taste," he wrote, "but it is also a veritable balm of the mouth, for the maintaining of all glands and humors in a good state of health and mental stability."[9]

As with anything that becomes popular, chocolate had its critics. Joseph Acosta, a historian writing in 1604, considered chocolate's use foolish and without reason. He described the drink as "loathsome . . . having a skumme or frothe that is very unpleasant to taste." In 1624, Joan Fran Fauch called chocolate a "violent inflamer of the passions" and suggested that monks should be forbidden from drinking it. Others blamed its evil effects on the sugar, saying it was a corrosive salt, a "hypocritical enemy of the body," the cause of English consumption and one of our "universal scurvies."

Today we blame chocolate for acne, migraine headaches, tooth decay and a myriad of other social ills. Eating chocolate makes children hyperactive, say critics. It is an allergen that can cause hives, cold sweats and nausea. It is a narcotic that has driven people to do insane things, like the chocoholic who devoured a two-pound box of Godiva chocolates she bought for her mother for Mother's Day—then another, and another. "Don't blame me," she said. "I just couldn't resist; it's the chocolate, it drives me nuts."

But chocolate affects more than just people; it has altered the histories of entire countries, influencing everything from social norms to tax policies to expansion.

Throughout the seventeenth and eighteenth centuries, chocolate was an important factor in European colonization. Spain initially ruled the cacao trade, with cacao groves in Mexico, Colombia, the Philippines and parts of the Caribbean. But every country that learned about chocolate wanted to secure its own supply. As Europeans colonized the tropics, they eagerly expanded cacao cultivation. From Central America, cacao spread into colonial Martinique and Saint Lucia, controlled by the French; Trinidad, the West Indies and Jamaica under the British; Curaçao and Venezuela under the Dutch; and Brazil under the Portuguese. As European influence spread, so, too, did the cacao trade. The British took cacao to Ceylon (now Sri Lanka), Réunion and Madagascar. The Germans introduced it to Samao and New Guinea. The Dutch planted cacao in Indonesia.

Cocoa beans became an important source of revenue for European governments. Britain, France, Spain and Germany all placed heavy taxes on the beans. Only in Austria, where chocolate wasn't overloaded with duties, could people outside the aristocracy afford to drink chocolate. A

German traveler to Vienna in the early 1700s wrote in his memoirs how shocked he was to see a Viennese tailor drinking top-grade chocolate. Vienna, he concluded, "was a den of Sybarites."

Throughout Europe, serving guests a cup of chocolate was a sign of social prominence and gentility. Artists reinforced this notion in their paintings, often depicting the royalty drinking chocolate and using chocolate as a general motif for nobility. Authors, too, used chocolate as a symbol for the upper crust. In *A Tale of Two Cities,* Charles Dickens portrays the drinking of chocolate as a luxury of the idle upper class.

In England, chocolate became so central to social life that by the early 1700s, London's chocolate houses had outstripped the popularity of the city's coffeehouses and taverns. Two of these establishments—White's and the Cocoa Tree—gained world renown, the five-star haunts of their day. Each drew its own specialized group of customers. At White's, the trendiest and most fashionable in society gathered for gambling, gossip and carousing. The place was famous for its high-toned, high-stakes games, a reputation that earned it a place in *A Rake's Progress,* William Hogarth's satirical engravings about English society.

GAMBLING AND CAROUSING IN WHITE'S CHOCOLATE HOUSE AS DEPICTED BY WILLIAM HOGARTH IN *A RAKE'S PROGRESS* (1733).

The Cocoa Tree was never as fashionable as White's, but it had its own distinction as the gathering place for Tory politicians. "A Whig will no more go to the Cocoa Tree . . . than a Tory will be seen at the coffee house of St. James's," wrote *The Tatler*, a prominent London newspaper. By 1746, the Cocoa Tree had developed into the quasi-official headquarters of the Jacobite party in Parliament. By then, the most successful chocolate houses had reorganized themselves as private clubs, laying the foundation for the London clubs that would serve as the city's male social bastion for the next two centuries.

By the close of the eighteenth century, chocolate was becoming ever more popular, but it was still available only as a beverage. Chocolate factories resembled little more than overgrown apothecary shops, and medical doctors and priests were the main manufacturers. Both professions advertised themselves as authorities on chocolate's virtues. Doctors, who were skilled with the use of a mortar and pestle, were particularly well suited to the job of hand grinding cocoa beans. Their involvement in the industry led to chocolate being called a confection; the word originally referred to a medicine made palatable by the addition of sugar and spices.

But not everyone who tried the drink found it fully satisfying. The chocolate of the 1700s tasted nothing like today's; it was strong, thick, bitter and loaded with so much fat that many people found it difficult to digest. Manufacturers tried cutting the drink with fillers—acorn powder, barley and rice—but these did little to lighten it.

True progress came only in 1828, when a Dutch chemist named Coenraad Van Houten, borrowing tools from the advancing industrial revolution, invented a hand-operated cocoa press. Traditionally, chocolate was made straight from the roasted cocoa bean, which was ground into a smooth paste. But with the help of his new invention, Van Houten was able to squeeze the heavy paste, filtering out about two-thirds of the cocoa butter. What was left behind was a "cake" that could be pulverized into a fine powder, known ever since as cocoa. Van Houten treated the powder with alkaline salts (potassium or sodium carbonates) to make it more soluble in water.

Suddenly, chocolate was much easier to stomach, and much easier to prepare. The chocolate pot fell out of use, and manufacturers stopped cutting their drinks with fillers. But the press did something else, as well.

The original paste had always hardened into a cake that was too dry and crumbly to be eaten by itself. (Which is why it was always dissolved in a liquid.) But now, Van Houten's presses were turning out rivers of creamy cocoa butter. If additional cocoa butter could be added to the paste, perhaps it would produce a softer, smoother tablet that could be eaten straight?

The first to try it were the English. The Bristol firm of Fry & Sons, which had been producing the drinking variety since 1728, introduced "eating chocolate" in 1847. It was very grainy and rather harshly flavored, but no one had ever tasted anything like it, and immediately manufacturers were racing to improve on Fry's creation.

As demand for the new confection rose, increasing the amounts of cocoa butter needed, its price climbed, and cocoa powder fell within economic reach of many more people. Now, cocoa powder was "common," and eating chocolate was for the elite.

New machines were developed to roast and hull and grind beans more efficiently, and special mixers were invented—called conches—to smooth the chocolate into a velvety mass. But no one succeeded in mellowing the bitter flavor until 1875, when Daniel Peter of the Swiss General Chocolate Co. joined forces with chemist Henri Nestlé, an expert in milk products, to produce Nestlé brand milk chocolate.

Over the centuries, many had tried to mix milk and chocolate, but no one had overcome the problem of combining fat-based chocolate with water-based milk. The key to Nestlé's success was using condensed milk—a drier, more stable form of milk, which Nestlé had invented. Peter added cocoa powder and sugar to the condensed milk to make it drier still, and kneaded the resulting "dough" to drive off the remaining moisture. This "milk-chocolate crumb," as it is known today, was then mixed with additional cocoa butter, chocolate liquor, vanilla, salt and more sugar, and the paste was then refined and ground for several days to make it smooth.

The process was laborious and expensive. From start to finish, it took Nestlé almost a week to perfect a single batch. There were other problems, as well. To produce sufficient quantities, Nestlé required more milk than was locally available. And the flavor of that milk often varied, depending upon the season and the cows' diet. Moreover, the demand for chocolate was greatest when milk supplies were at their lowest (in winter), and vice versa.

But these details could not diminish the impact of Nestlé's innovation. Overnight, milk chocolate became the rage, and manufacturers across Europe scrambled to duplicate Nestlé's success. The original formula was carefully guarded, so manufacturers began experimenting with new methods of drying out milk in order to mix it with chocolate. Some tried using powdered milk, which was becoming more readily available, while others began experimenting with their own milk condensing methods. Some of these experiments resulted in a "super condensed" milk, which was so low in moisture it resembled cheese and could be stored for long periods. In England, manufacturers began combining partially evaporated milk with sugar and chocolate liquor before drying out the mixture. The resulting crumb lasted even longer.

Each different method produced its own unique milk chocolate flavor, and people tend to prefer the chocolate they grew up with; so the British love the caramelized flavor of Cadbury, while the Swiss prefer milky Toblerone and Lindt, and the Italians like dark, creamy Baci. But it's a matter of personal opinion as to which is better. A common fallacy among chocolate lovers is that the only really "good" way to make milk chocolate is to use "fluid milk"—as though it were somehow possible to use milk that originally was *not* fluid. All milk starts out as a liquid, and all milk must be dehydrated before the chocolate manufacturing process is completed. The flavor of the finished product will vary depending on when and how the moisture was removed. If it is done before any chocolate liquor is present, the resulting flavor will be closer to fresh milk. But if the moisture content is still fairly high when the chocolate liquor is added, a fudgy, cooked-caramel flavor will result. And if the dehydration occurs more naturally over a long period of time, it will taste different than if the milk is dehydrated rapidly under high heat.

Milton Hershey understood none of this when he started experimenting with his own formula for milk chocolate in the late 1890s. He had tasted many European milk chocolates, and, with the help of his equipment supplier in Dresden, he supposedly visited milk-chocolate manufacturers in Britain, Germany, Switzerland and France. But he never worked for any of these companies, like Forrest Mars did, so he learned little about the actual manufacturing process—not that it ultimately would have mattered. For when Hershey decided to manufacture his own milk chocolate, he consciously decided not to follow the methods the Europeans had so laboriously perfected.

Given his success with caramels—where the addition of fresh whole milk had dramatically improved the quality of the candy—Milton Hershey believed he could outdo his European counterparts. So he ignored everything they had learned over the centuries and set out to re-create for himself what the masters had already perfected.

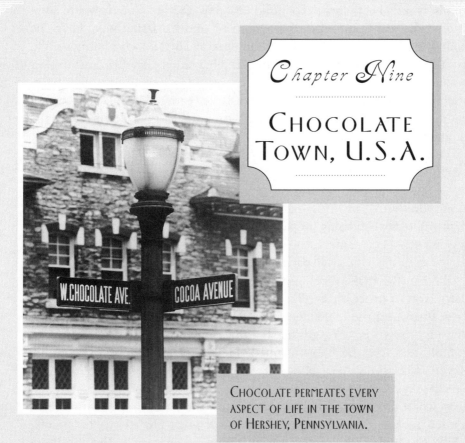

Chapter Nine

CHOCOLATE TOWN, U.S.A.

CHOCOLATE PERMEATES EVERY ASPECT OF LIFE IN THE TOWN OF HERSHEY, PENNSYLVANIA.

ERSHEY HAD NO understanding of chemistry to help him develop a proper formula for milk chocolate. His method was simply trial and error. He felt his way from experiment to experiment and paddled around for hours in the kettles with each new mixture. Before he began, he bought the most expensive, most impressive and most modern machinery he could find: condensing kettles to evaporate the milk, plow machines to knead the milk and chocolate into a dough, chasers to grind the mixture into a fine powder and mélangeurs to blend the mixture with additional cocoa butter. But no one showed him how to use this equipment, and the specific manufacturing process and ingredients were up to him.

To conduct his research in private, he moved part of his operations to the family's homestead, just a mile from the barren, rocky knolls where he planned to build his new factory and town. There, behind the old farmhouse where both he and his father were born, he built a creamery and a small experimental facility for condensing milk. To run the miniature factory, he installed an eighty-five-horsepower boiler, a deep-well pump and a water tank. He also built a new barn, which he filled with forty-eight head of Jersey cattle. The milk-processing equipment was shipped there, along with a few copper kettles from the caramel factory.

Working behind closed doors with a watchman on guard, Hershey began to experiment with various formulations, assuming it would take just a few months to finalize his recipe. He worked sixteen hours a day alongside four of his most trusted workers. At 4:30 A.M., they woke to milk the cows. Milton's mother served breakfast at 6 A.M., and then it was on to the creamery for work. Cleanup and the evening milking ended each day well after dark.

At first, the trials were simple. Milton knew nothing about running a dairy farm or processing milk, and he spent the early weeks just learning his way around the creamery. When he began experimenting with condensing, however, everything became more complicated—far more complicated than he had imagined. He assumed that the richest milk would make the richest chocolate, so he started working with cream. But the cream was almost impossible to condense without burning, and even when the condensing was successful, the fat content of the cream tended to keep the chocolate from hardening. He tried whole milk, which was better for condensing, but found that it made the chocolate spoil within a few weeks. Since he intended to ship his chocolate long distances, he needed a product that would last. Skim milk, it seemed, was the only answer. He installed separators and began churning out butter with the unused cream and condensed milk with the skim milk. Satisfied with the initial results, he replaced his Jersey cows with Holsteins, which tend to produce milk with less fat.

But he was far from inventing a final recipe. There was trouble with the sugar. When should it be added? Hershey supposed that the right time to blend it in was after the milk was condensed. But after months of trying, he discovered he could not get rid of enough moisture in the milk unless he added the sugar *before* condensing. The natural assumption—that if the sugar worked that way so would other ingredients—led Hershey off track again. He wasted many more months trying to add the cocoa butter in with the milk, but it always scorched in the condensing kettle. He tried adding dried and pulverized cocoa powder, but to make it mix he found he had to add water and then boil that out again, which added time and expense. He tried putting the warm chocolate liquor, fresh from the milling machine, into the milk, but the mixture curdled too easily.

After years of experimentation and hundreds of failed attempts, Hershey still didn't have a formula that he was happy with—and the pressure was beginning to mount. The chocolate business in the United States was booming, with new manufacturers popping up every day. Walter Baker was out in the lead, receiving half of the 24 million pounds of cocoa beans being imported to America annually, and rumor had it he was beginning his own milk-chocolate experiments.

Not only were his competitors moving ahead, but Hershey found himself running up against deadlines for completing the new factory and town. Even without the perfect milk-chocolate formula, his business was outgrowing the rented wing of the Lancaster caramel plant. He needed the new factory immediately, and he ordered construction to get under way.

Critics continued to pan Hershey's plans for an industrial utopia, predicting the factory "in the middle of the cornfield" was bound to fail. But Hershey persevered. He had sound reasons for locating in Derry Township. Out there, he would not need to compete with Philadelphia for his milk supply. Spring Creek and Derry Church Spring offered clean, steady sources of water. And the loyal, industrious Pennsylvania Dutch folk gave promise of a dependable labor force. There was already a railroad, and it was near the Hershey homestead. And although the site was comprised mostly of hills and rocks and stones, the landscape, too, could be put to advantage. Close at hand was a limestone ledge that would provide all the building material he needed.

On March 2, 1903, with Kitty and his parents anxiously watching, Milton Hershey broke ground on the factory, and all at once, Derry Church, a pastoral town in the Pennsylvania countryside, swelled with activity. Milton Hershey's quick step was everywhere, supervising the workmen and conferring with architects and foremen. This was *his* grand vision, and he intended to oversee it all. He involved himself in every aspect of the project, personally laying out the factory, the downtown and the neighborhoods. He christened the main thoroughfares Chocolate and Cocoa Avenues, and the lesser streets he named after varieties of cocoa beans: Java, Caracas, Areba, Granada and so on. On a gently sloping hill overlooking the factory, he laid plans for a new home for himself and Kitty, the twenty-two-room white porticoed mansion that would be called High Point.

From there, Hershey carefully surveyed all that was rising around him. The factory was top priority. The sprawling complex facing Chocolate Avenue stretched the length of two football fields, its sixteen single-story buildings radiating from a central corridor. Designed to accommodate 600 workers and produce millions of dollars of chocolate annually, Hershey wanted the factory as modern as possible. He bought more chocolate-making equipment from Germany and installed cocoa bean roasters, grinders, presses, conches and everything else he would need to make milk chocolate—once he discovered how.

An enormous engine room housed the power plant, equipped with two 600-horsepower John Best boilers—the most powerful on the market—along with a huge dynamo and force pump. Near the engine room stood two brick smoke stacks, with the letters HERSHEY running down each side, and two 50,000-gallon suction tanks sat to the south of the stacks. Another 50,000-gallon water tank towered over the east end of the factory, and at the western end of the complex were three more

THE HERSHEY CHOCOLATE CO. FACTORY, CIRCA 1915. THE IMMENSE PLANT PRODUCED MORE THAN 100,000 POUNDS OF CHOCOLATE A DAY.

buildings—the men's locker room, the women's locker room and, between them, a two-story executive complex.

Fifty laborers dug the plant's foundation while another hundred stonemasons cut the limestone for the factory walls. Plumbers, brick men, plasterers and carpenters—all worked seven days a week, fourteen hours a day, under Milton Hershey's constant attention. He involved himself in every step of the process, asking plasterers to show him how to use a trowel and bricklayers to explain how to slack lime for mortar. He met with the architects and surveyors daily and kept close tabs on Henry Herr, the civil engineer he hired to manage it all. Although Herr, a Lancaster native and graduate of Lehigh University, was the expert, it was Milton Hershey who signed off on every decision—and he had definite ideas about what he wanted.

Initially, Hershey put Harry Lebkicher, a longtime friend, in charge of building all the houses. But the first houses he erected along Trinidad Avenue alternated between two basic designs, and the second batch along Areba Street all looked alike. Hershey was furious.

"That's the way the slave dealers used to do it," he screamed at Lebkicher. "We don't want that here." He replaced Lebkicher on the spot, then ordered every house torn down. Hershey didn't want the town to feel cookie-cutter or industrial; he was building a community to be as pure and as wholesome as the chocolate that would be its foundation. And although aspects of the town were unabashedly commercial, Hershey never compromised on quality, beauty or character. He provided his residents with every amenity imaginable: indoor plumbing and electricity, a bank and a department store, new schools and entertainment.

His love of greenery was evident throughout. Every home had a tidy front lawn and a spacious backyard, and Hershey ordered trees, bushes and flowers planted along each street. The median that ran the length of Chocolate Avenue was so lavishly landscaped that it looked to all who entered the town as though they were driving through a garden. Having lived in both the city and the countryside, Hershey had developed a strong belief that urban life was unhealthy and morally debilitating. He felt that fresh air, unspoiled land and recreation were indispensable to a salutary existence, and he set out to sculpt a reality from this philosophy. Hershey left wide-open space—150 acres—for an enormous park at the center of town, equipped initially with a band shell, a boathouse and a baseball diamond. He also planned five eighteen-hole golf courses, a twenty-three-acre public garden inspired by the gardens of Versailles and a zoo that even today serves as a nature preserve for seventy-five species of North American wildlife. Outside the gates of the factory, Hershey ordered landscapers to erect a giant display of ornamental shrubs, spelling HERSHEY COCOA in ten-foot-high letters. Visible for miles, the sign still welcomes the town's steady throng of tourists.

For transportation, Hershey built a trolley system powered by electricity generated by his plant. For just a nickel, workers could ride the full thirty miles from Elizabethtown to Hummelstown, or stop at Hershey in between. Hershey also convinced the Philadelphia and Reading Railroad to serve his community with a new station at the foot of Cocoa Avenue and include a railroad siding for loading freight cars at the factory.

He then petitioned the U.S. postmaster for an official post office. For that, he needed a name for the town, so he sponsored a contest offering $100 to the winning entry. Thousands of names were proposed, including Dark Town, Drinkmore, Etabit, Grandoshus and Qualitytells, but the prize went to a woman from Wilkes-Barre who submitted "Hersheykoko." The U.S. postmaster balked at the name, however, saying it was too commercial. It was quickly shortened to just plain Hershey.

But it was a town in name only. The original 1,200 acres that Hershey purchased in 1902 was never actually incorporated; it remained part of Derry Township, named after the city of Derry, Ireland. As such, Hershey had no form of government or elected officials. In the early days, Milton Hershey served as constable, fire chief and mayor. And though he eventually hired others for some of these roles, he never relinquished final authority.

In the summer of 1904, the executive offices on Chocolate Avenue were finished and in December, the factory itself was completed. Work in the Lancaster caramel plant slowly ground to a halt, and by June 1905, equipment was being moved from Lancaster into the new chocolate works, "the most complete of their kind in the world," as they were advertised in the *Confectioners' Journal*.

The new factory was immense, designed for production on a massive scale. But so far, Hershey had been unable to perfect a process that would allow him to manufacture quality milk chocolate in such huge quantities. Since 1900, Hershey had been making small batches of milk chocolate at his Lancaster facility. Sales of the product were strong and his nickel milk-chocolate bar was proving more popular than his broad line of novelty items. But he was still struggling to find a milk-condensing method that would allow him to blend his chocolate and milk solution effortlessly. On some days, it seemed the milk would condense almost by itself;

but on others, it would come out lumpy or burned. And he was still having problems with the shelf life of his candy bars. He wanted a product that would last for weeks, but his current bars were spoiling far too quickly.

Hershey called in men from his caramel plant to help with his experiments at the Homestead. He had hired a professional chemist initially, but when the chemist burned a batch of milk and sugar that Milton was trying to test, it only confirmed his disdain for "experts." Hershey then brought in John Schmalback, a worker from Lancaster, who successfully condensed a kettle full of the same mixture in a matter of hours.

"Look at that beautiful batch of milk," Hershey said when the experiment was over. "How come *you* didn't burn it? *You* didn't go to college." Hershey was so pleased, he handed Schmalback a $100 bill.

But it took many more trials before Hershey hit on a workable solution: Using a heavy concentration of sugar, Hershey boiled the milk mixture slowly under low heat in a vacuum. When the batch came out, it was smooth as satin, like a batch of still-warm taffy. The concoction blended effortlessly with other ingredients, resulting in a chocolate that was light brown in color and mild to the taste. But something else had happened in the process that no one understood. In making the milk solution, Hershey had hit upon a method (as chemists would later explain) that allowed the lipase enzymes in the milk to break down the remaining milk fat and produce flavorful free fatty acids. In other words, it was slightly soured.

Whether Hershey noticed the off-note flavor in the final product is not clear. All we know is that the process was hailed as a triumph and was replicated in the plant, where Hershey began churning out milk chocolate with this unusual flavor, distinct from any of its European counterparts. And from the moment the public tasted it, Hershey's new chocolate was a success. No one in America had eaten anything like it, and by 1907, the year Hershey's Kisses were introduced, sales had reached nearly $2 million, far outstripping Hershey's own expectations.

After a while, Hershey began to pare down the number of products being made, focusing on a handful of items that could be mass-produced and sold nationwide at the affordable price of a nickel.

This strategy was radically different from the rest of the industry's. Until Hershey came along, no one had ever considered national distribution. Even Walter Baker's chocolate was known only as far as the Mississippi River. But Hershey wasn't content to limit his market; he wanted to sell his milk chocolate coast-to-coast. After all, Cadbury, Rowntree, Nestlé, Tobler and Lindt were all selling their chocolates across Europe.

Hershey also wanted to broaden the outlets where chocolate was being sold. He envisioned his nickel bars resting on counters at luncheonettes, grocers, bus stops and newsstands. This was a new concept in candy sales, which had previously been limited to candy stores and druggists. He singlehandedly developed these new outlets, distributing his products through the brokers who were emerging to serve the developing retail sector. It's thanks to M. S. Hershey that we can now find candy wherever we look.

These strategies emerged from Hershey's conviction that chocolate—so rich in nutrients and energy-giving properties—should be consumed by all. So he priced it cheap, forever altering the worldwide market. Henceforth, solid chocolate would be the province of the common man, available in every five-and-dime from Pennsylvania to Oregon. The Hershey name quickly became synonymous with the product, and today, nearly one hundred years after it was first introduced, "Hershey" means a chocolate bar to almost every American.

LEGEND HAS IT THAT WHENEVER MILTON HERSHEY SAW ONE OF HIS COMPANY'S NICKEL-BAR WRAPPERS ON THE GROUND, INSTEAD OF THROWING IT AWAY HE TURNED IT FACE UP—HIS WAY OF ADVERTISING.

The American public's love for Hershey's chocolate baffles European connoisseurs, who say Hershey's chocolate is offensive, if not downright inedible. Known in the industry as "barnyard" or "cheesy" chocolate, Hershey's unique, fermented flavor has never sold in Europe, despite attempts by the company to market it there.

"Milton Hershey completely ruined the American palate with his sour, gritty chocolate," said Hans Scheu,[1] a Swiss national who is now president of the Cocoa Merchants' Association. "He had no idea what he was doing."

Like most Europeans, Scheu despises the Hershey flavor and believes Milton Hershey could not possibly have intended to invent it.

"Who in their right mind would set out to produce such a sour chocolate?" he asked. "There is no way Mr. Hershey did this on purpose; it had to be a mistake."

Scheu backs up his view with a different version of history and says this is the story he had always heard about Hershey's chocolate: When Hershey was first starting out, he bought a tremendous amount of surplus powdered milk from a European supplier. By the time the milk was shipped to America, however, it had started to turn, becoming slightly cheesy. Hershey knew the milk was spoiling, but he refused to throw it away.

"He was a cheap Pennsylvania Dutchman; he didn't want to waste his money, so he used it in his chocolate, and that became the special Hershey flavor," said Scheu. "But I wouldn't call it special."

Jean Jedot of Jacobs Suchard recalls a similar tale.

"We always chuckle about his famous Hershey claim, how his chocolate was *special*," said Jedot, who has worked as a chemist in the industry for thirty years. "Everyone knows Hershey used spoiled milk to make his chocolate. That's what makes it so raunchy."[2]

Hershey officials declined to discuss the specific process that results in the Hershey flavor: "That's proprietary," declared former CEO Richard Zimmerman. "We don't discuss it or disclose it." But, he added, Milton Hershey never used spoiled powdered milk to produce his original chocolate formula.

"Mr. Hershey used only the freshest milk, which he learned to condense himself," Zimmerman said. "For anyone to suggest otherwise is preposterous."

Regardless of how the flavor was developed, it has become the undisputed Hershey signature, the prize the company values as its most important asset.

"Everybody at Hershey guards that flavor with their life," said Earl Spangler, who ran the chocolate manufacturing division from the 1940s through the 1970s. "It is taboo to mess with any part of that manufacturing process. I mean, you couldn't even change a screw without worrying how it might affect the Hershey flavor."

Although it is no longer true today, Spangler said no one in the factory during his tenure understood exactly what contributed to the Hershey taste.

"Science was not available in those days. You could not analyze it. You didn't know what chemicals were being formed. You just knew when you got it right and when you got it wrong.

"We always assumed that the copper kettles contributed significantly to that exclusive flavor and also the timing in the process of condensing that milk. But we never really knew for sure. That's why we were so afraid to touch it."

Over the years, this hands-off policy frustrated many of Hershey's engineers and chemists, who insisted there were better, cheaper ways to manufacture Hershey products. Louis C. Smith, who served as Hershey's chief engineer for more than thirty years, remembers arguing with management endlessly over Hershey's clumsy—almost amateurish—manufacturing methods.

Hershey's milk-condensing process is "the most inefficient process that you ever saw," said Smith. "For a mechanical engineer like myself, it almost destroys me to see that because I know they can do it much more efficiently and save piles of money.

"But the management would not accept a more efficient system because they said that it changed the flavor of Hershey's milk chocolate."

Smith argued that 99 percent of consumers would not notice any change unless they were eating the old Hershey bar together with the new.

"I still believe that," he said.

"But Mr. Hershey's recipe, you didn't fool around with that. There wasn't any question about it."

The only reason Hershey managed to maintain any consistency in the flavor, according to Smith, is not because of some carefully controlled and regimented manufacturing system, but because of the huge volume of chocolate produced—as much as 100,000 pounds a day.

"There was such a blend of different batches we could hide a lot of our mistakes," he said.

Zimmerman agreed that Hershey's manufacturing process is "a bit awkward and old-fashioned," but he defended the company's decision to keep it that way.

"Understand that in those days, the Hershey flavor was all we had," he said. "We didn't have Reese and we didn't have 5th Avenue and we didn't have the Peter Paul brands. We didn't have anything but the Hershey flavor. And we protected that like it was gold."

Today, the chocolate used in the company's original mass-produced candies—the Hershey bar, introduced in 1900; Hershey's Kisses, introduced in 1907; and the Hershey Almond bar, launched in 1908—is manufactured as it always has been, in strict accordance with Milton Hershey's original recipe. New products, however, like NutRageous and Reese's Pieces, are made from dry milk solids using more modern and efficient manufacturing techniques—although even this innovation was a struggle initially, according to Spangler.

He remembers heated arguments in 1970 between Hershey executives and British candy maker Rowntree Mackintosh PLC over Hershey's agreement to distribute Rowntree's Kit Kat in the United States.

"Rowntree had their own formulation for the coating on Kit Kat," remembered Spangler. "But we thought that since the taste of American chocolate differs considerably from the European, that maybe we should use a chocolate related more closely to our own Hershey flavor.

"But they really took issue with that. They didn't want their formulation contaminated one bit by the Hershey process. The product had to be produced specifically to their formulation, so that's what we're doing."

The experience with Kit Kat "opened Hershey executives' minds," said Spangler. "Suddenly, they realized that Americans would accept other flavors of chocolate besides the original Hershey. But that wasn't true in the beginning; it wasn't true for the first fifty years Hershey was in business."

By 1909, the Chocolate Camelot that had sprouted overnight from the Pennsylvania farmland was the talk of the state. The Pennsylvania legislature hailed Hershey's social experiment as a "model town" and declared Milton S. Hershey a visionary. Of the 1,200 acres of cornfields and pastures originally purchased for the creation of Hershey, fully half had been developed by 1913. The 150-acre Hershey Park was attracting more than 100,000 visitors a year. Residential construction was booming and services were being expanded to keep up with demand. Hershey built an inn and a restaurant, a gymnasium and a swimming pool as big as a small lake. He added attractions to Hershey Park, including a merry-go-round, a miniature electric train and a dance hall that became a popular Saturday-night destination, hosting some of the most famous orchestras around.

As the number of visitors increased so did the town's population. Drawn by stories of Milton Hershey's benevolence, farmers and tradesmen from miles around flocked to Hershey to live. By 1913, the total population exceeded 700 and continued to grow until it reached 2,500 in the late 1930s.

During Milton Hershey's lifetime, most of the town worked for him, and life in Hershey was the ultimate employee benefit. Hershey's workers shoveled the snow and removed the garbage. Hershey supported the volunteer fire company and supplied the utilities—the electric, water, sewage, telephone and steam pipes that carried surplus heat from the factory to the town's public buildings. Jobs were plentiful and taxes were nonexistent.

Monroe Stover remembers when his family moved to Hershey in 1911, renting one of the first houses on Areba Avenue. It was equipped with indoor plumbing and was electrified at the rate of $1 per month. Rent was about $15, Stover recalled.

"It was a small house for the nine of us," he remembered, "but it was our first modern home, and I'll never forget it. Moving to Hershey was like moving to paradise; no more outhouses or one-room schoolhouses or dirt roads. We had steam heat and electricity and telephones. And the streets were cobblestone. That was something."

The original forty-eight houses cost between $1,200 and $1,500 to buy. And although most residents preferred to rent their homes, Hershey encouraged buying and established a trust company in 1905 to make it easier for residents to get mortgages. He encouraged everyone to keep an account in his bank, and he set the example, placing his personal accounts there and investing $100,000 in trust company stock. The very first account went to William Malcolm Murrie, the firstborn son of William F. R. Murrie, Hershey's president, who deposited $100 in the name of the two-year-old boy. Mr. Murrie also had the honor of fathering the town's first baby, Marion Murrie, born in the Hershey Hospital on March 21, 1907.

The Murrie family, like most executives' families, lived directly across the street from the factory on Chocolate Avenue. Although their home was larger than average and had fancier appointments, it was still quite modest in size and property. Hershey tried hard to ensure that the hierarchy in the factory didn't spill over to the town; everybody in Hershey shopped at the same stores, attended the same churches and sent their children to the same schools. Despite these efforts, however, the town was not egalitarian.

Richard Murrie remembers one year in grade school when his teacher gave him top marks even though he had hardly completed any of his assignments. "My father found out that she was going easy on me, and he was furious," he remembered.

"It turned out my teacher wanted a job at the plant, and she figured that if she was nice to me she would get hired. My dad fired her, instead."

Richard said his parents tried to make sure he wasn't privileged; still, his upbringing wasn't that of a typical American boy. He remembers, for example, an afternoon when he was about five years old touring the plant with his father.

"I climbed up onto one of those giant mixers, the kind that smooths out the chocolate; and wouldn't you know, I fell in. I'll never forget that, swimming in that big vat of chocolate. Of course, my father got real angry and sent me home to get hosed off on the front porch. But it was worth all of his yelling. How many boys do you know who get to dive into a river of chocolate?"

MILTON HERSHEY'S UTOPIAN DREAM GAVE RISE TO THESE BEAUTIFUL HOMES ON JAVA AVENUE, PHOTOGRAPHED CIRCA 1919.

For most of the town's youth, growing up in Hershey was like living one long, sweet fantasy.

"Everybody kept chocolate in their cupboards," remembers Stover. "And we got to eat as much as we wanted. And every Saturday we'd go to the park. Nobody had to pay to get in, and the rides cost just a nickel. If you didn't have any money, you could swim in the pool or listen to the live music or watch the people. It was a great way to pass the day."

But life in Hershey wasn't all smiles and laughter. Living in town was like living in a fishbowl. Everybody worked together and socialized together. There was only one country club and one rotary. You never knew if your neighbor might someday be your boss.

"You had to get along with everybody," said Marlene Hubbard. "If you didn't like your coworkers, that was just tough. You couldn't get away from them; they were your neighbors and your fellow churchgoers. You couldn't go anywhere without seeing somebody you worked with or worked for."

For many, Milton Hershey's presence in town was also a bit overbearing. He would often tour the town in his chauffeured convertible Cadillac, making note of lawns that weren't mowed and homes that weren't being properly maintained. He liked to think his workers appreciated the services he gave them, and it is said he would ride the trolley—sometimes as early as five in the morning—to see how well it was patronized. He also occasionally hired private detectives to find out answers to questions that bothered him—like where the liquor was coming from during Prohibition and who was responsible for throwing trash on the grounds of Hershey Park.

Hershey's prying was nothing compared with the paternalistic oversight and control of some other industrialists. For example, Henry Ford conditioned his employees' wages on their good behavior outside the factory, employing a force of 150 inspectors in his "sociological department" to keep tabs on workers' hygeine, personal habits and housekeeping.

Nevertheless, several journalists who visited Hershey wrote stories highly critical of the way the town was run. *The Philadelphia Evening Times*—in an article that ended "Tell me truly, tell me please, Is Hershey a town or a disease?"—made Milton Hershey sound like a czar. *Fortune* magazine in the 1930s was equally negative, describing one of Hershey's most prized buildings—the Hotel Hershey—as "the Pennsylvania Dutch idea of Moorish architecture."

Hershey took great offense at these characterizations, telling close associates that no one outside of Hershey understood him; he simply wanted the very best for his residents and expected them to treat his investments with proper respect.

He did much to raise the standard of living among his thousands of employees. In addition to the town's lavish amenities, he gave his workers insurance benefits in case of sickness, accident or death, and he offered a generous retirement plan. He donated all of the buildings for the local schools and established a junior college, where tuition was free for all residents. He also gave $20,000 to each of the five local churches, and made certain his residents had access to the arts. His $3-million community building housed a theater as elegant as any on Broadway. The grand lobby was of Pompeian design, with marble walls three feet thick and a floor of Italian lava rock. Inside, the playhouse was extravagantly appointed, with gold trim and balconies. Over the years, the theater played host to some of America's greatest performers, including Fanny Brice and the Ziegfeld Follies, Roy Rogers, Blackstone the Magician and Virgil Fox. It became a regular stopover for touring Broadway shows, with headliners like Yul Brynner, Rex Harrison, Mary Martin and Alfred Lunt.

"Hershey's residents took all this for granted," said Stover. "We didn't know what it was like to live in a real small town. We had everything they had in the big city—maybe more."

And Hershey's philanthropy went far beyond the town. In 1909, he and Kitty set up a trust fund to found a school for poor, orphaned boys. The Hersheys themselves were childless, and Kitty said she wished to provide a haven for those in need of a good home and a better chance in life. Hershey provided the boys with everything he could to make their lives normal. He explained his generous giving this way: "Well, I have no heirs; so I decided to make the orphan boys of the United States my heirs. . . .

"The biggest influence in a boy's life is what his dad does; and, when a boy doesn't happen to have any sort of a dad, he is a special mark for destiny. I am afraid that most of our orphan boys have a bad time of it and that many never get the right start. They tell me that youngsters who go to prison never have a chance. Well, I am going to give some of them a chance my way."[3]

The backbone of it all remained the Hershey Chocolate works, where by 1911, annual sales had topped $5 million.[4] Although the factory was designed with mass production in mind, it was not fully automated, nor was it very efficient. It took the hard labor of 1,200 workers, six days a week, twenty-four hours a day, to produce the millions of candy bars that made Hershey possible. What workers remember most about life in the factory is not the privilege of eating all the chocolate they wanted, but the lifting, pushing, carrying and pounding that went into making each piece.

At first, there was a logical progression to the plant's layout: sugar, milk, cocoa beans, cocoa butter and other crude materials were handled at the farthest end of the plant; wrapping and shipping were headquartered at the opposite end; and in between, the rest of the process was arranged for orderly flow. But even before construction was finished, the company had outgrown this basic design and ad hoc additions were being built to supplement the space. In less than a decade, the Hershey factory expanded from six acres of floor space to thirty-six. The plant grew vertically as well as horizontally, requiring the installation of freight elevators and connecting corridors. The result: a tangled industrial maze that made orderly production almost impossible.

Even though the factory housed the best and most up-to-date chocolate processing equipment imported from Germany and Switzerland, it remained industrially unsophisticated. There was no means of connecting the various stages of production—from roasting, hulling and milling raw beans, to blending, smoothing and mixing ingredients and finally to molding and wrapping chocolate bars. Material handling was primitive, with no conveyor belts or pumps to direct the flow of ingredients. It was all done by hand using the most elementary equipment: bathtubs, buckets and spatulas.

Lawrence Pellegrini remembers his first job, unloading the 200-pound bags of cocoa beans, which came daily by rail from warehouses in New York, 500 bags to a car. If the storage room was full—which it usually was, although it held as many as 100,000 bags—he stacked the burlap sacks along the factory's main corridor, piling them to the ceiling in rows five and six deep. By elevator, the beans traveled to the fourth floor of the No. 24 building, where they were cleaned and shoveled into giant roasters, coal-fueled rotating drums capable of cooking 400 pounds of beans at a time.

Like coffee beans or peanuts, roasting cocoa beans is a delicate process that requires careful supervision to ensure peak flavor. Too light a roast and the beans taste raw; too dark, and they taste burnt. Fires, too, were a constant hazard. Cocoa bean shells, which tend to separate from the kernels during roasting, become highly flammable, like leaves in a forest. Too many loose shells and the entire batch would spontaneously combust, ruining not just the beans but also the oven.

Although Hershey's roasters were the best on the market, they were far from precise machines. There were no scientific controls for time, temperature, rotation or air flow. It required the skill and artistry of an experienced chocolate connoisseur to bring out just the right flavor. Several factors added to the difficulty of the task: First, cocoa is not a uniform raw material. The beans vary in age, ripeness, fermentation and moisture content, making an even, uniform roast nearly impossible. Second, the flavor that we recognize as "chocolate" is not really specific; so far, it has eluded analysis and identification, leaving it up to the roaster to know from experience when the batch has peaked.

In the early years at Hershey, this job belonged to George Bowman, an average factory worker elevated to this specialty by years and years of practice. With a team of a dozen workers manning the ovens, Bowman oversaw the roasting of tons of cocoa beans every day.

Working in the roasting room was one of the toughest jobs in the factory: sweaty, smelly and back-breaking. To clean the ovens, as required

A TURN-OF-THE-CENTURY COCOA BEAN ROASTER HAD TO BE FUELED WITH COAL AND LOADED AND CLEANED BY HAND. IT WAS A HOT, DEMANDING, DIRTY JOB.

several times each shift, the workers crawled inside and, on their hands and knees, vacuumed out the debris. During roasting, they were responsible for stoking the fires with coal and loading the drums with beans. The average roast took about an hour, and they ran ten roasts a day. By the second or third batch, the room would reach 120 degrees. And then there was the odor—a bitter, acrid smell so pungent it stung the nostrils.

"I couldn't smell anything but that odor for years," Bowman said. "It didn't matter if I was at the plant or at home or on vacation, I couldn't get that smell out of my nose."

Each variety of cocoa bean produces its own unique perfume, and each results in a different chocolate flavor in the final stage of production. Different types of beans also require different roasts, and Bowman knew them all. Forastero type beans, which are the basis of most commercial chocolate, require higher temperatures for a "full" roast, while criollo beans, which are highly aromatic, peak at much lower temperatures. To create the proper "notes" in the Hershey flavor, the different types of beans are blended after roasting according to a closely guarded formula.

Selecting the right mix of beans is considered by some connoisseurs to be the most difficult aspect of chocolate production. Over the centuries, the cocoa growing industry has tended to crossbreed varieties of beans so that today most beans are a hodgepodge of different flavor characteristics. This complicated genealogy, along with plagues of disease capable of wiping out entire crops, has made it nearly impossible to replicate flavors from the past and guarantee consistency in chocolate products. For example, scientists believe the original cocoa enjoyed thousands of years ago by Montezuma's court was a fine-quality criollo that has since died out. Some beans enjoyed by Spanish royalty in the 1600s have also disappeared, and while new flavor grades are constantly being researched and developed, there is no question that the chocolate we enjoy today has evolved significantly from its origins.

For manufacturers, this is a heavy burden. Hershey's researchers are constantly roaming the cocoa fields looking for varieties that will meet the factory's specifications. In recent decades, several strains in the original Hershey formula have vanished due to disease and irresponsible breeding, and replacing them is an ongoing challenge. Of course, it's not just Hershey that fights this battle; finding "the perfect bean" is the quest of every manufacturer in the world, the Holy Grail of chocolate. Hundreds of millions of dollars are spent each year on this research. Most large manufacturers, like Hershey, Mars and Nestlé, operate their own experimental cocoa plantations to study husbandry and disease. Many of their experiments have a direct impact on consumers.

For example, the introduction of the candy version of the Dove bar in 1992, Mars's first solid dark-chocolate candy bar, was made possible by the discovery in the late 1980s of a "secret" high-flavor bean that could be produced economically enough to be used in a mid-priced bar.[5] Typically, such high-quality beans are too expensive for any candy but the finest boxed assortments. But the Dove beans are different, and so prized by Mars that they have no official name and are never referred to directly in the company records. No one but a handful of top executives knows the origin of the beans or where they are being grown. Shipments, too, are encoded to avoid industrial espionage, according to a factory worker at the Dove plant in Burr Ridge, Illinois.[6] No one else at Mars would even confirm the beans' existence. John Mars boasted that the Dove bar is as "fine a quality dark chocolate as can be found anywhere in the world," but he left it at that.

Hershey, too, keeps its blends secret. According to former CEO Zimmerman, no one in the factory—not even the CEO—knows the proper proportions that must be combined to create the chocolate for a Kit Kat bar, a Hershey bar or a Reese's Peanut Butter Cup. (Each has its own distinctive blend.)

"These days it's all programmed into the computer," he said. "Nobody knows the correct recipe. Not even me—although I know where to go to find it."

In the early years at the factory, the only ones who knew the blend were Milton Hershey, William Murrie and the roasting operators who mixed the proportions manually before the beans were winnowed—a process that separates the cooled beans, as cleanly as possible, into useful kernels and disposable shells. The winnower cracks the beans by throwing them against a steel plate, and then, using a fan, it blows away the lighter shells, leaving the heavier kernels, or nibs, behind. Once cleaned, the nibs are milled in giant mélangeurs, round stone pots equipped with heavy granite wheels that crush the nibs into a liquid paste, producing chocolate liquor. The heavy, fatty liquor is then divided between two different manufacturing operations: cocoa and chocolate.

To produce powdered cocoa—used in beverages, baked goods, ice cream and chocolate syrup—some of the liquor was directed to vertical presses, where the cocoa butter was squeezed out through felt and canvas filter pads, leaving behind a partially defatted cocoa cake. Cakes that would become commercial cocoa were pressed until they contained about 24 percent cocoa butter. But Hershey also produced cocoa for use by tobacco companies, according to Howard Phillippy, former Hershey engineer.

This type of cocoa, which contained only 10 percent cocoa butter, was very dry by comparison, said Phillippy. "It was bought by the tobacco industry as an additive [to cigarettes]."

"It was supposed to make the smokes taste better," said Earl Spangler, former plant manager. "It helped cut the bitter flavor of the tobacco, and I think [the tobacco companies] believed it added a richness to the smoke, but I never tasted it myself."

These cakes, like the ones for cocoa, were hauled by truck to the canning department at the other end of the factory. Here, they were fed into crushers, which pulverized them into a microscopic powder that was easily airborne, making for hazardous working conditions. Those assigned to the department remember cocoa powder floating through the room in thick clouds, coating every piece of equipment and every employee in a fine layer of dust.

"If you worked in cocoa, every breath you took tasted like chocolate," recalled Henry Muller, who worked in the department for fifteen years. "You could wear a mask, eye goggles and gloves, and that powder would still get you. It was in your hair and your ears and under your fingernails and ground into your clothes. It was a very dirty job."

"You could always tell who worked in cocoa," said Rose Gasper, who began working at Hershey when she was thirteen years old. "They were the ones who reeked of chocolate—you could smell them coming a mile away."

Here, too, fires were a constant threat. The rapid pulverizing of the cocoa cakes created an enormous amount of static electricity, which was supposed to be dissipated by grounding magnets on the machinery. But if the temperature in the room rose above 80 degrees and the powder in the air reached specific concentrations, the cocoa became explosive. Muller said it was more dangerous to work in his department than in any other operation in the factory.

"One spark in the air under the right conditions could start a flash fire in seconds," he remembered. Women, in fact, were prohibited from these jobs out of concern for their safety. Instead, they were assigned largely to the chocolate-making operation, jobs that were less dangerous but just as physical.

It was this side of the factory that was open to outsiders. In fact, so many people came to visit the chocolate-making department that by

1915, a visitors' bureau was opened to provide formal guided tours. The public was not permitted to watch every stage in the production process, but they were allowed to view some of the most spectacular—starting with the Longitudinal department, which alone could fuel a child's imagination for years.

The room was so large you had to squint to see to the other end. But there was no doubt as to what was inside: chocolate. Giant vats of chocolate. Each one a lake, carrying some 10,000 gallons worth. Altogether, more than 300,000 gallons of liquid chocolate flowed through these vats, known as longitudinal conches. Lined up in double rows, one after another, they seemed to stretch for miles. As visitors watched, mesmerized, the conches performed a sort of industrial ballet, their enormous rollers mechanically swaying backward and forward, grinding the rich, brown liquid in each basin until it was smooth enough to be made into bars—a process that took three days and nights.

INSIDE HERSHEY'S LONGITUDINAL DEPARTMENT, HUNDREDS OF CONCHES PERFORM A MECHANICAL BALLET, SLOWLY GRINDING THE CHOCOLATE OVER THREE DAYS TO MAKE IT SMOOTH.

At this stage, all of the ingredients needed to make milk chocolate—the condensed milk and sugar solution, the spices and the additional cocoa butter drained from the cocoa cakes—were already mixed into the batch. Conching was not so much a matter of blending, which is done by mixers and refiners earlier in the process, but a means of "curing" the chocolate to the right consistency. Without conching, chocolate tastes gritty, a phenomenon that has puzzled scientists, since the particles at this point should be tiny enough to produce a smooth batter. But particle size doesn't seem to translate into fineness when it comes to chocolate—a conundrum that baffles manufacturers.

"All we know for certain is that without conching, the chocolate *just isn't* chocolate," said Hershey plant manager Ron Orlosky.[7] "But we still don't understand all of the changes that take place during conching. That's the big mystery of chocolate manufacture."

Scientists conjecture that when the chocolate paste is passed through refiners prior to conching, the particles (particularly of sugar) tend to be flat and sharp. In the conche, these edges are rounded or blunted by rubbing against each other and against the granite trough. At the same time, the blending process distributes the cocoa butter more evenly, allowing it to cover the entire surface area of the particles—all of which contributes to chocolate's velvety texture.

But other changes take place in the conche, as well. After this process, the chocolate tastes different somehow—connoisseurs describe it as more mellow. This is especially true of milk chocolate, which tastes flat or stale without conching. Tests have shown that during the days and days of conching, the pH in the chocolate rises and volatile acids and water are driven off. But other chemical changes take place that are less well understood, although they, too, serve to unmask the true chocolate flavor.

Visitors to the Longitudinal sensed the first hints of these changes in the aroma wafting from the basins. This was no acidy smell, like the smell in the roasting department. Here, the chocolate perfume was intoxicating, like opening a fresh tin of cocoa and inhaling deeply.

In fact, it is this delicious odor that permeates the entire town of Hershey—on muggy days it hangs in the air for miles around the factory. Local legend has it that the smell was the first crude attempt at subliminal marketing, Milton Hershey's way of increasing demand for his candy bars. But in truth, it serves a more practical purpose. The continual grinding inside the conches generates an enormous amount of friction heat; the only way to keep the room below 100 degrees is to pump the air out through giant vents in the ceiling, blanketing the town in a thick chocolate aroma—so thick that at times it seems just breathing the air can give you a cavity.

"Folks can usually smell Hershey long before they actually get here—it's the town's signature," said Stover. "But if you grew up around it, like I did, you really stopped noticing it after a while. It just becomes part of the scenery."

Like steel from the foundry and coal from the mine, chocolate from Milton Hershey's plant was nothing more than a commodity to local residents like Stover. It paid for the street cleaning and garbage removal. It provided the recreation and entertainment. It meant stability, wealth and jobs—lots of jobs. This was no automated process; it took thousands of people to operate the sometimes crude machinery that made Hershey tick.

Imagine emptying a 10,000-gallon conche with nothing but a bucket. Or wheeling chocolate from one end of the thirty-six-acre factory to the other, using a bathtub on wheels. Or knocking chocolate bars out of their molds with heavy metal hammers. It was cumbersome, tedious work.

Those assigned to the Longitudinal used giant spatulas to scrape down the sides of each basin and two-and-a-half-gallon buckets to drain the chocolate from the vats. To transport it to the molding room required bathtubs—old-fashioned steel tubs with claws—that became makeshift handcarts on wheels, carrying fifty gallons of chocolate from one process to the next.

"I don't think anybody could forget those bathtubs," said Lawrence Pellegrini, who began his career at Hershey in 1941. "They must have weighed over a hundred pounds when empty. And then you'd fill 'em up with chocolate and have to wheel 'em around without spilling. Now, that was a trick."

Once it reached the molding room, the chocolate was poured into heavy metal trays, each with deposits for thirty-six candy bars. Workers did their best to fill the deposits evenly, but precise measures weren't instituted until the mid-1950s. Up until then, an ounce was rarely an ounce, although a bar was more likely to be overweight than under. The temperature in the room was also erratic, a nightmare for the molding operators, since they needed just the right conditions for the bars to solidify properly.

To avoid shocking the warm chocolate, the trays had to be heated to between 80 and 90 degrees. Then they were filled and loaded manually onto a conveyor belt that led through a cooling tunnel some 200 feet long. But if the chocolate was too warm going into the tunnel, or cooled too rapidly inside the tunnel, streaks of white called "bloom" would appear on the candy's surface. Bloom is actually cocoa butter that has migrated to the surface of the bar and solidified. But because it looks like mold to consumers, it's a real hazard for chocolate makers.

The other big hazard in those early days was humidity.

"Too much moisture in the air and that chocolate would never come out of the molds," remembered Gasper, who began working in the factory in 1930 and retired in 1982. "You could hammer and hammer until your arm fell off, and that chocolate would just stick to the trays; it wasn't going anywhere."

Demolding the bars was the responsibility of a department called Knock Out, made up entirely of women, each wielding a hammer to literally knock the bars loose from their trays. Eventually, these jobs were replaced by vacuum pumps that lifted the bars out using suction, but until then, Knock Out was the loudest department in Hershey.

"You couldn't hear anything over all that banging," said Gasper. "There was no such thing as earplugs back then. You just had to get used to it."

Keeping up with the conveyor belt was chaotic, too. It took two women working in tandem to grab the twenty-pound tray, flip it upside down and start hammering out the candy. There was much debate over which part of the job was the hardest: the lifting and inverting, or the banging.

"You were always in such a hurry because of the conveyors—the chocolate would just keep coming out, and you would hammer your hand if you weren't too careful.

"I never broke a finger, just bruised and smashed, but I know a lot of women who did," said Gasper.

When the chocolate was arranged on pieces of cardboard, they were stacked onto skids, twelve high, and hand-wheeled to the wrapping room, two floors below. This was by far the busiest room in the factory, with hundreds of workers scattered around machines and tables, preparing the chocolate for shipment. And until the 1960s, it was strictly women's work.

"When I started, the girls ran the entire department—there were maybe 400 of us manning those machines and packing up chocolate," said Jean Ranerio. "About the only men around were the supply boys, who delivered the skids; the floor scrapers, who collected the scraps; and the elevator men."

Initially, wrappers were paid by the piece—a practice that encouraged speed and also shortcuts. To wrap a single Kiss was a delicate process: The tissues inserted in each one had a tendency to blow away and were difficult to handle. A proper wrap required picking up the tissue, laying it on the foil, placing the Kiss on top and twisting the whole package together. But this process took too much time. Some workers were known to pick up a Kiss, lick the bottom, dab it on the pile of tissues, then deposit that on the foil and twist.[8] Not exactly sanitary, but fast.

Wrapping candy bars was a bit more automated. Two women were required to run each specially designed wrapping machine—one feeder and one packer. The feeder loaded the bars one by one onto the lugs of

WORKING ON THE KISS WRAPPING LINE WAS MUCH LIKE THE FAMOUS SCENE FROM *I LOVE LUCY.* THE CONVEYORS SPILLED A TORRENT OF KISSES, AND THE FASTER YOU WRAPPED, THE MORE YOU WERE PAID.

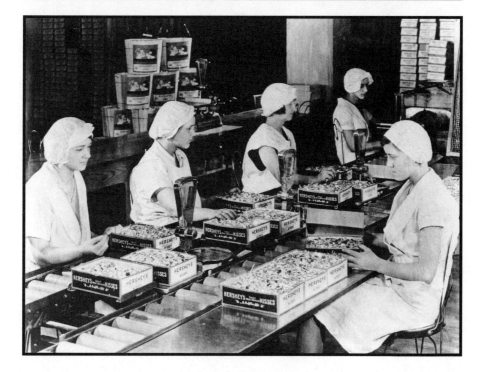

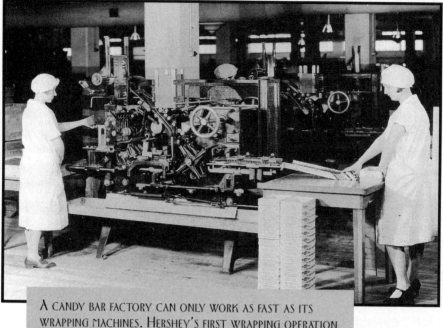

A CANDY BAR FACTORY CAN ONLY WORK AS FAST AS ITS WRAPPING MACHINES. HERSHEY'S FIRST WRAPPING OPERATION WAS THE MOST MODERN IN AMERICA, THOUGH IT WAS STILL ONLY SEMIAUTOMATED.

the wrapper, while the packer removed the wrapped bars and placed them in boxes for shipment.

Some women stayed in wrapping their entire careers, working thirty years or more with one machine. Over time, a relationship of sorts would develop.

"These women would come in early and they'd oil their machines and wipe them down and check the parts," remembered Ranerio. "Nobody else could touch their equipment; it was like their very own child."

All of the women wore crisp, starched white uniforms; in their silk stockings, white shoes, cotton linen hats and white dresses, they could have easily been mistaken for nurses.

"Everybody was neat and clean-looking—and those white uniforms against the brown chocolate—that was really quite a sight. It just made the chocolate stand out," recalled Ranerio.

In the 1970s, much to Ranerio's dismay, workers traded their whites for blue-green turquoise, and in the 1980s, they changed again to brown uniforms "that just don't have the same effect," she lamented.

Up until 1919, workers in the wrapping room were paid in the form of tokens, and output was measured at "the booth," a collection station in the middle of the floor. On payday, workers redeemed their tokens for cash. Depending on your speed, you could earn as much as $12 a week.[9]

The only woman who didn't collect tokens was Milton Hershey's mother, who never forgot her son's early failures and insisted on helping with the business. Mother Hershey, as everyone called her, lived across the street from the factory in the second-largest house in town. Every day, a girl from the wrapping room would deliver her a box of freshly made Kisses, along with tissues and squares of foil, and she would wrap them by hand in her kitchen. When she was done, she would sit on her front porch, her eye trained on the factory, drinking in her son's accomplishments—it was a satisfaction that Milton's father never had.

Unlike Fanny, Henry Hershey did not live to see his son's dream come to fruition. He passed away on February 20, 1904, one year before the opening of the new factory. When he fell ill, Milton happened to be traveling with Kitty in Florida, leaving only Henry's estranged wife at his bedside.

Although Fanny had joined Henry at the homestead when Milton moved his operations to Hershey, they had never reconciled their marriage. They barely spoke to each other and kept separate bedrooms on opposite sides of the farmhouse. The day Henry died, Fanny had her final revenge against the man she reviled: She took the hundreds of books in his library out to the field and burned them. The bonfire was visible for miles.

Chapter Ten

BITTERSWEET

A Kiss for You

HERSHEY'S MILK CHOCOLATE KISSES

KISSES WERE INTRODUCED IN 1907; THEIR TRADEMARK PLUMES WERE ADDED IN 1921 AS A MEANS OF DISTINGUISHING GENUINE KISSES FROM COPYCATS.

ALTHOUGH THE CHOCOLATE factory was at the center of his growing empire, Milton Hershey still did not involve himself in the plant's day-to-day operations. In fact, he often told his staff, "You do much better when I'm not around."[1] His focus was much broader than nickel candy bars; he was busy experimenting with new products, expanding the town and orphanage and traveling with Kitty. Like his father, Milton Hershey turned out to be a dreamer, but he had the capital and vision to make his dreams a success.

The town of Hershey was the best advertising money could buy. Millions of people visited the park and factory each year, attracted by the big bands, the amusements and the chocolate. And every one of them became a lifelong Hershey customer. Although not intended as such, the town became a far more effective marketing tool than billboards or printed promotions, which Hershey eventually stopped altogether. As word of his industrial utopia spread, so, too, did word of his chocolate bars. By 1915, Milton Hershey had established himself as America's candy man—a benevolent, soft-spoken, gentle uncle who made treats for children and gave orphans a home.

Having made his fortune many times over, he was content to see his money invested in others. His primary indulgence was Corona-Corona cigars, the best Cuban cigars he could buy, and he always had one in his mouth. As for clothes, his tastes remained modest. He was no sophisticate. His greatest thrill was being "first" in things—the first to own an electric car, the first to provide sewage to a town Hershey's size, the first to offer electricity to rural farm folk. But he shied away from publicity and was embarrassed easily when honored in public. He avoided self-promotion, and promoted his townspeople instead. He spent every Sunday when he was home with his orphan boys, and, next to Kitty, they received most of his attention.

Hershey told colleagues he wanted the boys to have everything he lacked in his own childhood—a sense of security, stability and an education. He believed strongly that environment, not heredity, determined the bent of a man's character, and he invested his fortune to ensure his orphans were given every opportunity.

The boys at the Hershey Industrial School lived on farms Hershey built in the surrounding countryside, with "house parents" to look after them. They worked on the farms as if they owned them, milking the cows, planting the fields and hauling in the grain. Hershey believed the experience would teach them responsibility and instill a proper work ethic, and he was strict when it came to how the farms were run. Whoever was in charge of the farmhouse had to have it in A-1 condition to avoid Hershey's ire.

"It didn't matter what time of day, before breakfast or after supper, you didn't know when Mr. Hershey was going to drop by unannounced," remembers house parent Henry Keener. "And he was the most meticulous fellow with himself. With his clothing, his mannerisms, everything. I never saw him in anything but a full-dress business suit, usually a dark suit. Never seen him in light clothing. [He always wore] a white stiff collar, and his tie was always in perfect place. He walked with a very spritely step. Nothing slouchy. Straight, upright, erect."

Hershey's exactitude was balanced by his warm generosity. The boys had spending money and clothes; they took vacations and spent Sundays

RESIDENTS OF HERSHEY AND SUR-
ROUNDING TOWNS WOULD GATHER IN
HERSHEY PARK TO ENJOY THE LIVE
MUSIC AND RECREATION, MUCH OF
WHICH WAS FREE.

in the park; they went to school, and when they graduated, they received $100, a new wardrobe and help in finding a job. Those who preferred to go on to college received full scholarships.

The initial enrollment of four boys quickly grew to over one hundred. Hershey turned the family homestead into the school's administrative office, and he built new educational facilities on the outskirts of town, including a large gymnasium, an auditorium and a library. When he was in town, he would always make time to visit the boys in their homes, and once a year he invited them all to High Point for a special breakfast of hot cocoa and toast. Out of respect, they called him Mr. Hershey, but they treated him like a parent. At times, their heartfelt adoration moved him to tears, although he would never openly admit the depth of his feelings.

Perhaps the only person who understood how important the school was to him was Kitty—the only one with whom he truly shared his thoughts. She encouraged his increasing philanthropy and supported him as he made each vision a reality. But she was no longer able to dote on Milton the way she used to; chronic illnesses had sapped her strength, leaving her crippled and short of breath.

Kitty's affliction upset Milton terribly. He sent for the country's best doctors to examine her and make a diagnosis. When they informed him in 1910 that her deteriorating condition was due to an incurable nervous disorder, he refused to accept their findings. He took Kitty to spas and clinics around the world, searching for a different answer. They traveled together to Florida, Arizona and Mexico, hoping she might respond to the warmth, but nothing helped. At a time when Milton should have been basking in his successes, he found himself wrought with grief and desperate to make his wife well again. He made her tonics and teas full of herbs he hoped would return her strength. He had the orphan boys plant gardens for her and sing for her—anything he could do to amuse her and lessen her pain.

In 1915, Kitty was on her way back from one of her long sojourns in Atlantic City when she took ill with pneumonia. Milton was summoned immediately. When he arrived at her bedside, he said she looked cheerful and radiant. He asked her what she would like, and she replied softly, "A glass of champagne."

Milton went out to get it, but when he returned the nurse said Kitty had changed her appearance. "I think she is gone."

On Saturday, March 27, 1915, a small funeral was held in Philadelphia and Kitty's body was interred there until a cemetery could be completed in Hershey. Twice a week for the rest of his life, Milton sent fresh flowers to her grave.

Although he had had many years to prepare for her death, Milton never came to terms with it. He told Murrie that Kitty had been stolen from him—an act of God he could never forgive. The two had been married just sixteen years, and she was only forty-two years old when she died. In her memory, he said he wanted to do something extraordinary. His thoughts naturally turned to the school.

The original idea for the orphanage had come from Kitty, and when it was founded, the Hersheys had endowed it generously. They set aside by deed 485 acres of farmland, which included the homestead, together with all the livestock, buildings and other personal property. With this original gift, the orphanage was able to establish itself as a model institution, providing food, shelter, education and encouragement to dozens of boys. But this was just the beginning.

After Kitty's death, in November 1918, Hershey donated his entire estate to the Hershey Trust for the benefit of the school, including thousands more acres of land and all of his stock in the Hershey company, which was valued at more than $60 million.

He made no public announcement about the gift. There were no press releases lauding his generosity. In fact, it was five years before the press got wind of the donation. On November 9, 1923, *The New York Times* ran a front-page story detailing Hershey's philanthropy, creating a sensation throughout the business community. Many industrial giants had set up foundations for charity, but most had willed their fortunes away upon their deaths. At sixty-one, Milton Hershey was still very much alive, and yet he had given away virtually everything he owned.

Hershey told Murrie he had no need for the money and saw no reason to wait to give it to others.

"He was a philanthropist in the true sense of the word," said Richard Murrie. "He got far more satisfaction out of [giving his money to the school] than out of spending it himself."

Today, Hershey's remarkable gift is worth more than $5 billion, making the school one of the richest private educational institutions in America. It is home to more than 1,000 students—girls as well as boys, of all races and religions. Most are not orphans, but instead come from broken homes in poor inner-city neighborhoods. Once in Hershey, they are treated to a lifestyle they have never known.

With an endowment that provides for $35,000 per child per year, the school is able to offer its students unheard of luxuries, like braces, brand-name clothing and college scholarships. The student-teacher ratio is about 9 to 1, and its educational programs and facilities rival those of elite preparatory schools like Choate and Exeter. The campus covers 3,200 acres of pristine, rolling countryside, and includes two state-of-the-art gymnasiums, an ice rink for skating and hockey and a $3-million showplace auditorium known as Founders Hall.

In the center of Founders Hall, inside a breathtaking marble rotunda that is the second largest in the world, is a bronze statue of Milton Hershey with his arm around a little boy. The inscription reads: "His deeds are his monument. His life is our inspiration."

Hershey's philosophies live on in the school's regimented programs. Students from Harlem, East Baltimore and South Central Los Angeles are boarded on eighty-nine farms that dot the countryside surrounding the town. And while they no longer milk the cows twice a day (the practice was stopped in 1989 because it interfered too much with extracurricular activities), they continue to be responsible for chores that help keep the farms running. Discipline is based on a strict system of demerits, which are enforced by fellow students, and there is an unbending daily routine, from reveille at 7 A.M. to lights-out at 9:30 P.M.

More than 80 percent of the school's graduates go on to college, and nearly all wind up law-abiding, successful American citizens.

The story of Kelly Corvese, a 1983 graduate, is typical: "My mother committed suicide when I was eight months old. My father was a gambler and never had enough money to feed my two older brothers and myself. If it wasn't for Milton Hershey, I'm sure I'd be on the streets, in jail or dead."[2]

Instead, Corvese is an editor for Marvel Comics. He says the ten years of house chores, schooling and barn work turned his life around.

Few outsiders are aware of this part of Hershey's legacy. The company doesn't advertise it, and the Milton Hershey School itself—because it has no need for fund-raisers or publicity—has remained out of the limelight. But the relationship between the two entities has a deep influence on the management of the business.

Because the Trust that runs the school is the company's largest shareholder and has voting control of the corporation, Hershey at times seems more like a private firm than a public one. It has no need to fear a takeover since it is highly unlikely that the school's trustees would sell their stake. On the other hand, this certainty of ownership keeps speculation in the company's stock to a minimum, leaving Hershey shares greatly undervalued.

"It is a strange relationship," admits former CEO Zimmerman. "We're public, and yet we're not like most public firms. How many businesses do you know that have an orphanage as the largest shareholder?"

Zimmerman stresses that the Hershey Trust controls the stock, "but they don't control the company."

"The school never tells us what to do," he said. "We run this business the way we think it ought to be run, and the Trust has no say in that."

On paper, at least, there are clear demarcations between the two. While several executives of the Hershey company serve as school trustees, the school typically has no other representatives on the Hershey board, and business decisions are generally not subject to control by the Trust. But it is impossible for the company not to be affected by the needs of the school.

"I think there are times when the ownership structure has influenced management decisions," said Jack Dowd, a former marketing executive. "Hershey has been slow to change, very cautious. And I think that's because they're afraid to do anything that might hurt the school."[3]

The fact that Hershey is majority-owned by the school "has an effect on the undertones of this place," acknowledged Kenneth Wolfe, the company's current chairman and CEO. "It gives you a warm feeling. I don't think of it in terms of sheer economic power, I think of it as sort of nice."[4]

Hershey Foods prefers not to hire the school's graduates: That, it reasons, would give students the impression that life is too easy. But a few graduates of the Milton Hershey School have made it big at Hershey. William Dearden, who served as CEO and chairman in the 1970s, was raised in the orphanage, as was Arthur Whitman, who served for thirty years as president of the Hershey Bank. And the current CEO of Hershey Entertainment and Resorts, J. Bruce McKinney, graduated from the school in 1955.

While he was alive, Milton Hershey served as chairman of the chocolate company, the Hershey Trust and the Hershey Estates, which ran the town and other noncandy enterprises. But he never actually managed any of these concerns; he left that to Murrie. And after Kitty's death, he seemed to distance himself even more, seeking new horizons far from Kitty's memory.

He spent most of his time in Cuba, drawn there by the sunny climate and the country's plantations, which provided Hershey with the bulk of the sugar needed to make chocolate. Demand for Hershey's products was reaching new highs—nearly 400 carloads full left the factory each week, bringing in sales of more than $10 million annually. At the same time, with World War I raging in Europe, it was becoming more and more difficult to obtain enough sugar to keep the factory running smoothly.

Hershey feared rationing might stop production entirely, so in 1916 he set out to secure his own sugar supply. In characteristic fashion, his solution took on grand proportions. Hershey purchased more than 65,000 acres of sugarcane fields between Havana and the port of Matanzas on the northern coast of the island. With permission from the Cuban government, he built a railroad connecting the two cities—a distance of more than fifty miles. At the midway point, he founded and built the town of Central Hershey, an exact replica of Hershey, Pennsylvania.

The houses included running water and electricity—luxuries previously unknown to all but the wealthiest Cubans. Hershey brought in doctors, dentists and teachers, and he built a baseball diamond, a nine-hole golf course, a racetrack and a country club to entertain his workers.

In 1923, a tragic train wreck on the Hershey Cuban Railroad killed thirty people and left several children orphaned, leading Hershey to repeat his experiment with the industrial school. In February 1925, the Hershey Agricultural School opened in Cuba, taking as its first students the boys whose parents had been killed in the accident. They followed the same daily regimen that Hershey had instituted in America, with classes to attend and fields to cultivate.

To finance this investment—which ultimately exceeded $40 million—Hershey sold securities in a newly organized company known then as the Hershey Corp., which owned all of the Cuban assets. At its height, it employed nearly 4,000 people in eight sugar mills, producing 31 million pounds of sugar annually. Until 1944, when he liquidated his Cuban holdings, Hershey owned the largest refinery on the island. He became one of the largest suppliers of sugar to the Coca-Cola Co. of Atlanta, Georgia, as well as supplying the Hershey Chocolate Corp.

His contributions to the Cuban economy earned him the highest award the Cuban government could bestow upon a foreigner. In 1933, at the Presidential Palace in Havana, Hershey was ordained with the Grand Cross of the National Order. In decorating Hershey, President Machado praised Hershey's efforts for the country, calling him "a magnificent ambassador."

Throughout the 1920s and 1930s, Hershey spent most of his time in the Caribbean, staying in an elegant hacienda in the old-world town of Rosario, just outside Central Hershey. His private room was open on three sides, with sweeping views of the ocean, the sugarcane fields and the refinery. Mother Hershey accompanied him on these trips until she died in the spring of 1920. After her death, Hershey spent most of his time alone.

Murrie ran Hershey, Pennsylvania, in Milton's absence, growing the business until sales reached more than $41 million in 1929.[5] World War I and the prosperity that followed had done much to popularize Hershey's products, which now included Hershey's chocolate syrup and the Mr. Goodbar. As the fall of 1929 approached, the factory was receiving 60,000 gallons of fresh milk daily from 8,000 acres of Hershey farms. The plant had not only continued to grow, but every department had been updated, making production far more mechanized and efficient.

For Hershey, and the rest of American industry, it seemed the good fortune would last forever. But the nation's exuberance quickly turned to despair after the stock market crash of October 1929 sent the economy into a tailspin.

THERE WAS NO SIGN OF THE
GREAT DEPRESSION ALONG
CHOCOLATE AVENUE IN 1933.

The years of the Great Depression took their toll on Hershey; revenue plummeted to a low of $21 million in 1933[6]—half what it was in 1929. But even with this precipitous drop in sales, both the town and the company weathered the Depression well. The company's fortunes were buffered by an even steeper drop in sugar and cocoa prices, which left the bottom line relatively unaffected. And protected from the ruin that faced so many other businesspeople, Milton made certain his townspeople did not suffer.

He maintained his rigid production schedule, cutting no wages and discharging no employees. Instead, he fought the Depression with his own building campaign, spending more than $10 million between 1930 and 1936 to add attractions to the town and expand the factory. The Hotel Hershey, the Hershey Sports Arena and Museum, the lavish Community Building and the Hershey Stadium were all products of this private "public works" program, as was a new office building of modern design—without windows and completely air-conditioned.

Those who lived in Hershey at the time say they have no memory of bread lines or unemployment.

"I remember hobos coming to our door begging for food," said Stover. "But we always had plenty ourselves. My parents kept their jobs. We kept our house, and we had warm clothes. No one in Hershey went hungry; the town was an oasis."

But as the decade wore on, feelings in Hershey began to change. The Great Depression fueled the labor movement, and around the country workers were becoming increasingly radicalized. Unions were bearing down hard on industries like steel and shipping, and rallying cries of "Let's organize!" could be heard everywhere. In Hershey, some workers chafed at Milton's paternalism, and he became the target of much criticism. Some complained that Hershey's sixty-hour workweek was too demanding, and they pointed to the rest of industry, where forty-hour workweeks were becoming common. Others charged that wages had failed to keep pace with the local economy.

Capitalizing on this unrest, "The Communist Party of Hershey, Pa." surreptitiously circulated a leaflet through the factory, accusing the company of starvation wages and ripping "the big bosses"—Murrie and Hershey—for their "high salaries and slave-driving methods." Members of the CIO held a secret meeting in nearby Palmyra to help workers organize, and in January 1937, workers demanded a 10 percent increase in pay. Murrie, acting in Hershey's stead, authorized only 5 percent, and frustrated workers began to rally behind the idea of a union shop.

Milton Hershey was baffled. He couldn't fathom the need for outside representation. His long trips to Cuba and absentee-management style had left him increasingly isolated from the workers on the production line, and he had remained completely unaware of the burgeoning discontent. Since the company's very creation, he had been viewed—and had always viewed himself—as a progressive businessman, offering good wages and steady employment to the workers in his idyllic company town. Hershey believed he treated his employees fairly and pointed to fringe benefits like free education and pensions as proof of his beneficence. That workers could see him differently was beyond his comprehension, but by the 1930s, the image of the industrial leader as benevolent parent was clearly unconvincing to many of Hershey's workers.

At midnight on April 2, 1937, approximately 600 workers seized the factory building, throwing out anyone who did not support the CIO. They put up barricades and chained the front doors; outside, picketers began to protest, chanting—to the tune of "The Old Gray Mare"— "Old Bill Murrie ain't what he used to be, ain't what he used to be, ain't

what he used to be." And though these workers represented only one-fifth of Hershey's workforce, they were now setting the agenda.

Caught off guard by the sudden turn of events, Hershey ordered his lawyers to negotiate with the strikers, but he himself did not get involved. He told a crowd of loyal workers, "My hands are tied," referring to his attorneys, who had warned him not to express any opinions.[7]

When five days passed without progress, Derry Township began to grow restive. Farmers from all around congregated in Hershey to express their anger at the strikers; every day, they were losing 800,000 pounds of milk—enough to supply a city of a million inhabitants. Army veterans, too, became incensed when the strikers lowered the national flag and ran up the CIO flag above it. To show their support for Hershey, the farmers and other loyalist workers staged a parade through the downtown. More than 8,000 people marched past High Point, the mansion Hershey had donated to the town as a public country club.

On Wednesday morning, April 7, the farmers and frustrated workers sent an ultimatum to the strikers: Evacuate by twelve noon or suffer the consequences.

When 1:00 P.M. came and there was still no response, the protesters turned violent. Hundreds of farmers stormed the factory gates armed with ax handles, ice picks, baseball bats, hammers and lead pipe. The strikers, stunned by the ferocity of the attack, fled to the locker rooms. The farmers in pursuit tore down fire hoses from the walls and charged in behind a barrage of water. The strikers broke and tried to escape. Some jumped through windows and were seized by the angry crowd below. Others tried to hide in the machinery. Eventually, the leaders were hauled out and beaten until they lay unconscious and bleeding.

No lives were lost, but many were wounded. The chief casualty was eighty-year-old Milton Hershey, who watched in shock from his suite of rooms in High Point.

"The strike changed him," said Richard Murrie. "He was deeply hurt and felt all he had done for the town had been forgotten. He cried bitterly after that."[8]

Eventually, the Hershey Chocolate Corp. signed an agreement with the American Federation of Labor, giving workers representation through the Bakery and Confectionery Workers International Union. Provisions were made for a forty-hour workweek and for wage increases, and the union was given authority to arbitrate future disputes.

Hershey signed the agreement without protest—although the sting of the strike never left him.

In the years that followed, he seemed to distance himself even more from the daily workings of the company and town. Although he shared an office with Murrie at the plant, he preferred his two-room suite in High Point, overlooking the ninth hole of the Hershey Country Club. There, he shuttered himself in for days on end, holding meetings at his bedside and entertaining only the closest of friends in the sparse adjacent sitting room. He rarely walked the halls of the factory anymore; a marked departure from the days when employees would signal his arrival by secret code—one hand above the head meant "the boss is coming," referring to Murrie, but both hands spread the alarm that "M.S." himself was on the way. And where once he could be found sifting through the garbage at the Cocoa Inn, making certain nothing was being wasted, he no longer roamed the streets of the town looking after its inhabitants.

Instead, he spent his waning years dabbling in experiments of all kinds. He was interested in irrigation, water and soil conservation and in selective breeding among the Hershey herds. He searched for synergies between his factory and his farms, trying to make candy from corn and other grains, using cocoa bean shells as fertilizer and chocolate as cattle feed. When he traveled—which was less and less—he examined unfamiliar crops and often tried to introduce them to the Pennsylvania climate.

Never satisfied with the conventional ways of doing things, he also continued his chocolate experiments, outlining procedures for adding oranges and bananas. He tried the same with celery, parsley and turnips.

"I can't tell you why he did things," said Lewis Maurer, who oversaw many of these experiments. "He just had an idea and wanted it done."

Hershey ordered Coca-Cola syrup added to skim milk; he wanted to see how it would taste. And in the early 1940s, he delved into the vitamin craze in his usual manner—purchasing a half dozen Zippy Juicers because he decided it was "much easier to drink raw vegetables than to eat raw vegetables." To make the drinks more palatable, he ordered Maurer to try using the juices in sherbet. No one had ever heard of onion sherbet before, but Hershey ordered it tried, along with beet, carrot, celery and others. Hershey thought the beet sherbet was so good, he added it to the menu at the Hotel Hershey, but somehow it wasn't too popular with the public and was quickly removed.

Those who were trying out these ideas ultimately decided that Hershey must have lost his sense of taste without realizing it. "After smoking six, eight, ten cigars a day, Mr. Hershey had absolutely burned out his taste buds," said former CEO Samuel Hinkle. "He couldn't taste or smell a thing."

Some experiments became quite elaborate, and colleagues admonished him for lavish spending on what seemed frivolous propositions. But he continued to pursue what intrigued him or mattered most to him.

During World War II, Hershey became concerned that rationing would prevent his boys from enjoying ice cream, and he ordered extensive experiments to develop a nondairy product that might substitute.

Two Hershey employees were assigned to the experiments full-time. Every morning, Charlie Miller met with Hershey at his bedside to discuss the previous day's work and make plans for the next. Hershey ordered him to experiment with ice cream made from oatmeal, mashed potatoes, sweet potatoes and cream of wheat—anything he could think of.

"He would dream about this and plan it," said Maurer. "He would eat oatmeal for breakfast and cream of wheat and he would imagine: Now, if that had sugar in it and was flavored and frozen, that might be pretty good ice cream."

The final formula included rice flour, dehydrogenated peanut oil, sugar, a little bit of salt and a little bit of seaweed (a standard stabilizer in food products). The company manufactured it in chocolate, vanilla and raspberry, and they sold the Victory Whip—as Hershey dubbed it—for six months, until Pennsylvania's state government began making some noise. The state's secretary of agriculture, it seemed, was not pleased to hear that Hershey had perfected an ice cream without milk, considering there were 10,000 dairy farms in Pennsylvania.

Maurer was sent to meet with the state's chemists to show them how Victory Whip was manufactured. Legend has it the agriculture secretary was so impressed, he took home three gallons and served them at a party, where no one guessed that it was fake ice cream.

Maurer said the product cost half as much as regular ice cream, and Hershey could have easily made money on it, but "he didn't want to upset the dairy industry.

"We kept that formula on the shelf, but we never did use it."

The experiment that most captivated Hershey involved the manufacture of cocoa butter soap, a folly that became legendary for the extraordinary size of Hershey's investment. At various times in the company's history—when demand for cocoa was high and demand for chocolate low—Hershey found himself saddled with an abundant supply of cocoa butter, sometimes as much as several million pounds. He became obsessed with finding an outlet for it, spending much of his time in his later years dreaming up uses for the white, creamy fat. When he settled on the idea of soap, Murrie and others tried to convince him otherwise. The soap industry was well entrenched in America. Horning in on giants like Procter & Gamble seemed an impossible proposition. But Hershey refused to listen.

He gave the project to John Hosler, who managed the Hershey Department Store. "I told him that I knew nothing about soap manufacture," recalled Hosler, "but he insisted that as I was the man who sold the soap I would know how to make it; and, if I didn't know, I could learn."

No one said no to M. S. Hershey, even if his judgment was increasingly questionable. So Hosler purchased $30,000 worth of equipment and set up a small soap-making plant behind the Cocoa Inn. He hired a local chemist, Gus Speicer, but he couldn't get the soap to congeal because of the richness of the cocoa butter. Hosler brought in an expert from DuPont, who took the ingredients back to DuPont's laboratories in Wilmington, Delaware. In two weeks, the young man returned with three small cakes scented with lavender to kill the chocolate odor. Within three months, the plant was manufacturing two different varieties at the rate of 120 cakes a minute.

"After we had run a million boxes of cocoa butter soap and filled our warehouse, Mr. Hershey came to me and said, 'Now that you have the soap, it's up to you to sell it.'"

Hosler convinced Hershey he was not the man for the job, and he hired three salesmen to go on the road with the product. But there were problems from the start. Initially, the soap was of very poor quality. It turned out traditional methods of manufacture were not adequate to get the lye to penetrate the cocoa butter. The result: Most of the cake was still free cocoa butter, not really converted into soap at all. Hershey hired more chemists and bought new machinery, and a new, more complicated manufacturing process was developed.

Hershey conferred with the soap makers at least four times a week, and while he understood none of the problems they were confronting, he kept on top of them, ordering them to try this or that and testing every batch on his own hands.

In his old age, he had developed the unsightly habit of picking at his hands with a penknife to remove the liver spots. He would work at them until they were raw, and then he would lather up the soap and rub it on his wounds, convinced it would heal them. He repeated this process over and over until, it is said, the liver spots were gone and his hands looked young again.

Certain of the curative properties in his soap, he tried to sell it to hospitals and beauty parlors. He talked the manager of the Waldorf-Astoria in New York into providing the soap to guests. But they were turned off by the strong chocolate odor that permeated each bar, and one even tried to bite the soap, thinking it was a new Hershey candy.

Sales were very slow, but Hershey kept the plant operating at full speed. Eventually, there was so much inventory it had to be stored beneath the auditorium in the Sports Arena. When the plant operators spoke up, complaining of all the money tied up in inventory, Hershey told them: "Don't worry about my money. You just sell all you can."

Hershey eventually persuaded Murrie to rent a store for him near the Ambassador Hotel in Atlantic City, and later on the boardwalk near the Steel Pier. Hershey spent much of his time there, selling the soap himself and enjoying the sea air. He liked the anonymity that Atlantic City offered him. He would often tell the customers as he was wrapping up a sale: "Mr. Hershey will be pleased, very much pleased, when he learns of your purchase."

The soap venture lost millions between 1936 and 1943, when Hershey finally withdrew his fifteen regional salesmen and called in all the soap trucks. But it never mattered to him. Financial success had not been his goal since the early days selling caramels in Lancaster, and even then, all he had really wanted was happiness. Except for the precious years he spent with Kitty, he never found it.

THE TUBES THAT WERE ORIGINALLY USED TO PACKAGE MARS'S M&M'S WERE MADE WITH MACHINERY SUPPLIED BY HERSHEY.

ORREST MARS, SR., always arrived at the M&M factory in Newark, New Jersey, just as the last wisps of night sky melted into the dawn. He loved this time of the morning, when the air was clear and his mind was free to wander. His best ideas were born just before sunrise: the pet food business, the Mars bar, and now, in 1940, his M&M's.

As he drove behind the low, narrow building that served as the headquarters for this latest business venture, he took note, as was his habit, of the cars that had arrived before his. Although no one was required to punch in before 7 A.M., including him, it had become customary for most workers at the plant to arrive well before dawn; that way, they were less likely to become targets for one of Forrest's morning tirades.

These explosive fits of screaming and cursing pierced the order of the factory floor several times a day. But the morning "flares," as the workers referred to them, were always the worst. It seemed anything could set him off when he arrived at the factory. An employee who forgot to wash his hands, a messy pile of papers on a salesman's desk or a speck of chocolate on a uniform could send him reeling into an abusive rage. Most workers eventually learned to shrug off these episodes, waiting patiently with heads bowed until the blood rushed out of Forrest's face and the taunts and name-calling ceased, almost as abruptly as they had begun.

But some days—when he called an associate an ass, or laughed mockingly at the results of the day's production, or hurled improperly wrapped packets of M&M's across the room—it was hard not to take these affronts personally. On these days in particular, workers tried to reassure one another—a pat on the back, a wink of an eye—that Forrest didn't mean to be cruel. He simply had very high standards, they would tell themselves. And, to be fair, he demanded as much from himself as he did from his employees, whom he insisted on calling "associates."

The address was meant to imply, somehow, that they were all in this venture together—that Forrest's success was their success, that his fortune was theirs, too. To that end, he tied everyone's salary, including his own, to the performance of the business—how much candy was produced, how much was sold and how much profit M&M Ltd. registered. On payday, Forrest's communal approach to business always rang true. When sales exploded, so did an associate's income, and when sales fell, the paycheck shrank accordingly. But on most days at the M&M factory, when Forrest was "flaring" and his workers stood quivering, the word *associate* rang empty, like a hollow candy shell.

Forrest's abusive attitude annoyed Bruce Murrie from the start. The initials M&M stood for Mars and Murrie, but so far the partnership existed in name only. Though Murrie had provided 20 percent of the capital for the venture, he received even less respect from Forrest than the workers on the production line. Forrest called him an associate, just like everyone else, and barked orders at him as though he were an office boy. It never occurred to Forrest to consult Murrie on business matters, and Forrest ignored any advice Murrie offered. With no authority and no specific responsibilities, Murrie passed his time reading and working through the latest *New York Times* crossword, generally trying to remain invisible.

Before joining Mars, Murrie worked as an investment banker in the Wall Street brokerage Reynolds & Co. There, he enjoyed a level of deference more typical of management: a private office, his own secretary, a company car and a lavish expense account. At Mars, there were no such perquisites. Forrest's idea of a fancy lunch was a roast beef sandwich and a pickle, which he ate standing up. He didn't believe in expense accounts or executive washrooms or reserved parking.

It was not exactly what Murrie had imagined when Forrest came to him a year earlier and begged him to join the business. Forrest said he would set Murrie up for life, painting an enticing picture of M&M's certain success and how much money they both would make. Murrie had always hoped for an opportunity like this; growing up in Hershey, as the second-eldest son of the company's president, he expected someday to have a starring role in Hershey's management, but knew he could never be the owner. After he graduated from the Wharton School of Business in 1938, his father sent him to get some entry-level experience at Reynolds & Co., a subsidiary of the metals giant that supplied the tinfoil wrappers for Hershey's chocolate bars. After Reynolds, Bruce expected to return to Hershey to help oversee the chocolate company's investments. But then came Forrest.

The only son of Frank Mars arrived in Hershey unannounced on a muggy August afternoon in 1939. He took the tour of the chocolate plant, lining up with the general public for the one o'clock walk-through. When it was over, he told the tour guide he wanted to see the president of the company. "Tell him Mars is here," he said emphatically. "That's all he needs to know."

Though he knew most of the Mars family, William Murrie had never met Forrest before. His dealings with the Chicago-based candy maker had always centered around Forrest's father. When Frank Mars died in 1934, Murrie attended the funeral, and he continued to call on the company personally, dealing directly with William Kruppenbacher, Frank's brother-in-law, who had taken over the business.

Murrie knew Forrest had broken off from his father and had taken Frank's recipes to Europe, so he was surprised to find the young man in Hershey demanding to see him.

He ushered Forrest into his oak-paneled office, where the double-sided secretary that he shared with Milton Hershey now sat half vacant. Murrie offered Forrest a seat on the leather wing chair facing his half of the desk, but Forrest declined. "I've been sitting on the train all the way from New York; I'd rather stand."

As Murrie started in with the usual pleasantries—inquiring about

WILLIAM MURRIE RAN THE HERSHEY CHOCOLATE CO. FOR MORE THAN FIFTY YEARS, BUT HIS CONTRIBUTIONS GO UNHERALDED, FOREVER IN THE SHADOW OF THE COMPANY'S NAMESAKE.

Forrest's family and his trip back to the United States—Forrest paced back and forth across the Oriental carpet. Abruptly, he stopped and turned to Murrie, interrupting him mid-sentence.

"Your son Bruce, what's he up to these days? He out of college yet?"

The question caught Murrie off guard; clearly, Forrest had something on his mind.

"He's in investment banking, working for Reynolds & Co."

"That's a waste. He won't learn a thing from those Wall Street types. They're nothing but flash."

"Is that so?" retorted Murrie, put off by Forrest's bluntness. "And just what makes you say that?"

"As my dad always said, you ain't worth nothing unless you understand product. Those Wall Street boys, they don't know a thing about product. They're playing a numbers game, and hell, anybody who can add and subtract can do that."

Murrie stared, not certain what to make of the thirty-five-year-old pacing in front of him. "Forrest, is there something I can help you with?" he asked, raising his eyebrows and picking up his unlit cigar. He never smoked them, as Hershey did, just chewed them. And he popped the Pittsburgh stogie into his mouth.

Relieved to get down to business, Forrest pulled a handkerchief out of his pocket and laid it on Murrie's desk. "Take a look."

Murrie saw a dozen brightly colored candies—violet, orange, yellow, red—each about the size of a fat nickel.

"They're chocolates," Forrest declared. "I've had 'em in my pocket ever since I left New York. Try one."

Murrie was impressed. A Hershey bar never would have withstood the train trip, not on a hot day like today. But Forrest's candies didn't seem to be affected by the heat. Murrie bit one open and examined the chocolate inside the thick sugary shell. "This is brilliant," he said, smiling. "Absolutely brilliant."

Forrest couldn't hold back any longer; he launched into his sales pitch with the force of a carnival hawker, waving his arms excitedly as he explained his plans to Murrie.

"We're gonna sell 'em all over the world. They'll be eating chocolate in Bombay, in the south of France. Just think of it. Chocolate that doesn't melt. Nobody would believe it, but there it is. I'm telling you, Mr. Murrie, *this* is a product."

Forrest told Murrie he wanted to start manufacturing right away. He already had a warehouse in New Jersey, and any day he was expecting a shipment from Italy of ten panning drums, the special machines that candy-coated the chocolates. All he needed now was a little more equipment, the ingredients—sugar and chocolate—and, he told Murrie, he needed a partner.

"This is a hell of an opportunity for one of your boys. With you supplying the chocolate and me supplying the product, we're virtually guaranteed success."

Forrest told Hershey's president he would treat Bruce like family and give him equal opportunity in the business. As far as ownership, it would be a limited partnership; Mars would put up 80 percent of the capital and Murrie's son 20 percent. But Bruce would serve as Forrest's No. 2, with the title of executive vice president. Even better, his name would go on the company and the product. "We'll call them M&M's, for Mars and Murrie. What do you think about that?"

The offer was irresistible. Murrie had devoted his life to Hershey, and he had worked hard to provide for his five children. But for all his hard work, he had no business to pass on to them, no lasting legacy for them to inherit. Now, Forrest was giving him the opportunity. The Murrie name would live on in the confectionery industry, and what's more, Hershey would have a new customer for its chocolate.

"You've got yourself a deal, young man," said Murrie, enthusiastically pumping Forrest's hand. "You go see Bruce in New York. If he's interested, I'll help you out all I can."

In the spring of 1940, M&M Ltd. opened for business. Bruce expected to manage the company, much the way his father had managed Hershey for the past fifty years. But as time wore on it became painfully obvious that Forrest never wanted a real business partner; he just needed Murrie's connections.

The rest of the nation's candy makers had had their supplies of chocolate severely rationed because of Hershey's wartime shortages of sugar and cocoa. But not M&M, which received as much chocolate as Forrest Mars ordered. Hershey engineers also helped design and install M&M's production equipment and continued to offer technical assistance. Without this special treatment, the company would have never gotten off the ground.

"My father made a tremendous sacrifice for M&M's," said Richard Murrie, Bruce's brother. "Hershey's resources were stretched to the limit; everything they had was going into the army's chocolate rations—engineering, equipment, workers, ingredients. The plant was operating around the clock—and they had special dispensation from the Labor Department to operate like that. But even though they were pushing hard, my dad made sure Bruce and Forrest got what they needed."

Richard Murrie described relations between the Mars and Murrie families in the early days as quite friendly.

"My father and Frank Mars became very close over the years. They had a serious business relationship—what with Hershey supplying [Frank] Mars all his chocolate—but they also admired and liked each other very much. . . ."

"[My father] figured my brother was in good hands with Forrest." But as Richard recalls the tale, the bitterness begins to show: "He didn't know Forrest was nothing like his father."

And Bruce Murrie never told his father how badly he was being treated. "I think he was afraid of disappointing him," said Richard Murrie. "My dad really saw this as the opportunity of a lifetime, and Bruce didn't want to upset him."

The elder Murrie had already lived through the biggest disappointment a father could face: the death of his oldest son, Malcolm, in 1936. Murrie had spent years grooming Malcolm to come into the Hershey business. He got him a job at the National City Bank of New York to start his rise to the top of the corporate ladder. But Malcolm contracted tuberculosis on a business trip to Brazil. The disease took his life within a year. Murrie's heartbroken wife died six months later, leaving Murrie alone to grieve for them both.

The loss was almost too much for Murrie to bear. He took to wearing nothing but black and often slept on the sofa in his office, not wanting to face the specters in his empty house. From then on, all Murrie did was work. He came into the plant every day, even on Sundays, when most of the town was in church. He had devoted a half century of his life to Hershey, and now the company was all he had.

Decades earlier, when the eighteen-year age difference between him and Hershey seemed so much greater, he assumed he would one day succeed Milton as chairman, taking over the company. But those dreams faded as the years rolled by and Hershey failed to retire. Now, Milton was in his late eighties and in deteriorating health; Murrie practically ran the entire enterprise without him, even as he knew he would never call the company his own.

It was Murrie who geared up Hershey for the coming war, and Murrie who made certain the soldiers ate only Milton Hershey's chocolate. When Congress threatened to shut down the candy industry in 1942, deeming it "non-essential" to the war effort, Murrie launched a campaign to convince Washington otherwise. Backed by the National Confectioners Association, Hershey successfully fought off attempts to ration much needed supplies, like sugar, corn syrup and cocoa beans, pitching chocolate as a vital source of nutrition for the nation's troops. Candy production continued uninterrupted throughout the war, with more than 70 percent going into soldiers' rations. The chief supplier, of course, was Hershey, with its Ration D, Ration K and tins of cocoa. By war's end, Hershey had produced more than one billion candy bars for U.S. soldiers.

But the victory was not to be enjoyed by Milton Hershey. Throughout 1945, he had battled old age, and on October 11, one month after he celebrated his eighty-eighth birthday, he suffered a severe heart attack. After lapsing into a coma, Milton Hershey died on October 13, 1945.

His death brought the town of Hershey and its surrounding communities to a standstill. Public schools and businesses closed upon hearing the news, and thousands of people made pilgrimage to the Hershey Industrial School, where the body lay in state in the foyer for three days.

So many flowers were left around the casket that they overflowed onto the steps outside—a blanket of red roses several feet deep. More than 1,600 people packed into the school's auditorium for the funeral service, led by ministers from all six Hershey churches.

Following the eulogy, 200 cars lined up behind the casket in a processional that stretched for more than two miles to the Hershey Cemetery, high atop a hill overlooking the town. There, Milton Hershey was laid to rest in the family plot, beside his wife, his father and his mother. Six students from the orphanage served as pallbearers, and following behind the casket were members of the board of managers. Out in front was Percy Staples, former head of the company's Cuban operations, who had recently taken the reins from Hershey. Beside him walked Arthur Whiteman, treasurer of the Hershey Trust Co. and former student at the Hershey School. Murrie walked immediately behind Staples, flanked by Ezra Hershey, a distant cousin of Milton's and treasurer of the Hershey Chocolate Co. This was the new order of Hershey management, evident to anyone who cared to take notice.

Milton Hershey had made the painful decision about succession one year earlier. At the same time, he signed a simple will of three directive paragraphs. The first reiterated his gift to the Hershey Industrial School, the second ordered all of his remaining estate be given to the Derry Township School District and the third named his executors. Nothing more was needed, for Hershey had relinquished his wealth long before.

"By the time Hershey died, he was for all intents and purposes a poor man," said Richard Uhrich, former executive of Hershey Foods. "There was nothing left in his own name—not his bank accounts, not High Point, not the stock. He had the shirt on his back and the cash in his pocket; that was about it."

Murrie would sometimes kid Hershey about his empty balance sheet, offering to buy him lunch at the Cocoa Inn or pick up the tab for his latest box of cigars down at the Hershey Department Store.

"I think my credit's still good," Hershey would tell him. "After all, I still have my name, and that ought to be worth something."

The passing of Milton Hershey was hardest on Murrie. After decades of working together, the two men had grown closer than brothers. They shared everything, professionally and personally, especially in their later years after each was widowed. They dined together daily whenever Hershey was in town, and not a week went by for more than fifty years without them at least speaking to each other. Until the very end, Murrie was the only one who could tell Hershey no and get away with it.

Theirs was an ideal partnership; Hershey manufactured ideas, while Murrie was the hardheaded businessman who made those ideas work. They would never have succeeded without each other, and what's more, they understood that.

With Hershey gone, Murrie felt an overwhelming emptiness. He and Staples didn't get along; they were opposites in every way—background, training, personal and managerial styles. Murrie was an extrovert, a consummate salesman, but he was no intellectual. He ran the company from his gut, making decisions on the spur of the moment and rarely delegating authority. Hershey set the direction but never questioned Murrie's business decisions, leaving him to do his job.

Staples was a different man entirely. An MIT graduate with a degree in civil engineering, he had been hired by Hershey in 1921 to oversee the Cuban enterprise. During his years in the Caribbean, Hershey had grown to respect Staples's careful planning and meticulous execution, his relentless, almost obsessive, pursuit of efficiency. But Staples was largely unknown to the executives in Pennsylvania, and it was a shock to all when Milton appointed him chairman of the company's board of directors and of the Hershey Trust Co.

Once in town, Staples kept to himself, a habit that only reinforced the gap between him and his Hershey colleagues. In his first months on the job, he absorbed himself with developing a chain of command. He wrote up organizational charts and detailed job descriptions and ordered reports and memos from every department. He went about his work deliberately, sitting at his desk for hours studying charts and accounting ledgers, a slide rule in one hand and a pencil in the other. He would organize his data until the numbers inevitably dictated a decision to him.

Upon Staples's appointment, Murrie considered retiring immediately, but he was terrified at the thought of not working. Seventy years old, with little else to do, he stayed on as president until his eyesight totally failed him.

On March 24, 1947, completely without ceremony, William Franklin Reynolds Murrie retired. Under his leadership, Milton Hershey's company had come to dominate the candy industry in America. The year he stepped down, the factory in the cornfields provided 90 percent of the nation's milk chocolate, and the company recorded sales of more than $120 million. In the end, his accomplishments shamed all of the tall tales he had spun in the pool halls of his youth.

$\mathscr{B}$ruce Murrie hadn't slept in a week, not since Forrest Mars had returned from Houston. It was always easier when Forrest was gone; the factory workers relaxed, Murrie could enjoy a cup of coffee or take an hour lunch break, and they all stopped looking over their shoulders. At times like these, Murrie almost liked his job. After the chaos of the first year, he had managed to stake out a small niche for himself, overseeing M&M's three-man sales force. He got the job initially by default; the military was M&M's biggest potential customer, and it was Murrie who had connections in the Department of War, through his father. After Murrie had closed a few deals, Forrest tacitly relinquished control over the sales operation.

Murrie spent most of his time on the telephone to Washington, D.C., lining up contracts with the quartermaster general. The air force quickly became the company's largest buyer, purchasing millions of M&M's for bomber pilots stationed in North Africa and the Pacific Theater. Not far behind was the army, which bought the candies for the C rations it distributed to soldiers in the Philippines, Guam and other tropical climates.

The business was going so smoothly that Forrest began taking interest in other matters, traveling across the United States looking for potential investments. His most recent preoccupation was a tiny rice-processing plant just south of Houston, where a new milling method was being tested. He had read about the plant in a five-line article in one of the patent journals he regularly perused, looking for ideas he could adapt to his candy companies. In this way, he had borrowed production techniques from the steel industry, the concrete industry and the pharmaceutical business. But the rice operation caught his eye for a different reason. Forrest was a staunch believer in making profit by adding value. He saw this as the underlying principle at work with candy bars, with M&M's and with all other great commercial successes.

"There's nothing new in a Milky Way," he would lecture his associates. "Before Mars came along, there was caramel, there was nougat and there was chocolate. So why does a Milky Way sell? Added value. You take what's out there and use it in a new way. You add value to existing products, and you make a profit."[1]

The owner of the rice mill had done just that: He invented a new process for milling rice that resulted in a more nutritious grain. He called the process parboiling, and it worked by steaming the rice while it was still in its hull; that way, the nutrients in the outer bran layers penetrated the grains. The resulting rice was not only better for you, but it cooked faster and came out fluffier than traditionally milled rice.

Forrest believed the improved rice could be branded and sold for a premium—a radical idea for a raw commodity like rice, which had always been sold by grocers in bulk, without packaging or fancy labels. But Forrest aimed to change that, and so, after buying the rice mill in 1942, he set out to learn everything there was to know about the rice industry.

He visited farmers in Texas, Mississippi, Alabama and Louisiana, searching for the perfect grain for his parboiling method. It was not an easy task; rice comes in hundreds of varieties. There is short grain, long grain and medium grain. There is white rice and brown rice, basmati rice and Indian rice. Each has a unique texture and flavor, and Forrest set out to review them all. He finally settled on a slightly sweet long-grain variety that was being produced on a farm not far from his plant. The farmer's first name was Ben; hence the brand name, Uncle Ben's rice. The man was real, but the warm, inviting portrait of "Uncle Ben" that Forrest used to decorate each box was fictitious, based instead on a waiter in a Chicago restaurant.

Forrest met the waiter while he was having lunch with adman Leo Burnett to discuss the launch of Uncle Ben's. Burnett believed in selling products with strong yet simple imagery that spoke to people in a friendly manner. In later years, he would go on to create such famous advertising characters as Charlie the Tuna, Morris the Cat, Tony the Tiger, the Pillsbury Doughboy and the Marlboro Man. But when he met with Forrest in 1943, he was just developing his advertising philosophy, which would later come to be known as the Chicago School. Forrest told Burnett he wanted every home in America cooking Uncle Ben's Converted Brand Rice for dinner, even though rice accounted for less than 10 percent of the nation's starch consumption.

Burnett considered Forrest's ambitious goal, then pointed to the waiter. "If you want everybody eating your rice, you better have somebody real friendly like him serving it," Burnett said, half-jokingly.

Forrest took one look at the broad-grinned, slightly balding black man who had been serving them lunch and called him to the table. He offered him $50 to sit for a portrait, telling him only that he wanted all rights to the picture. The waiter agreed, and in January 1944, Forrest introduced the nation to the now familiar orange box with the picture of "Uncle Ben." Today, the Houston rice plant produces 200,000 tons of rice a year, bringing Mars sales of more than $400 million. It has spawned an entirely new grocery category that includes such popular me-too products as Minute Rice, manufactured today by Kraft Foods, Inc., and Rice-A-Roni, a product of Quaker Oats Co.

But when Forrest Mars started, there was no competition. And that was just the way he liked it. Forrest knew that the best route to the top was the one that Milton Hershey had followed: Hershey was first to the market, and he quickly established his brand as the standard for milk chocolate.

"You gotta get in on the ground level," Forrest told his longtime accountant David Brown. "If you ain't first, why bother."

It was this drive to be No. 1 that he shoved down Murrie's throat day in and day out, especially after the end of the war, when military contracts for M&M's candies began to dry up.

"He was frantic about improving sales," remembered John Carmody, who worked in the plant in those early years. "He'd be screaming 'Get 'em out there, they ain't worth a dime sittin' in my factory [referring to the candies].' And everybody would scatter and get real busy like.

"You always knew when he was mad 'cause he had these marks on his forehead, birthmarks, I guess. And they would start pulsing and get blood red. Then his whole body would start shaking. It was scary to watch him when he was like that.

"Sometimes, he got so wild you could barely understand what set him off in the first place. He'd just be waving his arms and carrying on and screaming. And you'd have to stand there and take it."

The workers endured Forrest's tantrums because of the enormous salaries he paid them—two and three times what other manufacturing firms were offering. But there was a downside. Whenever M&M failed to meet its business targets—which was often in the years following World War II—Forrest cut employees' salaries proportionately.

He measured the cuts, and the company's performance, using an unconventional and rather obscure accounting system that he had read about in the British business book *Higher Control in Management,* by T. G. Rose. The system was designed for small businesses, and it aimed to go beyond the usual benchmarks—like return on sales, earnings per share and quarterly profit—to provide a more accurate picture of corporate performance. Forrest was so impressed with the concepts in the book that he based his entire management structure on Rose's principles. These unique performance standards still guide the company today, even though Mars has grown into an enormous multinational corporation.

Central to this accounting system is a figure known at Mars as ROTA, which stands for return on total assets. The assets are the machines, the factories and the offices—everything that Mars invests in to make the business run. For example, suppose Mars invested $100 million to build the M&M plant: For every $10 million of M&M profit, Mars would report a 10 percent return on its assets.

But that's a little misleading. After all, the M&M plant was built in 1941, and it cost a lot less to build a factory then than it does now. Publicly owned companies ignore this reality, reporting the original cost, less depreciation, on their books. But Mars values its assets at their current replacement cost. If Mars invested $100 million to build the M&M factory but estimates that building the plant today would cost $200 million, then for every $10 million of M&M profit, Mars would calculate only a 5 percent return on its assets.

By emphasizing ROTA instead of return on total sales or return on equity—more typical measures—Mars forces its managers to operate as efficiently as possible, making sure the family gets the most out of every investment. Each Mars division is expected to earn a pretax ROTA of at least 18 percent—a staggering figure by most companies' standards.

To meet the requirement, Mars spends hundreds of millions of dollars a year on automation, new factories and new equipment. For more than fifty years, Mars packaged its candy by hand like the rest of the industry. Today, virtually every plant has a completely automated packaging room, where the candy is boxed and readied for shipment, with equipment designed, and constantly improved, by Mars's own engineers.

Valuing machinery at its current cost gives Mars managers a tremendous incentive to continually replace old equipment with state of the art. The new machine is likely to increase productivity and, eventually, boost profits and ROTA. And since associate pay is tied directly to these measures, everyone is rewarded.

When it comes to sales, Mars also looks at the books a bit differently. It focuses on gross sales volume (GSV). Stated simply, GSV is the total sales revenue divided by the total population in each market. In Britain, where GSV is highest, Mars calculates that people spend an average of $40 per person per year on Mars products. Switzerland and Australia come in next at $28 and the European countries at $23. In the United States, citizens on average spend only $15 per person on Mars products.[2]

The family sees no reason why every country in the world can't eventually measure up to the Brits. To get the United States in line with the European countries would require a sales increase equivalent to the revenue generated by the entire M&M/Mars candies division today: $3.2 billion.[3] But the Mars family is undaunted. They want Mars to double the real size of the business (excluding inflation, that is) every seven years.

Forrest established these unique and demanding business principles during his years in England, and he brought them with him to the M&M plant in New Jersey—much to the chagrin of his workers. Although he tried to warn his hires about his strict business philosophy—telling them he ran a tight ship with no room for error—few understood what he meant until they were actually on the job.

"There were a lot of people who really respected what he was trying to do," said Carmody. "And he could convince you, you know. I mean, he wasn't just being a bastard to be a bastard; the guy had standards, and he wanted everybody pulling their weight."

But others couldn't take it. "The guy was certifiable; he was crazy," said Max Gluckman, who quit his job on the production line at M&M in 1954. "He treated everybody in the world like they were stupid—except him."

Murrie was completely unprepared for the hard, driving way of life that Forrest demanded. He had developed his image of management watching his father, and believed that rewards and perquisites accompanied executive status. At M&M, not only weren't there any perks, but there weren't any executives. Every employee was an "associate" who was expected to follow Forrest's prescripts. And if you failed to stick to the course, he came after you like a pit bull.

In the years following the war, Murrie took the brunt of Forrest's ire. With the military contracts disappearing, M&M needed to drum up new business and the pressure was on the sales team to make something happen. Murrie was putting in sixteen-hour days, trying to open up distribution channels and secure shelf space. But Forrest wasn't satisfied. He ordered Murrie to report to him every morning with the figures on the previous day's sales. If the numbers didn't match his expectations, he would humiliate Murrie by scribbling the word *Failed* in red ink across his reports and posting them in the men's bathroom.

The public floggings pushed Murrie past his limit. He refused to be treated like a peon, and he confronted Forrest in the summer of 1949, demanding some respect. The encounter escalated into an out-and-out brawl, with both men screaming insults and accusations.

The next day, Forrest Mars ordered Murrie out of the M&M plant, telling him that if he wanted to keep his job, he would have to go on the road as a salesman.

Murrie resigned, effective immediately.

Forrest eventually bought out Murrie's minority stake for $1 million, according to Richard Murrie. Asked if the price was fair, Bruce's brother shrugged. "Who knows? He paid my brother, and my brother got out. He just didn't want to work for Forrest anymore. Can you blame him?"

Chapter Twelve

SWEET HOME, CHICAGO

NOT MANY FACTORIES ARE BEAUTIFUL ENOUGH TO BE USED AS A BACKDROP FOR WEDDING PHOTOS; THE MARS PLANT IN CHICAGO IS A RARE EXCEPTION.

WHAT HAD STARTED at the turn of the century as a multitude of snug little kitchen businesses had become a booming nationwide manufacturing industry by the end of World War II. More than 6,000 candy firms shipped 2.8 billion pounds of confections in 1945.[1] That year, per capita consumption reached an all-time high of 20.5 pounds—a record that would remain unbroken for half a century.[2]

The heart of the industry was the city of Chicago, where a remarkable assortment of candy companies had set up shop by the 1930s, attracted by the shipping yards, the central location and the cool, crisp air that was so conducive to candy making. While Hershey, Pennsylvania, provided the bulk of the nation's milk chocolate,

Chicago, Illinois, provided everything else—from chewing gum and cordials to candy bars and caramel corn.

Today, Chicago's candy companies account for nearly one-third of the country's production. Almost a billion pounds of confections are produced in the city each year, bringing in revenues of more than $4 billion. At its peak, the industry employed 25,000 Chicagoans and the number of candy retailers and manufacturers in the city topped 300, including three of the biggest players—Brach's, Curtiss and Mars.[3]

It was here that the custom of giving candy as treats on Halloween developed. It was here that confectioners learned to place maraschino cherries inside chocolate cordials. And it was here that fortunes were made by candy makers like Milton J. Holloway, maker of Milk Duds, Slo Pokes and Black Cows; Leo Hirshfield, who invented the Tootsie Roll and Tootsie Pops; Andy Kanelos, maker of Andes Mints and other candies; and Salvatore Ferrara, whose Ferrara Pan Candy Co. makes Jaw Breakers, Boston Baked Beans, Red Hots and Atomic Fire Balls. All were immigrants who came to the United States with little more than a recipe and a dream.

"No matter where you turn in the confectionery industry, the mark of Chicago is there," said Susan Tiffany, executive editor of *Candy Industry Magazine*. "The city has a unique place in the history of sweets—it has provided us with everything from Tootsie Rolls to Mars bars to Jelly Bellies. Chicago has been candy land's great innovator."

Chicago has called itself the Candy Capital of the World since the turn of the century, and its residents have always eaten more candy than other Americans. In the 1960s, when national consumption hovered at seventeen pounds per person, Chicagoans ate more than twenty pounds each.[4]

"Chicago is a sweet-toothed town," says Ellen Gordon of Chicago-based Tootsie Roll Industries. "Perhaps it's because you can smell sweets everywhere. It makes your mouth water."

The city's candy-making industry dates back to 1837, the same year Chicago itself was incorporated. The first candy "factory" opened on South Water Street in the center of the young city, where John Mohr produced delicacies like macaroons, sugar wafers and pralines—the earliest commercial sweets, pre-dating even penny candies. Success breeds imitation, and within a few years two competitors had set up shop just down the street from Mohr, in what would become the city's wholesale market. These earliest retailers offered both bakery goods and confections.

As more and more immigrants flooded into the frontier outpost, turning it into a bustling center of commerce, they brought with them new candy-making recipes and memories of the fine candy shops they had known in Europe. By mid-century, with the development of the revolving steam pan and mills for powdering sugar, Chicago had become host to dozens of confectioners churning out now-classic penny goods like peppermints, Boston Baked Beans, rock candy and lemon drops.

In 1859, Chicago had ten brewers, nine vinegar makers and four pickle warehouses—but could boast forty-six different confectioners, according to culinary historian Bruce Kraig. He notes that Chicago's food history is "most often associated with the meat-packing industry and the grain industry, but the history of this town is much sweeter than that. . . . Confectioners helped define this city."

Chicago was a natural locus for candy makers. As the hub through which the Midwest's agricultural bounty flowed, Chicago offered confectioners ready access to important ingredients, like beet sugar, milk and corn syrup. By the 1850s, one-third of the nation's rail lines led through Chicago, a boon to manufacturers who needed fresh ingredients on a daily basis. The long, frigid winters also helped extend the manufacturing season, with confectioners producing goods from October through May. With all of these advantages, only much-larger New York City came close to rivaling Chicago's candy output.

Widely available candies in those early days were gibralters (lemon or peppermint hard candies), licorice ropes and pipes, chicken feed (known today as candy corn) and candy eggs filled with fondant, marshmallow or coconut. The origins of many of these candies are obscure, but Chicago's confectionery industry drew on the knowledge and skill of many different cultures. Italian immigrants, for example, brought the city their expertise in sugar coating, introducing rotating copper panning machines that could spin granules of sugar into layers of hard candy. Using sugar, food dyes and flavorings, the pans produced jaw breakers and fire balls. When nuts or pieces of fruit were added to the pan, the result was a candy-encrusted treat, like a Jordan Almond. Italians also brought the recipe for marzipan, a mixture of ground almonds, egg whites and sugar that could be molded into novelty shapes.

German settlers knew the art of spun sugar, used to create cotton candy and delicate swirls of hard candy, often found today as decorations on elegant desserts. They made the earliest lollipops by dipping slate pencils into spun sugar to create a handy confection. Greek immigrants introduced Chicago to baklava, a sugary pastry that was a popular early treat. The Dutch brought sugarplums—fondant mixed with nuts or fruits—and sugar wafers and marshpanes, an early version of the marshmallow.

As the industry grew, a host of ancillary businesses developed to serve it. Chicago became home to refiners of cane and beet sugar; makers of corn syrup, corn starch, fats and oils; processors of milk products, egg products and nut meats; and manufacturers of plain chocolate and cocoa.

In 1884, recognizing Chicago's increasing importance as the center of the industry, sixty-nine of the nation's largest candy makers met in the city to found the National Confectioners Association.[5] Chief among the concerns of these founding members was the growing problem of adulterated candies. Unscrupulous manufacturers would resort to any number of devious and even dangerous practices to sell their goods. Some, for example, varnished their candies with shellac to make them shinier and more attractive. Brick dust was added to some candies to make them redder, while other candies contained lead, insect parts and other contaminants. In 1886, the association successfully lobbied the New York legislature to pass the first laws prohibiting the adulteration of confections. This legislation was adopted by five other states (but not Illinois) and was incorporated into the nation's pure food and drug laws when they were finally passed by Congress a decade later.[6]

The city's flourishing candy industry, however, looked nothing like it does today. With few exceptions, candy producers before the turn of the century were still small operations, often with no employees outside the founder's family. Brands did not exist: Candies were sold generically, as horehound drops or peppermint sticks or jellies, with no indication of who manufactured them. This began to change as purveyors developed unique, individual offerings—often sparked by innovations in manufacturing techniques.

In 1885, for example, Chicago-native Charles Creator invented a combination peanut roaster and popcorn popper. The steam-driven marvel was mounted on a pushcart so the fresh-cooked snack could be sold in the streets. The Rueckheim brothers, German immigrants who had come to Chicago after the Great Fire, purchased one of Creator's machines to use at their popcorn stand. In 1890, they began experimenting with new ingredients, ultimately coating the peanuts and popcorn in thick, sweet molasses. They introduced their confection to the crowds gathered at the Columbian Exposition in Chicago in 1893—the same showcase that introduced Milton Hershey to chocolate. But the product went without a name until 1896, when a salesman, munching on a handful, exclaimed, "That's a crackerjack!" The brothers latched on to the words and began selling Cracker Jack to ballparks, where it was immortalized in the lyrics to Jack Norworth's 1908 song, "Take Me Out to the Ball Game." But what really got Cracker Jack selling was the "prize in every box" that the Rueckheims introduced in 1912.

Wrigley's Juicy Fruit gum is another famous confection that debuted at the 1893 Expo. Juicy Fruit was the foundation of William Wrigley Jr.'s extraordinary success, but Wrigley's interest in gum arose in a most circuitous manner. The founder of the nation's largest chewing-gum company had come to Chicago two years earlier with just $32 in his pocket. He was a traveling salesman, selling soap door-to-door. To help boost sales, he gave away a can of baking powder with every purchase. When the customers seemed more interested in the baking powder than the soap, he entered that business. When he again found he needed an incentive to boost sales, he started giving away chewing gum—and once again the incentive proved more popular than the product. Wrigley was no fool: This time, he dumped baking powder altogether and started to sell the gum. When the business ran into trouble, Wrigley again turned to incentives to boost sales, offering premiums—like lamps, razors and scales—to merchants to induce them to carry his gum. With the launch of Juicy Fruit and Wrigley's Spearmint in 1893, the business took off and by the turn of the century William Wrigley was one of Chicago's wealthiest businessmen. Wrigley was also one of the first American confectioners to take his products overseas, introducing his gum to Canada in 1910, Australia in 1915 and the United Kingdom in the 1920s. Today, Wrigley's gum is sold in more than one hundred countries, and Asia is the company's fastest-growing market. A century after its founding, the $2-billion company is still controlled by the Wrigley family, although much of its stock is now publicly held.

The early 1900s were a time of great change for the industry, as sales exploded and mass-production technology began to replace the traditional methods of hand-crafting candies. In 1903, the total value of candy shipments nationwide was less than $100 million. Two decades later that figure had almost tripled, boosted by World War I and the first great wave of industrial innovation.[7] With the introduction of the mogul, a fully automated machine that made soft chewy candies like gumdrops by the thousands, candies could be stamped out with a uniformity and efficiency entirely new to the business. The enrober, a

French invention that replaced manual chocolate dipping and coating, did for chocolate-covered candies what the mogul did for sugar candies. Now manufacturers could coat thousands of confections by machine in the time that it would take workers to hand coat a dozen.

With the availability of this kind of production equipment, the economics of the industry entered a new phase. A unique recipe was no longer enough to ensure success; entrepreneurs also needed a level of capital and technological know-how to compete effectively. Stricter regulations on business were also making it increasingly difficult for smaller and less sophisticated companies to survive. And kitchen enterprises found themselves facing even greater pressure with the introduction of the income tax in 1913.

"Now all the little mom-and-pop candy makers had to state their business, keep books, register trademarks, and generally conduct themselves in a businesslike manner," said Dick Peritz, Sr., of Fannie May Candy Shops, one of Chicago's first retail chains. "This shook a lot of people out of the business."[8]

Among those who successfully made the transition to this new competitive atmosphere was Chicago's E. J. Brach & Sons, which began as the Palace of Sweets on North Avenue. Emil J. Brach founded the company, with his sons Edwin and Frank, in 1904 with a capital of $1,000. Their candies were originally made to be sold in the store only, but they soon found that they needed outside sales to keep the business going. Emil started selling caramels to department stores along the Loop, and soon Brach's had established itself as a major wholesale supplier. But what made Brach's into an industry powerhouse was not a recipe or flavor or new confection. It was the company's advanced packaging equipment, which could wrap individual caramels, butterscotch discs and mints. Brach's method for producing individually wrapped candies eventually made it the nation's biggest seller of bagged sweets.

Bunte Brothers, another of Chicago's old-line firms, made its name with a different type of technological innovation. In 1905, the Bunte family originated a process for putting soft fillings inside hard candies—a feat that was impossible with traditional panning equipment. The firm grew to manufacture more than 500 varieties of suckers, and their wide line of candies is still being sold today.

In time, some of Brach's and Bunte's customers went into business for themselves. Walgreens opened its own candy factory, as did Marshall Field's, which produced the first Frango Mints—a Chicago delicacy—in its kitchen on the thirteenth floor of its flagship store. But as candy making became more commercial, there was a backlash of sorts. Chicagoans longed for the old-fashioned sweet shops that once lined the streets, a feeling recognized by Teller Archibald, who brought hand-dipped sweets back into vogue.

In 1920, Archibald opened the first Fannie May store on LaSalle Street, advertising homemade chocolates like Pixies, Debutantes and Turtles. He invented the grandmotherly character of Fannie May to give the shop that old-fashioned, homey appeal, and it was an instant success. By 1935, Fannie May's candies were being sold in forty-seven stores across the Midwest. The company later merged with East Coast–based Fanny Farmer to form the largest retail candy chain in the United States.

Other retail chains emerged from the Chicago scene, including Mrs. Snyder's Candy Shops, the Mrs. Stevens chain and Andes, now known nationwide for its line of mints. They all harkened back to Chicago's first famous candy shop, opened in 1871 by John Kranz.

Kranz came to Chicago from New York just after the Great Fire and opened the town's first candy emporium, a romantic fantasy decorated with flowing satin and snow-white animated swans.[9] His shop became renowned for its "mice," fanciful creations of sugar and dark chocolate in pink, brown and white, each beautifully wrapped in its own glossy box. Kranz's shop, which closed in 1947, set the standard for Chicago's candy retailers, who sold an incredible array of fine sweets, many found nowhere else in the nation.

The concentration of candy businesses in Chicago created a close but suspicious community. Companies often used the same suppliers and fought over the same customers. And given the similar nature of everyone's products, any competitive edge had to be milked for all it was worth. As in Europe, spying became endemic, and companies routinely pumped their suppliers for every detail they could learn about their competitors' operations.

"It was a highly secretive business," said Nello Ferrara of Chicago's Ferrara Pan Candy Co., founded in 1908. "With all the innovations and all the new machinery, everybody wanted to know what everybody else was doing. You had to guard your secrets with your life."

The atmosphere became even more competitive following World War I, which changed the nature of the candy business forever. To feed the nation's troops, the government needed cheap, high-calorie, non-perishable foods—in other words, candy. Following Hershey's lead, confectioners began wrapping their products in individual portions that soldiers could easily carry into battle. This practice gave rise to the "candy bar," which has remained the dominant form of confection ever since.

When the war ended, the Golden Age of the candy bar blossomed in Chicago, as confectioners vied to create ever more interesting, fanciful and popular products. Many of today's top-selling candy bars date back to this time.

The most impressive candy bar maker, by far, was Frank Mars. His opulent factory on the city's west side set the industry standard. Inside, the stained glass, fine oil paintings and Oriental carpets provided a country club atmosphere. But within the luxurious surroundings worked 1,500 employees, churning out 200 million pounds of candy bars annually, roughly half the nation's consumption.[10] And Mars was far from Chicago's only legendary bar maker.

Otto Schnering founded the Curtiss Candy Co. in 1916 in a back room over a plumbing shop on North Halstead Street. He produced his first candy bar, the Baby Ruth, in 1920. Named after President Grover Cleveland's daughter, it became a hit after Schnering chartered an airplane and dropped the bars by parachute over the city of Pittsburgh. He expanded his drops to cities in over forty states, making Baby Ruth a top seller by 1925. Bouyed by the bar's success, Schnering introduced his second candy bar in 1926, a chocolate-covered, peanut-butter-flavored bar called Butterfinger.

Chicago candy makers also began the practice of dubbing candy bars with outlandish and sometimes humorous names. George Williamson was the first. His "Oh Henry!" bar came out in 1920, named after a suitor who was pursuing one of Williamson's salesgirls. Every time the man came into the candy shop, the young woman would exclaim, "Oh, Henry!" Williamson also named a bar for Alfred E. Smith, the 1928 Democratic candidate for president. After Herbert Hoover beat Smith, sales of the Big Hearted Al candy bar rapidly declined, but the tradition of zany names kept going. Williamson manufactured a bar called Guess What? and one called That's Mine! In the 1930s, he added the Fat Emma and Oh Mabel!

Candy makers across the nation followed his lead, picking out any name that might appeal to customers. Smile-A-While, Snirkles, 10:30, Chuckles, Pep Up and Chewy Louie are just a few of the candies that appeared in the spirit of Williamson's. Other candy makers made their confections sound more like a meal. The Denver Sandwich, Chicken Dinner, Graham Lunch, Chicken Bone, Big Eats and Idaho Spud all debuted in the 1930s, when the Depression made a real dinner hard to

Candy Makes Friends

afford. Then there were bars named after popular characters and national crazes, like the Charleston Chew!, the Amos 'n' Andy Bar and Davy Crockett suckers.

By whatever name, candy received an unprecedented boost from World War II, when virtually all of the nation's candy production went into military rations. Among soldiers, per capita consumption reached fifty pounds a year, three times the pre-war average,[11] giving candy an entirely new image. When the war ended, soldiers brought their candy habit home with them, and the American public saw confections as the food that energized the troops—a belief popularized by industry advertisements. Candy purchases skyrocketed.

Before the war, candy was child's play. But after the war, men and women bought as much candy as children, and candy eating came out of the closet.

$\mathcal{A}$gainst this backdrop of extraordinary growth, sales of Forrest Mars's M&M's were disappointing. Success seemed guaranteed for products that had a customer base and brand recognition going into the war, but Mars's candies were unknown to the public, and Forrest grew increasingly frustrated by their failure to keep up with the industry leaders. Somehow, he had to create an awareness of M&M's in a marketplace already crowded with successful and satisfying products.

He started with the standard promotions—print ads in national newspapers and magazines, radio spots and billboards in big cities like New York and Chicago. The advertising copy was standard, too. A picture of a package of M&M's, some fluff on the quality of his product and a caption: "The candy that makes you smile." Sales increased to about $3 million in 1949[12]—not bad for a newcomer, but hardly in the league of the big moneymakers like Snickers, Hershey Almond and Baby Ruth.

Forrest was puzzled by the lackluster response. He knew his unique, multicolored candies were every bit as good as the best-sellers, but somehow he wasn't reaching the public. In 1950, he hired Chicago advertising giant Ted Bates & Co. to produce a detailed study of M&M's sales. Forrest wanted to know who was buying his product, who wasn't and why. Studies like these had long been prepared by sophisticated marketers like Kraft Foods and Procter & Gamble, but no one in the candy industry had approached marketing in such a scientific manner. Hershey saw no need for marketing at all, and while other players were creative in their appeals to the public, none of them was taking advantage of the developing techniques in market research. Most candy companies, no matter how successful, were still family-run, "seat-of-the-pants" operations. Forrest Mars believed in managing his enterprises by clearly defined, objective criteria.

The M&M study asked simple questions of potential purchasers, like: "Do you find this candy appetizing?" "Would you buy this candy for yourself?" and "Would you buy it for your children?" The results showed overwhelmingly that M&M's festive colors and bite-sized pieces had a special appeal to kids. In fact, when Bates followed up the initial study by comparing M&M's with other candies, children chose M&M's over every other chocolate candy they were offered. The problem was that children didn't control the family purse strings.

To solve the dilemma, Rosser Reeves, head of the ad agency, created one of the most famous tag lines in marketing history: "Melts in your mouth, not in your hands." The message was aimed at parents by way of their beloved, sticky-fingered, messy-mouthed children, and it was an instant success. The cartoon characters, Mr. Plain and Mr. Peanut, were added in 1954, when Forrest introduced the peanut version of his original candy. Shortly thereafter, Bates created the memorable television commercial of the M&M characters jumping into a pool of chocolate and then rinsing off in showers that coated them with their distinctive shells. The ad ran during popular shows like *The Howdy Doody Show* and *The Mickey Mouse Club*, and caught every child's imagination. By 1956, M&M sales had topped $40 million, ranking them as the most popular candy in America.[13]

By this time, Forrest's combined companies were far bigger than his father's business in Chicago. Besides M&M's and Uncle Ben's in America, Forrest's operations in Slough had grown into the fourth-largest candy company in Europe. Forrest also owned the largest pet food company in the world, with plants in England, France, Belgium, West Germany, Italy and Austria. And he claimed a host of lesser but still profitable enterprises, including a vending machine company in England, a candy firm in the Netherlands and substantial real estate holdings around the world. But still he wasn't satisfied.

Forrest Mars had always viewed the original Chicago factory as his own. After all, he was the one who convinced Frank to build it, and he was the one who gave Frank the idea for the Milky Way. The day he left the Chicago plant, splitting off from his father, he vowed to someday return, having shown his father that he was every bit as good a businessman as he. But Frank's sudden death had brought an end to those dreams of triumph and redemption. Instead of returning in glory to take over his father's business, Forrest was left to stare at the factory from the outside, far removed from its management.

Frank Mars had left the majority of his stock to his second wife, Ethel, and their daughter, Patricia (Forrest's half sister). Although Ethel was named president of the company, she left the management in the hands of her half brother, William "Slip" Kruppenbacher, who had joined Mars in 1930 as a salesman. Kruppenbacher served as the company's vice president and managing director while Ethel spent most of her time overseeing Frank's Milky Way Stables in Tennessee. She made a name for herself on the horse-racing circuit, taking third place in the Kentucky Derby in 1935 and 1937, and winning the race in 1940 with her horse Gallahadion, which paid off at a handsome 35 to 1. She frequently named her favorite horses after the company's candy bars, and one time the company offered the choice of a racehorse or $2,500 in a contest to name a new candy bar (the bar, named Two Bits, was pulled from the shelves because of lack of sales). But that was the extent of Ethel's involvement in the firm.

Under Kruppenbacher's stewardship, Mars Ltd. continued to expand, adding a half-dozen new products to its lineup. The Mars bar, with toasted almonds and vanilla nougat, debuted in 1936, inspired by the popularity of Hershey's Almond. The Forever Yours bar, a dark-chocolate version of Milky Way, came out in 1939. The Mars Cocoanut bar and the Ping bar were introduced in the 1940s, along with the Dr. I.Q. bar, named for a popular radio quiz show. But none of these candies could match the power of the company's major brands—Milky Way, Snickers and 3 Musketeers. And several of Kruppenbacher's launches completely flopped.

Forrest tried to convince Ethel that he was the one who should be running the business, but he got nowhere with his stepmother, who had always resented his reentrance into Frank's life. Forrest tried to convince Patricia to sell him her third of the business, seeing she had no interest in it besides her dividends. He offered to pay Patricia any amount, but she remained loyal to her mother and her uncle, neither of whom wanted Forrest involved with Mars, Chicago. Then, in 1945, Ethel Mars died and half of her stock passed to Forrest, as stipulated by Frank's original will. It was the break Forrest had been waiting for.

He used his inheritance to stage a bitter battle for control, taking on Kruppenbacher at every turn. He insisted that as a substantial shareholder, he should be given an office at the plant and access to the company's books. Kruppenbacher fought the proposal but was overruled by the board of directors, whose members believed they could appease Forrest by giving in to his demands. Instead, their plan backfired. Forrest used the office to keep tabs on current management, regularly assailing the board with acid-tongued memos about Kruppenbacher's performance. His memos accused Kruppenbacher of "slipshod management," decrying the "lack of oversight and wasteful business practices" that, he argued, were costing Mars millions.[14]

Forrest tried to convince board members to oust Kruppenbacher and install him as chairman. But the board split, and Forrest fell two ballots short of the necessary votes. Following the attempted coup, Kruppenbacher banned Forrest from the company's grounds. The move infuriated Forrest, and he instructed his attorneys to file suit against the management of the company for breach of fiduciary duty. By now, the dispute was so distracting to management that it was beginning to affect the company's sales, but Forrest didn't care. He told the board he would continue the fight until he had won some measure of control over the business. In 1950, after numerous board meetings where allegiances were tested, Kruppenbacher offered Forrest one-third of the board's nine seats.

Forrest used his newfound power to push Mars to expand. When the factory was originally built, it boasted state-of-the-art systems. But since Frank's death, Kruppenbacher had done little to update the equipment or enlarge operations, leaving Mars woefully lacking in technology. Instead of investing Mars's profits in the plant, Kruppenbacher had been stuffing them in the bank. Forrest convinced the board that it was a waste to have all that cash lying around doing nothing, and he proposed a $4-million addition to the original factory and a plant-wide update of all machinery.

In 1953, Mars announced a mechanized process for making candy bars. Previously, plant workers had formed bars in individual batches, much the way you might make a batch of brownies at home—except that at Mars, they would make thousands of batches of candy a day. Each time, they would mix the ingredients, let the bars cool, and then cut them by hand before dipping them in chocolate. It was highly inefficient.

The new equipment—based on systems Forrest had installed in England—allowed "continuous flow" production, slashing the total manufacturing time from sixteen hours to thirty-five minutes.[15] Metal rollers layed nougat onto a cold steel belt that carried the candy through each step in the process. First, the nougat passed beneath round, sharp cutters that sliced it into long strips. The strips were passed through a guillotine that cut them into bars, and then—for a Snickers—rolled beneath a machine that layered on caramel and sprinkled them with peanuts. The bars were then sent under a waterfall of chocolate, and over jets that sprayed chocolate onto the bottom. After proceeding through a long cooling tunnel, the finished bars were removed from the conveyor belt and taken to the wrapping room. Unlike Hershey, Mars was still wrapping most of its candy by hand in the 1950s—a task that employed over 1,000 workers. Forrest convinced the board to at least semiautomate the process, and new equipment was purchased from Germany to help prepare the candy for shipping.

The expansion was completed in 1959. The new factory covered 400,000 square feet of floor space, a jump of 35 percent. Mars also added badly needed air-conditioning and increased its office space. New semiautomated loading docks for trucks were built, along with two new outbound railroad tracks. Forrest's additions succeeded in making Mars the world's largest manufacturer of chocolate-covered candy bars. But

Forrest wasn't finished. He wanted complete control over the newly revamped company, and after Kruppenbacher retired in 1959, he made his move.

With three members of the board already in his corner, he went about convincing the other six that he should succeed Kruppenbacher as chairman and CEO. He won half the battle. In December 1959, Forrest was named chairman, but Patricia Mars's third husband, James Fleming, was installed as president and chief executive officer. The board, it seems, was not ready to concentrate all the power in the hands of one man.

The decision to install Fleming as head of the company was a disaster. Although he'd been with Mars for fourteen years, Fleming had spent most of that time as Kruppenbacher's crony. He knew little about actually managing a business, and what's more, he refused to cooperate with Forrest, whom he still saw as the enemy. The boardroom quickly became a battleground, with Fleming and Forrest duking it out over every decision. The two men disagreed on everything—the direction of the company, the advertising strategy, the distribution system, the pay scale, the hiring process. The reverberations were felt on every level of the business. Quality suffered, and sales plummeted from a high of $50 million in 1959 to $42 million in 1963.[16]

Patricia Mars watched helplessly as her husband ran the company into the ground. She herself was in no position to step in; not only did she lack the management skill, but she had been diagnosed with brain cancer and knew she would not survive much longer. In desperation, she called Forrest and begged for a truce.

Forrest flew to Patty's home in La Jolla, California, and painted a stark picture of the company's future. He told her Mars would go bankrupt in less than three years unless something was done to improve operations.

"Our father made the best damn candy bar on the market," Forrest reminded her. "He'd be sick to see what is coming out of that factory today."

With sales heading south, Fleming had cut back on expensive ingredients like chocolate and peanuts, and the results showed. The Snickers bar was half the size it used to be and the coating on the bar was so thin you could see through it.

"The business should stay in the family," Forrest insisted. "It should be run by a Mars."

Patricia listened to his arguments, and this time, she agreed to sell her shares. She asked only that Forrest keep her husband on the payroll, and that Forrest rename his umbrella corporation—Food Manufacturers Inc.—Mars, Inc., thereby preserving the Mars family association.

With more than 80 percent of the company in his name, Forrest had little problem convincing the rest of the board members to sell their shares. In December 1964, Forrest Mars, now aged sixty, acquired the remaining 20 percent of the company. He relieved James Fleming of his duties and took on the titles of chairman, president and CEO. Within days, life at the Chicago plant changed forever.

After ordering executives into the oak-paneled conference room, Forrest proceeded to share his plans for what he called the Mars candies division: "I'm a religious man," he told the crowd. Then, after a long pause, he sank to his knees and began the following litany: "I pray for Milky Way. I pray for Snickers. . . ." No one in the room dared move.[17]

These products, Forrest explained, were to consume the executives' every moment. Every bit of energy, every expense, every idea would be focused on the product. "That's what the consumer buys," he said. "And that's what creates profit. And profit is our single objective."

Soon after the meeting, Forrest ripped out the executive dining room, fired the French chef, tore down the office walls, stripped the oak paneling and sold the art collection, the rugs, the stained glass and the corporate helicopter. He then increased salaries 30 percent, replaced fixed annual compensation with incentive pay and handed each associate a time card.

The company was finally his.

Chapter Thirteen

BREAKING
THE MOLD

FORREST MARS, SR., WHEN
HE WAS IN HIS SIXTIES. THIS
PHOTOGRAPH HANGS IN
THE COMPANY'S OFFICES
IN SLOUGH AND MCLEAN,
THE ONLY PLACES THAT
HAVE BEEN PERMITTED TO
DISPLAY HIS IMAGE.

THE EXECUTIVES IN Chicago had all heard the stories of
Forrest Mars long before he took over as their boss. By the time he
finally gained full control of Mars, Inc., in 1964, he was already infamous in the industry. Not just because of his demanding, volcanic
personality or because he had kicked Bruce Murrie out of his business—a slap at Hershey that galled even Hershey's toughest competitors. But after rising to prominence in America and Europe,
Forrest Mars had snubbed the entire confectionery world by refusing
to join the industry's trade groups or attend any industry conventions. He shunned all inquiries by the trade press, declining to share
even the tiniest tidbit about his business or himself. Even in an industry where secrecy and paranoia ruled, Forrest Mars was extreme.

"In the candy business, nobody shared information; it was very competitive and everybody understood that," said Nello Ferrara of Ferrara Pan Candy Co. in Chicago. "But it was common decency to join the National Confectioners Association, to attend the conventions. Everybody was there—except him. He didn't participate in anything. He didn't pay the dues; he didn't help sponsor any industry initiatives. He wouldn't serve on any committees. It was a real insult to the rest of us."

The National Confectioners Association was founded in 1884 by a handful of candy manufacturers to foster industry self-regulation. By 1965, every major candy manufacturer and supplier in the United States belonged to the group, which held annual meetings to address problems plaguing the industry. Over the years, the NCA was responsible for federal and state legislation prohibiting adulteration of confections, for industry-wide public relations campaigns promoting the nutritional value of candy and for lobbying against excise taxes on confections. It was the NCA that originated the idea of tying candy promotions to such holidays as Valentine's Day, Mother's Day and Halloween. And it was the NCA that successfully fought the government's move to declare candy making a nonessential wartime activity.

The Mars company in Chicago had long been an NCA supporter, helping foot the bill for many industry-wide ad campaigns and encouraging confectioners to participate in Commerce Department surveys, which for decades served as the only real measure of industry growth and sales. In fact, one of Mars's vice presidents, Victor Gies, had been elected chairman of the board of the NCA in 1957. But when Forrest Mars took control of the company, he revoked Mars's NCA membership and ordered company executives to withdraw from all industry-sponsored activities. He also issued a directive prohibiting his associates from speaking with outsiders about the business.

"He clamped a lid down so tight over there, we used to joke he was making bombs, not bonbons," said Ferrara. "It was like overnight, whoosh, he changed everything. We used to play golf with the guys from Mars, used to socialize with them. But not after Forrest came in. The whole mood changed."

But if the public changes seemed dramatic, they barely hinted at the upheaval taking place within. By the time Forrest was finished, nothing would remain of his father's company but the products. Everything else would be remade in Forrest's image.

m

Charles Kaufman witnessed the restructuring of Chicago firsthand. Hired by Forrest in 1963 as the corporate vice president of research and development, his first assignment was to help Forrest complete the overhaul of Chicago's manufacturing facilities, including the critical task of ending the company's thirty-year relationship with Hershey.

"Forrest wanted me to investigate right away what it would take to make his own chocolate," remembered Kaufman. "It drove him crazy to have Hershey making his most important ingredient. He wanted to end that relationship as soon as possible; he didn't want to be dependent on anyone."

Frank Mars had always viewed Hershey as a partner, but not Forrest. To him, the Pennsylvania giant was Mars's major competitor, and it unnerved him to have Hershey controlling any aspect of his business. It was one thing to enlist Hershey's help for the initial startup of a company, as he had to with his M&M's and as his father had to when he launched the Milky Way. But it was quite another to continue to depend on Hershey once Mars was firmly established. More than that, it was inconceivable for Mars to continue to rely on Hershey given his plans for the future.

"The way Forrest saw it, he was going head-to-head with Hershey," said Kaufman. "How could he let them control his supply of chocolate?"

But his concern went beyond the danger inherent in relying on a competitor. Forrest believed that the only way to ensure the consistency and quality of his products was to be in command of every aspect of production. To this day, Mars refuses to contract out any part of its manufacturing needs, a common practice in industry. And the company refuses to participate in joint ventures for the same reason. "If we can't control it, we don't want it," said Mars top executive Phil Forster.[1] "It's impossible to maintain standards of quality if you're reliant on someone else for part of your operations."

Forrest first instituted this policy in the 1950s, when he stopped buying chocolate from Cadbury for his British operation. He knew he would do the same in the United States if he ever got control of his father's firm, and in 1965 he sent word to Hershey that he was going to phase out his purchases of chocolate coating.

The move stunned Hershey executives, who were caught completely off guard by the pullout. At the time of Forrest's decision, the coating business accounted for more than 30 percent of Hershey's sales, bringing in pre-tax profits of about $12 million. Sales to Mars, Chicago, made up the bulk of that business.[2]

"We were pretty surprised when Forrest announced he would stop buying our coating," remembered Earl Spangler, Hershey's plant manager at the time. "We couldn't make sense of it."

For Mars to manufacture its own chocolate, Forrest would have to invest a tremendous amount of new capital—as much as $20 million in equipment and supplies.[3] Hershey executives figured it would take him more than a decade to recoup his money.

"Forrest could buy our coating for a lot less than he could make it himself," said Spangler. "Economically speaking, it wasn't that feasible."

But Forrest never looked at it in those terms.

"Forrest was in the business for the long haul," said Kaufman. "He didn't care one bit about the short-term. If he was going to be a candy bar maker, he was going to do it right."

Today, Hershey executives downplay the impact of Forrest's decision on the company, saying it freed up capacity for the company's own products. "We were looking to get rid of the business anyway," said former CEO Richard Zimmerman. "The timing was really pretty good in that respect."

But the numbers paint a somewhat different picture. In the years following Forrest's move, Hershey's after-tax profits dropped from a high of $25 million in 1966 to less than $20 million in 1968. Some of the slide was due to a spike in the price of cocoa, but the loss of Mars's business was a factor as well.

"Those were very difficult years for Hershey," said marketing executive Jack Dowd. "The company was not waking up to the fact that in Forrest Mars they had a huge new competitor. They just didn't get it."

Forrest wanted not only to make his own chocolate, but to turn his father's company into a manufacturing powerhouse—a dynamo of quality and efficiency that would overtake Hershey and leave every other candy maker far behind. His drive for preeminence was not simply a matter of ego, but stemmed from his fundamental belief that success could be assured only by being the industry leader.

"He insisted on being number one," said Kaufman. "He didn't think there was any advantage to be gained whatsoever in being number two."

This philosophy grew out of his experience in England, where Mars products battled against Cadbury's and Rowntree's for every inch of shelf space. It was only after the Mars bar became England's best-seller that Forrest found it possible to get his candies prominently displayed. And each time Forrest expanded his market—taking candy and pet food into the Netherlands, France, Australia and the Middle East—he learned the same lesson, that being the biggest and most popular was the best way to get his products in front of the consumer.

"Forrest wanted to see Snickers bars and Milky Ways in every supermarket, drugstore and newspaper stand in America," said Chicago sales manager Larry Johns. "Every place there was a Hershey bar, he wanted a Mars product on top of it."

Forrest gave his engineers six months to figure out how to begin manufacturing chocolate that was on par with Hershey's and he ordered Kaufman to whip the rest of the Chicago plant into shape. As Kaufman remembers the factory, parts of it were still "vintage 1880," particularly the packing and shipping operations. And since the manufacturing line was limited by the capacity of the packaging equipment, improving those facilities was top priority.

"Forrest wanted the entire plant mechanized from top to bottom," said Kaufman. "He was gravely concerned about the quality of his products, and he believed in using the most modern equipment to ensure his standards were being maintained."

Not content with the speed and accuracy of the manufacturing machinery available at the time, Forrest employed a host of engineers to improve it and adapt it to his own purposes. He never took out patents on the changes, fearing that would only give his competitors ideas. And he insisted his engineers sign confidentiality agreements not to disclose any of Mars's secret innovations.

The result of this effort was the most efficient candy-making operation in the business. It was not long until Forrest's plants completely "outmanufactured" the competition, operating at speeds no one else could match. By the time he was finished with the Chicago plant, every step in the process—from the mixing of ingredients to the boxing of the bars—was done mechanically. He compressed twenty manufacturing lines into just five high-velocity operations, capable of producing 2,500 Snickers bars a minute, and Fun Size Milky Way bars at double that speed. It was all possible because of Forrest's high-tech wrappers, the only self-loading wrapping machines in the business.

"He was way ahead of everyone when it came to equipment," remembered Kaufman. "He had solved engineering problems that no one else had even considered tackling." Like how to pipe warm, thick

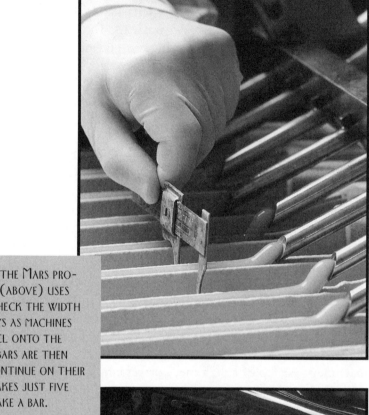

A WORKER ON THE MARS PRO-
DUCTION LINE (ABOVE) USES
CALIPERS TO CHECK THE WIDTH
OF MILKY WAYS AS MACHINES
SQUIRT CARAMEL ONTO THE
NOUGAT. THE BARS ARE THEN
SLICED AND CONTINUE ON THEIR
JOURNEY; IT TAKES JUST FIVE
MINUTES TO MAKE A BAR.

liquid chocolate from one end of the plant to the next, and how to evenly distribute ingredients like peanuts and caramel on each candy bar, and how to handle raw materials without exposing them to human contact.

Did you ever wonder how they get that tiny little *M* on the M&M? No other candy manufacturer had ever attempted to mark such a delicate product in this way, but Mars engineers developed a highly precise method to give the candies their unique look and ensure they could not be counterfeited.

Picture thousands of newly candy-coated chocolates spilling onto a conveyor equipped with tiny indentations, each the perfect cradle for a single M&M. As the conveyor shakes, the rainbow of naked candy shells settles in for a ride toward the printing press.

The printer's top roller is covered with the raised typeface of tiny *M*'s, which are coated with edible white dye. But this roller doesn't print the *M* on the candy; it would crush the fragile shell. Instead, it transfers the print of the *M* onto a second roller with a smooth surface. That roller passes over the centers of the speeding candies below and transfers the still-wet imprint onto the shells with just the right amount of force—not so much it crushes the candy, but enough that the *M* comes off, legs intact.

At the M&M/Mars factory in Hackettstown, New Jersey, it all happens at the rate of 200,000 M&M's a minute, or 100 million M&M's every eight hours. And 99 times out of 100, this remarkable proprietary equipment hits its target perfectly.

The way Forrest constantly upgraded the equipment and machinery required a tremendous ongoing investment. But, to this day, that is easier for Mars than for many other companies because Mars has never had any debt. And the family vows it never will. With no cash flow committed to banks and bondholders, Mars is free to reinvest every nickel of profits in its operations, keeping everything cutting edge. The Mars family rarely takes out dividends—indeed, doing so would result in needlessly large tax bills.[4] Instead, profits have always been pumped right back into the business, giving Mars a distinct advantage over the competition.

The giant mixers, conches and enrobers, the swift-moving conveyors, the miles of pumps and pipes that Forrest installed combined to give Mars, Chicago, the sleek look of a chemical-processing plant, rather than the overgrown kitchen that Forrest had inherited. To keep the plant operating smoothly, he retrained every worker on the floor, making each a mini-engineer, responsible for his own equipment—he taught them how to fix it, how to clean it and how to detect a potential problem.

"To work at Mars you had to do a lot more than make the candy," remembered Maryann Bishop, a line worker in the late 1960s. "We had to know everything there was to know about the production line. We had special training sessions at night and on the weekend, and everybody had to attend. It wasn't simple like just watching the candy go by and picking out the bad pieces."

Forrest put quality at the absolute center of the business, quickly reversing the downward spiral that had begun under Fleming. He boosted the chocolate coating on each bar, making it thicker than ever. He added more peanuts and more caramel to the Snickers, and increased the size of the 3 Musketeers. And when Chicago executives complained that the changes would slash profit margins, he gave them a half hour lecture at the top of his lungs.

"He screamed and screamed," recalled Larry Johns, head of Mars's sales department at the time. "I don't think I've ever seen anybody carry on the way he did. I mean, I didn't know it was possible to yell for that long."

Forrest believed that the only way to achieve success was to offer the consumer the best product on the market. Cost could never justify sacrificing quality. When other candy makers began replacing cocoa butter with cheaper fats like vegetable oil, Forrest refused. When others started using vanillin instead of vanilla, he refused. He insisted on the freshest ingredients, and he managed all of his factories so that raw materials arrived daily and were used immediately. He was obsessed with "incremental degradation," his term for the inevitable result if you substituted inferior ingredients. "Once you start down that road, there's no turning back."

When Forrest visited the factory, he didn't waste his time in meetings with managers—he headed straight for the factory floor, where he would inspect every inch of the production line. If he didn't like what he saw, everyone was sure to hear about it.

"He would climb up to the highest point, like to the top of the chocolate storage tanks, and he would take out his hand and wipe the top, looking for dust," said Bishop. "And if he found any, somebody was gonna get fired."

Since workers never knew just when the next surprise inspection might be, they kept the factory gleaming. Not a speck of chocolate marred the floor, not a uniform went unlaundered. Everything was slick, steel and polish. The sterile environment was like that of an operating room. Several times per shift, associates measured their work areas for bacteria, swabbing the equipment, the floor, their clothing.

Since Forrest couldn't be at every factory all the time, he insisted his managers walk through the plant hourly to be certain his dictates were being followed. And he encouraged everyone—from the line worker to the janitor—to halt production if they noticed something awry. Sometimes these problems were tiny details the consumer likely would never notice, like "scuff marks" on the end of a candy bar—evidence the bar didn't get a clean cut.

"My son is gonna rip this open and put it in his mouth so fast he won't even see the end," said a plant manager on a recent tour. "But that doesn't matter. It's my job to make sure that if he does look, all he sees is smooth chocolate."

Forrest was fanatical about scuff marks. He once ordered an entire production run scrapped because of the barely noticeable scratches in the chocolate coating. To him, the marks were evidence that his workers weren't paying attention—and that was a cardinal sin, punishable by firing.

"He absolutely could not tolerate a worker who wasn't taking his job seriously," said Kaufman. "For all the stories that have been told about him, I think this is what it boiled down to: He wanted everyone working as hard as he was. He wanted everyone pulling their own weight."

To further keep track of his factories, Forrest made a habit of buying Mars products from retailers to check the quality for himself. One hapless manager remembers being called out of bed in the middle of the night, with Forrest ranting on the other end of the phone. It seemed he had purchased a packet of M&M's at a Safeway outside of Los Angeles and some of the legs of the *M* were missing.

"He wanted me to track down the serial number and order a recall on the batch," said the worker. "But it was three A.M., for Christ's sake, and I told him I wouldn't do it."

"He said if I didn't get out of bed right then and get down to the plant, he would fire me. So I put my clothes on and went."

For Mars managers, phone calls like these were common. Working for Forrest meant being on call day and night, weekends and weekdays. It meant tolerating his sudden outbursts and foul language. It meant doing things that in other circumstances would seem completely outrageous—like tasting the dog food.

On visits to his pet food companies in Europe—and after he purchased Kal Kan in the United States in 1966—Forrest would hold court in the "cutting room" or testing center, where he would taste every variety of Mars's pet food and compare it with the competition, a practice that continues today.

"It tastes just like cold stew," John Murray explained during a tasting session at the Kal Kan plant in Vernon, California. "It's very meaty, moist and succulent."

The point of these human trials was not the flavor of the product—after all, a dog's palate and a human's are considerably different—but the overall quality of the pet food.

"If we don't get right in there, tasting, smelling, looking at the product, we're not qualified to judge it," said Murray. "We expect the consumer to feed this food to their pet. . . . If we don't taste it ourselves, how do we know we're offering the best product we can?"

This obsession with quality is evident throughout the business. Although no one in the company has *quality* in his or her title, quality control is everywhere. Mars was the first candy company to date its products and seize them from distributors if they had not sold in time. Forrest pioneered the use of computers on the production line to measure the consistency of his output. If a 3 Musketeers was a fraction of a gram too light, it was pulled from the line. If a Snickers didn't have exactly fifteen peanuts on top, it was rejected.

But these "faulty" products were not thrown in the garbage—that would be a waste, and Forrest hated waste almost as much as he hated sloppiness. Instead, each recipe was engineered to include a small percentage of "rework," scrap product that didn't cut the grade for sale to the public. On any given day in Chicago, there are dozens of giant bins filled with rejects that will get ground up and returned to the mix as part of the recipe. It was all part of Forrest's philosophy of keeping his businesses as efficient as possible.

In addition to using all of his factories twenty-four hours a day, seven days a week, Forrest saw to it that every input was fully exploited. At Uncle Ben's, for example, the rice hulls stripped from the unprocessed rice are burned to generate part of the plant's electricity. But the drive for efficiency doesn't end there—Forrest even found a use for the burned ash: He sold it to power plants, which use the rice ash to help burn coal more effectively.

Forrest carried his obsessions into the offices, as well. He insisted desktops be kept free of clutter, and he inspected associates' drawers, file cabinets and in-boxes, looking for signs of disorder. David Brown, Forrest's longtime financial officer, remembers a basket he used to keep on his desk filled with important papers.

"He dumped the contents on the floor because it wasn't neat enough," Brown said. "He wanted everything orderly—neat and efficient."

But the changes were more than cosmetic. Just as Forrest had revamped the factory, systematically improving every phase of production, he completely overhauled the company's approach to management.

The structure he installed in the Chicago plant is largely unchanged to this day, and it has been reproduced in each of the company's forty-one factories around the world. Everyone has the same size desk, everyone answers his own telephone and everyone is awarded a 10 percent bonus for punctuality. To encourage communication, managers sit in wagon-wheel fashion in the center of a large room, encircled by junior associates. The sales department is right next to the marketing department, which is right next to manufacturing and accounting. There are no offices, no partitions and no privacy. That way, Forrest reasoned, everybody in the company would know what everybody else was doing. Such openness applies to every aspect of the business.

At Mars, there is little regard for rank and no need for office memos or meetings. If you want something, you walk over to the boss and ask for it. If you have a problem, you gather your colleagues together and deal with it. Formality is frowned upon, and everyone, including the family, is addressed by his or her first name.

It all works, in part, because of Forrest's simple organizational structure. Although the company employs more than 28,000 associates, there is virtually no bureaucracy. The corporate ladder is divided into just six rungs, the top rung being occupied by the family itself. After the family come the company's executives, who total about 200, and next come the senior managers, of whom there are about 2,000. Considering Mars operates a global conglomerate with billions of dollars in sales, the number of "higher-ups" is astonishingly small.

"[Forrest] didn't believe in layers and layers of management," said David Brown. "He wanted lines of communication to be as direct as possible, and that meant flat, simple organization."

The company is divided horizontally, as well. Although comprised of many disparate parts, Forrest distilled the business's activities into seven distinct and universal functions: manufacturing, marketing, sales, research and development, goods and services, finance (accounting) and personnel. Each division—from pet food to rice to candy—was organized along these lines of management. Forrest kept tabs on everyone through a central committee made up of his top managers, each of whom oversaw one particular function. It was their job to make sure that the business operated according to his prescriptions and that his exacting standards were met.

Everything that the managers needed to know about running the business "the Mars way" was spelled out in a little blue book, just thirty pages long. Developed during his years in England and refined during the 1950s at the M&M plant in New Jersey, the book of "Forrest's Golden Rules"—as it was sarcastically referred to in Chicago—was a codification of all of Forrest's unique management practices, from the 10 percent bonus for punctuality to the calculations for ROTA. By looking at the manual, managers could figure out everything from pay raises to production targets. It was all there, laid out simply and elegantly, in neat little charts and tables.

By codifying his management philosophy, distilling it down to a systematic program, Forrest Mars freed himself from the drudgery of managing the business; that was for the hired help, not for an empire builder like him. What made Forrest's blood rush was the thrill of mastering new opportunities and taming uncharted worlds. Like Milton Hershey, he was driven by his visions; but where Milton Hershey saw utopia, Forrest Mars saw conquest. Once the battle was won, it was time to move on.

Forrest got involved with a division personally only if something was going terribly wrong. Otherwise, he left each business alone, giving total autonomy to the head of the unit. But if the unit manager failed to make his goals, heads rolled. According to former Mars managers, Forrest asked his executives on the day they were hired to sign a letter of resignation dated three years hence. If at the end of three years they had not met his business targets, the letter was put into effect.

It was a ruthless way to do business, but for Forrest, it was the only way that made sense. Forrest ran his businesses strictly by the numbers, but not in an accounting sense. He had always been impressed by the power of mathematics and economics, and he wanted to understand the relationships between the components in his business—how sales relate to marketing, production to sales, market share to profits. To do this, Forrest called on a highly sophisticated field of management known as "operations research." Pioneered by planners during World War II, operations research provided a mathematical framework for maximizing the results of a complex system, boiling vague questions of judgment or intuition down to cold calculations.

"It was a very sophisticated approach to management. Nobody in the industry was doing what he was doing; it was a very scientific, very orderly way of managing," said Kaufman, who worked as an industry consultant before joining Mars.

Forrest used his numerical models to understand the tradeoffs among ROTA, profits and sales, setting annual targets for each. If you met those targets it meant you were managing his business as efficiently as possible. If you failed, it meant he wasn't getting the most out of his investment.

"Forrest had very specific ideas about how to allocate resources," said Kaufman. "If you earned more than he wanted—or less than he wanted—then you weren't using his assets effectively, and he would have you canned." It's obvious why earning too little was condemned, but earning too much was no better. It meant you weren't spending enough money on marketing, promotions and other investments needed for long-term success.

Despite his harsh tongue and unforgiving approach, Forrest had a knack for finding and keeping outstanding talent—perhaps because of his unwavering focus on performance. Working for Forrest was not about personality or style; he didn't care what you looked like or who you knew. All that mattered was how well you could do the job. As untraditional and harsh as his management style was, nothing about it was arbitrary or subjective—a fact that won him much loyalty. Many of his top managers stayed with him their entire careers.

"Forrest got the best and the brightest," said Collin Pratt, who joined Forrest in Slough in 1936 and spent more than thirty years as one of his top lieutenants. "He gave everyone his system, but it was up to you to make it work. And he rewarded you well if you did."[5]

Pratt ran Forrest's British operation through World War II, and served as president of that division until 1973, when he retired a multi-millionaire. And he was just one of dozens of senior-level managers whom Forrest made very rich.

"Nobody could touch the salaries that Mars offered," said Claude Eliette-Hermann, who joined Mars in the early 1960s to head the French pet food division and eventually rose to oversee pet foods world-wide. "He was paying three times as much as the competition; it was very handsome compensation."

Forrest believed that to get the best, you had to pay the best, and the company continues that practice. A senior-level manager can bring home between $300,000 and $500,000 annually—salaries more typically associated with high-paying professions like doctors, lawyers and investment bankers.

Such attractive compensation makes Mars a popular employer. When the company opened a new candy plant in Waco, Texas, in 1981, thousands of people stood in line for hours just to submit job applications. Among MBA candidates, interviews with Mars are as coveted as interviews with IBM, Goldman Sachs or Salomon Smith Barney. And its reputation is global. In Denmark, Norway, Germany, Britain and France, Mars tops the list of high-paying employers.

But the generous compensation is only part of the success of Mars's pay structure. Forrest believed in setting compensation with the same objective standards used to judge the rest of his business. There are no individual merit increases and no rewards based on individual performance. It is a one-for-all, all-for-one system, with bonuses and raises tied directly to business goals.

Moreover, the company operates with only six pay levels, corresponding to the six zones on the corporate ladder. The pay scales within each zone are public, so everyone knows what everyone else is earning—incentive for advancement.

"People are always talking about how secretive Mars is, but once you get inside, there are very few secrets at all," said Mars vice president Mike Murphy. "It's a much more open atmosphere than you find at other companies. [Mars] lays it all out on the table, right from the beginning. You know what you're getting into, you know how far you can go and what you have to do to get there."

By paying associates at each level approximately the same amount, Mars finds it easy to move players around, a favorite pastime of the family. Forrest set the precedent early on, when he began bringing in associates from England to work at M&M in the United States. Today, it is not uncommon for a manager with ten years' experience to have lived in seven different countries, working seven different jobs. Mars believes such transfers help employees keep their edge.

"If you spend your whole life doing just one thing, you get narrow after a while," explains Phil Forster, who oversees the company's confectionery brands worldwide. "And if everybody is focused on their little piece of the pie, there's no one looking at the big picture."

Mars sees no reason why the vice president of sales for Pedigree dog food can't serve equally well as the vice president of sales for Snickers. Or why the head of marketing in Chicago can't one day be in charge of production in Slough. This crossbreeding, as it is known in-house, is one of the company's greatest strengths.

"We want ideas flowing backward and forward," said Forster. "A marketing guy will do his job a hell of a lot better if he knows what it takes to run the production line. The same is true if a sales associate spends time looking after the inventory."

With no other way to achieve status—no corner offices to covet, no limousines to aspire to, no corporate hideaways for favored executives—associates compare rank based on how many different jobs they've held. "You know you're getting good if you've served in four or five divisions," said associate Steve Greenly.

But while this constant shifting of personnel worked well within companies that Forrest built, it didn't sit well with the executives in Chicago. Shortly after Forrest consolidated his control of the Chicago plant, he began transferring workers in from his M&M division in New Jersey, part of his strategy for overhauling Chicago's corporate culture. But the transfers only increased tensions for executives who were already having a difficult time adjusting to life under Forrest.

"It was pretty obvious that he favored his employees at M&M," said sales manager Larry Johns. "They were getting all the top jobs."

The friction between the divisions made for very difficult working conditions, said Johns. And Forrest's abrasive style didn't help. In the years following the takeover "everybody in management was pretty unhappy," he remembered. "It was a very divisive time."

The president of Mars, Chicago—Duke Vance—and most of the top leadership had come into power during Fleming's administration, and Forrest made it clear he had little respect for them. Johns remembers a typical run-in between Forrest and William Suhring, who was head of marketing.

"Forrest Mars didn't like marketing people at all—I guess 'cause he thought he was the best marketer there was. Anyhow, he took off after Bill Suhring one day. Just laid into him for about forty-five minutes. He was saying, 'Bill, you're a nice fellow. You know I know you're a nice guy, and you have a nice family, but you're the dumbest SOB that I've ever known in my life. I don't know how I can live with you. You ought to get the hell out of here. Now don't get me wrong, Bill. I like you personally, but you're stupid.'"

Forrest was furious because he couldn't find a Milky Way bar in a store that he'd been in in Virginia.

"And I thought, well, this is how I can get Bill off the hook. So I said, 'Mr. Mars, excuse me, but that's not Bill's responsibility. That's mine.'

"And he turned around and pointed his finger at me, and he said, 'Then I ought to fire you, too!'"

In the end, Forrest didn't have to fire any of the Chicago brass. Within three years of his takeover, most of them left Mars for other companies. Some went to General Foods, some to Nabisco and some to Kraft. But two of them, Larry Johns and Bill Suhring, did the unforgivable: They crossed over into enemy territory and went to work for Hershey.

Chapter Fourteen

THE CARETAKERS

In 1936, the H. B. Reese Candy Co. operated just down the street from Hershey. Workers dipped the peanut butter cups into chocolate by hand before packing them for shipping.

*I*T WAS 1968, and Larry Johns, fresh from his job as head of sales for Mars, Inc., was sitting dumbfounded, listening to a Hershey district sales manager explain the job of selling Hershey bars. "This is one of the easiest gigs in the world," boasted the manager. "Why, most of the time, I don't even need to make calls; the orders just roll on in."

"I see," said Johns. "So how many Hershey bars did you sell last month?"

"How many bars? Why, I don't know. A couple thousand, I guess."

"But you can't say for sure?"

"Well, we don't keep track like that. I got in the usual orders, plus a few extra 'cause they're gearing up for Halloween. I'd say more than one hundred orders for August, and that's up five orders from last year."

Johns had never heard of a sales force that measured success by numbers of orders—an order could be ten bars or ten cases; a customer could place orders twice a week or twice a month; it told you nothing about how well Hershey bars were actually selling. But the district manager didn't care; his job, as defined by headquarters, was to get "orders." And for forty years, that's what the Hershey manager had been doing: dropping in on corner grocers, five-and-dimes and tobacco stands and taking orders for a box of candy bars here and a box there.

"The whole program was a curse," said Johns. "The salesmen were wasting their time in these little stores—mom-and-pop shops that Mars wouldn't be caught dead in—and they'd go there 'cause they knew they could get an order. It didn't make one bit of difference how big that order was; the only emphasis was on writing up the ticket."

When Johns came to Hershey, he spent his first months on the job touring the field, visiting the fourteen regional sales managers who oversaw Hershey's national sales division. And while he knew from his tenure at Mars that Hershey's sales force had its problems, with each stop on his tour he became more and more appalled at how out of touch and behind the times the Hershey team was.

"They had no idea what they were doing," said Johns. "They didn't know a thing about market share, they didn't know about their competition, they didn't have a clue what it meant to actually be a salesman."

Johns remembers district managers bragging that they carried twenty-four-count boxes in the trunks of their cars, just in case a customer needed one. "And I thought to myself, Jesus, who thinks in terms of boxes? I'm thinking in terms of carloads, truckloads—tonnage. And these guys are walking around happy that they're selling twenty-four bars at a time."

Johns watched in dismay, time and time again, as the Hershey reps took him along on sales calls: "They'd go visit Joe on the corner" and walk right by the Safeways, the Kmarts, the Stop & Shops—giant retailers that would sell cases, not boxes, of Hershey bars each week. When Johns asked reps why they ignored the big accounts, he was told "because they don't place the orders," which was true, since individual stores in large retail chains are generally supplied by central warehouses that buy goods from wholesale distributors. Nevertheless, every consumer products company in America made regular calls on retailers like these to secure the best shelf space, to set up special in-store displays, to convince local managers to advertise their products in the weekly circular. But not the men from Hershey.

"One guy even told me he'd been ordered to stay out of the supermarkets," said Johns. "It was ludicrous."

And the problems didn't end there. Johns knew from working at Mars that in markets east of the Mississippi River, the Reese's Peanut Butter Cup was Hershey's best-seller. But Hershey executives didn't even know that much, because the corporate office didn't keep track of sales by brand.

"They were keeping count of everything by pack type: How many six-packs sold, how many twelve-packs sold, how many thirty-six-count boxes, how many forty-eight-count boxes? But they had no idea which brands were actually selling and which weren't."

How Hershey could operate without fundamental information like market share was beyond Johns. It was the driving force behind every company he'd ever worked for.

"In Chicago, we knew every market by heart. We knew every place where Snickers was number one, where M&M's outsold Hershey's, where Milky Way lagged behind the Almond bar. This information was the lifeblood of our business."

To Johns, Hershey looked like a museum, a primitive operation about to run smack into the twentieth century, and he had to ask himself, "What happened?"

*A*t the height of Milton Hershey's reign, the people of Hershey worked in his factory, shopped in his department store and rode his trolleys. He supplied them with electricity and water, and they washed their clothes at the Hershey laundry. On weekends, they skated on his ice rink, rowed his boats on his lake, danced in his pavilion and played on his golf courses and tennis courts. When they died they were buried in a cemetery on land he donated.

In short, the town and the company were totally dependent on him. And when Milton Hershey died in 1945, the people who had come to rely on his generosity and vision seemed lost. They could not make a single decision without first wondering what "M.S." would do. In truth, no one could anticipate how Milton Hershey would have reacted as times changed, and so the rallying cry became "Milton Hershey would have never"—for it was easier to say what he wouldn't have done than to say what he would have done.

Too afraid to step into Milton Hershey's shoes, unwilling or unable to take any real initiative, Percy Alexander Staples spent his ten years as head of the Hershey enterprises in hiding. An introvert by nature, Staples spent most of his time holed up in his office alone, surrounded by stacks of papers. He rarely spoke to the company's employees or made public appearances. Rarer still was the sight of Staples about town. It was expected that if you worked in Hershey and lived in Hershey, you participated in the town's social and civic activities. Everyone, from the executives on down, attended Hershey's churches or joined Hershey's rotary or the garden club or the local VFW. But Staples and his wife, Eliza, kept to themselves. They didn't even buy a home in Hershey, preferring to rent a suite of rooms in the Hotel Hershey.

"It was as if they hadn't really decided they were staying," remembers Monroe Stover, who is Hershey's oldest resident, born in 1900. "They kept their distance, you know. They didn't even try to fit in."

Always more comfortable with reports than with people, Staples communicated with only a handful of top managers. But even they never knew what he was thinking or planning. "He was a mystery," said former CEO Richard Zimmerman. "He kept everything to himself." Considering Staples held all four top positions in the Hershey empire—chairman of the board and president of the Hershey Chocolate Co., president of the Hershey Trust Co. and chairman of the board of the Hershey Industrial School—his secrecy and isolation bred anxiety and distrust. Rumors abounded that Staples was planning to sell the company, and senior executives wasted much of their time fretting over the possibility. Their concerns were not without cause, for everything Staples did seemed to point in that direction.

He made it clear from the beginning that his overriding concern was the perpetuation of the Trust. But Staples interpreted that directive in an extreme, and extremely conservative, fashion. He focused on the financial condition of the Trust to the exclusion of everything else—the town, the company, the residents. Milton Hershey's broad vision of a grand utopia, where company and town worked in symbiosis, was reduced under Staples to a concern for the bottom line.

A pessimist by nature and fundamentally uncomfortable with risk, Staples was deeply troubled by the Trust's reliance on the chocolate company, and he was particularly concerned with the company's dependence on a volatile commodity like cocoa beans. He knew little about the cocoa markets when he took control, and as he studied their history, he found nothing to comfort him.

Cocoa bean prices tend to fluctuate wildly, and this was never more true than in the years following the war. The government set the price of cocoa at 8.9 cents per pound during World War II, but in 1946, the price gyrated from a low of 9 cents to a high of 27 cents. These dramatic swings made Staples extremely nervous. He became fixated on cocoa bean prices, worrying about them endlessly. He convinced himself that the world supply of cocoa beans would never keep pace with demand, a projection that, if true, pointed to disaster for company profits—and thus for the Trust.

Several factors contributed to his thinking. In the years following the war, diseases swept across the cocoa plantations of West Africa, Brazil, Ecuador and Venezuela, cutting world supply dramatically. The war itself also cut plantings because farmers, unable to ship their crops, cut production. As a result, in Staples's first year as CEO the cocoa market began a sharp rise that would last for his entire tenure. In the face of ever higher prices, Staples became paranoid. He focused his energies on anything that might protect the company against volatile swings in the market, setting aside millions of dollars in reserves and embarking on a costly campaign to build new storage facilities for beans.

Staples seemed oblivious to the great opportunities that the war had presented to Hershey. Soldiers brought their affection for Hershey's chocolate home with them from the war. Civilians, who had little access to chocolate during the war, also clamored for the company's products. Demand was so great that Hershey had to ration its supply to distributors.

Overseas, the United States was at the height of its influence, and all things American were cast in a rosy glow, admired in Europe and Japan. Hershey bars had traveled around the globe wherever American soldiers went, becoming not just a treat but a medium of exchange, the local currency. And at the same time, Europe's chocolate factories lay in ruins. It was the ideal time for Hershey to branch out into Europe, using its dominance in the American market as a springboard for worldwide expansion.

But at the very moment when Hershey could have been cashing in on the tremendous brand recognition it had earned during the war, Staples retrenched. He cut back on maintenance, refused to expand the factory and even resisted upgrading the plant to meet the skyrocketing demand in the United States. Instead, he poured all of his efforts, and Hershey's resources, into insulating the company from future cocoa bean price increases. The only capital project he was interested in was the construction of sixteen silos, capable of storing 64 million pounds of cocoa beans—a two-year supply. But even this wasn't enough to keep him from panicking when cocoa prices jumped to 58 cents a pound in 1954.

In a move that Hershey managers deemed heresy, Staples began preparing Hershey to purchase already-made chocolate supplies from other companies, hoping in this way to reduce its reliance on the cocoa markets. He started by importing tons of cocoa powder from Gill and Dufus, a British manufacturer, and chocolate liquor from the Dominican Republic and Ghana. Finally, in June 1956, Staples sent Sam Hinkle, who was then supervisor of the chocolate plant, and Elwood Meyers, the company's chief chemist, to Europe. Their mission: to explore the possibility of purchasing chocolate from Cadbury's factories.

Hinkle and Meyers returned from their trip on June 18, 1956. They

THE HERSHEY FACTORY LANGUISHED AFTER THE DEATH OF MILTON HERSHEY; THE COCOA DEPARTMENT, LIKE MOST OTHERS, REMAINED LARGELY UNCHANGED UNTIL THE 1960S.

were prepared to report to Staples that Cadbury was not only willing to sell chocolate crumb, but was also interested in selling cocoa powder.

The idea shocked Hershey's management. Milton Hershey had prided himself on making his very own chocolate from scratch. Buying ingredients from Cadbury would mean idling half the factory and diminishing the company's control over product quality. Moreover, Cadbury's chocolate had a completely different taste than Hershey's. No one had ever risked altering the Hershey flavor—it was the corner-stone on which the company was built. The resulting changes at Her-shey would be monumental.

As fate would have it, the deal never went through. On June 23, 1956, less than a week after Hinkle and Meyers returned, Percy A. Sta-ples died in his sleep at the Hotel Hershey.

After Staples's death in 1956, members of the Hershey Trust Co. board vowed that power would never be concentrated in the hands of one man again. At a meeting immediately following Staples's funeral, it was unanimously agreed that J. J. Gallagher, head of Hershey's sales team, should be chairman of the board of the Hershey Chocolate Corp., and Samuel Hinkle, plant superintendent, should be named president. It was a safe decision; both men had been with Hershey for more than thirty years, and they were intimately familiar with the chocolate com-pany's traditions.

Hinkle joined the company in 1924 as chief chemist and worked for twenty-four years in the Hershey laboratory, where he conducted exper-iments aimed at improving Hershey products. His greatest achievement was developing, in concert with the federal government, the formula for the Ration D bar. When Staples took over, he promoted Hinkle out of the laboratory and onto the factory floor, where he oversaw the manu-facturing end of the business. There he won the respect of the factory workers, and he was acknowledged by all in the firm as the expert on Hershey's production techniques.

Many of these techniques were now outdated, a fact driven home to Hinkle by his trip overseas. On visits to chocolate factories in En-gland, Germany and France he saw faster, more efficient, more versatile chocolate-making equipment that could greatly speed up Hershey's pro-duction. Now that he was chief executive, he set out to update every department in the plant, trying desperately to make up for the time lost under Staples. It was an enormous task, made harder by the physical layout of the factory, which wound like a maze through some thirty dif-ferent buildings.

Hinkle started in the Kiss department, where he authorized the overhaul of the packaging equipment to make the line faster. In 1962, he added automatic peanut sorters to the Mr. Goodbar line and installed the first "continuous flow" operation for making Hershey's syrup, replacing the old batch-by-batch method. Additional longitudinal conches were installed to boost total chocolate output, and new refiners and molding machines were added to the chocolate-bar line. He spent millions on construction to try to ease the bottlenecks that resulted from the haphazard layout of the factory, adding freight elevators and connecting buildings to ease the flow of production. But these were only stopgap measures—it was impossible to make real progress given the existing structure. It became clear that, if Hershey was going to meet demand for chocolate going forward, it would have to open a new factory, probably on the West Coast. It was a prospect that made everyone in Hershey extremely nervous.

As late as the 1960s, no one in Hershey—not even Hinkle—understood just how the unique flavor of Hershey's chocolate was produced. And since they didn't know how it was made, they were not sure they could re-create it. Hinkle assigned his best engineers and chemists to study the company's antiquated milk processing operation—which had not been touched since it was installed at the turn of the century—to pinpoint exactly what contributed to the Hershey taste. Some argued that it could never be reproduced in California or anywhere else because the flavor depended on the "special milk" from Pennsylvania cows. Nobody ever proved this to be true—and the argument was laughed at by some—but Hinkle wasn't prepared to take any risks. He recommended that Hershey open a small factory outside the country, to experiment, before investing $20 million in a California facility.

True to the company's conservative nature, Hershey chose Canada as the foreign country and in 1961 broke ground on a plant in Smith Falls, Ontario. In 1963, the first Hershey bars rolled off the line. But just as many had feared, the flavor did not compare with the original. Hershey first tried to correct the taste by trucking in millions of gallons of milk from Pennsylvania—an extraordinarily costly measure—but the "special milk" didn't help. Engineers and chemists then spent months working to replicate the original milk-condensing operation, copying every part piece by piece, down to the types of screws in the kettles. Eventually, they succeeded in re-creating Hershey's for Canada—only to discover that Canadians wouldn't eat Hershey's chocolate. Their palates were accustomed to the flavor of Cadbury's and of Rowntree's, which had operated plants in Canada since the early 1900s. Hershey's stiff, sour taste contrasted sharply with the mellow, cooked-caramel flavor of the British giants, and Hershey sales languished.

Meanwhile, having solved the milk dilemma, the company went ahead with plans to open a plant in Oakdale, California. But even today there are old-timers at Hershey who swear they can tell the difference between a piece of chocolate from Hershey and one from Oakdale.

"Most of the public would probably never notice the difference," said Monroe Stover. "But when you've been around the chocolate as long as I have, you can tell; it's subtle, but it's there."

Hinkle not only expanded production, but also took the first timid steps toward upgrading Hershey's management structure. Though he had been brought up within the company, he realized that the old style of management would not carry Hershey forward. At lower levels, promotions were based strictly on seniority, not merit. If you were there the longest, you got to be the manager. At the top, Hershey had always relied on the instincts and abilities of one or two leaders, but the company never had a cadre of professional managers to support it, nor were its leaders trained for the responsibilities they had to assume.

"After Mr. Hershey died, this company was governed by a small handful of people who made all the decisions at the top," said Earl Spangler, who would later become president of the Hershey Chocolate Co. "Hinkle realized that more was needed to run a company this size. But it took a long time before he was able to get a change in the management."

Staples had started the process, at least, by allowing Hinkle to hire several young college graduates—the first the company had recruited. Hinkle took the next small step, creating the company's first formal management training program. Under it, managers would spend years transferring across several company functions, so that they could learn the business from a variety of perspectives. But this was a painfully slow approach, and the opportunity was offered to just three hand-picked employees.

Hinkle also tried to extend the company's product line, with little success. Among the short-lived offerings: Hershey's Mint Chocolate and Hershey's Chocolate Covered Candy Coated Almonds (1959), Pennsylvania Dutch Sweet Chocolate and Hershey Squares (1962), Milk Chocolate Dainties, Easter Cuties and Hershey's Kool Glo Frostings (1965).

Hershey's only successful new product was not developed by the company, but acquired from outside, by buying one of the firm's best customers.

There was a long-standing relationship between Hershey and the H. B. Reese Candy Co. Harry Burnett Reese came to Hershey in 1917 to work as a dairyman for the Hershey farms, and in 1921 he went to work in the factory. But Reese was inspired by Milton Hershey's success, and was determined not to remain a factory worker for long.

"I remember one time he said that Mr. Hershey could sell seven carloads [of chocolate] a week. . . . He said he saw no reason why he couldn't sell a couple hundred pounds," recalls his son, Ralph.

Reese tried various confections in his kitchen, just as Frank Mars and Milton Hershey had. He made a coconut caramel bar, chocolate-covered dates, various crèmes and caramels and hard sugar candies.

"I remember he'd cook it on the stove till it was like taffy, then cool it on a marble slab, about three-by-three [feet], I guess. Then he'd take it off [the slab] and had a hook hanging on the wall in the dining room. [He'd] throw it over the hook and pull it like you pull taffy, then roll it out and cut little after-dinner mint size."

Reese struggled initially, supporting his family of six sons and seven daughters. But by 1925 he had developed a successful candy assortment that he sold to department stores in Lancaster. He capitalized on his association with the burgeoning chocolate company, advertising his candy as "Made in Hershey." In 1926 he built his own factory just down the street from the Hershey plant, and it seemed his operation would double in size every few years.

When the Great Depression came, the Reese company suffered big losses. But Milton Hershey helped his competitor survive, giving Reese free sugar and cutting the cost of chocolate. When the smaller company ran into production problems, Hershey also sent engineers to help Reese out. But Reese's big break came in 1941, with the wartime rationing of sugar. While the shortage meant crisis for most of the nation's confectioners, it forced Reese to refocus his business on peanut butter cups— which required less added sugar than anything else in his lineup. Reese began full-time production of peanut butter cups, offering them singly for a penny apiece.

The candy became enormously popular, and Reese discontinued all of his other products. By the early 1950s, the company ranked as one of the largest candy companies on the East Coast, with sales of $10 million annually. Reese was the second-largest buyer of Hershey's chocolate, behind Mars. The company began construction on a brand-new factory on the outskirts of town, designed with the latest in candy-making machinery. But in 1956, just as the factory was completed, H. B. Reese died, leaving his business in the hands of his six sons.

Without a clear successor, the company languished. The sons disagreed over how to run the business, fighting over management decisions and haggling over control. They soon found themselves in over their heads.

"The business . . . had outgrown the abilities of those who were attempting to run it, and I think they all recognized that in the early sixties," said Samuel Schreckengaust, Jr., counsel to the company.

Word went out that Reese was struggling and in the spring of 1963, several tobacco companies approached the family to discuss a buyout or merger. But Hinkle realized that Reese would be a much better fit for Hershey. Hinkle called Schreckengaust, and in June 1963, Hershey acquired Reese for $23.3 million. At the time, Reese boasted sales of $14 million.

The acquisition was one of the most positive steps Hershey management had taken since Milton's death. But after twenty years of slumber, it was far from enough.

MILTON HERSHEY WANTED TO PRO-
VIDE THE CHILDREN AT THE HERSHEY
INDUSTRIAL SCHOOL WITH THE
SECURITY HE NEVER KNEW AS A BOY.

OBODY IN HERSHEY, Pennsylvania, ever worried about selling Hershey bars. They sometimes worried about cocoa bean prices and sugar supplies and whether the Hershey Theatre should book Beethoven or Broadway for the upcoming season. But since the introduction of the nickel bar in 1900, nobody in the company gave a second thought to sales, which had climbed steadily upward for fifty years without coupons, newspaper ads, jingles or slogans. M. S. Hershey used to say the 5-cent Hershey bar sold itself. And he was right. By the 1950s, the bar was ubiquitous, as much a part of Americana as a hotdog and Coke at the Woolworth's lunch counter. Hershey was to the confectionery industry what Sears, Roebuck and Co. was to retailing. A chocolate bar just wasn't a chocolate bar unless it carried the maroon and silver label.

But times were changing, and no one in Hershey seemed to realize it except Harold Mohler. A graduate of Lehigh University in industrial engineering, Mohler had been recruited by Sam Hinkle in

1947 as part of Hershey's first attempt to professionalize its management by hiring young college graduates. When Hinkle became chief executive in 1956, he tapped Mohler as his assistant, grooming him to become the next CEO. As heir apparent, he was the first to enter the Hershey executive ranks without working his way up from the bottom.

His appointment had caused some consternation among the Hershey old-timers, who wondered what this college-educated industrial engineer could possibly bring to the corporation. But Mohler stood out to those who worked with him as a take-charge, no-nonsense leader who called the shots as he saw them. He was not a renegade but a motivator, who could walk the fine line between Hershey's past and Hershey's future.

In 1965, when Hinkle retired, Mohler took control of the company. Many pointed out that he had never met Milton Hershey personally, and some held that against him. But perhaps it was because of this that he was able to see Hershey for what it was, a company coasting on its reputation, stagnant and afraid of change. Unlike his predecessors, Staples and Hinkle, Mohler wasn't haunted by the ghost of M.S. He didn't see Milton Hershey in every decision he made, and he didn't concern himself with what Hershey would have wanted. He saw only a company adrift, not keeping up with the times and not even recognizing that it was being passed by. If Hershey was going to survive, Mohler was going to have to make major adjustments. But he would have to do it slowly, for Hershey wasn't ready for giant steps. The 5,000 workers who made up Hershey had been doing things the same way for a very long time, and real progress would take years. It was Mohler's job to set the wheels in motion, and he turned to William Dearden for help.

Where Mohler was seen as an outsider, Dearden was the ultimate insider.

On a brisk November morning in the middle of the Great Depression, a gangly, bewildered thirteen-year-old arrived at the beautifully manicured campus of the Hershey Industrial School (H.I.S.). After a brief interview with the schoolmaster, he received a tour of the pastoral fields and verdant hills that would be his home for the rest of his childhood. The setting, in the foothills of Pennsylvania's Blue Mountains, seemed unreal to a boy raised in a working-class section of Philadelphia. And as he later recalled, "Everywhere I looked I saw [signs with] H.I.S. I figured Mr. Hershey wanted everyone to know that the school was HIS property."[1]

Dearden will never forget that first day at the orphanage. It was the beginning of a whole new life, one that would bind him to Milton Hershey in ways neither could foresee. After the tour, he was fitted for a pair of warm pants and invited to the biggest feast he had ever seen. "Creamed rice was the vegetable, and there was apple pie for dessert," he said. "Where I came from, creamed rice *was* a dessert. It was like getting two desserts in one meal."[2]

Dearden, along with his brother and his sister, had grown up in the Frankford section of Philadelphia, where his father was an unemployed mill worker and his mother worked cleaning in the schools. After his mother died, in the fall of 1935, his father could no longer afford to feed or clothe his children. A neighbor had heard the incredible story of Milton Hershey's orphanage and suggested that Bill and his brother might find a home there. (Since the school did not then accept girls, Dearden's sister was sent to live with friends.)

Dearden had no idea what to expect from the school, but he found far more than a child of the Depression could have imagined. The more than one hundred students were well cared for, shielded from all traces of economic hardship. They got three good meals a day, lived in comfortable homes and were outfitted like upper-class schoolboys. As Dearden remembers, "You got two suits, and four or five pairs of shoes—farm shoes and house shoes and a pair of shoes for school and a pair you only wore on Sundays."[3]

For the next five years, Dearden lived on the Willow Wood farm, along with twenty-three other boys. Two sets of house parents looked after the students, making sure each stayed out of trouble, did his homework and performed his chores, and Dearden remembers them fondly. "You can't replace the love of a [real] parent under any circumstances," he said, "but there's a great and deep interest in the youngsters by the people who work at the school."[4]

In addition to a full load of courses, the students were responsible for all of the chores necessary to run the farm and maintain the house. That meant hoeing weeds and harvesting corn when "we'd have much rather been down at the swimming hole," Dearden said jokingly. "I worked in the house, as they say, making beds, mopping halls, washing dishes, all that kind of thing. Then, as I got a little older, I went into the barn to work, and that meant milking the cows in the morning and in the evening."[5]

Everybody complained about the hard load and long days, but graduates like Dearden credit the school with teaching them life lessons they would have never learned anywhere else. As Dearden tells it today, the school taught him that "work is a habit. If you learn how to do it, and learn how to focus on it, it stands you in good stead."[6]

There were privileges—trips into town on the weekends and summertimes spent on the lake, in the swimming pool and at the park. There were also weekly movies, concerts, theater, ice skating and a chance to go home each August. The younger boys received an allowance of 25 cents a week. Seniors got a princely 50 cents. "From that, you spent your 10 cents for the movies on Wednesday night, and you were also expected to save a little bit of money out of that allowance. That was to promote thrift and build a little nest egg for you when you left."[7]

Dearden's memories of the school include many of Milton Hershey himself. Because Willow Wood was located just behind Milton's trout hatchery, the boys in the home were often treated to visits by their benefactor. "When we saw the cloud of dust coming, we figured it might be Mr. Hershey, so the kids would run out to the road and wave to him. Sometimes, he'd stop and ask us how we were doing and talk a little bit. Other times, he might get out of the car and look around a little bit."[8]

On the Willow Wood farm, they experimented with raising soybeans, another of Hershey's pet projects, and Dearden remembers many visits from Hershey to see how the crop was doing. But even when he wasn't around, Milton Hershey was a constant presence in the minds of the young boys who owed their good fortune to his. "We were all proud of our association with him[, seeing him as our] foster father with a chocolate factory. We made up stories about him, saying that he was so rich he had a drinking fountain and a toilet in his car, and obviously he didn't, but they were the kind of things that kids made up."[9]

Dearden distinguished himself quickly at the school, building a reputation as a star athlete on the football and basketball squads. He was an active and popular student, singing in the glee club and working for the school newspaper and yearbook. The school had a vocational mission, and each student majored in a practical field. For Dearden, the choice was commerce, and he graduated at the top of his class.

The honor won him the opportunity to address his schoolmates at commencement exercises in 1940, where he delivered a speech on free enterprise in front of Milton Hershey himself. "When I got my diploma [Mr. Hershey] shook my hand very heartily and patted me on the back," Dearden remembered. "That had to be one of the best days of my life."[10]

After graduation, Dearden spent one year at the Hershey Junior College—a tuition-free institution also supported by the Hershey Trust—before moving on to Albright College in nearby Reading on a full athletic scholarship. In 1942, he enlisted in the navy, and received a year's education at the Harvard Business School, training to become a supply and disbursement officer. He served out the war on a tanker in the South Pacific and then joined Dun & Bradstreet.

In 1953, the administration of the school asked him to return to Hershey, offering him a job as assistant business manager. It was rare for any of the Hershey companies to hire a graduate from the school; Milton Hershey had always felt that giving his orphans jobs would make life seem too easy and would stir resentment from townspeople who already considered "Milton's Boys" privileged. But Dearden was an exception, having made a lasting impression on his teachers, many of whom saw in him the same leadership ability and strength of character as in Mr. Hershey himself.

At six feet five inches tall, Dearden was physically imposing. But he never talked down to his staff. A religious man, he looked people straight in the eye and invited conversation.

"He was taller than practically anybody else in town," said Zimmerman. "But while you were talking to him, he never seemed to be taller than you."

His skills at managing people impressed not only the school officials, but also members of the board of the Hershey Trust Co., who in 1957 tapped him to join the chocolate company as assistant to Hershey chairman John J. Gallagher. When Mohler took over as CEO in 1965, he named Dearden as his new director of sales and marketing, a position he created to try to shake up the status quo.

Dearden was the perfect candidate to wake Hershey from its decades-long slumber. Like Mohler, he realized how backward the company had become, but he could make changes without risk of mutiny. After all, it would be almost impossible for traditionalists to accuse the fair-haired orphan boy of betraying the Hershey legacy. As the old-timers would say, Dearden was an orphan who "bleeds Hershey blood."

$\mathcal{H}$ershey was the only company in the Fortune 500 that did not have a marketing department by the mid-1960s. Hershey himself had never felt the need to formally advertise his products, and those who followed after him were afraid to break with tradition. As late as 1960, Samuel Hinkle told *The Wall Street Journal* that Hershey didn't see the need for advertising. "Our minds are not closed to the advantages that might come from advertising," he said, adding, "We haven't convinced ourselves the time has come to use it."[11]

Hershey's attitude toward Madison Avenue had become a joke in the industry. The company continued to act as if it were the only force in the candy market. But now there was stiff competition from Mars, from Nestlé, from thousands of small candy companies with niche products that had found their way into the hearts of Americans. Hershey's sales weren't increasing the way they used to, and more adults than children were buying Hershey products—an ominous sign for the future. Advertising and marketing were the obvious way to reverse these trends.

Dearden's first act on the job was to bring in new talent from outside Hershey to help revamp the sales force and create a marketing department. His recruits were the first managers to enter Hershey with previous work experience. Traditionally, Hershey hired neophytes or promoted from within, fearing that anyone from another company might, in fact, be a spy looking to steal trade secrets. But Dearden realized that it would take experienced professionals to bring Hershey into the modern age.

His first hire was John Rawley, a marketing executive at Scott Paper. Rawley brought along his colleague Vern Tessier, a Scott Paper salesman. Together, they convinced Dearden to hire a third man, someone with advertising experience and an understanding of Madison Avenue. For Hershey, this was a monumental step, and it would require all of Dearden's finesse. The old guard at Hershey was already on edge, and word that Dearden was hiring an adman would have fired up the opposition before he even had his team on the field.

Working secretly through a headhunter, the company contacted Jack Dowd, a senior account executive at the advertising firm of Kenyon & Eckhardt. Dowd had twenty years of advertising experience and knew the ins and outs of the trade. He was well aware of Hershey's reputation and was intrigued by the prospect of working for the last advertising holdout in America.

"Everywhere you looked in Hershey you could see opportunity," said Dowd. "The company was sixty years behind the curve in advertising and sales. We were starting from ground zero."

But Mohler cautioned Dowd the day he was hired not to expect too much. "He told me Hershey still hadn't made up its mind about advertising. It seemed everybody in the world knew they were going to have to do it—except them."

Dowd's hiring was kept from the press because Dearden worried that every advertising agency in America would come calling on Hershey to try to drum up business. The company also kept the word *marketing* out of his title, calling him a products manager. But there was no question as to what he was supposed to do: prepare Hershey for the inevitable.

Dowd realized he would have to start at the most elementary level. No one at Hershey even understood what marketing was. "They thought it was what their wives did on Saturday with a shopping cart," remembers Dowd. "And that was the general impression throughout the company. They all knew what sales did; they went out and sold the stuff. And I think they had in the back of their head an image of us going to the store and buying it back again."

The broad definition of marketing is all of the steps involved in moving a product from the producer to the consumer, and advertising is just one component. Businesspeople often speak of the "four P's of marketing": product, price, package and promotion. Marketing departments are involved in everything from the creation and improvement of a product to the styling of the package, the determination of the price and the selection of distribution channels. Marketers are also responsible for developing the product promotions, like coupons in newspapers or discounts to wholesalers. And marketers work with advertising agencies to develop the product pitch.

Hershey had no one overseeing these various functions. Decisions regarding price or packaging were handled by dozens of different people with no coordination and little regard for how they might affect sales. Promotions were nonexistent, and although Hershey was busy developing new products, it had no consumer research to help it determine what people wanted to eat.

"This was very basic stuff; the ABC's of doing business," said Dowd. "But Hershey wasn't doing any of it."

Dowd found that in talking with the sales department, they didn't even understand who Hershey's customer was. "When I said *customer* I had a mental image of a kid trying to decide how to spend his nickel; a housewife pushing a cart down an aisle in the supermarket; a man grabbing a candy bar at a newsstand in the airport. Those were our customers, I told the sales force.

"But they saw the customer as the wholesaler and the corner grocer, since those were the guys they sold to. They didn't understand that just selling to them was not enough; that their job went beyond that, to reach the children and adults who were the ultimate consumers of the product."

The entire marketing process obviously needed to be revamped, but it was not alone. It seemed as though every department in Hershey was going to require a major overhaul if the company was to stay competitive. Nothing had really been touched since Milton Hershey's death—not the accounting systems, not the management practices, not the production techniques. There was just no understanding of modern business practices, remembers John Rawley. "The business was largely being run as Mr. Hershey had left it" in 1945, he said. Since that time, there had been very little pressure to change; after all the company was earning 20 percent pre-tax profits. But by the sixties, profits and sales were increasing more and more slowly. Mohler and Dearden recognized that they would have to make changes to turn Hershey around. Even so, neither had fully grasped the extent of the problems.

"Hershey couldn't have advertised if it wanted to," said Dowd. "There were no systems in place to back up the advertising if it worked. Besides, they didn't even know what products to advertise—the company just wasn't operating like a modern consumer products company."

Rawley, Dowd and Tessier began to lay the groundwork to remake Hershey in the image of Standard Brands, Nabisco or Quaker Oats, but it was slow going. The trio ran into resistance everywhere they turned.

When Rawley wanted to hire more business school graduates to join the marketing team, he went to the board to ask for permission to pay them $10,000 a year. This was 1966, and MBAs were getting at least that much. But Harold Mohler screamed: "Ten thousand dollars? I was forty-five before I made ten thousand dollars!"

After much wrangling, Rawley got the go-ahead to hire a dozen or so young, college-trained professionals. And Dowd began teaching them the basics. "I sat them down and said, 'Okay, we're going to write marketing plans.' And they just looked at me, like what? So I walked them through it."

A marketing plan listed objectives for each brand in the Hershey lineup. It asked questions like, What is the brand? What does it stand for in consumers' minds? What makes it unique? What is its sales history? What is its sales forecast? What can be done to expand the brand? By writing such plans, Dowd hoped to get Hershey to start to understand the way a consumer thinks, to approach selling from the consumers' perspective. For Hershey, this was an entirely new way of doing business.

In the past, decisions were made without such information, as John Rawley discovered when he approached a sales manager in 1965 about establishing sales objectives for the coming year. "He said, 'Oh, we can do that. That's easy to do.'"

The executive had his secretary retrieve a letter from his files, and he handed it to Rawley. Rawley read the letter in disbelief; it said simply: "Our objective for the next year is to increase sales 4 percent." That was it.

"Exactly the same letter went to every district, every region in the country," he said in horror. "The same letter had been used for eleven years, without any sales forecasting, any development of the growth or understanding of what brands were growing and what brands weren't."

The brand plans, Dowd hoped, would bring about realistic objectives, tailored specifically to each region of the country. A plan might tell the manager in Oregon to push Reese's because no one in Oregon had ever heard of Reese's, or it might tell the manager in Connecticut to push Hershey Almond because Nestlé's Crunch was beating Hershey in New England. And it would outline just what tools the salesmen should use to meet these objectives.

But to write such plans required information—lots of information about sales, about profits—and the company had always held this information very close to the vest. "Rawley had to fight like hell" to get figures, said Dowd. "The tradition of the Hershey Chocolate Corporation was that three or four people at the top had all the information and made all the decisions. It was a feudal company."

Dearden's recruits were Hershey's first middle managers. And it took quite a bit of convincing before the "lords of the manor"—as they were known to insiders—consented to share the information that Dowd and Rawley needed to do their jobs. For example, when Dowd joined Hershey, the company was manufacturing hundreds and hundreds of different items. They were making Mr. Goodbars in four-packs, in twelve-packs, in thirty-six packs; they were selling cocoa in five-ounce tins, in seven-ounce tins, in sixteen-ounce tins. "The size of the line was incredible," said Dowd. "Every time some little supermarket or distributor wanted a new pack type, the salesman would say, 'Okay, I'll see what I can do.'" The result was the most cumbersome operation Dowd had ever seen. Somebody had to take control and start rationalizing the line, but Dowd couldn't get any profit figures to help him make the calls.

"It was frustrating. I mean, here we were trying to get this behemoth under control, and they wanted me to do it without knowing the [profit] margins."

It was obvious no one before Dowd had seriously considered profits when deciding whether to produce a particular item. "Our policy was, if it's not making adequate profit—get rid of it," said Dowd. "Before, the policy was sell it; profit was not a goal."

Dowd remembers when Hershey's corporate secretary, Dick Uhrich, called him to discuss continuing a line of glass-jarred dessert toppings that was sold only in the Hershey gift shop to visitors of the factory. The company was running low on glass, and Uhrich wanted to know whether he should order more. "So I looked up the sales figures and they weren't anything to write home about, but I went up to see him and I said, 'What is the profit on these items?' And he wheeled around and opened a drawer and pulled out a very large book, thumbed through it, closed the book, put it back in the drawer, closed the drawer and said, 'Adequate.'

"And that was all I could get out of him. I didn't know whether adequate was 50 percent margin, 30 percent, 10 percent. I didn't know. How could I make a decision based on 'adequate'?"

Making matters worse, Dowd soon came to realize that the company had no information about its business beyond profit figures. The company's record keeping was rudimentary, covering only the fundamental accounting required for payroll, billing, shipping, etc. There was precious little information that would truly qualify as management information; there was no systematic budgeting, no cost accounting, no uniform inventory reports, nothing that would provide the tools needed to make basic rational decisions.

Samuel Tancredi, supervisor of Hershey's tabulating department, remembers how in the early 1960s each department was keeping its own inventory records. "And when they'd get together around the table to make decisions, they'd spend half the time arguing and trying to reconcile the figures." Tancredi began updating Hershey's record-keeping systems in 1963, installing new, more powerful IBM machines to help Hershey manage the enormous flow of numbers. And the company finally called in Arthur Andersen in 1968 to install a basic management information system. But when Dowd and Rawley started there was little information to work with.

Rawley went to Dearden to convince him that Hershey needed more data if he and Dowd were going to make any progress. He suggested investing in market share data being collected at the time by A. C. Nielsen. For a fee, Nielsen would survey stores around the country and develop a composite picture of Hershey's business. But Dearden balked at the suggestion, citing the enormous cost involved. To make the point of how critical such information was to Hershey, Rawley sent a memo to major consumer products companies across America, asking whether they purchased Nielsen data. When every survey came back yes, Rawley showed their responses to Dearden.

Hershey finally ordered the Nielsen surveys in 1967, and that May, representatives came to Hershey to present their initial findings. Mohler and Dearden were present for the meeting, along with Dowd, Rawley, Tessier and representatives of the sales staff. "Everyone was nervous," said Dowd. "We knew the picture wasn't going to be good, but we didn't know how bad it would be."

The first statistic that Nielsen presented Hershey was the percentage of products that were out of stock in stores nationwide. The number was obscenely high—30 percent.[12]

"I turned to Bill [Dearden] and said, 'Does this company realize what a disaster it is to have 30 percent out of stock?' Our products weren't even getting on the shelves! This was the worst possible scenario.

"I thought to myself, Jesus, what have I done? I'm going down with the *Titanic*."

Chapter Sixteen

THE GREAT AMERICAN CHOCOLATE BAR

HERSHEY DIDN'T ADVERTISE ITS PRODUCTS UNTIL 1970; IN THE 1990S, THE COMPANY SPENDS $200 MILLION PER YEAR TO TOUT ITS GOODS.

*I*T DISGUSTED BILL DEARDEN every time he walked into a Hershey, Pennsylvania, grocery store to find Mars candies—Snickers, M&M's, 3 Musketeers—displayed at the checkout counter, scornfully overshadowing Hershey's own products. Suddenly Mars was everywhere—in grocery stores, drugstores, vending machines, magazines, newspapers and on billboards and television. Worse still, he couldn't get that jingle, "The sweetest things on Earth come from Mars," out of his head.

Before Dowd and Rawley woke him up to the realities of retailing, he hadn't noticed any of these things. Now he saw that Hershey wasn't just in trouble, it was heading toward disaster unless drastic measures were taken. Dowd and Rawley could not do the job without help. They were going to need people who not only knew marketing but who knew the business of candy. And nobody knew the business better than the competition. Dearden knew this was radical thinking. But he saw no alternative but to raid the enemy camp.

Ever since Forrest's takeover of Chicago in 1964, Dearden had been hearing of executive disenchantment at Mars. He kept tabs on the company through Duke Vance, with whom he had developed a close relationship over the years.

"At the various conventions in the candy industry, we'd have our booths right beside each other," Dearden said, referring to Mars and Hershey. "Duke Vance, who was the president of Mars after Jim Fleming, was a great friend of mine. We knew their salespeople very well, and we worked very closely together because we were a major supplier of chocolate to them. . . . Obviously, when Forrest Mars came into the picture, he was an antagonist, and the whole approach [changed]."

When Dearden received a résumé from a Mars executive, he called Vance to check out the candidate's qualifications. Coincidentally, just weeks before, Vance had met with his top lieutenants to discuss which, if any of them, were going to stay at Mars. All but two announced intentions of leaving. So when the call came, Vance, who loathed Forrest Mars, was more than willing to help Dearden out.

"What do you think of this fellow?" Dearden asked, referring to the résumé on his desk.

"He's all right, but you don't want him. You want Bill Suhring."

"I can't afford Bill Suhring," Dearden replied. "You're paying him $35,000 a year. Even our president doesn't make that much money."

"I don't care," insisted Vance. "That's the guy you want. He's our top marketing guy, and we're all going to be fired by Forrest Mars, because he hates all of us. Why don't you try him?"

So in the winter of 1968, William Suhring, the head of marketing at Mars and the man behind the jingle, showed up at Hershey's doorstep. Larry Johns, head of Mars sales, followed soon after. Together, they introduced the aging, stately Hershey Chocolate Corp. to the cut-throat world of candy that Forrest Mars had created, where Willy Wonka is motivated by greed, rivalry, secrecy and paranoia and will do anything to get you to eat just one more of his chocolate bars.

Larry Johns learned his sales style from the masters at Procter & Gamble, selling soap in Detroit, one of their toughest markets. He spent three years with the marketing giant before joining the sales team at Hudson Pulp & Paper Corp. Before joining Mars in 1964, he worked for nine years at Armour Grocery Products. He wasn't particularly interested in working in the candy business, but the "money was unbelievable. . . . I couldn't turn it down." Hershey couldn't match Mars's salary, but the company promised Johns something he would never have at Mars—independence and a chance to be his own boss.

During his days at Mars, Johns never gave much thought to Hershey. Hershey may have seen Mars as competition, but to a Mars salesman, the feeling was not mutual. "I don't know how to say this, but we never considered Hershey competition," said Johns. "We never ran into a Hershey salesman anywhere."

As Johns got to know his sales force, he quickly discovered the reason. They were a collection of comfortable, old-time salaried employees, with little motivation and even less imagination. The average age of a district manager at Hershey was forty-seven, and the average age of a regional manager was sixty. "Procter and Gamble was half that. [Hershey] had very few college recruits. [Hershey] had very few college graduates, period."

The salesmen had no grasp of fundamentals like placing products at the height of a ten-year-old or monopolizing the candy racks with nothing but Hershey products. On one trip to the southeast region, Johns and a regional sales manager visited an A&P. There, he found Mars products prominently displayed at the checkout, right at eye level. The Hershey bars, meanwhile, were in the back of aisle ten, right next to the kitty litter. The candy bars were outdated, broken and covered in dust.

Johns returned to Hershey and demanded that Dearden fire twelve out of the fourteen regional sales managers. To his shock, Dearden refused, telling him: "They're doing what they were told to do. If they're doing it wrong, it's not their fault. After twenty years in this company you can't blame them. It's our fault." What they had been doing for twenty years, Johns learned, was going out in the field equipped with nothing but a customer list and a pad of paper.

"There was nothing in the manager's lexicon about training, motivating, compensating and spiriting salesmen."

Johns realized he would have to circumvent the archaic machinery of Hershey's higher offices and fix the company from the bottom up. He did this, first, by convincing Dearden to increase the salaries he could offer to lure savvy young men and women. Then he quickly promoted these foot soldiers up through the ranks. Next, Johns divided every district into two parts with two equal managers, one to oversee the mass merchandising—positions filled by those he had handpicked—and the other to oversee the wholesale operation.

Johns's goal was to saturate the retail market with Hershey bars the way Mars had always done with its products, so that when Hershey began to advertise, the merchandise would be on the shelves.

"The fastest way to kill a product is to advertise it and have consumers out there looking for it and not finding it," said Johns. "It was our job to get the product in the store. It was [Suhring's] job to get it out."

William Suhring, a Chicago native, was an MBA who started his career in the marketing research division of Lever Bros. He worked on Swanson chicken products back when Mrs. Swanson was still selling eggs from her farm in Omaha. He taught marketing for a while but returned to the advertising firm of Tatham-Laird in the mid-1950s. There, he consulted for Mars on a product called Mars-ettes, a cream-filled roll in caramel, mint and cherry. In 1958, Jim Fleming, then president of Mars, asked him to join the company.

Suhring spearheaded Mars's extensive promotions, including sponsorship of the popular radio program *Dr. I.Q.* He helped Mars formalize marketing studies of all of its brands, analyzing their weaknesses and strengths. He used the findings to jazz up the company's graphics and develop ads that clicked with the public. He also engineered Mars's discount program to wholesalers, which had helped ensure that Mars products were available from New York to Los Angeles. The six years he spent in Chicago, before Forrest's ascendance, had been fulfilling ones for him professionally. But after 1964, the atmosphere at Mars became unbearable. He remembered walking into Duke Vance's office and listening in on the squawk box as Duke talked to Forrest. "I heard Forrest say, 'Have you fired that son of a bitch Suhring yet?' Duke said, 'No, Mr. Mars. I haven't gotten around to that. In fact, I don't think I will. I think when Bill leaves, I'll go with him.' Mr. Mars would say something like, 'Well, that can be arranged, Vance.'"

While at Mars, Suhring had developed worst-case scenarios of what would happen if Hershey ever started to advertise. "We were concerned that if the sleeping giant ever flexed its muscle, it could cause chaos."

Now, Suhring found himself on the "other side," imagining quite different scenarios and doing whatever he could to wake the giant.

The first thing he did was work with Dowd to improve Hershey's line of products, getting rid of all the deadwood and revitalizing the images of its core products. For example, Hershey had a product called Dainties, which were baking chips just like Nestlé's. Dowd and Suhring didn't know what they were until somebody showed them the product. "Why don't you call them chips like everybody else?" Dowd asked Dearden. "Nestlé calls them chips, and they outsell us ten to one." Dowd changed the packaging and called them chocolate chips. But when Dearden saw the new package, he asked, in typical Hershey fashion, "Is it ethical to call them chips when our competitor is already calling them chips?"

Bemused, Dowd said, "You call Hershey milk chocolate, and our competitor calls it milk chocolate. I don't think it's unethical." But Dearden refused to approve the change, asking Mohler to take a look at it.

"So Harold came in and took one look at the package, and nobody had a chance to explain anything before he said, 'You're going to call them chips?' I said, 'Yes.' He said, 'Good!' And he wheeled around and left."

Suhring helped Hershey start down the advertising road, a move that had become all the more critical because Mars's sales were closing in on Hershey's. In 1966, Hershey was selling $150 million of chocolate while Mars was selling $90 million. By 1969, the companies were neck and neck.

The first step was picking an ad agency, and he and Dowd established a list of criteria: It had to be within one hundred miles of Hershey, Pennsylvania; it had to be big enough to handle a company Hershey's size; and whoever they chose had to be able to keep a secret because, as Dowd said, "We didn't see any reason why we needed to tell the whole world and have this process turn into a circus." For years the press had been speculating about whether Hershey would take the plunge into advertising, scrutinizing any and every movement inside the company.

Suhring chaired the search committee, which included Dowd, Dearden and Richard Zimmerman, who at the time was Mohler's assistant. The four men traveled to New York, meeting with four agencies in two days. Ogilvy & Mather stood out as the strongest, most knowledgeable and most aggressive candidate. In fact, the agency had handled the account of Mars, Chicago, for years, but when Forrest took over he fired them. "They were very disappointed that they had gotten the ax from Mars," said Zimmerman. "They knew why. When Forrest Mars took over he considered himself the world's smartest marketing man, and he decided they weren't doing a good enough job." Now, they were eager to get their hands back in the candy jar.

Ogilvy knew it would take their best work to convince Hershey. "We had to prove to Hershey that advertising would really pay off," said Ogilvy executive Lee Smith. "After all, every dollar they spent with us meant one dollar less for the orphans."[1]

Chairman David Ogilvy sent a team to Hershey to learn everything they could about the history of the town, the people and the factory. In early 1969, they presented their pitch to Hershey.

"It was clear they had done a lot of homework, and they really wanted our business," said Dowd. "Their presentation really blew us out of the water."

The first decision was what products to use in the initial campaign. The Hershey bar was the obvious choice, and Mohler and Dearden insisted that the Hershey Almond bar be included. But the other choices were less clear. Dowd and Johns pushed for Reese's Peanut Butter Cups because they were the company's best-seller in every market where they were introduced. The Hershey old guard resisted; Reese's was not an original Hershey product, and vanity kept them from wanting to push it. But Dowd eventually prevailed. There was a third campaign for Hershey's Instant, a product similar to Nestlé's Quik.

The goal was to develop campaigns that would appeal to young people. "The consumer had the highest respect for Hershey, [but] thought of us as stodgy and old-fashioned. . . . We wanted to balance that, accelerate things."

The campaign for Reese's was easy—to simply describe the product to the public. The result was the tag line "Two great tastes that taste great together." The commercials were built around a series of collisions. For example, in the first a construction worker falls into a manhole.

"You got peanut butter on my chocolate."

"You got chocolate in my peanut butter."

It was called the "manhole campaign"; unfortunately, everybody referred to it as the sewer campaign.

The ad for the Hershey bar was much more complicated because Ogilvy didn't want to tamper with America's nostalgic image of the product. "It's like when television first came out," said Dowd, "and people rejected certain characters because they didn't look like their radio personalities."

Calvin Miller, the creative director at Ogilvy, came up with a campaign with the famous tag line "Hershey's: the great American chocolate bar."

The Instant mix campaign had cows marching on Jefferson City, Missouri, demanding that children start drinking their milk.

They tested the ads in seven cities for six months, and the Reese's ad was so successful Dowd couldn't believe the test market numbers. "Sales of Reese's took off some 300 percent," said Dowd. "Nobody at Ogilvy had ever seen anything like it." Hershey bar sales also started moving slowly upward while sales of Instant stayed flat. Suhring recommended that Instant be dropped from the national rollout, but Mohler disagreed.

In 1970, when the ads were introduced nationwide, the response mirrored the test markets. The Instant campaign bombed, Reese's sales tripled within a year and sales of the Hershey bar rose 30 percent.

Dearden's troops were now Hershey's triumphant heroes.

"We had the tiger by the tail," said Dowd. "You could just feel the company about to take off."

But the euphoria was short-lived. Two years later, Mohler pulled the plug on the entire program.

Chapter Seventeen

HOT COCOA

THE CACAO TREE IS ONE OF
NATURE'S ODDITIES; GIANT
PODS SPROUT DIRECTLY
FROM ITS TRUNK, AND IT
BEARS FRUIT YEAR-ROUND.

*T*HE ANGER STILL shows in Jack Dowd's face when he talks about the decision to slash Hershey's advertising budget in 1972. "We were poised for a major breakthrough," he said of the months following the initial campaigns. "We could have had Mars on the run."

Instead, Hershey's sixty-year reign as king of the candy counter came to an end in the fall of 1973 when, for the first time, Mars surpassed Hershey in market share. The fact made headlines in Chicago, but nobody in Hershey even mentioned it. There were no stories in the local press, no meetings to announce the loss, no whispers over the lunch counter. It was as if they could keep it from being true so long as they didn't acknowledge it.

"It was a very difficult time for Hershey," remembers Earl Spangler, who was then plant manager. "We weren't used to being behind. Nobody knew what the future was going to be."

The disastrous decision to drop its new advertising campaigns was Hershey's reaction to a sharp, unexpected rise in cocoa and sugar prices on the world markets. For more than fifty years, Hershey had managed changes in the prices of its key ingredients by changing the weights of its bars—shrinking them as prices rose and expanding them as prices fell. The company also adjusted its wholesale prices slightly—but never enough to alter the final retail price of a nickel.

"For a long time, we believed the only option was to play with the weights," said Spangler. "We would change the weights as often as necessary to keep the price intact."

In the 1920s and 1930s, the nickel bar weighed in at a hefty 1.25 ounces. But as ingredient prices began to fluctuate wildly in the 1940s, '50s and '60s, the weight of the bar changed more than a dozen times, going as low as thirteen-sixteenths (0.8125) of an ounce by 1966. The shrinking bar brought much ridicule over the years, with the press comparing the size of a Hershey bar in the 1950s to a razor blade. A cartoonist, in a characteristic attack, depicted the Hershey directors in a meeting, with the caption: "Gentlemen, we can no longer sell a wrapper without a bar in it."

But the company ignored the criticism, believing that the nickel bar, Milton Hershey's great gift to the American populace, was sacrosanct. "The nickel bar was a Hershey institution," explained Spangler. "It was the lifeblood of the company."

As plant manager, it was Earl Spangler's job to keep on top of the ever-changing bar sizes. When the weight needed to be altered, he would order workers to retrofit the manufacturing lines with new bar molds and reload the wrapping machines with new bar labels. It was a time-consuming and costly process, although over the years it became easier as Hershey developed a stock of molds to accommodate the various sizes. The company tried not to change the size more than once a year, but at times even that was difficult.

"The pressure on the ingredient side was enormous in the sixties," remembers Spangler. "It seemed every time I turned around, there we were changing the molds."

By 1968, the Hershey bar was almost half its original size, and so small that even Hershey executives were embarrassed by it—the bars had shrunk to just eleven-sixteenths, or 0.6875, of an ounce.

The Hershey bar was "laughable," said candy bar historian Ray Broekel. "Sitting next to everybody else, it looked tiny."

"It got to the point where there was nothing more we could do," acknowledged Spangler. "We were no longer offering the consumer value for their money."

On November 24, 1969, Harold Mohler made the historic announcement that Hershey was abandoning the nickel bar, a constant of the candy business since its introduction in 1900. From now on, the standard Hershey bar would sell for a dime, and in exchange for the price increase, Hershey would boost the weight of its bar to 1.25 ounces.[1]

But consumers focused on the doubling of the price, and seemed unmoved by the increase in weight. That's because other candy makers —who had raised their prices to a dime much earlier—had candy bars that were still much larger than Hershey's. They could afford to offer larger portions because chocolate was not their main ingredient. A Milky Way, for example, contains less than half the chocolate of a solid Hershey bar. It is made mostly of nougat, which is nothing more than sugar, eggs, and air—all far less expensive ingredients.

"We couldn't win," said Hershey secretary Richard Uhrich. "In the consumer's mind, the Hershey bar was a nickel. When we raised the price to a dime, all hell broke loose."

It was the reaction the company had always feared. In the nine months following the price increase, sales of Hershey bars fell 30 percent. In the end, Hershey's policy of holding prices stable had backfired. If Hershey had maintained the weight of its bars, gradually increasing prices over the years, consumers might have accepted another penny or two markup. But the price had been constant for so long, consumers viewed it as an entitlement. Even today, there are those who remember wistfully the days of the nickel bar. Its passing seemed to many to mark the end of an era. Gone were the stability, security and prosperity of the post-war years.

The drop-off in sales in 1969 made Hershey's venture into advertising all the more critical. "We had to regain that lost ground," remembers Dowd. "The only way to do it was to start pushing our products like everybody else."

But just after the advertising campaign got under way, President Nixon announced the imposition of the nation's first peacetime wage and price controls, aimed at taming the unprecedented 4 percent inflation rate. The new regulations, which required food companies to get government approval for any change in the price or size of products, wreaked havoc on Hershey and other candy makers. As cocoa and sugar prices started to climb in the early seventies, there was little Hershey could do to cover its increasing costs.

"It was a nightmare," said Uhrich. "Getting permission to change the size of the bar required so much bureaucratic red tape. We almost couldn't do business."

Mohler was terrified that with Hershey hamstrung, the company would report its first-ever annual loss—and that was unthinkable. Hershey profits translated into dividends for the Trust, providing food, shelter and education for the hundreds of orphans at the Hershey Industrial School. Hershey's executives always knew that the company had a nobler mission than simply maximizing shareholder wealth, and with that mission came an added level of responsibility.

Mohler's solution was to preserve profits by slashing "discretionary" spending, like the company's new advertising budget. Although Mohler had been supportive of the company's new emphasis on marketing, he felt backed into a corner. The way he saw it, the company was about to spend tens of millions of dollars on promotions that had no guarantee of success. He could not bring himself to justify such spending when Hershey's margins were being squeezed so tightly. Moreover, he believed that advertising, while necessary, was not urgent. The campaigns canceled in 1972 could always be relaunched in better times.

The decision was handed down to Dearden unilaterally. And though Dearden knew it was a mistake, he never shared his misgivings with his staff, believing that it was his responsibility to support the decisions of his CEO. A rift at the top would have dire consequences for the morale of the new management team they had worked so hard to put into place. The announcement would be hard enough as it was.

Dearden called Suhring into his office to break the news, directing him to call a special meeting at which Suhring would inform the rest of the team. But Suhring balked, telling Dearden he could not relay such a decision.

"Advertising . . . is no different than putting a wrapper on a product," said Suhring. "It is a need. . . . You can't turn an advertising spigot on and off."

Suhring feared that every time there was some "extraordinary" circumstance, Hershey would look to advertising to make cuts—a prescription for disaster. Moreover, Suhring and his team had devoted every day of the past year to putting together an advertising strategy that could help turn Hershey's fortunes around. And now, just when their work was needed the most, the company was shelving the program. It seemed lunatic, and he even considered quitting in protest.

But as painful as it was, Suhring called the marketing and sales teams together in the spring of 1972 to make the announcement that Hershey would halt all advertising spending until further notice.

Looking back, he said grimly: "That was probably the blackest day of my entire work career."

Every candy company finds itself at the mercy of commodity pricing to some extent. The question is how to deal with the uncertainties when you depend on ingredients whose prices are about as predictable as the weather. It is not uncommon for cocoa bean prices to double or halve in a matter of months. In 1948, for example, the price of cocoa reached 46 cents per pound. The following year it averaged less than 22 cents, sinking as low as 17 cents per pound at one point. Sugar is also subject to constant price changes, although it is not quite as volatile as cocoa. (In the United States, the market for sugar is stabilized somewhat by government price supports. But on the world market, the price of sugar has continued to fluctuate.)

Commodities prices are determined much the way stock prices are, with buyers and sellers gathering through an exchange to bid on contracts based on their individual expectations. In the case of commodities, the buyers and sellers are end users (like Mars and Hershey), processors (companies that take raw beans and turn them into cocoa butter, powder and cake), speculators and representatives of cocoa-growing countries. In the United States, this trading takes place in the pits of the Coffee, Sugar & Cocoa Exchange in New York's financial district. The floor is a frenzied swirl of activity, with traders barking out buy-and-sell bids like auctioneers at a used-car sale. It is not a place for novices. The market is dominated by a handful of major players—Mars, Nestlé, Hershey and about a dozen or so other companies that deal in enormous quantities of beans and can move prices with a single bid. In a matter of seconds, millions of dollars are won or lost as these players react to the latest rumors of political instability in Nigeria or crop disease in Malaysia.

The candy bars displayed so alluringly on grocers' shelves begin their journey to America in the sweltering, steamy climates of Third World countries. Cocoa is grown only in a small band of tropical nations located within 20 degrees north and south of the equator. The biggest cocoa producers today are the Ivory Coast, Brazil, Ghana and Indonesia.[2] Thirty years ago, Ghana and Nigeria were the world's biggest producers, but disease and civil unrest have slashed their cocoa output substantially. The Ivory Coast now grows more than one-third of the world's cocoa beans, while Malaysia and Indonesia have recently become significant producers.[3]

Planted by villagers on small farms in West Africa, and on plantations by wealthy land barons in most of the rest of the world, cocoa is as important to the economies of these countries as oil is to the Middle East. On any given day in the port of Abidjan in the Ivory Coast, thousands of burlap sacks, each filled with 200 pounds of beans, await passage to the United States and Europe, where they will be transformed into rivers of chocolate. Cacao production accounts for half of the Ivory Coast's exports,[4] although the villagers who actually raise the cacao on one- and two-acre plots carved out of the jungle barely eke out a living. They have never tasted chocolate or seen a Hershey bar wrapper; they haven't the vaguest idea that the beans they sweat to bring to market are transformed in the industrialized world into frivolous indulgences that sell for 50 cents apiece. To them, cacao cultivation represents shelter and clothing. The Ivorian government estimates that half of the country's 14 million people live directly or indirectly on cacao production. The slightest drop in world demand sends this nation's economy reeling.

In the sparse, primitive villages that are scattered throughout the Ivorian breadbasket, the cacao tree grows amid the canopy of the rain forest. The groves are like the woods of fairy tales, shadowed and mysterious. Moisture drips from every leaf and branch, and the layer of mulch that litters the ground smells steamy and organic. Moss hangs everywhere, thick and verdant, and insects of all kinds swarm around the fragrant growth.

Against this backdrop, the cacao tree's lichen-spotted trunk and dark, twisted branches are rendered fairly inconspicuous. But it is the strange-looking, glistening fruit that gives away its presence and pulls you in for a closer look. Growing directly from the trunk, the football-sized cacao pods protrude like giant wax fruit in brilliant green, yellow, red, crimson and purple. Pools of sunlight filter through the large, flat leaves of the trees, illuminating the pods and making them shine.

The tree's exotic look is enhanced by the fleshy, orchidlike flowers that dot the trunk and the mature branches. Like the pods, the star-shaped flowers range in color from snow white to rosy pink, yellow and fiery red. Thousands of these flowers bloom on each tree annually, although only a small percentage ever fruits. It takes four to six months before a fertilized flower becomes a ripe pod. Beginning with a slightly elliptical form, the young fruit resembles a small cucumber. A fully grown pod is six to ten inches long and three to four inches thick at the center, with ridges like an acorn squash. Its skin is covered with warts and its husk is thick and woody.

The trees bear fruit year-round, although for cyclical weather reasons, two crops each year are recognized as standard. The "winter" or main crop is the larger of the two, harvested between December and March. Villagers cut the mature pods from the trees by hand, using a machete. It is a delicate task, with care taken not to bruise the trunk. The cacao tree is extraordinarily sensitive, known to botanists as the prima donna of the plant world. It grows best in low-lying areas, from 100 to 1,000 feet above sea level, and requires a minimum of forty inches of rain per year. Yet the weather must also be relatively static—heavy rains and winds can easily damage the pods. The soil requirements for the trees are also very specific; growth will be stunted if there is too much or too little nitrogen, or if the soil is too acidic or lacking other essential minerals.

Pests and diseases also pose a constant threat to the crop. The fungus known as witches'-broom has devastated cacao production in South America and the Caribbean Islands in recent years. It weakens old trees and kills young ones, causing losses of up to 50 percent of the harvest. Black pod disease, another fungal infection caused by too much rain and cool weather, has ravaged plantings in Africa, and is estimated to reduce annual worldwide production by 10 to 30 percent.[5] Black pod spreads at alarming speeds and can wipe out the entire cacao production of a country in just one season if it is not quickly contained. The same is true for the capsid bug, which attacks leaves, pods, young shoots and roots. Damage by the capsid in West Africa has been so severe that a hard-hit area is said to have been "blasted." Monkeys, squirrels, rats, parrots and woodpeckers are also enemies of the cacao tree, eating at pods and damaging tender plantings.

Well aware of the crop's vulnerabilities and of the impact a blight will have on the price of cocoa beans, chocolate manufacturers have led a massive effort to better understand cacao husbandry and disease. Hershey, for example, ran its own experimental plantation in Belize, known as Hummingbird Hershey Ltd., to study the effects of various pesticides and growing techniques on the output of the crop.[6] Mars runs a similar facility in the cocoa-growing region of Brazil, called the M&M/Mars

Almirante Center for Cocoa Studies. Scientists at the center are working furiously to help Brazilians contain an outbreak of witches'-broom that has reduced production from 400,000 tons to 220,000 tons since 1987 and dropped Brazil from first to third place among cocoa-growing countries.[7]

In March 1998, representatives from Cadbury, Nestlé, Mars and Hershey met with conservation groups at the Smithsonian Tropical Research Institute in Panama to discuss strategies for dealing with crop diseases like witches'-broom. The conference focused on new methods of sustainable cocoa farming, including shifting cocoa growing from large plantations to smaller farms within the rain forest. Recent studies suggest that *Theobroma cacao,* when grown in the shade of larger trees, requires fewer pesticides and is better protected from the devastating effects of sun, pests and fungal epidemics.

The Panama conference gave rise to a front-page story in *The New York Times* that direly predicted a shortage of chocolate in the near future. "Chocoholics Take Note: Beloved Bean in Peril," blared the *Times* headline. Hundreds of journalists followed the newspaper's lead, reporting that crop disease could drastically reduce chocolate supplies, and a national "chocolate scare" ensued.

But the press reports vastly overstated the problem. Consumption has outstripped supply by about 1 percent annually in recent years. But so far, large stockpiles of cocoa beans have been able to keep the price of chocolate steady. And the manufacturers are confident they can erase this deficit over the next ten years by improving production techniques.

"There isn't going to be any shortage," said Susan Smith of the Chocolate Manufacturers Association. "There's a lot of time to rectify the problem."

Still, disease has already wreaked havoc on economies like Brazil's. The world price for cocoa beans has declined from a high of over $5,500 per ton in the 1970s to less than $1,000 per ton today, largely due to a greater number of producers. The price drop, coming at the same time as Brazil's collapse in production, has cut the country's cocoa export earnings from more than $1 billion per year in the early 1980s to just one-fifth that level today. The effect has been calamitous.

The disease has displaced hundreds of thousands of workers who made their living in the nation's cacao groves, which are centered in the coastal state of Bahia. On the outskirts of Ilhéus, the region's main city, half of the cocoa-processing plants are idle, and estate mansions, once brimming with servants and riches, now sit empty amid uncultivated fields.

"The landowners are just letting the weeds take over their land," laments João Alves da Silva, who had worked in the now-abandoned cacao fields to support his five children.[8] The blight has left a tragic situation; more than 150,000 workers have been laid off by the plantations. Their families live in villages of plastic tents perched on the side of the road, and even if the outbreak of witches'-broom ultimately can be controlled, it is unclear how much their fortunes will improve. By then, there may not be a cacao tree left in Bahia.

If the local effect has been devastating, Mars scientists fear that the fungus plaguing Brazil could jump continents to Africa and Asia, threatening worldwide production. The company sees itself in the unique position of being able to fund and conduct the type of high-level, extensive research needed to prevent further catastrophe.

"What we're trying to do is something that's never really been done before, and that is a major resurrection of a significant growing region, some 600,000 hectares," said Martin Aitken, director of Mars's facility.[9]

There is a long history of chocolate manufacturers working to improve cultivation techniques. The practice was started by British confectioners at a time when many of the major cocoa-producing nations were British colonies. Indeed, cocoa production was introduced to most of these nations by the British, French and Dutch governments at the behest of their confectionery industries. The British established research facilities in Trinidad, Ghana (formerly the Gold Coast), Nigeria and Cameroon, among other places. This tradition has since been adopted by U.S. manufacturers, working under the aegis of the Chocolate Manufacturers Association and the American Cocoa Research Institute (ACRI).

The ACRI engages in a wide range of scientific study on behalf of the major players in the industry, which provide all of its funding. Its researchers have worked hard to develop means of dealing with all of the problems that beset *Theobroma cacao*. Present techniques for protecting and nurturing the crop rely on the proper application of a variety of pesticides, fungicides and fertilizers. But even where these measures are technically possible, many small cocoa growers lack the understanding or ability to carry them out properly. These chemicals are also very expensive, and many farmers are unwilling or unable to spend the money they require.

Hans Scheu, who oversaw the purchasing of beans for Nestlé

THE CHOCOLATE BAR ON THE GROCER'S SHELF BEGINS WITH A MACHETE'S SLICE IN THE TROPICS.

between 1962 and 1975, remembers how difficult it was to get farmers to adopt modern agricultural practices. "We spent millions of dollars in outreach in West Africa," he said. "But the money made no difference. No matter how many times we tried to tell the farmers how to spray and when to spray, we'd come back and there would still be no pesticides."

In any case, these modern growing techniques have come under increasing attack in recent years. After decades of chemical spraying, cocoa trees have become more and more vulnerable to disease and infestation, and growers on large plantations are finding it more and more difficult to maintain their yields. The use of chemicals has also drawn criticism from environmentalists, who charge that cocoa is being cultivated with irresponsible and unsustainable methods.

The Committee for a Safe and Moral Food, a new environmental advocacy group, has accused cocoa producers of destroying millions of acres of rain forest in the Ivory Coast, Indonesia and Brazil to make way for their crops. Dan Bradfield, executive director of the Committee, notes that cocoa production is "roaring toward a world production record" and suggests that all the talk about a cocoa shortage is merely a hoax by producers to cover up their "long record of environmental exploitation and destruction."

Ironically, cocoa is one of the few cash crops that can be grown within the rain forest, providing revenue and jobs in an environmentally friendly way. This fact has led to a growing number of "organic" chocolate products from companies such as Cloud Nine, Rapunzel and Newman's Own, which promote their products as healthier, eco-friendly alternatives to traditional chocolates.

The ACRI is also working to develop more sustainable means of cocoa cultivation. The group is trying to identify and enhance disease-resistant cacao trees. Other ongoing projects in this area include genetic engineering of trees to improve the durability, yield and flavor of the beans; grafting techniques to rapidly copy superior trees for quick dissemination; pollination programs to increase the number of flowers on each tree that develop into pods; and maintaining an extensive inventory of natural and cultivated strains to preserve the genetic diversity of the species.

Despite such efforts, cocoa farming remains a rather rudimentary operation in most of the world. After the pods have been cut down from the trees, the farmers slice them open with their machetes and scoop out the contents onto banana leaves or woven mats. The pods are filled with a thick, white mucilaginous pulp. It is believed that the pulp—which has a sweet-and-sour taste—is what first attracted animals and humans to the tree. South Americans still make a fermented drink from the pulp, which is considered a delicacy.

Embedded in the pulp are the treasured beans, each about the size of an almond. They vary in color from white to dark purple, depending on the variety and flavor. There are forty to fifty beans per pod, and it takes more than 350 beans to make a single pound of chocolate.[10] But fresh from the pod, the beans are far from being ready for market. First, they must be fermented and dried—a process critical to bringing out the chocolate flavor.

The beans and the pulp are dumped into wooden boxes, covered with leaves and left to sit for several days. During this time, microbes develop and feed on the pulp, converting it to alcohol. As the fermentation process continues, the beans change in color and flavor, losing much of their bitterness and beginning to take on the familiar taste of chocolate. Next, the beans are dried in the sun or sometimes in mechanical dryers, industrial-sized ovens that slowly bake the beans until their moisture content is less than 7 percent. Finally, the beans are bagged in burlap sacks, and in West Africa, they are largely sold to government-run marketing boards, relics of colonial rule.

The boards control the entire cocoa crop, arranging for its shipment and export to producing countries. Although the boards receive market price for their beans, they pay farmers only a fraction of what they earn, often less than half the world price. The rest is kept in the government's coffers.

More than 80 percent of the annual worldwide harvest—2.5 million tons of beans in 1997—is purchased by just a dozen or so companies.[11] In addition to the Marses and Hersheys of the world, there are giant food processors like Archer Daniels Midland and Cargill that convert beans into products used by the broader food industry. These giant purchasers play a cat-and-mouse game with one another, trying to minimize the price they pay on the commodities exchanges in London and New York. They have turned the purchase of beans into a cloak-and-dagger enterprise, depending on high-tech wizardry, intelligence reports and nerves of steel.

Each company guards its positions and intentions with the utmost care, the way the Pentagon guards its contingency plans. Hans Scheu, president of the Cocoa Merchants Association, recalls his days as a buyer for Nestlé, and still has trouble bringing himself to discuss any details of his purchases in the 1960s and 1970s. "I guess I can tell you now, [we bought] about sixty or seventy thousand tons," he said. Then, smiling sheepishly, he paused and added, "Actually, we bought a lot more than that. But it was a big secret. You don't go around telling everybody the quantities you buy because it just shows your vulnerability. There's a whole industry out there to make guesses at what Nestlé [and the other candy makers] are doing. But they can't get it accurate, the exact amount is a real trade secret."

A former Hershey cocoa buyer went even further, admitting that Hershey sometimes sold off its cocoa holdings to trigger a decline in the market. But the market didn't always respond to such tactics. After all, the other players in the market are no naifs. In fact, this trader alleged, the markets were being churned by a devious group of "high-rolling cocoa bean gnomes" based in Switzerland, Liechtenstein, Lebanon and the United Arab Emirates.

Whatever the truth of that claim, commodities trading has always been a dangerous game, a fact Milton Hershey learned early on. In 1936, Hershey watched the price of beans begin to climb, from 5.4 cents per pound to 6 cents, then 7. Concerned that his costs would sky-rocket, he dove into the market, purchasing enormous quantities of beans as the price continued to rise. By early 1937, when cocoa beans reached 13 cents a pound, his decision looked like a stroke of genius. But then the market turned.

As prices tumbled, Hershey scrambled to save his investment. He jumped into the market again, ordering his traders to buy more and more and more, hoping his purchases would stabilize the market price. As the year wore on, Hershey's stockpiles of beans grew as his bank accounts shrank. Desperate to keep his position alive, he turned to the banks, borrowing $17 million—an outrageous amount, equal to half a year of sales—to finance his speculation.

For a brief moment, it seemed Hershey had staved off disaster. But then rumors started swirling in the cocoa pits that the only thing propping up the price was Hershey's willingness to buy and store huge quantities of beans. Overnight, inventories poured onto the market and speculators sold short, betting he could not hold off a price collapse much longer. The market broke, and by the time it was over, cocoa bean prices had plunged to 4.89 cents per pound. Hershey's losses were staggering, at least on paper.

In the end, the huge inventory of beans turned into a major boon for the company. When World War II caused supplies to collapse and prices to soar, Hershey had a tremendous reserve on which to draw, giving the company the means to maintain production despite wartime shortages. But not all of Hershey's speculations had such happy endings.

In the 1920s, Hershey came close to losing the company, though this time the villain was sugar. During World War I, as sugar prices rose, Hershey launched his Cuban sugar operations, hoping to insulate himself from future market shortages. But by 1920, his mills were still not producing enough sugar to satisfy the company's needs. The price of sugar was rising once again, and Hershey began an earnest study of graphs and charts of statistics on the sugar market's fluctuations. He convinced himself that prices would keep climbing and by August, he was buying large quantities on credit, at prices as high as 22 cents per pound. When a trader offered him 23 cents for his contracts, he declined, holding out for 25.

But the market never reached that high. As the speculative bubble burst, Hershey was forced to close out his contracts for a paltry 2 cents. The losses were so massive that Hershey had to mortgage the company to the National City Bank. The bank imposed a manager who took charge of both the Pennsylvania and Cuban enterprises until 1922, when Hershey had recovered enough to refinance his debt.

At a dinner party years later, when a guest quoted some statistics to make a point, Hershey rejoined: "Statistics hell! Statistics lost me seven million dollars in seven days."

The company has since taken a more conservative approach to the commodities markets. Hershey's former secretary, who oversaw the company's bean purchases in the 1970s, said Hershey no longer speculates. "Mr. Hershey could have done that initially, when he owned the whole company," said Uhrich. "But not when they have stockholders and all that; they can't do that." Today, the company insists, it uses the commodities markets strictly to hedge its risks.

Twice a week, Hershey's Cocoa Bean Committee meets to determine how Hershey should react to the latest market developments. The committee consists of the company's top managers and commodities specialists, who keep in constant contact with Hershey's commodities buyers in New York. It is the committee's job to insulate Hershey as much as possible from the markets' constant volatility, and it does this largely through a risk-management technique known as hedging—the use of financial contracts to try to eliminate future gains or losses.

For example, by purchasing today the right to have beans delivered in the future—a "futures contract"—the company can lock in the current price, protecting itself from the threat of price increases. Conversely, if Hershey expects prices to drop in the future, it can sell its futures contracts. Another financial instrument Hershey can use is the "option," the right to buy or sell a commodity at a given price for a fixed period of time. A call option gives Hershey the right to purchase beans in the future at a price set today, protecting it from price increases. A put option gives Hershey the right to sell beans in the future at a price set today, protecting it from price decreases.

Ultimately, hedging cannot fully protect a company the size of Hershey, which purchases hundreds of millions of pounds of raw ingredients each year. If cocoa or sugar crops fail, world prices invariably rise and Hershey feels the pinch. But by combining these techniques, Hershey tries to stabilize the cost of its ingredients.

In contrast, Mars views the volatility of the commodities markets as an opportunity rather than a threat. Former Mars executives say the company earns as much money trading futures as it does selling candy and pet food. The company has an entire division devoted exclusively to analyzing the markets and predicting future price movements.

"Mars is very aggressive," said a former top executive. "They play the markets to win, not like other companies. They are very sophisticated, very high-tech. . . . [Forrest Sr.] prided himself in his understanding of the markets, and he made Mars tops when it came to working the numbers."

Forrest's approach grew out of his own early failures. Like Milton Hershey, Forrest gambled on cocoa futures in the 1930s and "nearly lost [his] shirt." He vowed that, thereafter, he would beat the markets by knowing more, and knowing it sooner, than anyone else. He hired "cocoa spies"—as they are known in the trade—to travel through Africa and South America, inspecting the crops and trading gossip with brokers and growers. And he employed scientists to study the way weather, plagues and pests affected the growth of the trees to help him make more accurate predictions.

In the 1960s, a Mars scientist named John Baker devised a very accurate method for counting the cocoa pods on trees in a few plantations and extrapolating that data to make predictions for the entire crop. In the days before satellite technology and computer simulation, his technique gave Mars an invaluable edge over the rest of the players.

Today, Mars has continued that tradition by staying at least two steps ahead of everyone else in the business. The company pioneered the practice of renting satellite time to watch the world's weather patterns. Mars also employs some of the most skilled statisticians in the world to help it predict the combined effects of weather, economic trends, consumption patterns, political developments and myriad other factors on cocoa, sugar and peanut prices. It has a staff of traders who do nothing but watch the markets, looking for opportunities to turn price movements into company profits.

On a visit by this author to Mars's headquarters in McLean, company officials shared some of their satellite images and spoke proudly of the computer models they had developed to forecast the quality and size of upcoming harvests. Though it seemed a highly uncharacteristic display of corporate confidences, Mars officials couldn't help but brag, knowing that I would not learn enough to be of use to the competition. At the time of my visit, the company was following the possibility of flooding in Georgia that would threaten the upcoming peanut crop. Acting on the latest information, the company had been shoring up its position.

Mars's scientists visit McLean once a month to share the latest data and forecasts with the Mars brothers and their top associates. Based on their presentations, the company develops its long-range strategy.

If Mars cannot get the information it needs on its own, it is not beyond asking the federal government for help. In 1981, Mars turned to the CIA for information about the cocoa and chocolate industry in the Soviet Union and Eastern Europe. In response to Mars's inquiry, the agency went against its own policies and prepared a special new report, entitled "Soviet Exports and Imports with Selected Commodities, 1970–79." The selected commodities were cocoa beans, cocoa butter and cocoa liquor.

In 1985, a reporter discovered this unusual exchange, and wrote a scathing article for *The Nation*, revealing the details of the special treatment Mars received and claiming that CIA director William Casey had personally ordered his staff to help the company with the information it was seeking. A former Mars employee explained that Forrest and Casey were friends.[12]

*M*ars's aggressive tactics have paid off handsomely over the decades. While the run-up in ingredient costs in the early 1970s led Hershey to run scared, pulling its nascent advertising, the wildly fluctuating cocoa and sugar markets gave Mars an opening to go for the jugular. With its commodities expertise—and the fact that its bars are made with cheaper ingredients than Hershey's—Mars was able to absorb the increased costs in a way Hershey could not. Instead of retreating, Mars pressed the attack, boosting its advertising spending and pushing Hershey to the back of the candy aisle.

This stunning offensive was the brainchild of John and Forrest Jr.— their first bold move after being handed the reins of the company their father had so brilliantly built.

MARS ATTACKS

Chapter Eighteen

OHN MARS NEVER knew what he wanted to do with his life. Growing up in the Mars household, the only thing he was sure about was that he would have to get a job. Though his father was one of the wealthiest men in America, John and his siblings knew nothing of riches growing up. There were no Lamborghinis in the Mars driveway, no kidney-shaped pools in their backyard and no servants in their home. In Forrest Mars's house, no one got anything he or she didn't work for. The Old Man ran his family the same way he ran his businesses. There were no free rides, no shortcuts and no excuses for failure.

Life with Forrest was one long lesson in perfection. If Forrest loved his children, he showed it by critiquing them at every turn. He never told his children he was proud of them. He never praised them or gave them credit for their accomplishments. And he rarely showed them affection.

Anything less than one hundred on a test, or, God forbid, a B on a report card, was met with scorn. As a child, Jacqueline fell in love with horseback riding. But when she didn't place first in a dressage competition, Forrest took her horse away. He was even tougher on his sons. John and Forrest Jr. could show no sign of weakness or emotion. And all of the children were expected to be unfailingly polite and perfectly obedient.

Forrest's approach to fatherhood is best captured in the scenes that took place night after night at the Mars dinner table. He turned meals into inquisitions, mercilessly cross-examining his three children about their schoolwork, friends, pastimes—every aspect of their lives. He would test them with logic problems, pose insoluble riddles, taunting and pushing them to prove themselves to him. To this day, John, Forrest Jr. and Jackie view mealtime as an ordeal. "The Mars children have a terrible time with food," said one intimate acquaintance. "They are all yo-yo dieters, they never sit down for a meal. They have awful recollections surrounding food and their father."

Friends say the brothers were relieved when Forrest packed them off to the Hotchkiss School, a prep school where they spent much of their youth. But even at Hotchkiss, the Mars offspring were haunted by their exacting father. He kept close tabs on their performance, threatening to disinherit them if they didn't live up to his expectations.

Moreover, their father's frugality was a constant source of embarrassment. While their wealthy classmates had plenty of spending money, fancy clothes and society lifestyles, the Mars boys lived like paupers. As one of their classmates recalls: "Nobody knew who Forrest [Jr.] was. You certainly couldn't tell from looking at him that his father and mother were wealthy. I used to think he was here on scholarship."

But Forrest's severity was not without purpose. Forrest had seen too many rich boys squandering their wealth during his days at Yale in the 1920s, and he vowed that his children would never follow that path. For all of his money, Forrest loved to tell his sons, "There is nothing like being broke." Forrest never stopped reminding his children that he had come from nothing, a poor boy in the backwoods of Saskatchewan. Like a broken record, he endlessly lectured them on how he had earned his way in life—the scholarship to Berkeley, his first job in the cafeteria, selling ties to the boys at Yale. He had earned his rewards through hard work and unwavering determination.

Forrest wanted his children to do the same, to forgo the trappings of wealth and the idleness that comfort and contentment can bring. And he succeeded. Today, the mere suggestion that John or his older brother could have lived a leisurely life is met with puzzlement by family members. "If you've figured out a way to make a living without working, I'd certainly like to know," John asked me, matter-of-factly.

Neither John nor Forrest Jr. was eager to enter their father's business, to work under his constant shadow and endure his unending criticism. But in the end they had little choice; so long as they were going to have to work, they might as well work for a company that they could one day own.

For Jackie, the story was slightly different. Friends say that although Jackie is extremely bright and capable, she was never encouraged to play an active role in Mars, though she owns one-third of the business, just like her brothers. It is only in recent years that she has joined the management team, taking the title of executive vice president in addition to her post as director. She spends her time looking after the company's marketing activities and helping set the direction for new products.

John and his brother are co-presidents, dividing responsibilities along lines of interest. Less outgoing than Forrest Jr., John is often described as the chief decision maker—the brains of Mars—and credited with leading the company's push toward global supremacy.

John says he decided to major in industrial engineering at Yale not because it was his father's major, but because "that was the only degree that didn't require writing a thesis." After serving in the U.S. Army from 1956 to 1958, he took his marching orders from his dad. His first assignment from Mars was to start a pet food company in Australia.

"Somebody handed me a plane ticket and said, 'Hey, that's what you do. You go to Australia,'" he recalled of his first days on the job. "I didn't go with anything. A ticket—a one-way ticket. And my wife turned up a couple of weeks later." To this day, one of his responsibilities is to oversee the company's pet food operations worldwide.

The route of Forrest Jr.—who oversees the candies division—wasn't so direct. A member of the Yale class of 1953, he majored in economics, and then served as a finance officer in the army. At the end of his tour, he joined the accounting firm of Price Waterhouse in New York, which had long done business with the family. In 1955, he married Virginia Mae Cretella, the daughter of a congressman from New Haven, Connecticut. They lived in New York for years before he finally launched his career with Mars.

Like his father before him, Forrest Jr. started out by building a business virtually from scratch. His first assignment, in 1960, was to oversee the opening of Mars's new headquarters—two rooms above a dress shop—on Fifteenth Street in downtown Washington. (Forrest Sr. chose to relocate to D.C. for several reasons: It was the capital, it had a new airport and it was close to his farm in The Plains, Virginia, where he loved to go fox hunting.) But a year later, he was dispatched to Veghel, in the Netherlands, where he built a new candy factory to serve the European continent.

Theo Leenders, who worked at the Veghel plant in those early days and is now a company manager, says Forrest Jr. would spend all night in the factory trying to impress the importance of quality and efficiency on his workers. "There they are, standing there in the middle of the night, and the boss comes along to chitchat. That really said something," recalls Leenders.

But no amount of hard work seemed to please Forrest Sr.

Never one to mince words, he would lash out in anger whenever he found the slightest flaw in either son's performance. These degrading scenes often took place in front of other executives, some of whom still retain vivid memories of Forrest Sr.'s tirades. "He was terrible to them," says one longtime associate. "He would shout and call them dumb and stupid. He would harangue them over the smallest detail. Everyone in the room would fall silent, and you could hear him screaming all the way into the factory. It was horribly embarrassing."

In 1961, three days before it was scheduled to open, the Veghel plant caught fire and burned to the ground. When Forrest Sr. heard the news, he flew into a rage. Although observers said the fire was beyond his son's control, Forrest Sr. demanded apologies over and over again. Forrest Jr. spent the next nine months rebuilding.

John received his own lessons in humility. Once, at a meeting of advertising executives in West Germany, Forrest Sr. ordered his younger son—who was twenty-nine at the time—to get down on his knees and pray for the company. John quietly obeyed, remaining on the floor for nearly an hour as the executives discussed the company's marketing strategy.

Former Mars associates say these experiences have haunted the brothers for years. It's taboo, they say, to even mention The Old Man in their presence. But Stegemann tells a different story. Forrest Mars, Sr., he says, was preparing his company for the future, and in the end he gave his sons the most generous gift he could: In the fall of 1973, he turned ownership of Mars, Inc., over to his children. It was a remarkable step.

One of the unmistakable traits of most successful entrepreneurs is a possessiveness, an insatiable need for control. The compulsions that bring men like Forrest Mars to the top, however, are too often also their undoing. Many a family dynasty has been wrecked by a domineering patriarch unable to pass the baton to the next generation. But Forrest Mars never wanted control for control's sake. Like Milton Hershey, Forrest was a dreamer, never one to be tied down to the mundane toil of running a company. Now that he had subdued his father's company and established Mars as a dominant power in the industry, he was ready for new conquests. And so he gave away his stock, resigned his offices and simply walked away.

"He recognized that as long as he was around, they could never take control," Stegemann said, "I don't think there are many people of his status around the world that have ever done that—said, 'Here's the end of the pool. I gotta kick you in it. Good-bye. I taught you how to swim.'"

*R*unaway inflation. Oil embargoes. Price controls. This was the terrain of the 1970s, across which John and Forrest Jr. had to negotiate their newly acquired company.

The stagflation of the 1970s was brutal for many businesses, but there were troubles unique to the candy industry. Consumption of candy was up, but cocoa crops were down, driving the price of chocolate steadily upward. While every candy maker was feeling the crunch, what was trouble for some firms was opportunity for others.

When the Mars brothers heard that Hershey had canceled all of its advertising, they knew they had been handed a gift. It had always been their father's goal to be the No. 1 candy maker in America, and Hershey had given the brothers the chance to accomplish what their father never had. Revenues were down, and they were new at the helm, but the brothers agreed to take a calculated risk. With Hershey in retreat, Mars would go after the U.S. market as forcefully as it could. In 1972, the brothers ordered a massive increase in advertising and promotions, determined to wrest sales from Hershey no matter what the cost.

The marketing blitz was backed up by the most aggressive sales force in the industry. They were a sophisticated, determined and motivated crew, famous in the candy industry for their gutsy brand of retail warfare. For John Strong, the head of Mars's West Coast region, those days were a dream, a whirlwind of energy and excitement. Strong called in his "warriors," as he referred to them, and ordered them to press the attack; for the next three years, Strong's men pushed Mars candy into every possible outlet while pushing Hershey out.

"We were like armed thugs out there," Strong said. "We had Hershey running scared."

Strong's men traveled from store to store across Washington, Oregon and California, slashing open case after case of candy bars and piling them up onto the shelves as fast as their box cutters could fly.

"We were brash. We were tigers," Strong remembered, "kicking them around and pressing and pushing and stacking and whacking."

Strong and his men rarely came across Hershey reps. Perhaps it was because the Hershey guys were never in the stores, but Strong recalled one day, in a Safeway out West, when the Hershey rep saw him coming and disappeared—hiding in the canned goods aisle.

"So I thought I would have some fun, and I walked back there and asked him what the hell he was doing back in canned foods. 'The candy is over here,' I told him. I thought the poor guy was going to shit a brick.

"And do you know what he did? He asked us—I mean *he* asked *us*— is it all right if I put these Reese's boxes up here on the top shelf?" Strong told the rep to go ahead, but the minute the Hershey salesman walked out of the store, Strong stashed the Reese's boxes in the back.

This was the way Mars operated all around the country. Recognizing that some 70 percent of all candy is bought on impulse, Mars salesmen persuaded merchants to put candy displays near the cash registers. And there was nothing a Mars guy wouldn't do to get his products on those racks, whether that meant sending free candy bars to the store manager's children or "accidentally" knocking Hershey bars off the shelves. Whatever it took, they were going to make sure that when you reached for a piece of chocolate, your hand would find a Mars product rather than a Hershey bar.

The Mars strategy was successful, although no one knows how much profit Mars sacrificed during the tumultuous period between 1970 and 1974. Analysts estimate that Mars lost tens of millions of dollars, but what they bought with that money was the position as America's No. 1 candy maker. Mars's triumph made headlines around the country. They had finally put Hershey in its place, and it looked as if the brothers had arrived.

Mars's ascendance, however, came at a uniquely difficult time for everyone in the candy industry, as issues that had been brewing for years finally erupted in the sugar scare of the seventies.

Ever since chocolate came to Europe, it had suffered its detractors, who tried to link it to all sorts of evils—from illness to obesity to tooth decay. But the public paid little attention. Now, however, chocolate was making conspicuous and persistent appearances on Saturday morning TV—stirring pleas no parent could ignore—and a general backlash against the industry had begun, fueled by government studies and attacks in the media.

The Center for Science in the Public Interest (CSPI), a nonprofit health advocacy group founded in 1971 by Michael Jacobson, was the catalyst for the controversy. Jacobson targeted the candy industry in the same way he has recently targeted the nutritional content of movie pop-corn, Chinese food and McDonald's products. In 1972, he coined the phrase "junk food" in reference to candy and other unhealthy snacks. These two words knocked the industry upside down over night. Jacob-son went on to say that candy was full of "empty calories"—another of his famous expressions and a claim that Mars and others in the candy business would go to sometimes ridiculous lengths to disprove. Clearly, the industry had run up against a food fad, one of those periodic crazes that rule over the diets of Americans, and the impact of the sugar scare was extraordinary, with per capita candy consumption dropping by 25 percent in the early 1970s.

But concerns and scares about the nutritional content of candy and chocolate were nothing new.

In the United States in the early 1900s, there were charges of lead in chocolate. Dr. John Kellogg (of the famous cereal family) refused to serve cocoa at his Florida sanitarium because, he said, it was poisonous. In England in the 1940s, there were charges that arsenic in cocoa was killing people. And in the mid 1970s, Mars pulled its red M&M's from the market, following FDA reports linking certain food colorings to cancer.

To help fight such perceptions, the industry sponsors studies on the various effects of food on the human body. Hershey has long been a

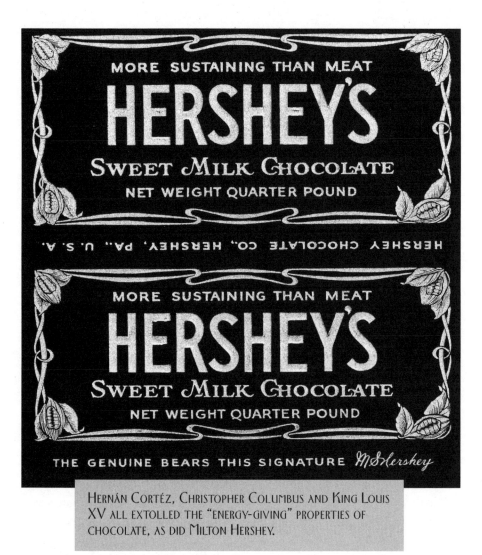

MORE SUSTAINING THAN MEAT

HERSHEY'S
SWEET MILK CHOCOLATE
NET WEIGHT QUARTER POUND

HERSHEY CHOCOLATE CO., HERSHEY, PA., U. S. A.

MORE SUSTAINING THAN MEAT

HERSHEY'S
SWEET MILK CHOCOLATE
NET WEIGHT QUARTER POUND

THE GENUINE BEARS THIS SIGNATURE *M S Hershey*

HERNÁN CORTÉZ, CHRISTOPHER COLUMBUS AND KING LOUIS XV ALL EXTOLLED THE "ENERGY-GIVING" PROPERTIES OF CHOCOLATE, AS DID MILTON HERSHEY.

major contributor to the Nutrition Foundation, which has conducted extensive research on candy and health.[1] In the 1950s, the company even provided wall posters to schools, extolling the wholesome virtues of the cocoa bean and chocolate. The National Confectioners Association and the Chocolate Manufacturers Association were the prime sponsors of a 1994 scientific conference at the University of Texas Southwestern Medical Center aimed at understanding some of the special properties of cocoa butter and chocolate. They found that stearic acid, a major fatty acid in cocoa butter, does not raise blood cholesterol, and that milk chocolate as part of a daily diet did not raise blood choles-terol levels in healthy men, even suggesting that chocolate might lower cholesterol levels. The results appeared on the front page of *The New York Times,* in the health section of *The Washington Post* and on more than fifty major television stations across the country.

These claims gained added support in 1997, when researchers (not funded by the chocolate industry) found that chocolate contains phenol, an antioxidant found in red wine that is believed to reduce the risk of heart attacks. In a letter published in the British medical journal *Lancet,* the researchers reported that "chocolate can contribute a significant por-tion of dietary antioxidants, and the pleasant pairing of red wine and dark chocolate could have synergistic advantages beyond their comple-mentary tastes."[2] However, as Andrew Waterhouse, one of the scientists who produced the study, is quick to add, the calories and fat content of chocolate keep it from being a health food. "We certainly aren't suggesting that people start eating chocolate to prevent coronary heart disease."[3]

But the industry has long extolled the health benefits of confec-tionery. At the turn of the century, Milton Hershey lauded the virtues of milk chocolate in literature for his product, writing: "Hershey's steril-ized milk chocolate is specifically recommended for cyclists, athletes, Ladies and Children. It is most sustaining, being amalgamated by a spe-cial process with the finest fresh milk. Every hygienic care is taken in the selection and treatment of the cows who supplied the milk by the com-bination of the two substances of which it is composed (chocolate and milk). It makes a delicious article of food."[4]

Hershey always made a distinction between chocolate and candy. To him, chocolate was "not merely a sweet" but a nutritious food. He often stated that an ounce of chocolate provided more energy than a pound of meat, and he forbade anyone in his factory from referring to chocolate as candy. In 1926, he tried to convince the federal government that chocolate should be taxed as a food rather than candy, making his point in an inches-thick brief written to the Supreme Court of the United States. Although he backed his claim with historical "proof and opin-ion," the Court held that chocolate is candy, at least for tax purposes.

In a more recent effort to defend gumdrops and malted milk balls, the National Confectioners Association claimed that candy "is good for you—it doesn't cause acne; it doesn't make you fat; and chocolate actu-ally prohibits tooth decay."[5] In 1966, the NCA went so far as to suggest

that candy could actually help people lose weight. "The plain truth is that the problem of overweight is directly related to overeating generally," an industry spokesman told the *Chicago Tribune*.[6] "It is also a fact that because candies raise the blood-sugar level, which makes them excellent fatigue fighters, people can depress the appetite. Therefore, candy is a good reducing aid." One survey showed that 56 percent of registered dietitians ate chocolate once a week themselves, and claims that candy actually helps people stick with their diets persist to this day.[7]

In the 1980s, the industry released a brochure entitled "A Chocolate a Day Keeps the Diet Blues Away." It included dieting tips and calorie counts of different chocolate products. Other such brochures compared chocolate and candy to foods like carrots, bananas, raisins and peanut butter in terms of providing essential nutrients as part of a daily diet.

For every charge leveled at candy and chocolate—concerning their role in obesity, illness and tooth decay—the industry has shot back with everything from scientific studies to slick marketing ploys, and at times the tactics and rhetoric have reached desperate levels.

Mars, in particular, responded to CSPI's attacks by going on the offensive, giving its advertisements a brand-new face-lift. In its more inspired moments, Mars made Snickers and Milky Ways appear as wholesome and nutritious as an apple or a bowl of oatmeal. Their message was clear: Candy is good for you. "A Snickers really satisfies" . . . so go ahead and eat one. It's made from milk, fresh eggs, peanuts and other nutritious ingredients. It is energy-packed food—"a Snickers a day helps you work, rest and play."

In another ad, they were brazen enough to show a glass of milk "magically" turning into a Milky Way bar. The Federal Trade Commission took exception to the ad, resulting in a consent order under which Mars agreed not to misrepresent the nutritional value of its products.[8] Still, Mars continues its efforts to link candy and health. In the 1980s, Mars began to feature athletes eating Snickers bars in their commercials. The company is also a major sponsor of the World Cup soccer championships, and even paid $5 million to have Snickers and M&M's named "the official snack foods of the 1984 Olympic games."

The industry spends just as lavishly to ensure that its voice is heard by our elected officials. The National Confectioners Association employs a full-time lobbyist, Steve Lodge, who is active on legislative matters ranging from sugar and peanut price support programs and nutrition labeling laws to international trade. The association is very popular on Capitol Hill for the many candy-related perks it provides to members of Congress and their staffs. Every Secretary's Day, for example, the NCA delivers bags filled with chocolate and candy to the secretaries in each congressional office. In recent years, the association has also sponsored

MILTON HERSHEY FORBADE HIS WORKERS FROM CALLING CHOCOLATE "CANDY"— TO HIM, IT WAS A WHOLESOME AND NUTRITIOUS FOOD.

an elaborate Halloween party for congressmen and their families, in which thousands of pounds of candy are distributed.

The association also stocks the Senate Candy Desk, a repository of confections always available on the Senate floor in case an elected official or aide needs a quick energy boost. When Senator John McCain passed control of the Candy Desk to Slade Gorton in 1989, he quipped, "It was an incredibly sweet experience on my tour of duty. . . ." (According to the NCA, both senators have been active supporters of its positions on sugar and trade.)

And candy manufacturers don't limit their lobbying efforts to the government. In the early 1990s, thousands of dentists received newsletters from the Princeton Dental Resource Center with reports on dental health and fighting cavities. The center asked the dentists to pass them on to their patients. The newsletters contained the rather surprising news that eating chocolate could be as beneficial as eating an apple a day. What the dentists weren't told was that the Princeton Dental Resource Center was primarily financed by Mars.[9]

The attorney general of New York responded by suing the Princeton Center for misrepresenting dental information. The center paid $25,000 and agreed to disclose its relationship with the candy maker in future publications.[10]

But this wasn't the company's only misstep in addressing public health concerns.

When Mars retired its red M&M's, it was responding to growing fears of carcinogens in our water, food and air. In 1976, the FDA released a series of studies linking cancer with food colorings, including red dyes #2 and #40. The brothers reacted by yanking red M&M's from the market—even though the candies never contained the dyes in question. Unfortunately, instead of reassuring consumers that M&M's were safe, the move only succeeded in arousing the belief that M&M's had been bad for us all along.[11]

It took more than ten years for Mars to return the red candies to its lineup. All that time, associates and customers screamed about the bland, boring mix of M&M colors and beseeched the brothers to reverse their decision. But John and Forrest Jr. didn't listen. Then, in 1982, a student from the University of Tennessee founded the Society for the Restoration and Preservation of Red M&M's. He began a letter-writing campaign and gave dozens of interviews to the media. The public outcries grew, fueled by Mars's decision in 1985 to include red M&M's in its Christmas holiday assortment. With great fanfare, in 1987, the company finally reintroduced the red M&M to its regular lineup.

But Mars associates and industry insiders were unimpressed. They said Forrest Sr. would have never pulled the red M&M in the first place, bowing to public hysteria the way his sons had; but by then, everyone around the brothers must have realized that things had changed at Mars. They were not, after all, like their father.

The years of subservience and chastisement have taken a terrible toll on John and Forrest Jr. To this day, neither will talk about the man who built the company they now lead, and any mention of him in their presence invites a harsh rebuke.

When the brothers took control of their father's company they knew they could not repeat his act of creation. Instead, it was up to them to preserve and expand their father's empire without marring the intricate systems that kept it running smoothly, without changing its vital and essential nature.

It was a difficult tightrope to walk. On the one hand, they wanted to assert their independence. On the other hand, they could not risk the type of radical changes that are often used to signal the arrival of a new regime. Moreover, they had not risen to the top by demonstrated merit, but by virtue of their birth. Proving themselves to the company's associates was an imperative. And it was not just to the company's workers that they were trying to prove their worth. They wanted to show their father, too, that they deserved the gift they had been given. For John and Forrest Jr., the goal was parental respect, a reward that would remain ever elusive.

The determination to prove themselves led the brothers to a style of management that was nothing like their father's. Where Forrest Sr. had always set the destination and let his managers find their own way, the brothers, in an effort to assert their leadership, clamped down on the company, diving headlong into every detail of the business. They routinely second-guessed managers, and insisted on personally approving every decision that was made. Where Forrest Sr. was a strategist, John and Forrest Jr. acted like tacticians.

"Working for John and Forrest Jr. is not like working for a bunch of anonymous stockholders," said one former Mars executive. "These guys were all over you all the time. There wasn't a decision that was made that didn't have their mark."

Executives who had sometimes gone years without a meeting with Forrest bristled at his sons' hands-on style. At times, the insistence on control reached absurd levels. One hapless manager at the McLean headquarters remembers raising Forrest Jr.'s ire simply by moving a potted plant that was blocking his view. When Forrest Jr. saw the plant in its new location, he shouted, "Who moved that potted plant? No one moves anything around here without my permission."

The humiliated associate returned the plant to its original spot, and meekly asked Forrest to okay the move. "Certainly," Forrest Jr. replied, his point made.

According to former Mars associates, Forrest Jr. has a temper like his father's. On a visit to a factory in Europe, he walked over to an associate who was talking on the phone and asked to speak to him.

"Hold on. I'm on a business call. I'll be right with you," the associate told him.

Furious, Forrest Jr. swept everything off the associate's desk, and shouted, "When the boss speaks to you, you drop the phone."

The associate was fired on the spot.

John is not nearly as explosive as his brother, although he, too, can be difficult to work for. Once, when John was meeting with an architect to discuss the building of a new plant, he looked over the detailed drawings. Ignoring all of the elaborate planning, John picked an insignificant detail on which to drill the architect: "Why is the stair rise five inches?" he demanded. When the architect could not provide a satisfactory answer, John tore up the plans and told him to start again.

Ed Stegemann says incidents like these are merely an act; underneath, he says, they are warm, reasonable, even charming. "They're rhetoricians," Stegemann said. "They'll do whatever it takes to get the point across. If that means chewing out a manager, so be it." Stegemann jokes that a successful Mars manager must be one part Teflon, one part steel.

In fact, there are few shrinking violets in the company. Workers on the factory floor are as quick to criticize Mars as the managers; no one—including the family—is beyond reproach.

"Everyone here is a pain in the ass," noted Phil Forster, a thirty-year veteran. "That's what keeps us sharp."

But while the brothers kept a tighter grip on the company than Forrest ever did, they never dared stray from his stated principles. In fact, they codified his management philosophy in a handsomely printed, twenty-four-page brochure that can be found on desks and tables in every Mars factory around the world.

This bible of corporate rectitude, known to insiders as "The Five Principles of Mars," espouses lofty-sounding themes: Quality, Responsibility, Mutuality, Efficiency and Freedom. (One Mars manager, eager to show off her dedication to the principles, named the conference rooms in her building after them; during our interview, we sat in Responsibility.)

While the principles are easily dismissed as platitudes, they capture some real aspects of the business under the brothers' leadership.

Principle number two is Responsibility. "As individuals," the brochure states, "we demand total responsibility from ourselves; as associates, we support the responsibilities of others."

Forrest Jr. once put it this way: "We are responsible to our associates, for without them there would be no Mars. In fact, my brother and I believe we work for our associates, and not the other way around."[12] Though this sounds like motivational rhetoric, the brothers do work awfully hard. They spend 70 percent of each year traveling the globe, checking on operations. And when they're in McLean, they often work eighty-hour weeks.

"Their dedication to the business is mind-boggling, when you think about it," said Leenders. "How many people do you know worth billions of dollars who would spend their days going in and out of factories?"

Associates are expected "to take on direct and total responsibility for results, exercising initiative and making decisions as their tasks require," the brochure continues. As a symbolic reminder, the brothers Mars have positioned a butcher's block in the middle of the second-floor office in McLean. Attached is a plaque that reads: "Head on the block responsibility."

The notion of responsibility blends into principle number three, Mutuality, which simply means, "everybody wins." The brochure insists that each business encounter—with the consumer, another associate, a supplier, a distributor or the community at large—should benefit everyone concerned; then it poses this rhetorical question: "If we are selfish in these relationships and give less than fair benefit in return, how long can this continue?"

The fifth principle, and probably the one closest to the brothers' hearts, is Freedom. In the pamphlet, it's explained this way: "We need freedom to shape our future; we need profit to remain free." What it really means, however, is privacy—in every facet of the business. The brothers believe the best way to determine the company's future is to remain private, and privately held.

Being out of the Wall Street spotlight means Mars doesn't need to be concerned with achieving consistent financial returns. "There's no SEC, no stockholders that have to be answered to, and if John and Forrest want to make investments at the expense of short-term profits, they can and they're able to and they do," said Al Aragona, the retired president of Uncle Ben's.

But the privacy issue extends beyond business decisions to the company's public relations—or lack of public relations. If Mars doesn't have to communicate with the world, it won't. The only thing Mars wants the public to pay attention to is its products.

This is a company that, until recently, wouldn't even share its financial statements with its bankers for fear that information might leak. Company treasurer Vito Spitaleri says Mars "has gotten more sophisticated" about releasing information to those who need it, like bankers and lawyers. But despite its decision to open the company to me, Mars hasn't overcome its deep-rooted aversion to publicity.

Although family members agreed to be interviewed, they refused to be photographed.[13] Edward Stegemann, Mars's general counsel and an adviser to the family, insisted that a tape recording of Forrest Sr.'s voice be destroyed, lest it fall into the wrong hands. And until I presented Mars with an accurate portrayal of the tremendous size of its business, officials lowballed sales figures and downplayed the number of associates worldwide.

Stegemann patiently explains that the brothers' precautions are necessary. A couple of times a year he finds strangers lurking outside the McLean headquarters. The brothers have been threatened with kidnapping—at times, forced to hire round-the-clock body guards for protection.

Generous as Forrest's gift might have appeared, the Mars children know that it was no simple blessing.

"[John and Forrest Jr.] work harder than I do," said Mars senior executive Phil Forster. "They work harder than anybody else in this company. And all they get is grief."

Chapter Nineteen

A LEGACY LOST

MILTON HERSHEY'S HIGH POINT MANSION WAS HOME TO THE HERSHEY COUNTRY CLUB STARTING IN 1930 AND WAS MADE INTO CORPORATE OFFICES IN 1978.

ONCE A MONTH, or more often if he could find the time, William Dearden would take his lunch break in the Camelot Room of Founders Hall. The dining hall could have easily been mistaken for a fancy restaurant or private club, with its dark wood paneling and King Arthur motif, were it not for the hundreds of boys and girls laughing and talking as they ate. Dearden loved nothing more than these visits. He would pick a table at random and join the students in conversation. With his ready smile and gregarious charm it was easy for the children to forget that he was a big shot at the company, and they treated him like one of their own. Together, they would joke about the food, complain about the teachers and groan about the chores.

The students liked to listen to Dearden reminisce about his own days as a boy at Willow Wood and hear the tales of his encounters with Mr. Hershey. In the three decades since Milton Hershey's death, the stories about him had grown more and more elaborate, blending fact and fiction in a way that continued to fascinate and awe the students. Many of the tales centered around his supposedly endless wealth: Milton Hershey gave every boy who graduated $10,000 and a gold watch, went one story. Another told of his gold-plated china and hundreds of servants. The conversations reminded Dearden of his own childhood, when he would dream chimerical dreams about the man who had made his life possible.

His musings about Mr. Hershey no longer took on the patina of childish fantasy, but they were no less reverential. Since joining the company, Dearden's appreciation of Milton Hershey's accomplishments, and gratitude for his remarkable charity, had only deepened.

"Milton Hershey was a giant of a man," Dearden said, in homage to Hershey's character and accomplishments. "He taught me to be concerned with people, not just with business. He taught me to be caring toward the helpless."

For Dearden, the connection to Milton Hershey was personal and direct. "At the school, we all thought of him as our guy. He was concerned, and we all knew it. He came to every graduation, every homecoming. He picked up the tab for everything. Because of Mr. Hershey, we never thought of ourselves as poor orphans."[1]

The students of the 1970s might have shared this gratitude toward Hershey in the abstract, but they could not relate to him as a real person. He was a legendary figure, too far removed from their reality to be an inspiration. But in Dearden, they found that same sense of caring and hope and promise, proof that no matter their backgrounds, with the school's help they, too, could rise to the top.

After eleven years in the executive suite working beneath Harold Mohler, Dearden had been named CEO of the corporation on March 1, 1976. As he went to work each day from his modest house at 405 Homestead Road—the street that led to Hershey's boyhood home—the appointment still struck Dearden as unreal, an act of Providence. He saw his ascendency as confirmation of his life's mission: to repay Hershey for rescuing him.

Dearden knew that he was taking charge of the company at a difficult time. In addition to soaring cocoa prices in the early 1970s, sugar prices ran wild, increasing from 10 cents per pound in 1973 to 66 cents a year later.[2] As commodities prices soared and inflation ravaged the economy, Mars had the flexibility and financial strength to respond in ways that just weren't feasible for Hershey. As Dearden recalled, "During this period of the price controls, Mars really stuck it to us, because having no shareholders, being a private company, they could do anything they wanted to. . . ."[3]

But Hershey did not have that freedom. "Not only for our shareholders in general," said Dearden, "but obviously the big income to operate Milton Hershey's school came from dividends from Hershey Chocolate. . . . We couldn't afford to lose anything, and we had to make a profit somehow."[4]

As a result, Mohler had raised the price of the old "nickel bar" from 10 cents to 15 cents, reducing its weight at the same time. Not surprisingly, sales plummeted and profits went with them.

As bad as it had been, the company never actually sustained a loss under Mohler. In 1973, however, things had become tight enough for the company to cut its dividend, reducing the Trust's income for the first time in its history. It was only a temporary measure, but the market trends all seemed to reinforce the sense of dread that this painful decision engendered. When Mohler announced his decision to relinquish control, in 1975, Dearden faced enormous challenges: Hershey was now the No. 2 player, its management was stolid and unimaginative and its product line was stagnant.

It was Dearden who would revive Hershey, remaking it as a modern Fortune 500 company. With Richard Zimmerman, president of the corporation, at his side, he started asking the fundamental questions that for so long had gone unvoiced: What kind of company did Hershey want to become? What were its goals and priorities? Where did it want to put its resources? For the first time since Milton Hershey's death, the company had a leader who understood the importance of vision.

Two months after taking the helm, Dearden gathered eight of his top managers and led them in a quest to chart Hershey's course. The corporate planning committee—a hand-picked team that represented the company's future, including Zimmerman, Spangler, Suhring, Johns and Dowd—escaped to the Poconos for a week of reflection, self-criticism and planning. This April retreat has since become a Hershey tradition, an integral part of its management process.

Before the retreat, the company had no formal planning process, and certainly no written strategic plan. The only starting points from which the committee could work were the marketing plans that had been put together by Suhring and Dowd. Like those plans, the corporate plan would set goals for the company for the next ten years and outline the methods by which these goals would be achieved.

As Dearden's assistant, John Rawley, recalls, the plan that emerged from the retreat was a "Model T at best, but it was a start. It was qualitative in nature. It had no numbers in it. It simply addressed what we . . . as a group . . . hoped this institution would be in the future."

Nevertheless, the plan broke new ground. Among its contributions to the corporation were the creation of Hershey's first research and development department, a human resources department, a legal department and a corporate communications department to handle public relations. The group also addressed the need to systematize the purchase of commodities, to expand the company globally and to identify and train promising junior managers.

But the central insight to emerge from the retreat was a recognition that Hershey needed to diversify its operations and reduce its dependence on cocoa-related products. As of 1975, over 90 percent of the company's sales and 96 percent of its profits came from chocolate.[5]

Under Mohler, Hershey had acquired several noncandy businesses, including the San Giorgio Pasta Co. and Cory Food Services, a coffee business in Chicago. But as Dearden recalls, these acquisitions were made without forethought or planning. Hershey purchased San Giorgio in the sixties because, as Dearden said, "It was a go-go period. . . . Everybody seemed to be acquiring everybody else." A business broker approached Hershey shortly after the Reese acquisition and invited the company to put in a bid for San Giorgio. There was no evaluation of the business, no strategy that led Hershey to decide that this was the right market to invest in. It happened "by accident, with this fellow dropping in."

Dearden wanted to build on these initial forays. Growth would come from acquisitions, but Hershey was concerned that attempts to buy candy companies would draw the ire of federal officials who were aggressively enforcing the nation's antitrust laws. And the company desperately needed some cushion against the vagaries of the commodities markets. So Dearden determined to make Hershey into a major food company, with interests in a wide variety of product categories. His goal was for nonconfection products to account for at least 30 percent of total sales.[6]

In April 1978, Hershey bought the Procino-Rossi Corp., a pasta manufacturer, and it added the Skinner Macaroni Co. of Omaha in January 1979. These acquisitions have since become the cornerstone of

Hershey Pasta, a division that contributes $300 million in sales annually, making Hershey the nation's largest pasta maker.

Hershey also reorganized itself to reflect its new focus on nonchocolate enterprises, calling itself the Hershey Foods Corp. Beneath this new corporate umbrella Hershey established two divisions, one for candy and one for everything else. Earl Spangler was put in charge of chocolate operations, while Richard Zimmerman took primary responsibility for the company's nonchocolate businesses.

Dearden assigned Dowd the critical task of developing brand-new products, ones that could help turn the tide in the battle with Mars. He also moved a number of key executives into the corporate parent, including Bill Suhring, who became the head of corporate development. From his new post, it was Suhring's job to identify businesses for Hershey to acquire. Among the firms he targeted were American Beauty Macaroni, acquired from Pillsbury, and Y&S Candies, a leading maker of licorice.

Hershey's diversification effort climaxed in 1979, with the acquisition of the Friendly Ice Cream Corp., a Massachusetts company that operated over 600 family-style restaurants in New England and the Midwest. To finance part of the $164-million purchase, Hershey turned to the public debt markets, issuing $75 million in long-term bonds. The company explained the purchase as part of its program to diversify "within the food industry, but into areas that aren't tied to the importation of foreign commodities, such as cocoa beans."[7]

The company also began its first ventures into the international candy market, establishing a division to pursue joint ventures and export opportunities abroad. Hershey purchased a 20 percent interest in A.B. Marabou, the largest candy maker in Sweden. And Hershey entered into an agreement with Mexico's Anderson, Clayton & Co., S.A., to establish a joint venture called Nacional de Dulces. The company also began exporting products to Japan, the Philippines and China.[8]

No one but Dearden could have initiated such monumental changes. He made the tough calls; but more important, he sold his decisions to the managers who would have to carry them out. He knew how to play the role of quarterback, how to set the play in motion, then step back and let the team take over. But he was not a distant man, he was the kind of CEO who left his door open, who toured the factory on a regular basis, just as M.S. had.

Dearden's experience in the Hershey Industrial School had taught him tremendous discipline, but it had also helped him develop the interpersonal skills that would prove invaluable during his tenure as CEO. Dearden was the kind of guy who would meet you once and never forget your name. He sent hundreds of personal notes to his staff, each one handwritten, praising them for their work. He had the kind of warmth and caring that could come through even when he was chewing you out, and because you knew he respected you, you could not help but admire and respect him. He was not a man of consensus, however, but a charismatic figure who inspired trust and confidence in his followers. A deeply religious man, Dearden held strong convictions about business, about God and about family. He was, like Milton Hershey, a man of vision.

Dearden's leadership won him widespread praise in the business press, which referred to him as "Hershey's Savior." Lengthy tributes to the man who had risen from the orphanage to the CEO's office appeared in magazines and newspapers, putting the company in the limelight for the first time since Milton Hershey gave away his fortune. The company's new profile was further buoyed by the reactivation of the marketing campaigns that had been shelved in 1972.

But while Hershey's image was improving in the media, its reputation at home was suffering. As the company increasingly acted like a typical, profit-driven corporation, it extricated itself ever further from the affairs of the town. When Milton Hershey first sold stock in his company to the public in 1927, he separated out town-related enterprises into a company he called the Hershey Estates, now called Hershey Entertainment and Resorts, which is owned by the broader Hershey Trust. But as long as Milton Hershey was in charge, the separation was never really complete.

In the years after Hershey's death, however, the company and town slowly started to move apart. It was subtle at first, like when the company stopped providing the town's garbage pickup, snow removal and electricity. Over time, as the factory grew, much of the greenery that had enhanced the downtown was reduced to asphalt so the company could provide parking for an increasing number of workers and tourists.

The first public protests were raised in 1963, when the Trust donated $50 million and one hundred acres of land to Pennsylvania State University for the creation of a new medical school. Many believed that if Milton Hershey were still in charge, that money would have been used to improve the two-year Hershey Junior College, which provided a free education to town residents and company employees.

Instead of being expanded into a four-year institution, though, the junior college was closed down. "The community was outraged when that happened," said L. Eugene Jacques, the superintendent of the Hershey schools. "They jammed the auditorium for public meetings. The school board was completely blamed for it, [but] the school board had no choice. They had no money for the junior college. So it was a very nasty situation."

The medical center completely changed the nature of the town. Suddenly, there were thousands of new residents who had nothing to do with the chocolate company and had little in common with the town's established citizenry. Many of these newcomers were highly paid doctors, and some residents believed they brought with them a sense of superiority.

"With the medical center, everything changed," said Philomena Castelli. "They started building fancy houses up in the hills and they wanted [advanced placement] classes in the schools. . . . There was an 'us and them' kind of attitude."

"You had an influx of new people who had a different approach to what was going on in the community," explained Jacques, the school superintendent. "We had many more students after that who were academically inclined, whereas previously there had been many students going into vocational education. Their parents also placed many more demands on the school district."

But the Trust's officers defended their decision to fund the Milton S. Hershey Medical Center, saying it has provided a boost to the local economy, ensured first-rate health care for residents and honored the memory of the town's beloved founder in a manner consistent with his beliefs.

The tension between the town's traditional blue-collar base and its new wealthy suburban enclave only aggravated feelings that the Hershey enterprises no longer cared for the town as Milton Hershey had. For many, these suspicions were confirmed in 1970, when the Cocoa Inn was torn down. Though the building was in need of major repairs, it was a historic landmark—once serving as Hershey's drugstore, department store, bank, post office, restaurant and hotel.

As Millie Landis, a long-time Hershey resident, recalled, "The Cocoa Inn was the center of everything. It was always, 'Meet you at the Cocoa Inn.' You could stop for an ice-cream cone at the drugstore there, or go in the lobby where you might see someone famous in town for a show. It was the bus stop, the newsstand. It was where the townspeople ran into each other and exchanged greetings."[9]

When the Hershey Entertainment company demolished the structure rather than restoring it, many in the town felt it was a betrayal of the Hershey legacy.

This sense of betrayal was heightened later that year, when the park, which had been so central to the town's identity, was closed. In its place arose a commercial, Disney-style theme park surrounded by a chain-link fence.

In the old days, residents could stroll through the park, taking in the scenery or enjoying a picnic. Many spent their weekends rowing boats on the lake and dancing to the bands, and while they had to pay for rides and games, much of the entertainment was free. The new Hersheypark wasn't about recreation for residents and workers; it was about making money, a fact that chafed at residents.

"Milton Hershey was a man of great principle," said Patty Shearer, who has lived in Hershey since the 1930s. "He built this town for a purpose, not for a bottom line. But the company can't see that."

The same year the park was transformed, the company stopped offering free tours of the factory to the public, inviting visitors instead to "Chocolate World," a simulation ride that takes you step-by-step through the candy-making process. Though Chocolate World is supposed to give visitors a sense of life in the factory, it is no comparison to the real thing.

"When you walked through that factory your mouth would start to water," remembered Shearer. "It was that smell, and the sight of all that chocolate, and those candy bars coming off the line. I remember thinking to myself, 'Who eats all this stuff?' I mean, there was so much of it—it was incredible."

Initially, visitors to the factory were allowed to take candy right off the conveyor belts. This got expensive, however, and soon the company began handing out bags of candy and cups of cocoa at the end of the tour. Today, visitors to Chocolate World are treated to one miniature-size candy bar apiece, just enough to entice them to spend their money in the supermarket-size gift shop at the end of the ride, where Hershey sells all of its products, plus a dazzling array of Hershey drinking cups, Hershey's Kiss banks, Hershey T-shirts and sweatshirts, Hershey tote-bags, Hershey pencils, Krackel place mats, Mr. Goodbar key rings, playing cards, bumper stickers, visors and calendars. Chocolate World drew more than 2 million visitors in 1996, and the attraction underwent extensive renovations in 1998 to further enhance its appeal.

More of the town's unique character was effaced in the spring of

1980, when the community center was closed to the public, save its handsome theater. In one stroke the town lost its bowling alley, indoor swimming pool, gymnasium, pool hall and party room. The library, at least, was moved to another building. "The loss of the community center was a real blow," said Monroe Stover. "It was the heart of the town. . . . It gave Hershey a special feeling—a feeling of place, of belonging. It made Hershey unique."

The community center is now known as the Hershey Foods Corp. Administrative Office, and it accommodates 200 top staff members of Hershey Chocolate North America. At each entrance to the facility, signs now read: "Hershey Foods Corp. Employees Only: Identification Required."

The company's top executives adopted an even more hallowed site as their home—Milton Hershey's High Point Mansion. The move came in 1977, when Hershey Entertainment, faced with mounting bills to repair the structure, considered tearing it down. When Dearden heard of the proposal, he was heartsick.

"The building called High Point, which was Mr. Hershey's home, was almost sacred ground, as far as I was concerned," Dearden said. "It was his home. Many of his major decisions in developing the business over the years were made right here by him."[10]

Dearden proposed renovating the building for his newly created corporate staff. The old bedroom and sitting room, where Milton Hershey lived out his final years, became Dearden's personal office.

Dearden explained these various changes as a necessary evolution. While the town "is still a major concern to Hershey Foods because Hershey is our home, too, increased citizen interest and involvement in local affairs was necessary for the healthy growth and development of the community. On the other hand," he said, "we hope that Hershey citizens realize that for the healthy growth and development of our company it is necessary that we also open our eyes to opportunities and concerns beyond the horizon of Hershey."[11]

Residents understand that the company can no longer provide unlimited support for the town, but they are disappointed by what they see as the abandonment of Milton Hershey's ideals. As Hershey resident Landis said: "I'm not bitter. I'm sad. You can't blame anybody for what's happened. We had no right to expect what we had. But if Mr. Hershey could see this town today, he'd be very, very sad. He had great pride in these buildings. There'll never be another man like him."[12]

From Milton's old desk, Dearden charged ahead with the company's makeover. His first priority was to wrest market share from Mars, and he summoned every one of his employees to the task—posting market share data in every bathroom to make his point.

"Dearden really focused Hershey on the competition," said Johns. "There was a lot of talk in those days about where Mars was and where we were. It made everyone a little nervous. For the first time, the workers realized the company wasn't bullet proof. We couldn't just take the future for granted."

By the end of the decade, Dearden's leadership seemed to be paying off. The company's diversification promised to stabilize the bottom line, and in the meantime, market share had started to rebound. But just as the first positive results were coming in, Mars hit Hershey with a devastating surprise.

In 1980, in an effort to lure consumers back into the candy aisle, and to keep the pressure on Hershey, John and Forrest Jr. took the unprecedented step of increasing bar sizes by 20 to 30 percent while holding the line on wholesale prices. The company took out full-page advertisements in the nation's leading newspapers to tout the change, which was a welcome gesture after a decade of shrinking candy bars and ever higher prices. Sales of some Mars products jumped by as much as 50 percent.

"They clobbered us," said Spangler. "They could afford to, and there was nothing we could do."

Chapter Twenty

NICE PEOPLE DON'T EAT CHOCOLATE

MARS COULD NOT HAVE IMAGINED THE OPPORTUNITY IT MISSED WHEN IT TURNED DOWN STEVEN SPIELBERG'S OFFER FOR M&M'S TO BE E.T.'S FAVORITE CANDY.

N ICE PEOPLE DON'T eat chocolate: Such was the prevailing wisdom of the 1970s. In the decade of leisure suits and disco, chocolate had become a pariah, a tawdry indulgence for middle-aged traveling salesmen, pimply overweight teenagers and lonely housewives watching the afternoon soaps.

For Al Pechenik, president of Godiva Chocolatier, Inc.,[1] and consumer of a half-pound of chocolate a day, this cheapening of chocolate's image was almost blasphemous, a cultural and culinary embarassment. Pechenik believed Americans had never understood chocolate. How could they, when the taste most Americans associate with chocolate is that of a Hershey's milk-chocolate bar, what Pechenik and other world-renowned chocolatiers describe as "barnyard" chocolate. Pechenik, who took the helm of Godiva in 1974, eight years after the family-owned Belgian candy maker was purchased by Campbell Soup Co., knew he would have to transform chocolate's image if Godiva were to be successful.

So began the chocolate revolution, an extraordinary change in American tastes and perceptions.

By the early 1980s, chocolate was everywhere. Elegant chocolate boutiques appeared on the chic shopping boulevards of Beverly Hills and New York, catering to customers who wanted to choose their bonbons one at a time, like jewelry. Avant-garde restaurants loaded their menus with decadent, artery-clogging chocolate desserts, each one a meal in itself. Imported chocolates once rarely seen except at duty-free shops were now popping up in places like Boise, Idaho, and Springfield, Missouri. Tony stores like Neiman Marcus and Bloomingdale's opened chocolate departments right next to the lingerie and evening wear.

"In the 1980s we saw a new chocolate snob emerging," said Alice Medrich, owner of Cocolat, a small chain of upscale chocolate shops in San Francisco. "It used to be that people would ask me 'What's a truffle?' Now they ask me, 'Who makes your truffles?' "

Much of the credit for America's newfound obsession with chocolate goes to Godiva's Pechenik. He realized, when observing the success of products like Campari, that Americans can be enticed to buy anything if the image is right.

"Americans are ruled by status," said Pechenik. "It's the Mercedes syndrome." Like a luxury automobile, chocolate—with its rich history, aristocratic tradition and alluring flavor—is a perfect vehicle to sell status. And so Pechenik set out to restore chocolate's luster. His first Godiva ad, in 1979, showed four truffles elegantly arrayed on a Limoges dish, with the simple caption, "Dessert." Shortly thereafter, he broke new ground in pricing, paving the way for tariffs of $20 a pound and up. The effect was electrifying.

Between 1980 and 1985, per capita chocolate consumption jumped by two and a half pounds. Candy eaters everywhere were coming out of the closet, declaring chocolate as essential as milk, bread and eggs.

Overnight, Pechenik remade boxed chocolates—reduced in America to the staid Whitman's Sampler—into treasure chests of expensive, exotic delights. Wrapped in distinctive gold foil and fine silk ribbon, with ingredients listed in French and English, the Godiva chocolate box was irresistibly rich and alluring.

Between 1979 and 1983, the company opened 1,200 outlets nationwide, each as sumptuously decorated as the candy boxes they sold. Consumers flocked to Godiva stores to handpick their chocolate by the piece and by the pound, and company profits soared 400 percent.[2] With Godiva's success, the race for chocolate cachet was on. Hundreds of competitors opened their own shamelessly extravagant boutiques with foreign-sounding names like La Maison de Chocolate and Du Coco Monde. In New York, the standard was set by the chic chocolate houses of Teuscher, Krohn and Chocolaterie Corne de la Toison d'Or. Their superpremium candies sold at the extortionate price of $40 a pound, elevating chocolate's status to that of caviar and champagne.

The timing couldn't have been more perfect for Hershey. The company spent most of the 1970s fighting just to hold the line on sales. It was the most turbulent decade in the company's history. Spiraling cocoa bean prices and inflation forced Hershey to raise the price of candy bars three times during the 1970s. With each jump in prices, consumers turned away from Hershey products. By the end of the decade, when Mars clobbered Hershey by increasing the size of its bars, Hershey seemed completely adrift. But the company had gotten a taste of what advertising and marketing could do and was preparing to push ahead—just as America was rediscovering its love of chocolate.

Dearden put Jack Dowd in charge of marketing research. It would be his job to find out what the public wanted to eat and how Hershey could satisfy consumer cravings. If Hershey's existing products did not fit the bill, it would be his job to come up with new ones.

Hershey had never asked these questions before. Until now, most of Hershey's new products had been copycats of successful brands from other companies. For example, in the 1950s, Hershey came out with its answer to M&M's, called Hershey-Ets. A few years later, the company launched Hershey's Instant, a me-too version of Nestlé's Quik.

The products that Hershey didn't copy from other companies, it bought from them, like Reese's Peanut Butter Cups. The Kit Kat was a successful product manufactured by Rowntree in England. In the 1930s, Hershey licensed the right to manufacture it in America, along with two more of the company's most popular candy bars—Biscrisp and Aero. Such licensing agreements were popular during the first half of the century, when it was difficult for companies to make an investment abroad themselves. Forrest Mars, for example, licensed the recipe for the Mars bar to a Danish candy maker in the 1930s.

In 1978, Dearden ordered Dowd to come up with ten new products for Hershey's lineup in the next three years. This would have been a stunning order at *any* candy company; coming up with new products is one of the hardest things to do in the candy business. And Hershey, in particular, had never built any expertise in developing new products. But Dearden needed anything and everything that the company could possibly find for its fight against Mars.

So it was up to Dowd to try to turn Hershey into an innovator, anticipating consumers' tastes before even they knew what they wanted. It was a difficult job. Dowd recalls working in Hershey's windowless office building. When it was built it had seemed a modern architectural triumph, but by the end of the seventies it had come to symbolize the company's insularity. Without windows, said Dowd, "I couldn't even tell what people across the street were doing and thinking and wanting, let alone what the people in Albuquerque and Dubuque wanted."

Developing a new candy is not nearly as simple as sitting down in the kitchen and mixing together ingredients to see what tastes good. It takes three to five years to successfully develop and introduce a new product, so it's essential to anticipate consumers' preferences down the line. Dowd likened new product development to shooting ducks. "You can't shoot where the duck is; you've got to shoot out front where he's going to be."

The product must appeal to consumers, but that is just a start. It also has to be able to last for twelve weeks on the grocer's shelf. It has to be a recipe that can be manufactured efficiently given the current technology, and one that can be made up time and time again with the same results. It takes chemists and nutritionists and engineers and marketers all working together to come up with new products that sell.

And even a product that seems to have all the bugs worked out can turn up a surprise. Shortly after Dowd arrived, the company had to abandon its chocolate marshmallow cups. "We had that for a few holiday seasons," recalls Spangler. "We had trouble with that exploding. When it was transported across the Rockies, that altitude."

Dowd and a team of a half-dozen marketing people began studying different candy ingredients to determine which were the most popular. They found, for example, that raisins are among the least popular candy additives, while nuts—especially peanuts—are the most popular.[3] Then they began to experiment with product combinations, but many of the recipes that Dowd and his team tried simply couldn't be translated into mass-produced candies on a factory line. It's a common problem in candy land.

When Hershey first took the license for the Biscrisp bar from Rowntree, it was one of Rowntree's best-selling items. But Hershey had no end of problems with the manufacturing. The product was a cookie-centered chocolate wafer bar that required a tremendous amount of man power to produce. The cookies had to be baked in special ovens, then cut by hand with fine-tooth saws. Molds were then dipped in chocolate, and the cookies were hand-placed inside the molds. Finally, the extra chocolate had to be scraped off the cookies, again by hand, using tiny spatulas. It was a tedious, cumbersome process, and Hershey finally had to shut the line down because it couldn't make the bar profitably. The company had no idea when it first purchased the license that the Biscrisp would be such a headache to produce.

The same was true for the Kit Kat bar, initially. Hershey engineers couldn't figure out how to keep the chocolate from making the wafer soggy. They had to bring Rowntree engineers over from England to help them solve the problem, and to teach them how to evenly coat the wafers and how to keep the cookies from breaking up in the chocolate molds.

Dowd identified several more brands that Hershey could license, and he and his team suggested making a handful of other new products from scratch. Among the offerings was a product that looked very similar to M&M's, except that it had a peanut butter center. The product was perfect for Hershey. The company still had panning machines left over

OVER THE YEARS, MARS AND HERSHEY HAVE COPIED EACH OTHER'S PRODUCTS. HERSHEY STILL SELLS HERSHEY-ETS ON SPECIAL HOLIDAYS.

from the days of its failed Hershey-Ets. "The difficulty with Hershey-Ets was that when we said, 'We have a product called Hershey-Ets,' people would say, 'What is it?' And to define it you had to use the competitor's name. That's a pretty difficult situation." But the company still had the equipment and the expertise in candy coating. Dowd saw the opportunity to use them for an entirely new approach.

With the idea in hand, Dowd faced the technical problem of developing a workable peanut-based center. That was not as easy. Experiment after experiment failed, because the oil in the peanut butter tended to separate out from the solids, then migrate into the candy shell and make it soggy. After months of work, Dowd's team turned the problem over to outside scientists who developed a special peanut meal. They called it "penuche"; not really peanut butter, but a peanut butter–flavored sugar filling with the consistency of chocolate.

The new product had no actual chocolate in it—a fact that was debated for quite some time. But members of the Hershey team wanted the M&M feel without having it seem too much like an M&M. That was the mistake they had made with Hershey-Ets. This time, they would be capitalizing on the popular Reese brand. They would stress the peanut butter filling and manufacture the candies in the Reese colors of orange and brown. The new product would not be stamped with a letter, and would be slightly smaller than M&M's. But there was no question that it was intended to compete with them, even though Hershey managers to this day deny that they were going after Mars's best-selling product.

"Reese's Pieces are nothing like M&M's," said Dowd. "The taste sensation is completely different. This is not a chocolate product."

The test runs of the product were difficult. First, Hershey had trouble with the consistency of the penuche. They wanted it smooth, but the sugar kept crystallizing and making it taste grainy. Then there was the question of the shell—how thick it should be. Too thin a layer and it would crack during shipment, but too thick and it would become brittle, breaking up into sharp pieces in the mouth. There was also a problem with the colors—how many should there be, and what hues should they use. The first oranges were almost fluorescent, the second batch looked too tangerine. Dowd wanted the colors to match the Reese's packaging identically . . . but that meant using an orange that was very similar to an M&M orange, and many working on the product thought that was taboo. In the end, Dowd succeeded in producing an array of colors that complemented the brown and orange of a Reese's wrapper. All that was left was the name of the product.

Dowd knew it had to be associated with Reese's—he was counting on that association to help the product sell. In marketing lingo, this was a "line extension"—using the name and image of an already popular brand to launch a new product. The new candy would be associated with the Reese name in the minds of consumers, so if you were a fan of Reese's Peanut Butter Cups, you might try this other product, too. The name that Dowd initially suggested was "PBs," but the company couldn't use that name because the trademark was already held by Mars. Dowd then suggested Reese's Pieces, and the name stuck.

The new product was successfully introduced in four test markets in 1979. The sales department did a superb job of getting distribution, the advertising support was effective and consumers seemed to take to the new candy. Hershey started to build a production line devoted to Reese's Pieces at its new factory in Stuart's Draft, Virginia. But just as the company was putting the finishing touches on its multimillion-dollar investment, sales for Reese's Pieces started to decline.

"Not at an alarming rate, but certainly at a disturbing rate." Dowd and the others were disappointed and worried. They thought Reese's Pieces would be an instant success. After all, Reese's was an extraordinarily popular brand.

Even with this warning, Hershey chose to launch Reese's Pieces nationally in 1980. Dowd told Dearden not to worry—advertising and promotions would help pick up the pace. But after a year on the market, sales were still lagging. Dowd knew he would need something—some gimmick, some special hook—or the product wasn't likely to survive. The answer to his dilemma came from a very unexpected place.

In October 1981, Tony Pingitore, one of the new-products specialists, received a call from Universal Studios. It seems they were filming a new movie about a space creature that befriends a little boy. The script called for M&M's to be used to lure the creature out of the woods and into the little boy's house, but when Universal asked Mars for permission to use M&M's in the movie, the candy company refused.

Now Universal wanted to use Reese's Pieces instead. Universal pitched that the movie would sell Reese's Pieces, and wanted Hershey to promote the movie with its candies. Dowd didn't know what to think of the offer; nothing like this had ever been tried before. But he was curious. By chance, he was traveling to California one week later for a meeting of the board of directors of the Association of National Advertisers. He figured that as long as he was going to be in San Francisco anyway, he would fly to L.A. to talk with Universal representatives. But he was so wary of the offer that he paid for the trip to Hollywood himself, not even wanting to bill it on his expense account.

On any other business trip Dowd would have checked into a Holiday Inn, but since he was dealing with the glamorous executives of Universal, he booked a room at the Beverly Hilton. That night he received a call from a vice president at Universal, asking him to "do breakfast." So at 7:30 A.M. they met in the lobby. To his surprise and amusement, Dowd ended up stuck with the bill for breakfast. But his hosts then whisked him away in a limousine for a VIP tour of Universal Studios.

After the tour he was escorted to the Universal building, where he met with attorneys to discuss the terms of the agreement. For six hours they talked. "There was no coffee offered, no tea offered, which is just as well because there were no bathroom breaks either."

Although Steven Spielberg was directing the film, Dowd didn't meet him that day. Spielberg was in the Muir Woods filming the landing of the UFO for the movie. Kathleen Kennedy, Spielberg's co-producer, told Dowd the story of the alien who lands in a California suburb and is befriended by a nine-year-old boy. Dowd knew Spielberg had had some successes, but his last movie—*1941,* starring John Belushi—had been a bomb. Dowd was concerned that *E.T.* would also fail. "We didn't want some 'monster that ate Chicago–type movie.' We didn't want to frighten our consumers. We wanted to entertain them."

Kennedy explained that the creature would be lured into the little boy's house by a trail of Reese's Pieces. The vice president of Universal told Dowd that they had decided to go with Reese's Pieces after his son suggested the product.

Dowd was impressed with what he heard, and came to an agreement with Universal: Hershey would back up the movie with $1 million worth of promotions and, in return, Hershey would be able to use *E.T.* for its own advertising.

"So I came home," Dowd said, "and told the staff what we were going to do, and that we were going to spend a million dollars on a movie that I couldn't show them the script for, that was going to employ a little green creature from outer space that I couldn't show them a picture of. I didn't even know at that point what E.T. would look like."

Everyone in the room thought Dowd had lost his mind. When Earl Spangler, then Hershey president, asked Dowd if he was sure this was going to work, Dowd said, " 'Oh, of course.' Because what else could I say? I had already signed up for it." Spangler told Dowd that he would not authorize any additional money for the promotion. Whatever was spent would have to come out of the existing budget. And he warned Dowd, "You had better produce a bottom line by the end of the year."

In a few weeks, Universal sent Dowd a picture of E.T. and the little boy to use on the promotional materials. "I proudly showed the picture at a staff meeting, and Earl said, 'That is the ugliest creature I have ever seen in my whole life.'" Dowd said nothing as the room burst into laughter, but silently he began to wonder if he'd made the right decision after all.

"I spent weeks daydreaming about that little green creature," said Dowd. "It was hard to imagine that my entire career was going to come down to this little alien."

When the movie was ready to screen, Tony Pingitore went to New York to view it. When he returned to Hershey he assured Dowd that the film was great. Earl Spangler asked, "Is it going to sell any candy?" Dowd assured him it would, although "that was more of a prayer than an answer."

Dowd was launching the biggest PR offensive for a single brand in Hershey's history. The Stuart's Draft plant worked overtime for two months to get enough product into the pipeline to support the campaign. Meanwhile, posters and stickers proclaiming Reese's Pieces as "E.T.'s favorite candy" rolled off the presses, ready to be bartered to consumers for proof of purchase seals. Reese's Pieces, never before sold in cinemas, suddenly popped up in the display cases of 600 theaters scheduled to premiere the movie. Plans were laid to spend the $1 million that Dowd promised Universal over a six-week period coinciding with the opening of the film.[4] Dowd prayed that his gamble would pay off.

The night of the movie's premiere in Hollywood there was a special showing at the Hershey Motor Lodge Theater. Everyone who had worked on the project—the manufacturing people, the technical people, Hershey brass—came to watch the film. Dowd sat anxiously in the back. When the movie was over and the lights came up, nobody said a word. Then suddenly the room burst into applause. Dowd ran out to the lobby so that he could watch the faces of the crowd as they left the theater. Many of them were tearstained. Dowd remembers Earl Spangler leaving the theater, his eyes red and swollen. "And I said, 'Is he still ugly, Earl?' And Earl said, 'Ah, he's beautiful.'"

The movie set all-time box office records, and the publicity was incredible. Sales of Reese's Pieces took off, tripling within two weeks of the film's release. Distributors reordered as many as ten times in that fourteen-day period. Movie-house owners devised their own gimmicks with the candy, such as Guess-How-Many-Reese's-Pieces-Are-in-the-Jar contests and the "extraterrestrial cookie" studded with the candy.

"It was the biggest marketing coup in history," Dowd recalls now, proudly. "We got immediate recognition for our product, the kind of recognition we would normally have to pay fifteen or twenty million bucks for. It ended up as a cheap ride."

After the unrivaled publicity surrounding the Reese's placement, word quickly spread that Mars had been offered the movie deal and had blown it off. Mars was kicking itself. But this gaff reflected the caution that had become the trademark of the Mars brothers. Since taking control of their father's company in 1973, John and Forrest Jr. had developed their own oppressive management style, one that was slowly squeezing out any spark of innovative spirit at the company.

Like their father, John and Forrest Jr. were tyrants. They were inordinately demanding and they had wild, unpredictable tempers, rebuking associates at the slightest provocation. But unlike Forrest Sr., they often seemed irrational in their approach to management. They transferred associates without explanation, played favorites with executives and pitted divisions of the company against one another. At times, their antics seemed to have no ultimate purpose except to let everybody know they were in charge.

Managers who had bristled at Forrest Sr.'s outbursts, but excused them out of respect for his accomplishments, could not accept the same behavior from his sons. They had not earned the right to be SOBs, and instead of inspiring loyalty and devotion, their manner bred paranoia and insecurity.

Working at Mars was enough to make anyone neurotic, as Charles Somborn, a former sales associate, recalls: "At my last big national sales meeting [in 1985], they were giving out ties with the Mars logo if you had a special recognition coming. It meant a lot to a salesman to get one of those ties. [Forrest Jr.] got up to make the presentations, and made a complete ass out of himself. He gave all poor and negative reviews and comments to the award recipients. It was unbelievable. We all just stared, silent."

The brothers were loose cannons, and as John Strong recalled, people ran scared, spending "a lot of time in hiding." As a result, problems were often buried rather than acknowledged and solved, and managers squandered time, resources and opportunities to protect themselves from the wrath from above.

Strong remembers a typical scene from the mid-1980s, at the Skittles and Starburst factory in Waco, Texas. Inventory had piled up, and executives panicked when they heard John Mars was coming down to inspect the plant.

"If John were to come into a warehouse and see a tremendous stockpile of product, he'd probably order the plant shut down, saying, 'Until you get that stuff moved out of here, you won't make any more.' So there was this big tour, and John was coming to Waco. The guys in Waco moved all the product into other warehouses where they knew John wouldn't go. It was unbelievable—just mountains and mountains of [product] they hid from him. They had like six or eight months' inventory, but all John saw was just a few little cases.

"I'm saying this to tell you the mind-set over there, to tell you how people are responding [to the brothers]."

Somborn said the brothers' management style drove him from the company. As he summarized it, "They are the seagull management team. They swoop down, shit and fly away."

As a result, nobody at Mars wanted to be responsible for making any decisions. And at the same time, it seemed as if the Mars brothers themselves were hunkering down. While other companies spent the 1980s capitalizing on the chocolate craze, the brothers appeared unwilling to make any changes in their father's business. And so the company grew increasingly cautious and unresponsive to the market. In a remarkable reversal, Hershey was now playing the role of innovator, while Mars seemed caught up in its own past successes.

The brothers resisted ideas for any new products, choosing instead to endlessly repackage and reformulate the company's established offerings. For most candy companies, a product that grossed $20, $30 or $40 million was considered a blockbuster. But Mars viewed things differently.

"For a while at Mars everything had to earn a hundred million dollars or more," said a former Mars marketer. "The brothers couldn't see the value of smaller launches. They just didn't hold up when compared [to M&M's]."

The company avoided niche products, and the brothers killed any launch if sales failed to meet their extraordinarily aggressive goals. Every product was measured against the success of Snickers, which sold $400 million annually. "Snickers is the best-selling bar in the country, and there can only be one of those," said a former Mars executive. "But the brothers never understood that."

For the first ten years of John and Forrest's tenure, the company tended to limit its new-product introductions to candies that were already successful in England. The company brought over Starburst Fruit Chews, known in England as Opal Fruits. The Twix bar was another British import.

One of the few truly new products Mars introduced was the Summit bar, a wafer and chocolate candy bar meant to compete against Hershey's Kit Kat. But when Summit sales stalled at $40 million in 1985, the brothers ordered it off the market. The company also pulled the plug on Royals, mint-flavored M&M's aimed at the adult market. Like Summit, Royals were canned because they failed to match the sales of original M&M's. The only successful introduction in the 1980s was Kudos, a chocolate-covered granola bar launched in 1986.

In the same period of time, Hershey not only scored its remarkable success with Reese's Pieces but continued to pick up market share with a bevy of smaller successes, like Whatchamacallit, New Trail bars, Hershey's Chocolate Milk, Skor and Take Five. "Hershey wants to have as many products out there on the shelf for the consumer to choose from as possible," said former CEO Richard Zimmerman. "New-product launches are the key to getting consumers excited about candy and eating our products." The strategy worked: Between 1979 and 1984, new products surged from 7 percent of Hershey's sales to nearly 20 percent.[5]

In defense of the brothers' conservatism, Ed Stegemann said, "We just don't go out and throw things on the wall and see what sticks."

But former Mars marketing managers say the company squandered dozens of opportunities to expand market share because the brothers demanded so much research and proof before they were willing to give products a green light. "Mars tested and retested new products. They conducted market study after market study. They would spend millions of dollars just to find out if the product would succeed, and then the brothers would [complain] that they were spending too much on research," remembered one former manager. It was a Catch-22.

According to Sharon Hennessy, a Mars manager in England, the 1970s health scare over sugar consumption had a lot to do with Mars's timid attitude. "The entire United States was saying sugar promotes tooth decay. It's no wonder they were afraid to invest hundreds of millions of dollars into the business." But that timidity lingered long after public attitudes had changed.

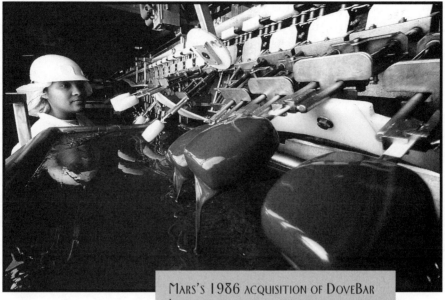

MARS'S 1986 ACQUISITION OF DOVEBAR INTERNATIONAL WAS A DARING MOVE AT A TIME WHEN MARS MANAGEMENT APPEARED OTHERWISE MORIBUND.

The mentality of the company's research and development division raised another barrier to new-product development. The R&D department had always been focused on solving problems related to the manufacturing process, rather than trying to develop new candies.

But final responsibility for the company's weakness in product development rests squarely with John and Forrest Jr. They tended to make decisions based on their own personal preferences, and, having spent their childhood in England, their tastes were not compatible with those of Americans. "I venture to say that there isn't a product that ever goes out that Forrest, John or Jackie haven't personally shaped, touched or tasted," said one Uncle Ben's executive. "Their name is on the product, so that's the way it is."

The brothers didn't eat peanut butter growing up, so they never recognized its allure for Americans. Fanfare, a European candy bar made with hazelnut paste, is a family favorite. Americans hate hazelnut paste, and tests of Fanfare have always failed in the United States. But that doesn't stop the brothers from repeatedly proposing hazelnut products, each of which fails at the product testing stage.

John Mars tells a slightly different story. "Mars didn't launch new products because Mars doesn't have a lot of new products to launch. Neither do most other companies. There's nothing new in the candy world. All these products have been done before."

Instead of focusing on innovation, the Mars brothers have grown the company through global expansion, taking M&M's, Snickers and Milky Way around the world.

A CHOCOLATE-
COVERED WORLD

FORREST MARS'S DREAM
WAS TO SEE M&M'S
ON SALE THROUGHOUT
THE WORLD. BY 1992
HIS DREAM HAD COME
TRUE, ALTHOUGH IT
TAKES MORE THAN A
DAY'S WAGES FOR THE
AVERAGE CHINESE
WORKER TO AFFORD
A PACKAGE OF THE
PRECIOUS CANDIES.

*I*T IS A TYPICAL day inside the Mars plant. The pit, desks arranged in standard wagon-wheel fashion, is abuzz with activity as associates discuss the day's production. Dotting the room are little tables, each with a full complement of Mars products. This is to encourage associates to snack, a means of keeping tabs on overall quality. But it's not a free-for-all. To keep it polite, there is also a little knife and cutting board, and each associate is expected to slice off a dainty sample.

There are few pictures on the walls, and no marks of individuality decorate the desks—no family photos or good-luck charms or bulletin boards with little cartoons. As at every plant, there are dozens of copies of "The Five Principles of Mars" strewn about, on conference tables, filing cabinets, in the entryway. Most workers are dressed in their starched whites, uniforms provided by the company and laundered daily. Some are wearing hard hats, and everyone has their first name emblazoned on their coats. There is no way to tell who is in charge—who is an executive and who is a janitor. There is also no way to tell that you are in a factory located in the former Soviet Union, just 120 kilometers outside Moscow.

For the citizens of Stupino, a smallish industrial community on the banks of the Oka River, the arrival of the Mars plant has meant salvation. Stupino was once part of Russia's vast military establishment, closed to outsiders and left off maps of the country. With the collapse of the Soviet Union in 1990, the town's economic base all but disappeared. But now, with Mars as its industrial backbone, Stupino has become part of the global capitalist system.

The 100-acre plant, opened in the summer of 1995, produces nine different candy products, from Mars bars to Milky Ways. Mars also manufactures a hard mint candy called Rondos and a hazelnut chocolate bar called Topic. The $140-million plant employs 650 workers and can produce 70,000 tons of candy a year.[1]

The plant is the physical embodiment of what the press has pejoratively called "the Snickerization of Russia"—a brilliantly conceived campaign to win the imaginations and taste buds of the former Soviet citizens.

The highlight of the campaign came on a bitterly cold morning in the middle of a particularly vicious Moscow winter, when thousands of Russians lined up in the pre-dawn hours hoping for their first taste of a Snickers bar. Mars had been advertising for weeks that it was coming to town, bringing Milky Ways and M&M's to sweet-starved Muscovites. With billboards and heavily televised charity programs, the company had been teasing the populace with mouthwatering pictures of its products and a promise that they would be available on January 4, 1990, at a store created especially for the occasion. The night before the opening, a line began to form, composed of eager Russian consumers, their pockets stuffed with rubles to buy their very first Western confectionery. By the time the doors were unlocked the line stretched for more than a quarter mile, and extra Russian police were on hand to make sure the crowd did not get out of control. Despite a limit of four candy bars per customer, Mars sold more than twenty tons of chocolate in two days, an auspicious

Игра или дело – ешь «Марс» смело!

Сливки, жжёный сахар и
толстый слой шоколада

MAIDEN SOVIET

NOT LONG AFTER THE COLLAPSE OF THE FORMER SOVIET UNION, MARS ERECTED
BILLBOARDS LIKE THIS ONE THROUGHOUT MOSCOW, ATTRACTING THE ATTENTION
OF CHOCOLATE-STARVED MUSCOVITES.

beginning for the first Western candy company to offer its products
within the once Communist state.

It was a remarkable coup, the culmination of the company's "Presence Program." This public relations campaign had begun on November 17, 1989, in Moscow, with the announcement that Mars would be
appointed the exclusive supplier of candy to the All Union Children's
International Theme Park, a Disney-style amusement park and pet project of then president Gorbachev. With the coming of Christmas, Mars
launched its first television promotions, using the theme "All the World
Loves M&M's." Mars wanted to capitalize on the fact that this was the
first officially endorsed Christmas since the Russian Revolution. The
company threw Christmas parties for disadvantaged children in Moscow,
Leningrad and Orsk, including a rock party for 4,000 teens. These
events attracted extensive television coverage, boosting familiarity with
the Mars name across the Soviet republics.

The campaign culminated in the two-day sale on Kalinin Prospekt, a major shopping area near the Kremlin, providing Russians with a unique opportunity to try Western candy. Other companies were avoiding the Russian market because the country did not permit foreigners to take profits out in hard currency. In other words, if you brought in your products and sold them for rubles, you had traded good merchandise for worthless paper. But Mars had solved this problem by trading its candy for Soviet shipping rights. The deal gave the company a one-time shot to get tons of candy into Moscow, and while it did not generate any profit, that's not what it was about.

"We wanted maximum exposure for our product," said David Badger, the Mars executive who orchestrated the Russian invasion. "We wanted everyone talking about Mars."

When Russia opened its currency market in 1992, allowing companies to exchange rubles for dollars, Mars was ready to capitalize on its investment. Since that winter day in 1990, sales in the former Soviet Union have exploded, reaching more than $300 million annually. In 1994, the company began construction of the Stupino factory, and within thirteen months, it was up and running. In 1997, Mars recorded its first profit from the plant, though Badger declined to give a figure.

The speed and determination exhibited by Mars in opening the Russian market has stunned its rivals. Today, there isn't a kiosk in the country that doesn't carry a full line of Mars products. The company is spending $25 million a year in advertising, and it has captured more than 40 percent of all candy sales, making it the largest confectioner in the market.[2]

The Snickers bar and Mars bar rank among the best-selling candies in the former Soviet bloc countries. Badger, who is one of Jacqueline Mars's ex-husbands and still considered a member of the Mars family, finds the success of the company's brands inspiring. "There is no question in my mind [now] that our major brands, Mars, Snickers, Twix, M&M's know no boundaries. The consumer demand for sweets is universal."

It had always been Forrest Sr.'s dream to see Snickers bars on sale in China, in Russia, in Pakistan—all over the world. "The only big business has got to be an international business," said Forrest Sr. "Mars is going to be in Russia some day. We'll be in China. You need simple businesses if you wish to go for the world . . . candy bars are probably the easiest way to start."[3]

From the company's beginnings in Slough, England, Forrest Sr. had started a push to the Continent, building pet food plants in France and

Germany and candy factories in France and the Netherlands. But it was up to John and Forrest Jr. to carry out his lifelong ambition, building Mars, Inc., into a truly global empire.

As the Iron Curtain fell, Mars put David Badger in charge of breaking open Hungary, Romania, Czechoslovakia, Russia and Poland. Adhering to their father's principle that being first in the market was paramount to success, the brothers ordered Badger to set up distribution lines as fast as borders opened up.

In the summer of 1991, just as Prague was getting its first taste of Western commercial culture with the opening of stores like Benetton and Nike, I traveled with Mars associates as they planned their initial assault on the city. Though Czechoslovakia had been liberated from Communist rule one year earlier, the city was only starting to see real changes. Prague had its first billboard—an ad for Panasonic—but there were still no fast-food chains, no department stores, and only one Western-style hotel. Consumer goods were largely local or East German imports and, most important, good chocolate was nowhere to be found.

"People here haven't tasted real chocolate since before World War II," said Roland Von Moos, Mars's point man in Czechoslovakia.

"Try it," Von Moos continued, handing me a native candy bar. "It will make your mouth pucker." I bit it, then quickly spat it out. The chocolate was incredibly gritty, almost like eating sand.

This is what brought Mars so eagerly into the region. Before the war, the nations of Eastern Europe were some of the biggest candy consumers in the world. Their confectioners were renowned for their fine chocolates and superb cordials, but this legacy was lost during four decades of Communist rule.

A whole generation had come of age without ever tasting fine candies—and without ever even hearing of Mars. But for Milada Novakova, the name had a special resonance. So scarce was candy of the quality we take for granted, that the twenty-five-year-old Czech, daughter of a university professor, remembered clearly a childhood trip to East Germany when her father had bought her a packet of M&M's on the black market.

"I will never forget eating those candies," said Novakova. "They were the most sumptuous thing I'd ever eaten."

By chance, when Badger was visiting Prague in 1990 to scout out the market, he hired Novakova as his tour guide and translator. Within a day, he had invited her to join the company, making her the first employee of Mars, Czechoslovakia. Novakova helped Mars set up an office and began searching out possible retail outlets for the company's products, including its rice and pet foods. She was joined six months later by Von Moos, a young, energetic associate who had worked for Mars in Zurich.

The week that I arrived, Phil Forster, the brothers' second-in-command and Mars's chief of brands worldwide, was also in the city. I accompanied the three of them as they scouted Prague for places to advertise Mars products. Pointing to a large, dingy brick wall, just off the main shopping district, Forster turned to Von Moos and said, "How much do you think they'll want us to pay for that space?"

Von Moos looked puzzled for a moment, and then realized that where he saw the side of a decaying building, Forster saw a bulletin board waiting for his message. As we strolled along Wenceslas Square, Forster pointed to location after location where Mars products could be showcased. "Look at those umbrellas," said Forster, referring to the sun shades over a sidewalk café that carried the Cinzano label. "Those should be Mars umbrellas."

At one point, Forster took out a wad of cash from his pocket, handed it to Von Moos and sent him into a store to ask for permission to place Mars billboards in the window.

He took note, as we were strolling, of how many pets he saw in the streets. "There's lots of customers here," he said, pointing to a pile of evidence that had been left beneath a tree. I didn't follow what he meant until he added, "People don't generally take notice of these things, but I do. We actually count the dog [droppings]."

Mars's ground-level efforts in Prague have been duplicated in Hungary, Romania and Poland. In each country Mars began by forming a distribution network to get its products in front of consumers. Massive advertising campaigns were backed by skilled negotiations with local governments to help ensure Mars's success. In Hungary, for example, Mars first entered the market in 1989, after negotiating a deal to exchange imports of candy for exports of animal parts that the company could use for its pet food business. "At the time there were restrictions on how much we could bring into the country without bringing [product out]," explained Ed Stegemann. "We were lucky in that they had something we needed." The restrictions on the Hungarian market have since disappeared, but because Mars was one of the first Western candy companies in Hungary, it remains a market leader.

The entrepreneurial approach that Mars used to break into the Eastern bloc reflects the company's overall strategy for global expansion. At Mars there is no grand blueprint for taking the company around the world. Mars enters new markets as opportunities arise, sending in one or two associates to scout out product potential and organize distribution. Over time, as sales expand, the brothers boost their investment until the new market is self-sufficient.

Unlike Coca-Cola or General Foods, Mars has never established an international board of directors to preside over its global operations. Instead, each individual business unit is designed to be completely self-contained, connected to McLean only through its products and principles. The Mars brothers rely on local talent to get products into the marketplace and, except for the company's flagship brands, design advertising for their consumers. And although John and Forrest Jr. travel the globe themselves, carrying ideas from one country to the next and broadly overseeing local decisions, that is the extent of any corporate involvement.

In this way, Mars has expanded to include more than seventy independent business units from Helsinki to Hong Kong. Today, Mars is the global market leader with 15 percent of worldwide candy sales. It is particularly strong in the market for candy bars, where Mars controls 28.5 percent of the U.S. market and 27.5 percent of the U.K. market, and is among the top three players in the Netherlands, France, Germany, Italy and Australia.[4]

Individual units never advertise their American origins, preferring instead to let each business unit blend into the local environment. Still, the brothers have inculcated the Mars culture in every one. Walk into the Mars office in Strasbourg, France, for example, and there is the staff sitting in open offices, meeting in glass-enclosed conference rooms. The Five Principles are expounded in fluent French by associates who see Mars, Inc., as a French company. And they're not alone. In virtually every country where Mars markets its products, few people realize it is an American firm—which is just the way the brothers want it.

The global flavor of Mars is evident throughout the company. Mars managers typically speak at least three languages, and most speak five or six. There are Japanese associates running the Japanese offices and Dutch associates running the Holland offices. There are also Brits in the United States and Germans in Spain.

"We're one of the few truly international companies managed by international people," said Phil Forster, a Brit. At one time, he bragged, foreign-born executives actually outnumbered Americans 2 to 1. Forster himself speaks seven languages and has lived in at least as many countries.

The company's individual business units manufacture dozens of local products. In Australia, for example, Mars makes millions on sauces and spices sold under the Master Foods label. In Germany, the company recently started selling freshly made pasta in grocery stores, an enterprise Mars hopes will become as popular as Contadina has in the United States.

The brothers are always looking for the next local product to take around the world, and they are constantly exchanging products from country to country. It was in this way that Forrest Sr. originally built the business in England. He introduced the British to a product he called Maltesers, a malted milk-chocolate candy he copied from Whoppers in the United States. And he brought over two types of medicated cough drops, which he called Tunes and Lockets, copied from Luden's and Halls.

The corporate philosophy behind the Mars approach is known to associates as "the transfer of best practice," meaning simply that what works in one country will work in another, as Forrest Sr. proved when he took the Milky Way overseas. Following in his footsteps, John and Forrest Jr. preach that if Americans eat Uncle Ben's rice, so, too, will the Pakistanis. And if an advertisement is effective in England, it will also work in Brazil.

Not that every transfer has met with the same success. A granola product similar to Kudos was a flop when it was introduced in Germany. A line of Asian foods called Suzie Wan, popular in Australia, failed when it was introduced in the United States. But as overseer of all Mars brands—which number more than one hundred worldwide—Forster asks his managers to say why their products *shouldn't* become global. It's the opposite of the approach traditionally taken by many American executives, who ask managers to justify why a brand deserves to be marketed abroad.

From pet food to rice to candy, all of Mars's best-selling brands are sold around the world. This push to make key products as multinational as possible has been a top priority for the brothers since their father stepped down. But pursuing this goal has required an enormous investment in marketing and advertising.

It used to be that a Snickers bar was known by many different names in many different countries. For example, in Britain a Snickers was known as a Marathon and M&M's were known as Treets. (Forrest Sr. originally changed the Snickers name because the word rhymed with *knickers,* and he didn't want his consumers to make such an association.) But in the last ten years Mars has relaunched all of its major brands, giving them the same name and the same advertising pitch in every country. Smaller brands are still marketing on a local level, giving Mars the flexibility it needs to respond to national tastes while allowing it to capitalize on economies of scale when marketing its flagship brands.

"Twenty-five years ago I could have advertised in Holland that the Mars bar was giving you energy and in Belgium I could have advertised the Mars bar was a sleeping pill, and nobody would have known because people couldn't see each other's television or read each other's newspapers," said Theo Leenders, the Mars executive who oversaw the company's Olympics sponsorship. "But with the advent of CNN and satellites and . . . the Olympics, we realized we had to harmonize our brands."

Candy wrappers also used to differ from country to country, but Mars has changed that as well. And the company has spent millions of dollars teaching consumers how to pronounce the names of its candies. The name M&M's, for example, caused a lot of confusion overseas. "In Italy we showed them the pack of M&M's and asked customers to pronounce it, and they'd say, 'mmm, mmm.' Or 'umee, ur, umee.' They never said M&M."

The name and wrapper changes often lead to a drop in sales, at least initially. "It's difficult overnight to convince consumers that the same brand they've been buying for twenty-five years will still be the candy they want but with a different name," said Leenders. "But we felt it was critical to create truly global brands to get the synergies from advertising and promotions."

Mars's sponsorship of the 1984 Olympics helped wake up the company to this reality. There were no Mars brands that could be advertised at the games that would be recognized in every nation. Now this is no longer the case. In 1988 and 1992, Mars was a worldwide sponsor of the games, spending hundreds of millions of dollars in Olympics-related promotions, and it could support this investment with its major brands, Snickers and M&M's. Today, the company is a major sponsor of the World Cup, a position made possible by these global brands.

The "best practice" approach is in sharp contrast to that of Mars's top international competitor, Nestlé S.A., which routinely enters new markets by acquiring local food companies or by signing joint manufacturing agreements, often outspending Mars on the front end by hundreds of millions of dollars. Before entering a new country, the Swiss giant will map out its marketing plan and schedule mass production, always bringing in its own Swiss or German managers to oversee the market. The strategy has made Nestlé the world's biggest food manufacturer, with 1997 worldwide sales of $46.7 billion dollars.[5]

In the last ten years, Nestlé has gone on a buying spree never before seen in the food business. The company goes head-to-head with Mars in pet food and candy, and it has strengthened both divisions with its recent spate of acquisitions. In 1994, the company acquired Alpo, which competes against Mars's Pedigree brand dog food in the United States. In 1988, in a spectacular bidding war that turned the British candy market upside down, Nestlé purchased Rowntree, the nation's second-largest chocolate maker. Italy's Perugina has also recently been merged into the Nestlé fold.

Nestlé chairman and chief executive Helmut Maucher, the engineer behind these acquisitions, says it is his goal to see Nestlé conquer the world. The company already has more than 400 plants in sixty countries, with 195,000 employees. Its global advertising budget is nearly $2 billion. It is the most multinational of the world's multinational food giants: In most every aisle, in most every supermarket, in most every country, you can find something Nestlé makes. And Maucher predicts that Nestlé sales will reach 100 billion Swiss francs ($60 billion at today's exchange rate) by the year 2000.[6]

Despite Nestlé's consistent success, Mars associates believe strongly in their entrepreneurial style. And in any case, as former associates point out, the Mars culture leaves its owners little choice. An acquisition of any size would require Mars to assimilate hundreds or thousands of new employees into its no-frills, hardworking environment. It is much easier to recruit locals who are open to the Mars way of doing business than to teach the company's principles in the aftermath of a takeover. In addition, the brothers are reluctant to spend the vast sums necessary to buy a business, fearing they would stretch the company too thin or force it into debt. "Once we become like P&G, Nestlé or General Foods, we're dead," says Forster. "We don't buy and sell, we build."

The strategy is perfectly suited to Mars, and the brothers have stuck to it with admirable tenacity; but like any business strategy, it comes with a downside. Mars's aversion to acquisitions has made it difficult for the company to compete against global operators like Nestlé and Kraft Jacobs Suchard, a division of Philip Morris, America's biggest tobacco and food processor.

Neither of these companies operates within the strict constraints that bind Mars. As a result they are able to grow more rapidly and expand into new markets more quickly. When Nestlé wanted to enter the candy market in Hungary, it bought a local chocolate factory, a move Mars never would have considered. The company did the same thing in Poland and the Czech Republic. And Jacobs Suchard, backed by its giant corporate parent, has swallowed a half-dozen confectioners in recent years, including some of Europe's premier companies like Cote d'Or and Van Houten.

Everywhere Mars executives turn these days, they are staring in the face of stiff competition from players with far more resources than themselves. Just five months after Mars opened the Stupino plant in Russia, Cadbury opened its own Russian factory in the Novgorod region south of St. Petersburg. The $120-million plant is Cadbury's most modern facility in Europe. Meanwhile, Jacobs Suchard has purchased a small candy plant in St. Petersburg, and Nestlé has acquired two regional Russian candy makers in the southern city of Samara, on the Volga River. Having merged them into a single company, called Rossiya, Nestlé is now trying to build brand recognition with a national advertising campaign.[7]

These multinational behemoths are extending their control over the candy market worldwide. Dominic Cadbury, chairman of Cadbury Schweppes, estimates that the leading five manufacturers account for half of the world's candy sales, and he expects their share to reach 60 percent by 2006.[8]

Overall, Nestlé sells about 10 percent of the world's candy. It is a leader in Europe, controlling one-quarter of the British market, thanks to its 1988 purchase of Rowntree. Although the company lags behind Mars and Hershey in the United States, it is not content to remain an also-ran. In 1989, Nestlé spent $370 million to buy RJR Nabisco's Baby Ruth, Butterfinger and Pearson confectionery businesses, boosting its market share from 7 percent to 12 percent. And aggressive advertising has since raised its share another 3 points.[9]

Philip Morris's Kraft Jacobs Suchard has a market share of about 6 percent worldwide, with many established global brands, such as Toblerone, Tobler bars and Milka. The company expanded rapidly in the late 1980s, purchasing over $1 billion worth of businesses.[10]

Concerns over these global rivals are what motivated Mars to adopt such aggressive tactics in the former Soviet Union and Eastern Europe. "Our mission was to achieve a dominant position in all relevant product categories in each and every country," said Badger. "We realized that the opportunity might never exist again, as our competitors' brands were virtually unknown."

Mars wanted to put itself in the same league as Pepsi, Marlboro and McDonald's—Western brands with cachet and instant recognition throughout the former Communist states. And it has succeeded.

"What we've done in Russia is nothing short of miraculous," said Mike Davies, who is responsible for developing new markets. "Nobody knew our brands. Nobody had tasted a Mars candy. And now, Snickers is a Russian word."

Industry analysts agree with Davies's assessment, calling Mars's success in Russia one of the company's greatest triumphs. "Mars opened up that market overnight," said Nomi Ghez, of Goldman Sachs. "They paved the way for confectionery brands throughout the Eastern bloc countries."

The one glaring absence from this heated international competition is the Hershey Chocolate Corp. Although it has tried many times to expand globally, each attempt has ended in failure. Indeed, the company has squandered unique opportunities that might have made another company the world leader.

No company has ever been as poised to take advantage of global brand recognition as Hershey was in the years following World War II. The war made Hershey famous from Japan to North Africa to Paris and London. What's more, Europe's candy companies were devastated by the war. Hershey had one of the only fully operational chocolate factories in the world in 1945. But in a remarkable display of provincialism, Hershey's management failed to recognize the tremendous opportunities at hand.

The company simply ignored the overseas markets, choosing instead to focus on satisfying demand for chocolate at home. "There was a tremendous shortage after the war in America," said former Hershey CEO Richard Zimmerman. "And it was all we could do to keep up with the domestic market."

It was a mistake from which the company has never fully recovered. "There was a lack of intellectual capacity. . . . There was no recognition of just how powerful these brands and these products could have been," said Zimmerman. "It's a decision that we'd all like to do over, but that's not for us to really consider. We were dealt a hand, and now we have to play that hand." Zimmerman believes that if Milton Hershey himself had been alive following the war he would have pushed the company to go abroad. "He traveled quite a bit," said Zimmerman. "He was more worldly focused."

Hershey had a second great opportunity to develop an international

presence in 1969, when executives of Cadbury came to the United States looking for a merger partner. Maurice Jeffery, the head of research and development for Cadbury, met with Harold Mohler and several other Hershey executives to talk about the potential benefits of a merger. Mohler was intrigued by the idea, but it was another victim of Hershey's retreat in the wake of the cocoa price spike in the early seventies.

"The two together would have been a major powerhouse," said Jeffery, who authored a report within Cadbury recommending the merger. "Hershey was very much a manufacturing company, and Cadbury on the other hand was very much a marketing company. It would have been the perfect fit." Jeffery said the recommendation was not acted upon because of the turmoil Hershey faced in the 1970s. "The timing was all wrong," he said. "If only we would have started talks sooner, I think today we would see Hershey worldwide."

$\mathcal{T}$he list of Hershey's international failures goes on and on. Start in Canada: After spending millions of dollars on research to perfect the Hershey flavor at its Smith Falls plant, the company learned that Canadians did not share the tastes of U.S. consumers.

Hershey has been no more successful south of the border. Although it has tried to sell its products in Mexico for decades, Mars's market share surpassed Hershey's in the very first year it entered the market. And the story played out the same way in Japan. In 1979, Hershey entered into an agreement for a Japanese company to import, make and sell Hershey products, but the confectionery company, Fujiya, never had much success. Mars has since surpassed Hershey in Japan.

The Mexico and Japan experiences are typical. Whenever Hershey has tried to introduce its chocolates abroad, foreigners have rejected the Hershey flavor. "A Hershey bar is stiff. It does not melt like European chocolates. It tastes stale," said Hans Scheu of the Cocoa Merchants Association. "It doesn't have the smell or the feel of a real chocolate bar." Still, even Scheu has to admit he likes a Hershey Almond bar. "When Mr. Hershey combined that sour chocolate with almonds, he really had something," he concedes.

Lisbeth Echeandia, the publisher of *Confectioner* magazine, tells of taking Reese's Peanut Butter Cups to a seminar in Germany on American products. "The Germans couldn't believe Americans would eat it. They were tasting the candy and spitting it out." According to Echeandia, "The world out there eats Hershey chocolate and goes, 'Yuck.' They're going to have to come up with another answer."

Hershey executives have talked about launching their Symphony chocolates overseas, since Symphony is a more European-style candy. But Echeandia predicts Symphony will fall flat in Europe. "Compared to the cheapest chocolate bar in Europe, a Symphony is nothing special."

And the problem is not just the famous Hershey flavor. For Hershey to become global, "they're going to have to change their whole mindset," said Echeandia.

"Hershey has always been seen as backward," agrees Scheu. "They don't understand the world market at all." In fact, Jay Carr, appointed by Hershey in 1993 to be its vice president in charge of international operations, doesn't even speak a foreign language. "How can they really have hopes for global expansion when he can't even communicate?" asked Jeffery, who is currently a consultant in the industry.

Recognizing that it lacks the expertise and products to expand globally on its own, the company has tried acquiring overseas companies. Hershey put high hopes on a planned acquisition of Freia Marabou, a Norwegian chocolate company with a strong presence in Scandinavia, but the company lost out in a bidding war against Philip Morris. Hershey continued its efforts, however, buying a German praline maker,

Gubor Schokoladen, and an Italian sugar confectioner, Sperlari, Srl. But Hershey simply found itself unable to compete in the European markets and in 1996, after years of disappointing results, sold both companies for a loss of $35 million.[11]

Having failed in Europe, Hershey is now pinning its hopes on Latin America. In 1998, the company appointed a new head of international operations, Patrice Le Maire, who had successfully restructured Procter & Gamble's export division. Le Maire promptly moved Hershey's international headquarters from Pennsylvania to Miami, Florida, to be closer to Central and South America. Le Maire believes Hershey has a better chance to expand its global sales by focusing on these markets, where the competition is less entrenched.

As it stands, Hershey exports products to more than ninety countries. But these sales are "very modest indeed," admits Hershey's current CEO, Kenneth Wolfe, representing less than 4 percent of the company's total revenues. Hershey has no manufacturing facilities overseas and no offices outside the United States.

Hans Scheu summed it all up nicely. "Hershey is not a player. Nobody on the world scene gives Hershey a second thought."

Helmut Maucher, Nestlé's chairman, echoes this sentiment, saying he does not consider Hershey competition. Although Nestlé competes against Hershey in North America, Hershey's lack of overseas success keeps it from registering on Maucher's radar screen. "When I think about chocolate, I think Mars and Philip Morris."

The inability to compete globally has important ramifications. Without an overseas presence, Hershey is often left out of the major developments in chocolate. The industry is centered in Europe—that's where all the production technology comes from, where all the innovations regarding manufacturing take place. And while Mars and Nestlé and Suchard and Cadbury are constantly bumping against each other and pushing each other to greater efficiencies, Hershey is left completely out of the loop.

Louis Smith, who oversaw Hershey's research and development in the 1960s, always argued for Hershey to have an office in Switzerland in order to keep abreast of the latest innovations. "You don't know what's going on unless you're there," he said. "There's no substitute for being there. Absolutely none."

And the United States is basically a mature market, which will expand at only moderate rates in the years to come. The growth markets are all overseas, particularly in the Far East, where chocolate consumption is expected to expand at astronomical rates for the foreseeable future. China has a population of 1.2 billion, who consume an average of less than one ounce of chocolate each year, compared with three pounds in Hong Kong—and over twenty pounds in Europe. While it will take time for the market to reach its full potential, the process has already begun: Chocolate consumption in China more than doubled between 1988 and 1994, from 9,500 tons to almost 22,000 tons.[12]

Cadbury has recently built a large plant near Beijing in cooperation with the Chinese government; although the plant is expected to lose money for years, Cadbury views it as an important long-term investment. The company already has factories in Malaysia, in Indonesia, in India. Mars has had a plant in Beijing since 1992, producing M&M's and Galaxy brand chocolate, a popular British line. And Nestlé has announced plans to open two factories in China, one for ice cream and one for chocolate and powdered milk.[13]

Together, these three companies are the major challengers for dominance in Asia. For the moment, however, there is plenty of business to go around, as the companies' advertising efforts combine to expand the market. But as these companies establish their brands in the markets of the future, Hershey sits at home and watches.

The company seems to have resigned itself to the unpleasant reality. Unlike Mars and the rest of the confectionery leaders, Hershey no longer sees global expansion as a top priority. "I think we have to label it as a goal . . . but it's going to be difficult," said Zimmerman. "It will take us maybe a quarter of a century [to get our foot in the door].

"We can be a very successful company in North America without being in Europe," he concluded optimistically.

Chapter Twenty-two

RAISING THE BAR

THE BATTLE FOR SHELF SPACE IS THE FINAL FRONTIER OF THE CHOCOLATE WARS. MANUFACTURERS PAY RETAILERS MILLIONS OF DOLLARS TO HAVE THEIR PRODUCTS PROMINENTLY DISPLAYED.

WILLIAM DEARDEN SAYS he remembers an interview that Milton Hershey once granted a Cuban journalist. When asked whether he regretted never having children, Hershey replied: "Yes, I do regret that, and I do wish that I had a child of my own." He told the reporter that if one of the orphans were his own flesh and blood, he'd give him everything he had. But, he added hopefully, "Maybe someday one of those boys will end up running my business."[1]

The ten years that Dearden spent as Milton Hershey's successor were a turning point in the company's history. Hershey spent the early eighties turning up the heat on advertising and introducing a flurry of new products aimed at taking sales away from Mars. By the time Dearden retired, in 1985, the two companies were in a dead heat. Hershey had shed its moribund image and emerged as a vigorous challenger for Mars's throne.

It was Dearden's way of saying thank you.

"Looking back over my life, I say to myself sometimes, 'Where would you be today had it not been for the school?' I'd have probably never finished high school, would have never had the opportunity I had to go on to college and graduate school and the navy.[2]

"I think that maybe one of the most important thrills in my life is having had, through coincidence, the opportunity to repay a subjective debt that I felt I owed Mr. Hershey for what he did for me as a boy."[3]

As Richard Zimmerman took Bill Dearden's place, his first priority was reclaiming the top spot in the candy industry. The Lebanon, Pennsylvania, native had joined the company in 1958, as an assistant to then president Hinkle. A quiet, reserved man, he had always worked in Dearden's shadow, spending most of his career in Hershey's nonchocolate ventures. But now that Zimmerman was in charge, he was determined to prove that he could lead Hershey's core candy business, orchestrating its bid to finally overtake Mars.

He declared that he was ready to increase the company's debt to 40 percent of its capital, if he could find the right acquisition. He negotiated the purchase of RJR Nabisco's Canadian candy and nut operation for $140 million. He also acquired Dietrich Corp., maker of Luden's cough drops, Mellomints and 5th Avenue chocolate bars, for $100 million. These acquisitions were made possible, in part, by the Reagan administration's relaxed stance toward antitrust law.

"This was an enormous boon to our business," said Zimmerman. "It allowed us to concentrate on what we knew best and to grow our business very quickly."

Zimmerman also pushed for at least one new, hot product each year. In 1988, Hershey introduced Bar None, a peanut chocolate wafer bar. The company expanded its presence in grocery stores by introducing a line of Hershey puddings to complement its chocolate milk.

But the biggest coup of all came later that year, when Hershey purchased the Peter Paul brands—Almond Joy, Mounds and York Peppermint Patties—from British giant Cadbury Schweppes. To pay for the acquisition, Zimmerman jettisoned the Friendly chain of restaurants, whose sales had been ailing.

With the acquisition, Hershey boasted half of the top twenty brands in the United States, and its share of the total candy market eclipsed Mars by more than 2 points, 21 percent to 18.5 percent. "I've been number two and number one," said Zimmerman after the acquisition. "Number one is better."

Mars executives say that Hershey's move came as no surprise to them. The prior year, they say, the brothers had passed up the same opportunity, leaving the door wide open for their American rival. Nevertheless, the merger struck a nerve.

Given its corporate culture and management philosophy, Mars had made only one significant acquisition: DoveBar International, Inc., a family-owned Chicago company that had taken the country by storm with its hand-dipped ice-cream bars. And Mars had introduced only a handful of new candy products in the United States over the years. The company's last successful launch was Kudos, the chocolate and granola bar that hit the market in 1987. Before that, there had been little beyond Twix, Skittles and Starburst, all launched years earlier.

If Mars were again to overtake Hershey, John and Forrest Jr. decided, they would have to make fundamental changes in the business. For fifteen years, the brothers had struggled to measure up to their father's expectations while adhering faithfully to his management gospel. Now they'd have to rethink the way he did things.

In seeking a new approach, the brothers relied heavily on the judgment of Alfred Poe. Hired in the early 1980s for a top spot on the Kal Kan marketing team, the thirty-two-year-old Poe was one of the company's youngest recruits. But it was more than just his youth that set him apart.

At six feet four inches, Poe towered over most of the other executives. Aggressive and boastful, he loved to recount the story of his rise from Brooklyn's low-income housing projects to Harvard, where he earned his MBA. One of the company's few black managers, he laced his speech with street talk that contrasted sharply with the Mars brothers' style. And to top it all off, there were his flamboyant trappings: a fashionable wardrobe and a sable brown Porsche 944.

Yet it was precisely because he was different that, in November 1988, Poe was tapped to help Mars reclaim its candy crown. He became the head of marketing at Mars.

Two years earlier, at Kal Kan, Poe had made a number of remarkable recommendations. Because the U.S. pet food division was struggling, Poe and others suggested that the recipes be changed and that the higher-quality European formula be used to make the company's dog and cat food for the American market. To coincide with the changes, Poe suggested that Kal Kan adopt the brand names—Pedigree and Whiskas—that had been so successful abroad. He believed that by folding all the dog food products under one umbrella brand and all the cat food products under another, the company would need just two marketing campaigns to sell the whole range of chow, and the increased name recognition would benefit all of the products.

Few in the company thought the brothers would go for these changes. Forrest Sr. would have never considered such an outlandish idea. Everyone knew that a brand was sacrosanct; it represented just one kind of product.

But what if Poe and his allies were right? Kal Kan controlled just 7 percent of the U.S. pet food market,[4] and it was losing ground fast. The cost savings would be tremendous in the long run, so the brothers took the chance. They renamed their entire dog food line Pedigree and their cat food line Whiskas.

WORKERS UNROLL A MASS OF TAFFY THAT WILL BE SLICED INTO BITE-SIZED PIECES AND BECOME STARBURST FRUIT CHEWS. THE TAFFY ROLLS EACH WEIGH MORE THAN ONE HUNDRED POUNDS.

Critics inside and outside the company blasted the change as too risky and expensive. But consumers weren't buying criticism, they were buying pet chow. The deluge of advertising caught their attention, which was exactly what Poe was hoping for. The results were phenomenal. By 1989, Kal Kan's market share had nearly doubled. And so it dawned on the brothers Mars: If many different varieties of dog food could all be marketed under the same name, the possibilities for expanding the company's other key brands were endless.

In 1989, spurred on by Poe's success, Mars associates launched the biggest blitz of new treats since the Great Depression. Snickers branched out into Peanut Butter Snickers. Kudos suddenly became Butter Almond Kudos and Cookies and Creme Kudos. Skittles, Starburst, Combos and Twix all burst out in new flavors. Even M&M's got a face-lift, with three new varieties—peanut butter, almond and mint—being rolled out.

Other sweets also made their debuts. PB Max, a peanut butter cookie combination; the solid dark-chocolate Dove bar; and the coconut-filled Bounty bar—which until now had been marketed only in Canada and Europe—were introduced, competing head-on with Reese's Peanut Butter Cups, the Hershey bar and the Mounds bar. The Mars marketers also resurrected—in a new, improved version—a bar called Forever Yours that had been pulled from the market in 1979 because sales hadn't met the brothers' extravagant expectations. This time they called it the Milky Way Dark. And the company also unveiled the revolutionary lower-in-fat Milky Way II.

Poe's formal responsibilities were limited to the Mars division, but his ideas sparked innovation in all sections of the company. In 1989, the makers of the Dove bar created an ice-cream version of the 3 Musketeers. Snickers and Milky Way ice-cream products soon followed.

To match the product innovations, Poe and his team of marketing managers beefed up ad spending in 1989 and 1990 and added new twists to the company's standard marketing approach. For example, Snickers hadn't been advertised in years; it was such a hit that Mars had just let it sell itself. But Poe persuaded Mars to pay more than $2 million for the worldwide rights to the Rolling Stones song "Satisfaction" to promote the company's leading product.

And in a coup that stung Hershey, Mars entered into an agreement with the Walt Disney Co. to become the only supplier of candy and snacks to Disney World's Magic Kingdom, Epcot Center and Disney

MGM Studios, which have a combined draw of more than 60 million consumers a year. Along with the contract, spearheaded by Poe, Mars and Disney rolled out a multimillion-dollar, multimedia Halloween sweepstakes called "Mission from Mars." The 1990 ad campaign was one of the company's most ambitious marketing events in years.

The very title, "Mission from Mars," was a departure from standard company practice: Forrest Sr. had never emphasized the Mars name over the brand name. Poe's group pushed on. They created Mars's first-ever umbrella ad campaign, which showed people of all ages eating Mars and Milky Way bars and used the theme "Making Life a Little Sweeter—Mars."

Poe believed it was time for the company to start thinking like the huge corporation it had become. Seen as a visionary by some and a pain in the neck by others, he believed—above all—in change. It was his ticket up the Mars corporate ladder. But it turned out to be his ticket out as well.

Over the years, Poe had been courted by dozens of corporate head-hunters, all of them attracted by his dynamic style and his status as one of the top-ranking black men in American business. But he had ignored their generous offers. After all, he was earning more than half a million dollars a year at Mars. More important, he had been given free rein to explore his creative ideas, to buck the company's conservative traditions and to use all the marketing power he could muster to overtake Hershey.

Then—just as Mars was poised to recapture the No. 1 spot—the Mars brothers announced new responsibilities for the company's sales personnel and called for the Uncle Ben's, Kal Kan and Mars divisions to coordinate their sales efforts for the first time. The restructuring—which had been discussed for more than three years before being imple-mented—was one of the most sweeping changes to take place at Mars in thirty years. Under the new system, it would be up to sales to achieve the company's top-line results each quarter—a responsibility that once belonged to Poe and other marketers like him. Sales would also take over all advertising campaigns, leaving marketing with the somewhat amorphous task of building business over the long run.

John and Forrest Jr. signed off on these changes because they believed that the marketing managers were becoming too powerful and the sales division should shoulder more responsibility. As head of marketing, Poe had spoken out against the shift in power, saying it would ultimately hurt the company's brands. But when the brothers asked him

AL POE IS NOT YOUR STANDARD-ISSUE CORPORATE EXECUTIVE— BUT THEN, FEW TOP MARS MANAGERS ARE.

to oversee the transformation, he obliged. They told him it was a promotion.

Until he saw Mike Murphy backstage at San Francisco's Moscone Convention Center in August, Poe even believed it.

Poe and Murphy were among a dozen executives preparing to address the 2,500 sales associates gathered at the convention hall to be told of their new assignment. Poe had spent every summer weekend and most of his nights preparing for the historic meeting, an uncharacteristically glitzy affair complete with a theme song, a stage show and a rare address by the brothers. But it was Murphy who was being congratulated in the corner by his colleagues. It seemed the longtime Mars manufacturing vice president was being promoted to head the Kal Kan division, replacing the president, who had announced early retirement. It was the job Poe had always wanted.

"I spent four years with Kal Kan and three years with Pedigree—I'm the best in the business in pet care," he said. "I wrote the master plan in 1986 that [Kal Kan] is using now. That is common knowledge. And when they gave that job to Murph, I said, 'Okay, I see how this works.'"

Three months later, Poe quit his job to accept a position with Campbell Soup Co. as president of Vlasic Foods. Ironically, Poe's departure came just weeks after Mars learned that it had officially regained the lead from Hershey. A survey by A. C. Nielsen in October 1991 showed Mars with 28.2 percent of the U.S. candy market, compared with Hershey's 26.2 percent.

Poe's abrupt resignation rocked McLean, which had advertised him as the future of the company, the next general manager of the M&M/Mars candies division. Mars general counsel Ed Stegemann, in explaining Poe's decision, said he really wasn't sure why Poe left, and suggested that he took the job because his wife wanted a change.

From his new post at Campbell's, Poe laughs at that notion. Campbell's "made me an offer I couldn't refuse," he said. "Here, I can be my own boss. That is the selling point—that someday, I have the chance to be the CEO."

It's a sentiment echoed by other former Mars executives who, like Poe, left the company in the last decade to pursue other paths to the top. "The brothers don't know how to delegate," said one former executive. "Sure, they give you responsibility. But they keep the authority. In the end, you realize, you'll never make your own decisions."

Poe said he wasn't given the sales force job because the Mars family was uncomfortable with his radical style. And although he was told he would someday become head of M&M/Mars, he said he came to understand that there wasn't enough room in the executive suite for his ideas and those of the Mars family.

Ed Stegemann scoffed at this notion. "Sure, the [brothers] have the final say on business decisions, but that doesn't mean they control every little part of the business. They're open to ideas—you just have to prove your case. . . . It is *their* money."

In the course of the early 1990s, more than a dozen top executives, with an average tenure of twenty-five years, left Mars, Inc. In interviews with several of them, there was a recurring sentiment: It's not that we don't love Mars and respect the company and appreciate what the brothers did for us; it's that they don't know how to share power.

"In the end," said Poe, "every discussion that I couldn't win ended on, 'Well, it's my rubber ducky.' Not, 'What if I trust you and you are right.'"

Most of these executives left over disagreements about how to expand the business.

At Hershey, there were no such disagreements. The company made it clear that it never wanted to be outdone by Mars again. To fight back against the stream of new products arriving from Mars, Zimmerman launched an assault of his own, bringing out the two best-selling items Hershey has seen in decades: Hershey's Cookie 'n' Mint bar and Hershey's Hugs.

The Hershey's Hug, billed as a miniature Kiss "hugged" on the outside by white chocolate, was designed to capitalize on the immensely popular Kiss brand. In 1989, Kisses ranked as the nation's fifth favorite candy with annual sales of $400 million.[5] It seemed a natural move to introduce Hugs, and the company was certain it would be a hit, expanding the company's already prodigious 41.7 percent market share in chocolate candies.

But if Hugs was predicted to bring such sweet success, why did it take Hershey so long to launch it? The story behind Hugs shows just how difficult it is to create a new candy. More important, it shows the way once sleepy Hershey has learned to respond to the competitive realities of today's marketplace.

The white- and milk-chocolate drops were the result of more than fifteen years of pondering, testing and planning. It took major leaps in manufacturing technology, a virtual overhaul of Hershey's approach to new-product development and tens of millions of dollars to get Hugs to market.

"All things considered," said Joseph Viviano, president of Hershey's confectionery division. "I think we got this to the market pretty fast."

Hershey first took ownership of the Hugs trademark in the late 1970s, knowing full well that the combination with Kisses was a natural. But coming up with a product that fit that name was another matter. After all, just what does a Hug look like? How should it taste? Should it be marketed with Kisses or stand alone? Would a product like this cannibalize Kiss sales or provide a boost to the existing brand?

In 1982, a new recruit to Hershey's product development team thought he had the answer to all these questions—although his idea eventually resulted in an entirely different Hershey product. Hugs, as proposed by twenty-eight-year-old Dennis Eshleman, would be a

Hershey's chocolate Kiss with an almond tucked neatly inside. It was the perfect embodiment of the name and, what's more, it was a product with a virtual guarantee of success. History had proven that nutty versions of America's favorite candies—Hershey's Milk Chocolate with Almonds, Mars's Peanut M&M's and Cadbury's Almond Joy—all sell nearly as well as the original. There was no reason for Eshleman's version of Hugs to be different.

But getting an almond inside a Kiss stumped Hershey's engineers. The company produces Kisses at the rate of 33 million a day. They're manufactured just the way you might imagine: Dime-sized steel tubes pump out perfectly measured dabs of still warm chocolate onto a conveyor, much the way a cake decorator squeezes out icing. To create the familiar Kiss shape, the tubes pull away from the belt just as the chocolate is deposited. The conveyor quickly carries the bite-sized drops through a cooling tunnel to solidify the chocolate before it has a chance to droop.

Adding an almond to this process would be impossible. Not only would it distort the Kiss shape, engineers could never ensure that an almond would wind up inside each candy. Clearly, a new manufacturing method would have to be developed, a process that took Hershey engineers another three years.

The new technology remains one of the company's most closely guarded secrets. Outsiders are not allowed to view the entire process, which is described only in the most basic terms. Instead of extruding Kisses, the new technique deposits the chocolate into Kiss-shaped molds. The molds are cooled slightly, forming a hard shell of chocolate around the inside. Once the shell is formed, the molds are flipped over, spilling out the excess chocolate. The centers of the molds are then filled with a mixture of almond halves and chocolate and cooled again. Once the Hug is dumped out of the mold, it's impossible to tell the difference between it and the original.

But as Eshleman was developing the packaging for the product in 1986, new questions were raised about its identity. The manager responsible for the brand declared the product didn't "feel" like a Hug but more like a Kiss with almonds. She suggested Hershey save the trademark for a whole new product line that would complement Hershey's Kisses.

Suddenly, Eshleman was back at square one; only this time, the possibilities seemed endless. A Hug could be any shape, any flavor. So which was the right one?

For a while, Hershey tried out chocolate teddy bears, which were sold to visitors at Hersheypark. But the bears, and all the other shapes that weren't like Kisses, seemed to lack emotion, said Eshleman.

"All those feelings and associations you get from looking at a Kiss you just can't get with some neat shape you make up and decide to call a Hug," said Eshleman. "It would have been nice to think that we could have done the same thing Milton Hershey did seventy-five years ago and created something brand new, but it just didn't work."

With the emphasis shifted from shape to flavor, the answer to Hugs suddenly became obvious. In the long history of candy making in America, there remain only a handful of ingredients that haven't been fully exploited by confectioners. White chocolate is a big one. With the new technology created for Kisses With Almonds, it was possible to do almost anything with the Kiss, including putting a miniature milk-chocolate Kiss inside and a white-chocolate one outside.

For their part, Hershey's research and development scientists had long been testing various types of white chocolate—which is made of cocoa butter, sugar and milk, and actually has no chocolate liquor in it. They immediately began trying combinations of the mini-Kiss surrounded by a white Kiss, but the balance wasn't easy to find: Too much white chocolate and it might not appeal to American tastes, too much milk chocolate and it tastes just like the original Kiss.

Then there was the issue of eye appeal. The white chocolate outside looked bland, boring. Todd Johnson, a scientist on the R&D team, suggested a plain white Kiss might even be mistaken for fancy soap, the kind you keep in the guest bathroom. Something had to be done.

"Somebody suggested putting stripes on it, chocolate stripes," remembers Eshleman. "It turns out the stripes have become an integral part of what Hugs is all about, although we didn't quite realize it at the time."

In 1991, when Hershey finally believed it had achieved the ultimate Hug, the product was sent to consumers for testing. "We knew right away we had a hit on our hands," recalls Kathie Rhyne, the marketing executive directly overseeing the Hugs brand. "The tests went better than we expected."

The results of the year-long experiment showed Hugs would be popular with adults and kids alike, a critical factor to any new candy's success, since fewer and fewer consumers are under the age of thirty-five. More important, the test showed sales of Hugs wouldn't hurt sales of Kisses, but help them.

Now, said Rhyne, it was time for the really hard work to begin. Hershey wanted to get Hugs to market by August 1993, only a year and a half away. It was a tight time schedule considering the company had no room in its current plant to manufacture the product, and only a sketchy idea of the equipment it would need to produce it.

Logistically, too, Hugs promised to be a nightmare. Every indication was that Hugs would be as big a hit as Hershey's Kisses With Almonds, which, when they were launched in 1990, couldn't be produced fast enough to meet demand. Hershey executives didn't want to repeat that mistake, which still burns in the minds of the company's suppliers and customers.

Rhyne knew she would need everyone's cooperation if Hershey were going to pull this off. The Hugs assembly line was going to be located in Hershey's new 350,000-square-foot West plant, which was under construction in Hershey, Pennsylvania. Coordinating the new plant, the new manufacturing line and the sale of a brand-new product left no room for miscommunication, finger pointing, turf wars, personality clashes or any of the other myriad problems that can plague a new-product launch. She needed a team—a new concept for the executives at Hershey, whose corporate practices have never been too flexible.

"We needed to break down the barriers between departments," said Rhyne. "We didn't have time for R&D to pass this off to engineering and have them hand it to manufacturing. Everyone needed to work together like clockwork."

And they did. After spending three and a half days locked in a resort in the Poconos, the forty key players in the Hugs launch agreed to a common mission statement, with specific sales targets, deadlines and manufacturing goals. Moreover, they agreed to have their performance evaluated as a group, not as individuals. Nine members of the team, including representatives from sales, manufacturing, logistics, marketing and engineering, would meet regularly to hammer out problems and discuss strategy. The broader team would be kept fully informed of their progress and meet once each quarter.

"There were times we really wondered whether we were going to make it," said Ron Orlosky, operations manager at the new Hershey plant. "One month before we turned the lights on in that building, we were presenting Hugs to buyers. That had me pretty worried."

Ron Lott of engineering recalls putting in the Hugs machinery before the roof was even on the new factory. "Without the team, we never could have made it work," Lott said.

Since May 1993, the Hugs line has been running twenty-four hours a day, seven days a week, to meet demand. The product has sold more than $100 million each year[6] since its introduction, a nice payoff for one of the most innovative ideas to come out of Hershey in recent memory.

The Hershey Cookie 'n' Mint bar achieved similar success when it was introduced in 1991, and was quickly followed by the Hershey Cookie 'n' Creme bar. These new products helped Hershey regain the lead from Mars, less than a year after Poe and his team celebrated their victory.

*M*ars has not yet adjusted to the realities of this new, invigorated Hershey. "No one at Mars is used to being number two," said Whitney Hill, who worked at Mars for more than thirty years. "They're still acting as if they own the candy aisle."

Many former associates say that Mars developed an arrogance after its years of unchallenged leadership, taking for granted its superiority over the competition. John Strong, who continues to work in the industry as a food broker, says Mars seems to have lost the aggressive edge and inventive nature that drove the company to the top. "They're walking around, patting each other on the back, and bragging to each other about their numbers. In the meantime, they're losing perspective."

Poe's team had taken some important steps, but the company has been unable to maintain the momentum. One of Poe's most important initiatives—introducing products to compete head-on with Hershey's top brands—has stalled. Mars hasn't launched a single new candy bar since the debut of PB Max, and the company has pulled many of its line extensions off the market, including Peanut Butter Snickers and Forever Yours. The only peanut butter product left in Mars's repertoire is Peanut Butter M&M's, and even that candy is struggling.

After reaching a peak of $78 million in 1991, Peanut Butter M&M's sales dropped to just $34 million in 1993. Mars has tried several times to relaunch the brand—giving it new packaging and backing it with aggressive promotions—but sales only started to move back up after Mars copied the coloring and styling of Hershey's Reese's Pieces package.

The desperate attempt to remake Peanut Butter M&M's in the image of Reese's Pieces has sparked a lawsuit between the two companies that is scheduled to go to trial in the spring of 1999. Hershey is accusing Mars of infringing on its famous trademark, and Mars has countersued.

The court proceedings mark an unprecedented public airing of the companies' bitter rivalry.

In a court affidavit, Robert J. Shelton, the Hershey manager responsible for the Reese's brand, states: "By copying the Reese's trade dress, including the virtually identical shade of orange, Mars is capitalizing on Hershey's goodwill and substantial investment in [Reese's]."

Hershey lawyers point out in their court filings that every version of Mars's new packaging for Peanut Butter M&M's has copied some element of Reese's. The package Mars used in its test marketing, for example, displayed the M&M logo in yellow outlined in brown (just like Reese's). The package used for the product's introduction had the words "peanut butter" written in brown, framed by an oval with a yellow background (just like Reese's). And the newest version of the package utilizes the same exact color scheme as a Reese's label—a vibrant orange background with brown writing and yellow highlights. Both products also tout their peanut butter flavor in similarly sized and similarly placed ovals.

"In a blatant attack on Hershey, Mars is purposefully exploiting the enormous popularity of [Reese's] by mimicking the unique Reese's color scheme that consumers universally associate with the Reese's products," wrote Hershey's lawyers in a brief filed with the court. "Moreover, the evidence points strongly to the conclusion that Mars adopted the Reese's color scheme, not by coincidence, but as part of a deliberate attack on Reese's market share and in an effort to boost sales of a Mars product whose very survival was in doubt."

So far, the strategy has worked. Sales of Peanut Butter M&M's have increased ever since the new package design was introduced. In fact, the copycat packaging has been so successful, Mars is now using it on its latest version of M&M's, introduced in the summer of 1998. These M&M's—which have crisped rice inside the chocolate—taste a lot like tiny candy-coated Nestlé's Crunch bars. And in keeping with the new strategy, the packaging neatly imitates the red, white and blue color scheme of a Crunch wrapper.

Such desperate and unimaginative tactics reflect a sense of apprehension that seems to have engulfed Mars. Sales associates who have left the company all say the same thing: The reorganization of the company's sales and marketing structure in 1992 has been a failure; scores and scores of associates have left Mars in frustration, and the company is suffused with a vague sense of unease.

As John Strong says: "It's like a cancer over there. You don't hear people talking in a positive tone about the company."

That feeling has only been heightened by the recent departure of several top executives, men the company has depended on for decades. Phil Forster, one of the most powerful executives in McLean, retired in January 1998. The heads of Kal Kan and Uncle Ben's rice have also recently departed.

Mars associates say the company is adrift, searching for direction. The Mars brothers have failed to set priorities, to give associates clear marching orders. And given the power structure at Mars, no one else can do it for them.

"The problem is, there isn't really anyone at Mars right now who can stand up to the [Mars] family and say what needs to be done, to get the family to set priorities and stop contemplating its navel," says an insider. "There is a passion to do things, but there is a question whether the family is willing to recruit the right people or give the current people the freedom to initiate."[7]

The lack of vision has finally begun to surface in Mars's sales figures. Though Snickers is still America's best-selling candy bar, the brand has been consistently losing share since 1994. M&M's has also failed to keep up with the overall growth in the candy market.[8]

Mars has begun aggressively advertising its flagship brands in an effort to regain momentum. The new ad campaigns, which are receiving rave reviews from Madison Avenue, are the creative handiwork of ad giant BBDO. The witty, tongue-in-cheek commercials are designed to be "more entertaining, with more of an emotional connection with consumers . . . less didactic," explains Mars vice president Paul Michaels. Mars handed its accounts—worth $400 million a year—over to BBDO in 1995, after it split with longtime ad agency Bates Worldwide. Mars fired Bates in protest when the founder and chairman of the agency, Maurice Saatchi, was ousted by dissatisfied shareholders.

Analysts say the switch to BBDO is one of the most positive things to happen at Mars in decades. Under the creative direction of the new agency, Mars has revitalized M&M's image and introduced the brand to a whole new generation of candy eaters. The addition of the blue M&M and the revival of the animated M&M characters have endeared the fifty-year-old product to today's five-year-old consumers.

BBDO's advertising has been on the air only since September 1996, but Mars is already seeing results; both M&M's and Snickers sales are climbing. And while this is promising for the company, it should be no surprise: Mars continues to have incredibly strong brands and extraordinary manufacturing prowess. Despite the criticisms of the brothers' management style, Mars has seen its revenues increase at an average rate of 14 percent each year since they took control, and Mars is still the No. 1 candy company in the world. But, inside the company and out, everyone knows that Mars is not fulfilling its immense potential.

"Mars has a number of tough challenges on every front, but there are opportunities," said one current executive. "The real issue is leadership. The Mars [family] needs industrial-strength therapy to get them to harness what the company is capable of doing."[9]

Chapter Twenty-three

CORPORATE CANDY

EIGHTEEN OF THE TOP TWENTY CANDY BRANDS ARE MANUFAC- TURED BY HERSHEY AND MARS. THE EXCEPTIONS: BUTTER- FINGER, A NESTLÉ PRODUCT, AND TOOTSIE ROLLS.

OR MOST OF us, just looking at a box of Jujyfruits— those jaw-achingly chewy candies—conjures up memories of Satur- day afternoons spent in the movie theater watching Warner Bros. cartoons and Disney features. But the company that makes these fruit-shaped sweets, Henry Heide Candies, Inc., dates back to even before Edison invented the Kinetoscope. Henry Heide was a German immigrant who opened his first candy shop in New York City in 1869. For well over a century, generations of the Heide family have continued the tradition of candy making, turning out Jujyfruits, Drops, Red Hot Dollars, Mexican Hats and Jujubes—named for the juju gum that is the main ingredient.

Philip Heide, great-grandson of the original founder, talks proudly of his family's heritage. "We're the oldest continually operating candy company in America," said Heide in an interview in 1992. "The recipes for our candies go back before the turn of the century, before most other candies were even invented." Heide and his brother, Peter, grew up in the plant operated by their father. Their lives revolved around sweets. They were popular with their friends because their dad owned a candy company. They can remember going into the factory and eating Jujubes fresh off the line. Philip spoke wistfully about how few companies like his are left in America. "The family-owned candy company is fast becoming a relic," he said. "There aren't many dinosaurs like us around anymore." When asked if Heide would survive the chocolate wars, Philip sighed and said with a look of deep concern, "I hope so."

Three years later that hope was dashed, when Hershey acquired Heide for $13 million. In explaining the sellout, Philip Heide said his company could no longer afford to compete against the big players in the industry. "Economically, this made the most sense for our business." Philip Heide has since joined Hershey's sales staff and Peter Heide is overseeing the firm's manufacturing for Hershey.

Hershey bought Heide as part of an aggressive plan to expand into nonchocolate candies. In recent years, the company has extended its market by introducing dozens of sugar-based candies, and Heide's facilities were ideal for making products like jelly beans and gummy candies.

To pursue its new strategy, Hershey has been actively buying small, successful independents. The Heide acquisition was only one of a half-dozen takeovers by Hershey in the last decade. In 1996, the company purchased the brands of Leaf North America, including Jolly Rancher, Whoppers, Good & Plenty, PayDay, Heath, Milk Duds and Xylifresh gum. These new products have expanded Hershey's growing array of sugar-based treats. The company now makes Twizzlers brand licorice, Amazin' Fruit gummy candy, TasteTations hard candies and a line of soft, chewy caramels, introduced in 1997, which harken back to Milton S. Hershey's first success, his Crystal "A" candies.

Market watchers say the nonchocolate segment is the battleground of the future. Hershey's recent forays into this arena have already increased its space on the candy rack fivefold, and the company shows no sign of slowing its expansion. In March 1988, Hershey put new muscle behind Leaf's Jolly Rancher brand of hard candies, introducing Jolly Rancher Jolly Jellies. Hershey also has major plans for Heide's Wunderbeans.

Mars is anxiously trying to duplicate its rival's success. In 1997, the brothers launched their first sugar candy brand since Skittles, more than a decade earlier. The new Starburst Fruit Twists and Starburst jelly beans are going head-to-head with Hershey's Twizzlers and Wunderbeans. Mars is also testing a new line of hard candies to compete against Taste-Tations; these candies would also capitalize on the Starburst name.

Until the early 1990s, the chocolate giants showed little interest in sugar-based confections, considering it a low-profit, low-profile business. But Americans' latest nutrition fad suddenly has made this long-ignored segment very popular. As Lisbeth Echeandia explains, sugar candy can be labeled fat free, and "these days, that's very appealing."

Hershey's aggressive expansion has been directed by Kenneth Wolfe, who replaced Zimmerman as chairman and CEO in 1994. Wolfe, a thirty-year Hershey veteran, has changed much about the company since taking over the corner office. The soft-spoken leader is quick to point out that Hershey has boosted revenues from $3.5 billion in 1993 to $4.3 billion in 1997, while earnings have grown from $193 million to an impressive $336 million. Wolfe boasts that Hershey's stock price has reached unprecedented highs since he took the helm, growing 44 percent in 1997 alone. He is at ease talking about things like profit growth, P/E ratios, return on capital—Wall Street terms his predecessors took little interest in.

"I'm a different person than Dearden, Zimmerman or Mohler," Wolfe said in a 1998 interview. "I perhaps am a little more conscious of our stock price and what we have to do to improve the stock price, to give value to our shareholders."

The way he talks, Wolfe could be the CEO of any Fortune 500 company. He is very aware of the connections between Hershey and the financial world; he regularly spends time talking with stock analysts and investment bankers; he plays down his small-town roots (born in Lebanon, Pennsylvania, just miles outside of Hershey); and he wears the power executive's uniform: dark pinstriped suits, monogrammed cuffs, gold-rimmed glasses.

Whereas William Dearden had run the company from Milton's High Point Mansion, Wolfe conducts his business each day from a modern glass-and-brick office complex atop a hill across from the Hotel Hershey. The complex, an example of uninspired corporate architecture, was built in 1991 to house Hershey's burgeoning bureaucracy. Milton Hershey's mansion is now home to the Hershey Trust offices, and Milton's second-floor suite of rooms has been restored to its original state, though you need special permission to view it. Wolfe doesn't get there very often; he's too busy planning the company's future.

Wolfe states matter-of-factly that he sees his job as running "this business in a way that will generate the maximum value." To do that, Hershey is "going back to our roots," he said. "We are primarily a confectionery company."

Industry analysts have watched the recent changes at Hershey with excitement. "This is not the staid old candy company [of days gone by]," said Leonard Tietelbaum of Merrill Lynch. "Hershey is making a run for the candy aisle." Analysts say they expect Wolfe to sell the company's pasta business in the near future so that all of the company's efforts can be concentrated on candy.

But with each move that makes Hershey bigger, more and more small companies are squeezed out of the business. James Hanlon, former president of Leaf, bemoans the rise of the candy behemoths. "Pretty soon there'll be no one else left," he said in 1992, foreshadowing Hershey's acquisition of his own brands. "There'll be no independents. No small niche players. Everybody will be either Hershey, Mars or Nestlé."

Analysts agree that mergers and acquisitions will continue to shrink the industry. "It used to be that anybody with a good recipe and a catchy name could get their product into the candy aisle," said Echeandia of *Confectioner* magazine. "But that's not true anymore. You need muscle, lots of muscle and deep pockets to compete against the Mars and Hersheys of the world."

At one time, the seasonal candy market was almost exclusively dominated by small, family-owned businesses like Bob's Candy Canes, which makes nothing but the Christmas tree decorations, and Palmer Chocolates, which sells Easter treats like giant bunnies and hollow eggs. But in the past decade, Mars, Hershey and Nestlé have stormed the seasonal trade, hawking their own year-round brands in special holiday colors and packaging.

These seasonal sales are big business; nearly half the candy purchased each year is bought in connection with the holidays. Christmas, Halloween and Easter each bring in nearly $1 billion in wholesale revenue, and Valentine's Day adds another $700 million.[1] The candy giants' new aggressiveness in this market has wreaked havoc on smaller companies, who have suddenly seen the shelf space for their most profitable products disappear.

The small players say it's becoming impossible to prevail against the marketing savvy of Mars and Hershey salesmen, who have sophisticated data to show retailers that their products are the most profitable. "Why should the store manager put a Goo Goo Cluster on the shelf when he's got Mars and Hershey breathing down his neck with stats that show their products will outsell a Goo Goo Cluster, ten to one," explained Echeandia. Little companies are relegated to selling their products at rural truck stops and gas stations.

But for consumers, there are some benefits to consolidation. Since Hershey purchased Leaf, for example, the company has invested generously in brands like PayDay, vastly increasing distribution of products that had been languishing.

"When Leaf had PayDay, they weren't doing anything with it," said Wolfe. "We're breathing new life into the brand; we've got the resources to do that."

But ultimately, as in the much heralded and closely watched "cola wars," the battle between the industry titans ends up killing the little guys, while the giants grow ever stronger. As the two contenders compete for shelf space, they leave no room for smaller companies or regional competitors. "The public's choice of candy is getting steadily narrower as Mars and Hershey take over," said Ray Broekel, the candy bar historian.

The two giants now control approximately two-thirds of the candy aisle, and their dominating presence is making it harder and harder for less prominent companies even to get their products in front of the customer. It has reached the point where candy companies that want to compete against Mars and Hershey must actually pay retailers just to get them to put their products on the shelf.

The dual trends toward consolidation and homogenization appear unstoppable. In 1997, Americans consumed 25.6 pounds of candy per capita, and the retail value of candy sales reached $28 billion—both all-time highs.[2] As a result, the candy industry has been reporting record profits, so you might expect more and more companies to enter the market. In fact, more and more independents are dropping out. The roster of companies attending industry trade shows is steadily shrinking, and only a handful of new independent brands have been launched in recent years.

For candy maker Salvatore Ferrara II of the Ferrara Pan Candy Co. in Chicago, the trend is alarming. Ferrara's grandfather, after whom

Salvatore was named, started the business in 1908 after coming to the United States from Italy. In a partnership with his brothers-in-law—the Buffardis and the Paganos—the Ferrara Pan Candy Co. grew into an American icon.

The company made the original Atomic Fire Balls, Jaw Breakers, Boston Baked Beans, Lemonheads and Red Hots. In the Forest Park, Illinois, factory where these candies are made, you can almost smell history. Some of the equipment dates back to the firm's founding, including the ancient, hand-hammered copper pans that have rolled the ingredients together for decades.

The 450 people who work at Ferrara see the industry trends but pray that Ferrara can stay just the way it is. "This company is different because of the family orientation. Everybody here can feel that aspect of the business. It's personal. It's warm. You know they're going to take care of you," said Raymond Johnson, one of the factory workers.

But there are signs that times are changing at Ferrara. In 1991, the company hired its first nonfamily member into a top managerial position. Steve McMichael, a former executive of E. J. Brach Corp., is Ferrara's vice president in charge of sales. It has also hired a director of marketing from outside the ranks.

"We don't want to lose our family orientation, but at the same time we recognize we have to be flexible for the future," said Ferrara. "If we can't do that against giants like Mars and Hershey, we're finished." The venerable family-owned company, with its proud history and its well-worn equipment, cannot rely on tradition. It has to keep running, learning and evolving if it is to continue into the next generation.

"To survive in the long run we're going to have to expand," said the Ferrara president. "We're going to have to acquire other businesses and get aggressive. Otherwise we won't have the clout we need to get our products to the consumer."

Ferrara has watched Hershey's expansion into sugar candies with concern, but not resignation. Ferrara has struck back in its own style. Rather than acquiring other firms, Ferrara has negotiated a series of high-profile licensing deals to link its candy with Hollywood movies and cartoons. The family-run business became the sole purveyor of dinosaur-shaped candies in conjunction with the Steven Spielberg hit *Jurassic Park*. They spent $2 million on promotion for the *Jurassic Park* line. The company has agreements with Walt Disney Co. and Hanna-Barbera productions to sell fruit snacks in the shape of characters like Chip and Dale and the Jetsons. The company is also starting to market co-branded products. For example, it recently introduced Sun-Maid chocolate-covered raisins and Planter's chocolate-covered peanuts.

"This is the modern way for more sales and bigger market share," said Ferrara. He also knows his company will have to widen its distribution from drugstores and convenience stores into supermarkets if its brands are to survive.

Between 1994 and 1997, Ferrara sales have more than doubled. The company is working hard to boost its brand recognition, a move Ferrara sees as critical to the future of the business. Steven Parker, a candy buyer for Walgreen Co., said this strategy is working. "They've upgraded their image tremendously. Now you know the products are Ferrara Pan candies."

But the statistics are stacked against companies like Ferrara Pan. According to John Ward, a professor at Loyola University in Chicago, only 35 percent of all family businesses make a successful transition from first to second generation, and only 15 percent make it to the third. Less than 1 percent of family businesses are passed to the fourth generation.

At one time 95 percent of candy companies were family-owned, but now it's only 60 percent, keeping in mind that "family-owned" doesn't always mean "little." Mars is family-owned. So is Tootsie Roll.

"The dilemmas faced by family businesses are very unique," said Craig Aronoff, director of the Family Business Forum, a think tank on family-owned businesses. Problems with succession and sibling rivalry can doom even the most successful family firms. "In a family-run business there are people playing many different roles, and it is sometimes hard to keep those roles straight." Many candy companies have already succumbed to these pressures. The H. B. Reese Co. was a prime example, deciding to sell to Hershey only after a bitter battle for control among the siblings who inherited the company from their father.

These issues loom large for the Mars family. All together, John, Forrest Jr. and Jackie have ten children and seven grandchildren, and at any one time, as many as half a dozen Mars offspring are likely to be working in the company. Although they're outwardly treated no differently from other associates, it's clear, say managers, that someday this generation will assume control. But how and when the brothers will pass the baton is anyone's guess.

That's "the big unknown," said former top executive Claude Eliette-Hermann. Senior executives have tried for years to get an answer to that question, he said, but the family is playing it "very close to the vest."

Former associates maintain that Forrest Jr., now in his sixties, has been trying for years to retire and leave the company in the hands of brother John. But, they say, his desire for control is too great; he just can't let go.

Pointing to this, some associates are concerned about the company's future. They say it won't be as easy for the brothers to simply walk away as their father did, because this would leave Mars, Inc., in too many hands.

The rumor in the industry is that John, Forrest Jr. and Jackie are forbidden—as a condition of their ownership—to sell any part of Mars. But whoever inherits their stock, one industry leader says, may do whatever he or she pleases with the business. The family would not comment on any of this.

The family patriarch, Forrest Sr., seems to have little faith in the next generation of Mars children, and he is concerned for the company's future. So concerned that in 1992—at eighty-eight years of age and nearly twenty years removed from active management in the company—he met with Nestlé chairman Helmut Maucher to discuss a merger. Forrest had never been interested in keeping Mars private if that wasn't ultimately best for the company. The only thing he cared about was seeing the business thrive. If that meant a merger with Nestlé, so be it.

Over lunch at the Hotel President in Geneva, the two men debated the advantages of combining their strengths. Hank Vogel, who at the time was Jackie Mars's husband, accompanied Forrest on his trip to meet with Maucher. Vogel says Forrest was very interested in working out a deal with Nestlé whereby his sons would continue to manage the company until their retirements, but the company would not pass to the next generation. But, Vogel says, when Forrest Sr. discussed the possibility of the merger with his children, John and Forrest balked. Angry that their father had initiated discussions with Nestlé behind their backs, they insisted that it was their company now, and they would do with it what they wanted. The brothers reportedly felt that selling out to Nestlé would be an admission of defeat. Their sister, Jackie, was in favor of the deal. But then again, she has not invested her life in the company the way her brothers have.

Officially, Nestlé and Mars deny these talks even took place. When asked if John and Forrest Jr. were considering selling the firm, Ed Stegemann laughed and said that was the last thing on their minds. They didn't put all this hard work into the company just to turn around and hand it over to someone else.

Forrest Sr. has told friends that if he had it to do over again, he's not sure he would give the business to his children. "They think they can't run it into the ground, but they can," he told Hank Vogel. Forrest's sentiments were echoed by a prominent marketing industry newsletter in 1994, which gave Forrest Jr. its "worst marketer" award. The Delaney Report cited Forrest Jr. "for allowing Mars to continue to lose ground in the candy battle with [Hershey]. For permitting management turnover at high levels to continue unabated during the past three years, which has caused disruption in the ranks. For a lackluster new product program."[3]

Of course, the real question is not the ability of John and Forrest Jr., but that of the next generation. Of the ten grandchildren, Jackie's three children are said to have shown little interest in the business. Forrest Jr.'s oldest daughter, Victoria, has worked in the company's pet food division in England. His daughter Pam, according to Ed Stegemann, is running the Mattoon, Illinois, pet food factory and doing "a damn good job." Linda Mars, John's only daughter, has been working to develop new markets abroad. John's son Mike, who graduated from Duke in 1991, has been working in the Hackettstown plant, and some believe he could be the one to run the company someday. But others in the company believe that John's eldest son, Frank, is the chosen heir.

Frank's career looks a lot like those of his father and his grandfather. The young Yale graduate has built his own business in the suburbs of Phoenix, where he manufactures Styrofoam packaging specially designed to keep chocolate products from melting in transit. He sells the packaging to two Mars divisions, along with other packaged goods companies. He lives in a sparsely furnished apartment, and he tells friends he's "just an average guy." And, squarely in the tradition of the secretive world he could inherit, he doesn't talk about the future of Mars.

It has been a quarter century since Forrest Sr. gave up the business, and the years have taken their toll. He is in good health for a man of his age, although he spends most of his time in a wheelchair, the result of a stroke he suffered in 1994. He and his companion, Janet (a former Mars secretary), seldom travel abroad anymore, though they spend winters in Miami.

While his various projects kept Forrest busy through the 1970s, they proved unable to absorb his energies and attention for more than a few years. In 1980, bored with retired life, he invited some of his old colleagues to join him in building another candy company. Forrest named the business Ethel M Chocolates, after his mother. The new factory, located in Las Vegas, makes fine liqueur-filled candies.

Forrest established the venture in Nevada because it is one of the few states that allowed the sale of liqueur-filled cordials. He has been trying ever since to expand the number of states where it is legal to sell his new products. He took the fight to state legislators in Texas, where a group called Children Against Alcohol in Chocolates lobbied strongly against the Mars product and won. Their major source of funding? Insiders say it was Hershey.

Despite the loss, Ethel M has gotten off to an impressive start. Within a few years of its opening, the company had reached annual sales of $150 million, from seventy Ethel M stores throughout the West.

This success should come as no surprise; Forrest Mars runs Ethel M the way he has run all his businesses. He lives in a penthouse above the factory and spies on his workers through one-way mirrors. Employees call him the "phantom of the candy factory."

CHAPTER 1: BAR WARS

The account depicted here is based on interviews with dozens of sources, including current and former Mars associates, current Hershey employees and scientists and chemists who have consulted for either one company or the other on developing non-melting chocolate. The specific account of Omar Sharir was provided in an interview with Theo Leenders in the summer of 1991. Mike Davies shared the story of the "SuperSavers" program and Mars's efforts to turn the gulf crisis into an opportunity. The account of Ed Stegemann's reaction to the gulf crisis was provided by sources close to him who asked to remain anonymous. William McComis of the Battelle Memorial Research Institute provided invaluable insight into the race to develop non-melting chocolate, and many scientists in the field contributed their knowledge and understanding of chocolate's chemistry to the account provided here. The details of the unfolding war were taken from newspaper accounts in *The Washington Post* and *The New York Times*. Attorneys familiar with the GAO dispute provided details of that legal battle.

1. The name "Omar Sharir" is a pseudonym, used to protect the employee's identity.

2. Mars's internal sales figure, provided by Mike Davies in an interview with the author.

3. Several sources close to Stegemann have shared information on his background, including that he once served as a U.S. intelligence agent. Stegemann himself declined to discuss matters he deemed "personal."

4. Details of Hershey's Field Ration D provided by Samuel Hinkle in his unpublished manuscript, pp. 414–15, pp. 387–88.

5. Malcolm Gladwell, "A Chocolate Advance of a High Degree: New Confection Resists Melting," *The Washington Post*, May 3, 1988.

6. Ibid.

7. Ibid.

8. Ibid.

9. Information on the availability of Mars products was provided by the company and confirmed in interviews with U.S. soldiers and Pentagon officials.

10. Interview with author, December 1993.

11. GAO case file #B-245250.

12. Ibid.

13. This refers to the size of the wholesale market in 1996, as reported by the U.S. Department of Commerce. The size of the retail market that year was $21 billion, according to the National Confectioners Association.

14. Interview with author, May 1991.

15. I conducted the interview with Stegemann and wrote the brief story that appeared in *The Washington Post*.

16. Interview with author, January 1994.

CHAPTER 2: CANDY FROM STRANGERS

Over the course of eight years—between 1989 and 1997—I interviewed more than 200 people intimately familiar with the candy industry in the United States. This overview is based on those interviews and my own personal observations, made during tours of various candy factories, including those of Mars, Hershey, Tootsie Roll, Ferrara Pan, NECCO and Heide. Much of the historical information included here came from the National Confectioners Association (NCA) and the Chocolate Manufacturers Association (CMA). Lisbeth Echeandia, publisher of *Confectioner* magazine, provided an invaluable perspective on the industry, as did Richard O'Connell, who for thirty years ran the NCA and the CMA. Ray Broekel, a noted candy bar historian, also provided historical information based on his own archival collection of candy bar wrappers and trivia. Broekel is the author of two books about candy bars that were particularly helpful in my research—*The Great American Candy Bar Book* (Boston: Houghton Mifflin Company, 1982) and *The Chocolate Chronicles* (Illinois: Wallace-Homestead Book Co., 1985).

1. Hinkle manuscript, p. 778.

2. Based on statistics compiled by A. C. Nielsen, Information Resources, Inc., and DEBS/Candi Snacs Vending Data. This 75 percent figure is what the industry refers to as the "front end"—the share that Hershey and Mars have of the typical candy rack at the grocery or drugstore checkout or vending machine.

3. Ronald Kessler, "Candy from Strangers," *Regardie's Magazine,* August 1986.

4. I tried repeatedly to interview Mars and Hershey executives on the record about the GAO dispute, but all attempts were met with "no comment." Even ex-employees were uncomfortable talking, saying the incident was too recent and too painful.

5. After initially declining to be interviewed, current Hershey CEO Kenneth Wolfe agreed to a one-hour telephone interview, which took place on January 16, 1998.

6. Sheehan left the NCA in 1996. He was replaced by Jim Corcoran.

7. Interview with author, August 1989.

8. Interview with Lynn Dornblaster of *New Product News,* which tracks the number of new consumer goods introduced annually.

9. Interview with Mars research and development executive Allan Gibbons, July 1991.

10. Ibid.

11. Hershey has since purchased Leaf, thereby acquiring the Heath brand. Analysts speculate that Hershey will eventually drop Skor in favor of the better known Heath.

12. "Candy Almanac," published by the National Confectioners Association, Virginia, n.d.

13. Information collected from various Hershey insiders.

14. The description of how Mars deals with outside contractors was provided by several ex-employees and confirmed by one contractor who was assigned to fix machinery in the Hackettstown facility.

15. "Welcome to Lollipop Land," *Ingram's Magazine,* December 1992.

16. Broekel, *The Great American Candy Bar Book.*

17. Interview with author, January 1994.

18. Interview with author, June 1993.

19. "The Confectionery Elite," *Confectioner* magazine, May/June 1997.

20. Sales figure for M&M's provided by Mars insiders. Sales of Camel cigarettes and Maxwell House coffee were each less than $2 billion in 1997, according to published newspaper accounts.

21. *Confectioner* magazine estimated sales of Reese's Peanut Butter Cups at $500 million in 1997. That year, sales of Advil were estimated at $431 million and sales of Ivory Soap at $98 million.

The portrait of the company rendered here is based largely on personal observation. Between 1990 and 1992, I toured the company's factories around the United States and Europe, watching firsthand how Mars operates each of its divisions: pet food, rice and candy. I was given unrestricted access to the firm's employees and was also permitted to interview John Mars and his brother, Forrest Jr. To complete my picture of Mars, I also interviewed numerous ex-employees. In all, I spoke with more than 150 people intimately associated with the company. I also drew on the handful of profiles written about Mars, including Thomas W. Lippman's two-part series that appeared in *The Washington Post* on December 6 and 7, 1981, and Ronald Kessler's cover story for *Regardie's Magazine* that appeared in August 1986.

The statistics found in this chapter were provided by Mars insiders, including sales figures and data on the size of the firm. Though Mars has always tried to downplay the size of its business, I believe the figures used here are accurate. Where possible, the numbers were confirmed with knowledgeable outside sources. In some instances, I discovered major discrepancies. For example, Ed Stegemann told me repeatedly in interviews that Mars had sales of $9 billion in 1991. But in a meeting with associates, Phil Forster said sales that year were $12 billion. When asked about the inconsistency, Stegemann acknowledged the higher figure was correct. In company literature printed in 1997, the company is reporting 1996 sales of $12 billion. But a high-ranking executive with access to the proper information put sales for 1996 at more than $18 billion. He said it was standard company practice to underreport sales figures, noting that such information would be material to Mars's competitors.

1. The Mars family ranked third on *Fortune* magazine's list of the world's wealthiest people in 1989. The family has since been bumped down the list, but continues to rank among the top fifteen.

2. According to *Fortune* magazine's Fortune 500 list for 1998, RJR Nabisco sales were $17.1 billion, McDonald's sales were $11.4 billion and Kellogg's sales were $6.8 billion. Hershey Foods reported annual sales of $4.3 billion in 1997.

3. Figure provided by former Pedigree associate.

4. Budget figures from "100 Leading National Advertisers," *Advertising Age,* www.adage.com/dataplace/archives/dp031.html.

5. Bill Saporito, "Uncovering Mars' Unknown Empire," *Fortune,* September 26, 1988.

6. Thomas W. Lippman, "The Mars Empire: How Sweet It Is," *The Washington Post,* December 7, 1981.

7. Vogelsinger has since been rehired. She played a significant role in convincing Mars to provide photographs for this book and arranging an interview with executive David Badger to discuss Mars's recent global activities.

8. Some of the photographs taken for *The Washington Post Magazine* cover story were subsequently provided to me by Mars for use in this book.

9. Though Mars declined to cooperate with the writing of this book, the company agreed to an interview with executive David Badger in January 1998, just as the manuscript was nearing completion. The company also provided many of the photographs that appear in the book.

10. John Gorham, "The Billionaires," *Forbes,* July 6, 1998.

11. Sales of PB Max provided by former Mars marketing executive, who asked to remain anonymous.

12. Interview with author, December 1991.

13. Interview with author, July 1990.

14. Sales figures for 1973 provided by Forster.

CHAPTER 4: MELTS IN YOUR MOUTH

The account of Forrest's discovery of M&M's came from a videotaped interview that Forrest Mars, Sr., made for the family's personal archives. Sales figures for the candy were provided by company sources and confirmed with available market data.

CHAPTER 5: TO THE MILKY WAY AND BEYOND

The history of the Mars company detailed here was compiled from the following sources: the family's personal archives, numerous former employees of the Slough factory and the Chicago factory who asked to remain anonymous and the following Mars associates: Ed Stegemann, Phil Forster, John Mars, George Greener, David Brown, Charles Kaufman, Paulette Perkins, Hans Fiuczynski, Al Aragona, David Badger, John Murray, Al Poe, Michael Murphy, Ron Smiley, Robin Pedler, V. J. Spitaleri, William Hellegas and Mike Tuttle.

The account of the relationship between Frank Mars and William Murrie came from interviews with Hershey employees who worked at the company during the 1930s and 1940s and from members of the Murrie family.

1. Al Chase, "Standard Set by Mars Plant Built in 1928," *Chicago Tribune,* November 15, 1953.
2. Interview with author, March 1993.
3. Richard Murrie, "The Story Behind a Hershey Bar" (senior thesis, Princeton University, 1939).
4. Forrest has acknowledged working at two Swiss chocolate factories. The specific factories were identified by a source close to him.
5. Hinkle manuscript, pp. 58–59.
6. Firsthand observation from tour of the Elizabethtown factory.
7. The Cadbury and Rowntree families have denied this claim.

    ⋮

CHAPTERS 6 AND 7: THE CANDY MAN AND SWEET DREAMS

The history of the Hershey company was drawn largely from materials at the Hershey Archives. I relied heavily upon two unpublished manuscripts that detailed Milton Hershey's boyhood and the development and management of the company between 1875 and 1950. Samuel Hinkle, former Hershey CEO, wrote his memoir of the company upon his retirement from the firm. The information contained therein was drawn directly from company documents and Hinkle's personal observations. The Wallace manuscript was written in 1955 by Paul Wallace, who was hired by the Hershey Trust to write an autobiography of Milton Hershey. Wallace had access to the records of the Hershey Chocolate Corp., the Hershey Estates and the Hershey Trust Co. He also relied heavily on the recollections of Hershey's friends.

To fill out the picture of Milton Hershey and his company, I also reviewed the oral history collection of the Archives and conducted dozens of my own interviews with Hershey residents and employees (past and present). I also read through one hundred years' worth of newspaper clippings about the company in *The New York Times, The Wall Street Journal, The Philadelphia Inquirer* and other newspapers. Other people closely associated with the company provided invaluable information, including members of the Murrie, Reese and Stover families. My portrait of M. S. Hershey would not have been complete without the additional insights provided by Hershey archivist Pam Whitenack.

There have been numerous books written about the history of chocolate, but the following were invaluable in the writing of this section: L. Russell Cook, *Chocolate Production and Use* (New York: Books for Industry, 1972); Marcia and Frederic Morton, *Chocolate: An Illustrated History* (New York: Crown Publishers, 1986); Allen M. Young, *The Chocolate Tree: A Natural History of Cacao* (Washington, D.C.: Smithsonian Institution Press, 1994); and Sophie D. Coe and Michael D. Coe, *The True History of Chocolate* (London: Thames and Hudson Ltd., 1996). Also helpful were A. W. Knapp, *The Cocoa and Chocolate Industry* (London: Sir I. Pitman & Sons, 1930); W. T. Clarke, *Literature of Cocoa;* and Richard Cadbury (Historicus, pseud.), *Cocoa: All About It* (London: Low, Marston, 1896).

1. Associated Press, "HMMMM: Sensuous M&M ad receives green light," April 27, 1998.

2. Information on the caffeine content of chocolate provided by the National Confectioners Association, which says that levels of caffeine range from 2 to 23 mg. in a 1.4-ounce bar of milk chocolate. A cup of coffee, by comparison, contains 150 to 200 mg.

3. Christine Chianese, "Briefer Madness," *The Sciences,* March/April 1997.

4. Carl Bergen, "Chocolate and Mood," *Popular Science,* September 1982.

5. "Backgrounder on Phenylethylamine," press release provided by the National Confectioners Association, Virginia, n.d.

6. Judith Stone, "Life-Styles of the Rich and Creamy," *Discover,* September 1988.

7. Suzanne Hamlin, "It's Hard to Ignore Cravings: Researchers Can't Resist," *The New York Times,* February 22, 1995.

8. Ibid.

9. Marcia and Frederic Morton, *Chocolate: An Illustrated History* (New York: Crown, 1986), p. 28.

CHAPTER 9: CHOCOLATE TOWN, U.S.A.

This chapter also draws heavily on the Hinkle and Wallace manuscripts, and on other materials found in the Hershey Archives. The description of the development of the Hershey flavor came from these sources and was further detailed in interviews with numerous industry sources. Several "chocolate experts" were particularly helpful, including Reg Olson,

Maurice Jeffery, Malcolm Blue, Allan Gibbons, Earl Allured and George Greener.

The account of how cocoa beans have changed over the centuries is drawn from interviews with industry experts and from Young's *The Chocolate Tree*. The discussion of the importance of "conching" is drawn from Cook's *Chocolate Production and Use* and from numerous chemists who specialize in the manufacture of chocolate.

1. Interview with author, January 1993.
2. Interview with author, April 1994.
3. James C. Young, "Hershey Unique Philanthropist," *The New York Times*, November 18, 1923.
4. Hinkle manuscript, p. 174.
5. Interviews with Mars sources.
6. Ibid.
7. Interview with author, May 1993.
8. This method of wrapping Kisses was told to me by various women who worked in the wrapping room in the early part of the century.
9. Workers were paid 10 cents for every 20 dozen Kisses wrapped, according to Pam Whitenack of the archives.

CHAPTER 10: BITTERSWEET

The description here of the Milton Hershey Industrial School (known today as the Milton Hershey School) is drawn from various sources, including the school's own literature and the school's newspaper, *The Spartan*. Mark Cohen's well-researched article in *The New York Times*, "Uncle Milty's Lost Kids," August 1, 1993, also informed my writing. Details on the founding of the orphanage came from the Murrie thesis and press reports in *The New York Times* and *The Philadelphia Inquirer*, in addition to the Wallace and Hinkle manuscripts.

The account of Hershey's activities in Cuba was informed by the Hinkle manuscript and by Joseph Richard Snavely's book, *An Intimate Story of. . . . M. S. Hershey* (Hershey: J. R. Snavely, 1957).

The account of the strike and Milton Hershey's later years were drawn from the oral history collection at the Hershey Archives, the Wallace and Hinkle manuscripts and various press reports.

1. Wallace manuscript, p. 122.
2. Kelly Corvese, Letter to the Editor, *The New York Times*, August 29, 1993.

3. Interview with author, April 1994.

4. *The New York Times,* July 21, 1984.

5. Hinkle manuscript, p. 346.

6. Ibid., p. 366.

7. Wallace manuscript, p. 325.

8. Interview with author, February 1994.

CHAPTER 11: M AND M

The account of Forrest Mars's "flares" is based on interviews with more than two dozen people who worked for him in the 1940s and 1950s, and confirmed in on-the-record interviews with David Brown and Hank Vogel.

The account of Bruce Murrie's relationship with Forrest was provided by Richard Murrie and other members of the Murrie family who asked not to be identified. Others close to Bruce Murrie also spoke about his years at M&M, including workers at the plant who remembered him.

The description of the meeting between Forrest Mars and William Murrie is based on interviews with the Murrie family and on interviews with people close to Forrest Mars. The dialogue recorded here was confirmed by Richard Murrie, based on his memories of his father's stories.

The account of the death of Milton Hershey and the subsequent reign of Percy A. Staples is based on press reports and materials from the Hershey Archives, particularly the Hinkle manuscript. Samuel Hinkle had firsthand knowledge of Staples, having worked for him directly.

Forrest's discovery of the parboiling method for Uncle Ben's rice and his founding of that company is based on interviews with Ed Stegemann, Phil Forster, Charles Kaufman and various Uncle Ben's executives.

The description of Mars's accounting methods comes from interviews with current Mars personnel.

The account of the breakup between Mars and Murrie is based on information obtained from sources intimately familiar with both parties.

1. From an interview with a close associate of Forrest Mars who recalled many of his early business philosophies.

2. Figures provided by Mars in 1992.

3. Figure for 1994, provided by source intimately familiar with M&M/Mars division.

The depiction of Chicago's central role in the candy industry is drawn from numerous sources, including interviews with industry old-timers Nat Sloan, Nello Ferrara, James Hanlon, Ellen Gordon, Dominic Antonellis, Edgar Goldenberg and others who asked to remain anonymous. Also helpful were industry experts Susan Tiffany, Ray Broekel, Susan Smith, Richard O'Connell, Larry Graham and Lisbeth Echeandia. Food historian Bruce Kraig contributed greatly to my understanding of the candy business's role in the city's economy and Broekel's *The Great American Candy Bar Book* provided invaluable information on the history of some of Chicago's early confectioners.

The account of Forrest Mars's takeover of the Chicago factory is based on interviews with more than a dozen people who worked at the plant at the time and on an article in *Fortune*, May 1967, that detailed the events leading up to Forrest's victory.

1. Commerce Department annual survey of the industry.

2. Ibid.

3. Tracy Poe, "Sweet Home Chicago: Candymakers Made City Their Capital," *Chicago Tribune*, July 16, 1997.

4. Louis Dombrowski, "Candy Makers Unspoiled by Sweet Smell of Success," *Chicago Tribune*, May 1, 1962.

5. The NCA moved its headquarters to northern Virginia in 1981.

6. "100th Anniversary of the National Confectioners Association," (NCA brochure), 1983.

7. Ibid.

8. Alan Gross, "Sweet Home Chicago!" *Chicago Magazine*, February 1988.

9. Poe, "Sweet Home Chicago."

10. Al Chase, "Standard Set by Mars Plant Built in 1928," *Chicago Tribune*, November 15, 1953.

11. "100th Anniversary of the National Confectioners Association."

12. Sources familiar with the history of M&M's.

13. Ibid.

14. Sources familiar with the memos.

15. Myron Banks, "Mars to Expand Factory," *Chicago Tribune*, April 6, 1958.

16. Elwood Berman, "Mars Embattled over Succession," *Chicago Tribune*, June 10, 1959.

17. Sources who witnessed the meeting.

The description of what happened after Forrest Mars took over the Chicago plant is based on interviews with more than two dozen people intimately familiar with the events that took place there between 1959 and 1969. Many of these sources witnessed firsthand how Forrest Mars set about changing the character of the plant and instituting his own unique formula for success. The specific account of how Forrest ran his businesses was confirmed in interviews with dozens of past and present Mars executives, including Ed Stegemann, David Brown, Charles Kaufman, V. J. Spitaleri, Phil Forster, Robin Pedler and others who asked to remain anonymous. I also drew on the profile of Forrest Mars, Sr., written by Don Gussow, publisher of *Candy Industry Magazine*. Gussow interviewed Forrest personally, and is the only journalist ever to do so. In tours of Mars facilities around the world, I witnessed how Forrest's principles are carried out today.

The account of Forrest Mars's breakup with Hershey was provided by sources close to Forrest and confirmed in on-the-record interviews with Hershey executives. Some Hershey executives acknowledged that the split was painful for Hershey while others denied that this was the case. The company was either unwilling or unable to provide data that would show the specific effect of the split on the bottom line. I calculated the result based on numbers provided to me by Mars sources and on information provided by Richard Murrie, who collected data on Hershey's coating business for his college thesis (see note 3 on page 330).

1. Forster retired from Mars in January 1998.
2. Murrie thesis.
3. Estimate provided by industry experts.
4. In recent years, the Mars siblings have taken out larger dividends, according to court papers filed in relation to Jackie Mars's divorce. Those papers show that in 1988, Forrest Jr. received a payment of $75 million. (That year, Forrest Jr. divorced his wife of more than thirty years, paying her a divorce settlement of $50 million, according to court papers.) Jackie Mars received a similar amount in 1990. But as a general practice, the siblings rarely tap the company's wealth.
5. Richard Ferguson, "At Mars, Sweet Success," *The Times* (London), May 8, 1953.

CHAPTER 14: THE CARETAKERS

The depiction of the Hershey sales force in the 1960s is based on extensive interviews with Larry Johns, Jack Dowd and Earl Spangler and on the oral history collection of the Hershey Archives. In addition, this chapter draws heavily on the Hinkle manuscript, which details events at Hershey through 1965.

The portrait of Percy Alexander Staples is based on numerous interviews with Hershey executives who knew of him or who worked for him, and on the Hinkle manuscript. Details of the rise and fall of the cocoa markets are provided by Hinkle, as is the account of Staples's obsession with cocoa bean prices. Hinkle himself wrote of the trip to Cadbury to investigate the purchase of Cadbury chocolate, and he detailed his own tenure as CEO of the company.

Details about the H. B. Reese Co. were obtained in interviews with members of the Reese family, and from the oral history collection of the Archives.

CHAPTER 15: MILTON'S BOY

The profiles of Mohler and Dearden provided here are based on interviews with dozens of Hershey sources and on materials from the Hershey Archives, including William Dearden's oral history, given September 29, 1989. Dearden declined to give a personal interview, citing his poor health. (He was diagnosed with Hodgkin's disease in the mid 1990s.) To provide a fuller picture of Dearden, I read numerous articles that have been written about him and found the following pieces to be particularly insightful: Jane Shoemaker, "How an Orphan Grew to Head Hershey Foods," *The Philadelphia Inquirer*, March 14, 1976; Charles Shaw, "Hershey School Grad Heads Hershey Corp.," *Lancaster Intelligencer Journal*, March 19, 1976; Salim Muwakkil, "Enthusiasm in the Executive Sweet," *Success Unlimited*, December 1980.

The description of Hershey's approach to marketing, sales and advertising is based on extensive interviews with Jack Dowd, Larry Johns, Earl Spangler, Richard Zimmerman and Dick Uhrich, and on the oral history collection of the Hershey Archives.

1. Shoemaker, "How an Orphan Grew to Head Hershey Foods."
2. Ibid.
3. Shaw, "Hershey School Grad Heads Hershey Corp."

4. Ibid.

5. Dearden's oral history, p. 3.

6. Shaw, "Hershey School Grad."

7. Ibid.

8. Dearden's oral history, p. 7.

9. Ibid., p. 8.

10. Ibid., p. 7.

11. "Record '60 Profit Indicated for Hershey Chocolate," *The Wall Street Journal,* December 28, 1960.

12. Interview with Dowd and confirmed with other sources.

CHAPTER 16: THE GREAT AMERICAN CHOCOLATE BAR

The account of Dearden's raid on Mars came from Dearden himself and was confirmed in interviews given to the Hershey Community Archives by Larry Johns and William Suhring.

The description of Hershey's venture into the world of advertising and the development of the company's first advertising campaigns was gathered in interviews with Jack Dowd, Larry Johns, Earl Spangler, Richard Zimmerman, Dick Uhrich and numerous other sources familiar with these events. Various executives from the advertising firm of Ogilvy & Mather spoke on condition of anonymity and confirmed the scenes depicted in this chapter.

1. Jack H. Morris, "Big Chocolate Maker, Beset by Profit Slide, Gets More Aggressive," *The Wall Street Journal,* February 18, 1970.

CHAPTER 17: HOT COCOA

The portrayal of Hershey's approach to the cocoa bean market is based on interviews with more than a dozen people familiar with the company's strategies, including cocoa traders, cocoa growers, cocoa brokers and Hershey executives who have participated in decisions to buy or sell cocoa options.

Information on Hershey bar prices and sizes was provided by the company.

The effect of Nixon's price controls on Hershey is based on information provided by Uhrich, Dearden, Zimmerman and Hinkle.

The description of the inner workings of the cocoa market was gathered from interviews with Hans Scheu and with various cocoa brokers and traders who asked to remain anonymous. Material for this chapter was also drawn from *Cocoa: A Trader's Guide* (Geneva: International Trade Centre UNCTAD/GATT, 1991) and *Fine or Flavor Cocoa: An Overview of World Production and Trade* (Geneva: International Trade Centre UNCTAD/GATT, 1987). I also visited the floor of the Coffee, Sugar & Cocoa Exchange, to witness trading firsthand. Additional information about the cocoa crop was drawn from Young's *The Chocolate Tree* and from Cook's *Chocolate Production and Use*. Scientists at the American Cocoa Research Institute were also very helpful in supplying information about the dangers to the cocoa crop from disease and pestilence, and on specific undertakings to help protect the crop in the future.

The account of Mars's cocoa purchases and approach to the market comes from numerous Mars sources, including those who have traded cocoa on Mars's behalf.

1. Though the press described the 1969 move as a price increase, Hershey officials took umbrage at that characterization. The company had been making both nickel and dime bars, and Mohler simply discontinued the nickel bar, making the ten-cent bar the standard.

2. Statistics provided by American Cocoa Research Institute.

3. Ibid.

4. The World Factbook: Côte d'Ivoire (http://cliffie.nosc.mil/~nawfb/factbook/iv=e.html).

5. *Cocoa: A Trader's Guide,* p. 133.

6. Hershey closed its Hummingbird Hershey research facility in 1988.

7. Susan Tiffany, "CI Conversations," *Candy Industry Magazine,* April 1997.

8. James Brooke, "Where Cocoa Was King, the Weeds Take Over," *The New York Times,* August 23, 1995.

9. Susan Tiffany, "CI Conversations."

10. Statistics provided by Chocolate Manufacturers Association.

11. *Cocoa: A Trader's Guide,* p. 27.

12. Jay Peterzell, "No Bars for Mars at the CIA?," *The Nation,* September 14, 1985.

CHAPTER 18: MARS ATTACKS

The account of Forrest Mars's relationship with his three children is based on numerous interviews with people close to the family, including relatives who asked to remain anonymous and Jackie Mars's ex-husband Hank Vogel. I also drew on two profiles that have been written about the company, the *Regardie's Magazine* piece by Ronald Kessler and an article in *Fortune* magazine by Bill Saporito, "Uncovering Mars' Unknown Empire," September 26, 1988. Numerous Mars employees also talked about the Mars family relationships and their effect on the business, including David Brown, Al Poe, George Greener, Phil Forster, Ed Stegemann, Robin Pedler and more than a dozen others who asked to remain anonymous. The brothers themselves declined to talk about their relationship with their father. They did, however, provide details of their rise through the corporate ranks.

The depiction of John and Forrest Jr.'s management styles is based on interviews with more than fifty Mars associates, from those on the production lines to those in the headquarters at McLean. The descriptions provided were remarkably consistent, and each anecdote included here was confirmed by at least two independent sources.

1. Hinkle manuscript, p. 122.

2. Ibid., p. 149.

3. Andrew L. Waterhouse, Joseph R. Shirley and Jennifer L. Donovan, "Antioxidants in Chocolate [Letter]," *Lancet,* September 21, 1996.

4. Matt Kramer, "Lift a Wineglass to Toast Chocolate's Myriad Charms," *Portland Oregonian,* January 12, 1997.

5. Brochure published by the NCA in 1982.

6. James Gavin, "Candy Industry Outlook Bright," *Chicago Tribune,* December 6, 1966.

7. Survey in *Confectioner* magazine, March/April 1995.

8. "Mars Agrees to Soften Ads for Milky Way Bars," *The Wall Street Journal,* August 26, 1970.

9. Barry Meier, "Dubious Theory: Chocolate a Cavity Fighter," *The New York Times,* April 15, 1992.

10. "Dental Center Financed by Mars Settles Lawsuit," *The New York Times,* June 4, 1993.

11. David Owen, "Seeing Red," *Atlantic Monthly,* October 1988.

12. Copy of a 1988 speech to business students at Duke University.

13. After extensive internal debate, the company agreed to provide a photo of Forrest Mars, Sr., for this book.

The account of William Dearden's tenure as CEO is based on extensive interviews with Richard Zimmerman, Dick Uhrich, Earl Spangler, Larry Johns, Jack Dowd and Pamela Cassidy. Dearden's oral history also contributed to my understanding of him, as did numerous published articles. Dearden's move toward strategic planning, his approach to acquisitions, his reorganization of the company into Hershey Foods Corp. and his effort to diversify the corporation were all discussed at length with more than a dozen past and present Hershey employees.

The account of the changing nature of the relationship between the company and the town is based largely on the oral history collection of the Hershey Archives and on numerous interviews with Hershey residents. I also drew upon Bill Ecenbarger's piece in *The Philadelphia Inquirer Magazine* entitled "Semi-Sweet Times in Chocolate Town," published August 22, 1982.

1. Salim Muwakkil, "Enthusiasm in the Executive Sweet," *Success Unlimited,* December 1980.

2. Ibid.

3. Dearden's oral history, p. 29.

4. Ibid.

5. William Dearden, "Strategic Planning Should Be a Top Management Team Effort," *Progressive Grocer,* November 1983.

6. Muwakkil, "Enthusiasm."

7. "Hershey to Buy 40.5% of Friendly Ice Cream Corp.," *The Wall Street Journal,* December 27, 1978.

8. Muwakkil, "Enthusiasm."

9. Bill Ecenbarger, "Semi-Sweet Times in Chocolate Town," *The Philadelphia Inquirer Magazine,* August 22, 1982.

10. Dearden's oral history, p. 34.

11. Ecenbarger, "Semi-Sweet Times."

12. Ibid.

CHAPTER 20: NICE PEOPLE DON'T EAT CHOCOLATE

The description of the revolution in chocolate during the 1980s comes from numerous sources in the industry, including Elaine Gonzalez, Malcolm Blue, Al Pechenik, Barbara Albright, Michel Guerard, Richard O'Connell, Alice Medrich and Milton Zelman. I also drew on numerous published articles that documented America's growing chocolate obsession, including *Newsweek*'s 1983 story "America's Chocolate Binge," and *People* magazine's 1982 story "The Sweetest Game in Town." Both articles provided invaluable information on chocolate's evolution from drugstore window to chic boutique.

The account of the development of new products is based on dozens of interviews with candy industry insiders, including scientists and chemists from Hershey and Mars. The specific story of the development of Reese's Pieces and its inclusion in the Steven Spielberg movie *E.T.* came from interviews with Jack Dowd, Larry Johns, Earl Spangler, Richard Zimmerman and several Mars sources who asked not to be identified.

The discussion of Mars's approach to new-product launches is based on interviews with past and present Mars associates, and on interviews with John Mars, Ed Stegemann and Phil Forster.

1. Pechenik stepped down as president in 1983.
2. "America's Chocolate Binge," *Newsweek*, April 4, 1983.
3. Despite this finding, Mohler ordered production of chocolate-covered raisins, a Hershey product that was very short-lived.
4. "Life Is Sweet for Jack Dowd," *People*, July 26, 1982.
5. N. R. Kleinfeld, "Hershey Bites Off New Markets," *The New York Times*, July 22, 1984.

CHAPTER 21: A CHOCOLATE-COVERED WORLD

The discussion of Mars's overseas expansion is based on personal observation and on interviews with David Badger, Ed Stegemann, Phil Forster, John Mars, Robin Pedler, Theo Leenders and Mike Davies. I toured Mars facilities throughout Europe and personally witnessed Mars's unique approach to global marketing. I also saw firsthand the groundbreaking events in Prague and spoke at length with David Badger about Mars's strategies in Eastern Europe and the former Soviet Union. Badger provided many of the figures pertaining to Mars's activities in these regions.

Information on Nestlé and Kraft Jacobs Suchard came from published articles and interviews with past and present employees. In addition, I interviewed Nestlé chairman Helmut Maucher at length about his approach to management and his visions for Nestlé in the future.

The discussion of Hershey's failures overseas is based on interviews with Richard Zimmerman, Kenneth Wolfe, Jay Carr, Louis Smith and other Hershey employees. Maurice Jeffery, Elaine Gonzalez, Lisbeth Echeandia and other industry experts contributed to my understanding of Hershey's troubles abroad.

1. Badger interview, January 1998.
2. Ibid.
3. Video made for family's personal archives.
4. Figures provided by Mars and based on data collected by A. C. Nielsen.
5. Dow Jones Newswires, "Nestle's Sales Surged 16 percent Last Year to $46.7 Billion," *The Wall Street Journal Europe,* January 22, 1998.
6. Interview with author, March 1992.
7. John Thornhill, "Sweet Taste of Success," *Financial Times,* January 3, 1998.
8. Speech to industry given at World Cocoa Congress, February 1996.
9. "Nestlé Shares Surge," *Confectioner* magazine, June 1990.
10. "Kraft Jacobs Suchard Takes Bite Out of Market," *Financial Times,* September 21, 1992.
11. Hershey 1997 annual report.
12. Chad A. Dorn, "China: A Boom Market for Confectioners," *Candy Industry Magazine,* November, 1, 1996.
13. Ibid.

CHAPTER 22: RAISING THE BAR

The account of Richard Zimmerman's tenure as CEO comes from lengthy interviews with Zimmerman himself and with numerous Hershey executives who worked closely with him.

The discussion of Mars's attempt to win back the lead from Hershey in 1989 and 1990 is based on personal observation and lengthy interviews with executives from M&M/Mars in Hackettstown, including Al Poe, William Hellegas, Mike Murphy and Hans Fiuczynski.

The account of the making of Hugs is based on interviews with Dennis Eshleman, Jay Carr, Joseph Viviano and Todd Johnson.

1. Dearden's oral history, p. 39.
2. Ibid., p. 38.
3. Ibid., p. 39.
4. Figure provided by Mars.
5. Based on annual confectionery survey published by *Confectioner* magazine.
6. Ibid.

7. "Forrest Still in the Woods," *Delaney Report,* December 1, 1997.
8. Noreen O'Leary, "New Life on Mars," *Brandweek,* May 6, 1996.
9. *Delaney Report.*

CHAPTER 23: CORPORATE CANDY

The account of Forrest Mars's meeting with Helmut Maucher was provided by Hank Vogel, who accompanied Forrest Sr. on the trip. Information about the next generation of the Mars family is based on interviews with people close to the family and former Mars executives. The account of Forrest Mars in Las Vegas is based on interviews with employees at Ethel M.

1. Data provided by the National Confectioners Association.
2. Ibid.
3. The Delaney Report Quarterly Awards, March 21 and October 3, 1994.

ACKNOWLEDGMENTS

This book would not have been possible without the cooperation of the men and women who work inside the nation's candy factories. I am eternally grateful for your help, your insights and your patience. Over the course of nine years, I have spoken to hundreds of you, and while many of you asked not to be mentioned by name, please know that I am indebted to you for breaking your code of silence. To those of you who contributed on the record, I am even more grateful. You lent credibility to this story and risked your own reputations in talking with me.

I cannot begin to name everyone who helped me in this venture—I owe thanks to far too many. But there are a few people I must mention specifically, for without their efforts, this story would never have been written. I must first thank the Mars family and Ed Stegemann for agreeing to open their world to me and letting me document what I saw. I believe I lived up to my original promise: to write a fair, thorough and accurate account of the Mars business. I know it is hard to be judged by an outsider, and I am certain my perceptions of your business differ from your own, but I did my best to write a balanced appraisal and to respect the personal privacy that you value so highly. I must also thank Sue Vogelsinger and Barbara Parker for their tireless efforts on my behalf and for never wavering as my advocates. And I would especially like to thank Phil Forster, Robin Pedler, David Badger, Hans Fiuczynski, Al Poe, David Brown, Charles Kaufman, John Strong, Theo Leenders, Hank Vogel, Mike Murphy and George Greener for permitting me to take up so much of their time. As for the countless other Mars executives who spoke to me, you know who you are and I thank you.

In the Hershey organization, there are many who devoted their memories to this book and who believed that this project was worthwhile. Foremost among them are Richard Zimmerman, Monroe Stover,

Dick Uhrich, Larry Johns, Jack Dowd, Richard Murrie, Earl Spangler, Peter Shearer, Rose Gasper, Lawrence Pellegrini, Elwood Meyers, Jean Ranerio, Philomena Castelli and Mary Pearson. I would like to extend a special thanks to Pam Whitenack and the Hershey Community Archives for enduring my endless queries and providing invaluable details about Milton Hershey's legacy. Without Pam and her vast store of knowledge, this story could never have been brought to life. And I would also like to thank John Long, Kenneth Wolfe and those people in Hershey Foods Corp., who cooperated with me and made this project possible. To the residents of Hershey, Pennsylvania, who gave me so much of their time and who opened their homes and their lives to me, I also thank you.

Others in the candy industry who offered generously of their knowledge include Lisbeth Echeandia and her husband, Jim, both of *Confectioner* magazine; Susan Tiffany and Patricia Magee of *Candy Industry Magazine;* Larry Graham, Susan Smith, Steve Lodge and William Sheehan of the National Confectioners Association; Ray Broekel, whose candy bar books and newsletters were of tremendous value; James Hanlon, Philip Heide, Nat Sloane, Dominic Antonellis, Nello Ferrara, Ellen Gordon, Mindy Goldenberg, Joseph Blommer, Paul Brock, Spaulding Goetze, Jack Zachary, Arnie Jellison, Michael Rogak, Elaine Gonzalez and Maurice Jeffery. Thank you all for sharing so generously.

I would also like to thank my editors at *The Washington Post,* particularly Peter Behr, David Vise, Leonard Downey, Robert Kaiser, Linton Weeks and Bob Thompson, who believed in this project and who gave me the time and support to finish it. I am also forever indebted to my editor at Random House, Jon Karp. Jon was a tireless support and a brilliant editor who always understood the scope and depth of what I was trying to accomplish. I would also like to thank Ann Godoff, Harold Evans and Cathy Hemming for their support and enthusiasm. Others at Random House who helped me complete this project: Beth Pearson, production editor; Nora Reichard, copy editor; Barbara Bachman, designer; Andy Carpenter, art director; Sally Marvin, publicist; and Leah Weatherspoon, serial rights manager. To all of you, I owe a great debt.

Finally, on a more personal note, I would like to thank my friends, my parents, my grandmother Norwitz and my extended family for their patience and understanding during the years it took me to finish this project. I could never have done it without you, and I thank you for believing in me when I could not believe in myself. I am forever indebted to Marcy Heidish and Joan Matheiu, writers who gave me wisdom and courage when I needed it most. And to Kelly McDevitt,

Diane Mattinly, Amy Wahl, Diane Bozeman and Courtney Navarro, I thank you for your research assistance, your time and your patience. To Brad McKee, Brad Risinger, Elisabeth Sperling, Ruth Farber and Rick Horowitz, I would like to say thank you for reading the manuscript and giving me your criticisms. You are true friends.

And most of all, I have to thank my husband, Marshall, to whom I owe a particular debt of gratitude. You read and reread the manuscript, offering invaluable wisdom and editing; you took care of our daughter when I was working eighteen-hour days; and for some reason, you never stopped saying "I love you."

Finally, to my grandfather David Norwitz, I want to say a special thanks for taking me to the candy store every Saturday when I was child, and for giving me the countless personal memories that helped inform my writing.

ILLUSTRATION CREDITS

THE ILLUSTRATIONS AND PHOTOGRAPHS IN THIS BOOK ARE
REPRINTED COURTESY OF THE FOLLOWING:

pages ii (top and bottom), 71, 76, 80, 81, 83, 86, 87, 103,
106, 110, 115, 119, 123, 127, 128, 131, 133, 139, 141,
150, 195, 200, 207, 219, 236, 250, 253, 259, 273:
Hershey Community Archives.

pages ii (left), 33, 43, 45, 49, 147, 163, 179, 184 (top and
bottom), 281, 283, 285, 295, 302, 305: Author's collection.

pages iii, 27, 269: Hershey Foods Corp.

page 19: *Chocolate Fantasy* watercolor by Patrick D. Clark;
courtesy of Patrick D. Clark.

page 62: *Brockhaus's Encyclopedia.*

page 91: Portrait by Jean Baptiste A. Gautier-D'Agoty;
courtesy of the Sterling and Francine Clark Art Institute,
Williamstown, Massachusetts.

page 99: The Museum of London.

pages 171 (left and right), 227, 243, 252: National
Confectioners Association.

page 299: *The Newsstand* © 1985 Ken Keeley. All rights
reserved, Cue Bee Publishing.

page 313: Photo by Michael Macioce.

INDEX

Bunte Brothers, 168
Burnett, Leo, 157
Bush, George, 8
Butterfinger bar, 170, 293, 315
Byrd, Adm. Richard, 10

C

cacao trade:
 and colonization, 98–101, 235,
  237–38
 and commodity pricing, 232–41
cacao trees, 92, 227, 232–37, 241
Cadbury Brothers Ltd., 65, 66
 in Asia, 298
 and conservation studies, 234
 and Hershey, 25, 39, 295
 and Mars, 181
 and Peter Paul, 25
 in Russia, 293
Cadbury, Dominic, 293
Cadbury Dairy Milk Bar, 65, 66, 102,
 110, 203
Cadbury family, 65, 69
Cadbury Schweppes, 39, 293, 300
caffeine, 96
candy:
 adulterated, 166
 generic, 166
 grazing of, 46
 as impulse purchase, 31–32
 individually wrapped, 8, 30
 ingredients in, 50, 251
 liqueur-filled, 324
 medicated, 77, 78, 290
 mood-altering chemicals in, 95–98
 nonchocolate, 316–17
 nostalgia for, 19–20, 25
 and nutrition, 96, 250–51
 perishable nature of, 51, 272
 recipes for, 27
 temperature of, 50
 and weather, 50
candy bars:
 first, 50, 169–70
 global markets for, 289
 and military, 169–70, 171
 names of, 170–71; see also specific names
 size and price of, 228–30, 268

candy corn, 165
candy industry:
 added value in, 156
 advertising by, 243, 252
 in Chicago, 163–77
 and commodity pricing, 231–42
 competition in, see competition
 confidentiality agreements in, 28, 62
 consolidation in, 28–31, 168, 318–21
 control of, 20, 24–25
 espionage in, 62–63, 169, 241
 family-owned firms in, 21, 28–29
 global, 25, 263, 283–98
 government regulation of, 20, 30, 168,
  262, 300
 growth of, 163
 joint ventures in, 181, 263, 291
 licensing agreements in, 271, 273, 291,
  320
 lobbying by, 253–54
 local products in, 54
 marketing in, see marketing
 national distribution in, 109–10
 national tastes in, 63, 65, 66, 102, 113,
  296
 new products introduced in, see new
  products
 niche companies in, 28, 318
 secretiveness in, 20–29, 30, 36, 121,
  169, 179–80
 self-regulation in, 180
 sugar scare in, 249–55, 280
 trends in, 26, 249, 316–17, 320
 at turn of century, 50–51
 see also chocolate business
capsid bug, 233
caramels:
 chocolate coating for, 86
 Hershey's Crystal "A," 79, 316
 invention of, 26
 Lancaster Caramel Co., 79–80, 81, 83,
  87–88, 105
 milk-based, 78, 102
 paraffin in, 78
Carletti, Antonio, 94
Carmody, John, 158, 160
Carr, Jay, 296
Carrier, Willis, 11
Casey, William, 242

Castelli, Philomena, 9, 265
Central Hershey, Cuba, 137–38
Chappel Bros., 67
Chappie pet food, 67
Charles I, king of Spain, 93
Charleston Chew!, 29, 171
Charlie and the Chocolate Factory
    (Dahl), 61–62
Charms Co., 29
chewing gum, 167, 316
Chicago, candy industry in, 163–77
chocoholics, 95
chocolate, 91–102
  and acne, 24
  baking, 86
  chemical components of, 64, 95–96,
    97, 250–51
  at Columbian Exposition, 85, 88
  consistency in, 120
  detractors of, 98, 249–55
  FDA standards for, 16
  flavor variables of, 119, 121
  global market for, 91
  in history, 91–94, 98–101
  as love potion, 94–95, 97, 98
  as luxury product, 74, 91, 99, 269–271
  medicinal properties of, 94, 95, 100
  melting point of, 8, 10–11, 12, 16
  milk, *see* milk chocolate
  molecular structure of, 92
  as mood enhancer, 95–98
  "mouthfeel" of, 13, 16
  non-melting, 10, 12, 15, 16, 46
  and nutrition, 250–51
  organic products of, 237
  professional tasters of, 63–64
  "refreshing," 46
  "subsistence," 8
  unsweetened, 86
  white, 309
chocolate business:
  and commodity pricing, 231–42
  competition in, *see* competition
  early years of, 87
  growing business of, 105
  national distribution in, 109–10
  see also candy industry
chocolate liquor:
  beans ground into, 85, 121

milk added to, 102
and milk-chocolate crumb, 101
research on, 12
in secret processes, 27
Chocolate Manufacturers Association,
    24, 235, 250
chocolate pots, 93–94, 100
chocolates, boxed, 30, 270–71
chocolate wars, *see* competition
CIA, and cocoa trade, 241–42
cigarettes, cocoa added to, 122
Clark bar, 30
Cloud Nine, 237
Coca-Cola Co., 22, 96, 138
cocoa, 100–101
  production of, 121–22, 231–38
  as raw material, 119
  for tobacco companies, 122
  unsweetened, 86
  wartime supplies of, 152, 153
cocoa beans:
  crossbred, 120
  as currency, 93
  fermentation of, 237
  ground into paste, 100
  in history, 92–94
  in manufacturing process, 63
  "perfect," search for, 120–21
  perfumes of, 120
  prices of, 199–200, 228, 231–42, 247,
    260
  research on, 12, 120–21, 233–35, 237
  as revenue source, 98–99
  roasting of, 118–19
  secret varieties of, 27, 120,121
  shells of, 118–19, 143
cocoa butter:
  fat content of, 91–92, 101
  flavorists and, 64
  melting of, 11
  and milk chocolate, 101, 104–5, 124
  molecular structure of, 12
  removal of, 100–101, 121
  research on, 11–13, 250
  soap from, 144–46
  substitutes for, 10–11, 186
  in white chocolate, 309
Cocoa Inn, 265–66
Cocoa Merchants Association, 238, 296

Great Britain (*cont.*)
  peanut butter unpopular in, 39
  taxes in, 69
Greener, George, 62–63
Greenly, Steve, 193
Gubor Schokoladen, 297
Guittard, Etienne, 74
Gulf War, 4–8, 10, 13–18
gummy candies, 26, 316

H

Haley, Mark, 51
Hanlon, James, 318
Harris, George, 47
Harrison, Rex, 117
hazelnuts, 39–40, 281
Heath bar, 25–26, 30, 31, 316
Heide family, 31, 315–16
Hennessy, Sharon, 280
Henry Heide Candies, Inc., 31, 315–16
Herr, Henry, 107
Hershey, Catharine Sweeney (Kitty), 72,
  81–82, 83
  and Fanny, 81, 87
  illness and death of, 134, 137
  marriage of, 81
  married life of Milton and, 82, 84,
  105
  and Milton's philanthropy, 133
  residences of, 106, 259, 267, 317–18
Hershey, Ezra, 154
Hershey, Fanny, 104
  death of, 138
  and Henry, 74–76, 79, 82, 87, 129
  and Kitty, 80–81, 87
  and Milton's business, 77, 78–79, 80,
  84, 87, 129
Hershey, Henry, 74–78
  death of, 129
  as entrepreneur, 75, 76, 77–78, 89
  and Fanny, 74–76, 79, 82, 87, 129
  and Milton, 76–78
Hershey, Milton S., 71–82
  birth of, 74
  business disliked by, 83, 87, 131, 137,
  142, 247
  as candy maker, 72–73, 76–79, 84,
  86–87, 102, 104, 121

childhood of, 75–78
chocolate discovered by, 84–85
death of, 153–55, 197–98, 214
early years of, 54, 71
as entrepreneur, 73, 78, 83, 89,
  109–10, 131, 158, 239
experiments of, 142–46
and Henry, 76–78
and Hershey bar, 50, 108–9, 228
and Hershey model town, 105–8,
  113–17, 137, 198, 265, 266
and Kitty, *see* Hershey, Catharine
  Sweeney
and Lancaster Caramel Co., 79–80, 81,
  83, 87–88
later years of, 71–72
legacy of, 23, 260
manufacturing process of, 63, 64–65,
  201
marriage of, 81
mental breakdown of, 78
and milk chocolate, 61, 74, 90, 102,
  103–5, 108–13, 158, 251
and William Murrie, 47, 72, 73,
  154–55
and orphan boys, *see* Hershey Industrial
  School
paternalism of, 116–17, 140, 299
personality of, 73, 132
philanthropy of, 113–14, 117, 132–33,
  134–37, 139, 197, 260
retirement plans of, 88–89
travels of, 80, 81, 82, 84, 138, 140
utopian dreams of, 89–90, 267
Hershey, Pennsylvania, 103, 131–32
aroma in, 124–25
and Communist Party, 140–42
community center in, 267
construction of, 105–8
development of, 113–17
early plans for, 89–90
and Great Depression, 138–40
and Hershey Estates, 137
and Hershey's death, 153–54, 197–98
rift between company and, 264–67
Hershey, Serena, 75–76
Hershey Agricultural School, Cuba, 138
Hershey Almond bar, 113, 174, 224,
  296, 308

O

O'Connell, Richard, 24–25, 26
Ogilvy & Mather, 223–25
Oh Henry!, 30, 170
Olympics sponsorship, 253, 291
Opal Fruits, 26
Operation Desert Shield, 8
Orlosky, Ron, 124, 310

P

Parker, Barbara, 36
Parker, Steven, 321
PayDay, 30, 31, 316, 319
PB Max, 39, 303, 311
peanut brittle, 26
peanut butter, 39, 273
Peanut Butter M&M's, 311–12
Pearson candy, 293
Pecan Pete, 29
Pechenik, Al, 269–70
Pedigree, 35, 192, 302
Pellegrini, Lawrence, 118, 125
Pennsylvania State University, 264–265
penny candy, 19–20, 165, 204
Pentagon, *see* military, U.S.
penuche, 274
peppermint sticks, 51
Peritz, Dick, Sr., 168
Perugina chocolates, 292
Peter, Daniel, 61, 101
Peter Paul/Cadbury, 25, 32, 300
pet food industry, 35, 67, 173, 187–88, 245, 292, 301–3
Petfoods Ltd., 67
PEZ Candy, Inc., 21–22
phenylalanine, 95–96
phenylethylamine (PEA), 96
Philadelphia and Reading Railroad, 108
Philip Morris, 292, 293, 296, 297
Phillippy, Howard, 47, 122
Pingitore, Tony, 275, 277
Piomelli, Daniele, 96
Planter's chocolate-covered peanuts, 321
Poe, Alfred, 39, 301–7, 311

Pratt, Collin, 69, 191
pretzels, 35
Procino-Rossi Corp., 262
Pullman, George, 89

Q

Quetzalcoatl, 92

R

Ranerio, Jean, 126–27, 128
Rapunzel, 237
Ration D, 8–11, 153, 201
Ration K, 153
Rawley, John, 212, 214–15, 217, 219, 262
Red Hots, 50, 164, 320
Reese, Harry Burnett, 204–5
Reese family, 204–5, 321
Reese's Peanut Butter Cups, 204
  acquisition of, 271
  ingredients of, 121, 296
  marketing of, 224–25
  popularity of, 32, 224, 275, 303
  production of, 195
Reese's Pieces, 48, 113, 280
  E.T. and, 273–78
  and lawsuit, 311–12
Reeves, Rosser, 172
Reynolds & Co., 148–49, 150
Rhyne, Kathie, 309–10
rice industry, 35, 156–58, 173
Riker Electric automobile, 85–86
RJR Nabisco, 293, 300
Rogers, Roy, 117
Rolling Stones, 303
Rose, T. G., 68, 158
Rowntree & Co., 47, 65, 69
  chocolate flavor of, 203
  and Hershey, 271, 272–73
  international sales of, 110
  and Nestlé, 292, 293
Rowntree Mackintosh PLC, 113
Royer, Joseph R., 76–77
Royer's Ice Cream Parlor and Garden, 77
Rueckheim brothers, 166–67
Russell Stover Candies, Inc., 30

Russia:
  Cadbury in, 293
  Mars in, 35, 283–86, 287, 294, 295

S

Saatchi, Maurice, 313
San Giorgio Pasta Co., 262
Scheu, Hans, 111, 235–36, 238, 296, 297
Schlang, Elliott, 29
Schmalback, John, 109
Schnering, Otto, 170
Schreckengaust, Samuel, Jr., 205
serotonin, 96, 97
Sharir, Omar (pseud.), 3–6, 14
Shearer, Patty, 266
Sheba, 35
Sheehan, William, 24, 26
Shelton, Robert J., 312
Sifers, Russell, 28
Skinner Macaroni Co., 262
Skittles, 44, 303, 317
Skor bar, 25–26
Slo Pokes, 164
Smile-a-While, 29
Smith, Lee, 223
Smith, Louis C., 112, 297
Smith, Susan, 234
snacks industry, 41
Snavely, Frank, 88
Snavely, Martha, 77, 79, 84
Snickers, 186, 253
  in global markets, 14–15, 35, 282, 286, 290, 291, 295
  Hershey's chocolate in, 9, 59
  invention of, 57–58
  line extensions of, 303, 311
  success of, 174, 279, 303, 313, 314
So Big, 66
Somborn, Charles, 278
Spain, chocolate in, 93–94, 98–101, 120
Spangler, Earl:
  on E.T., 276–77
  on Hershey management, 203, 261, 263
  on Hershey taste, 111–12, 113

on related businesses, 58, 122, 182, 268
Spanish Civil War, 46, 69
Speicer, Gus, 144
Sperlari, Srl., 297
spices, in milk chocolate, 124
Spielberg, Steven, 276, 320
Spitaleri, Vito, 258
Staples, Eliza, 198
Staples, Percy A., 154, 155, 198–201, 203
Starbar, 29
Starburst Fruit Chews, 26, 44, 280, 302, 303, 317
Starlight mints, 30
Stegemann, Edward J., 34
  on global markets, 288
  and Gulf War, 4–6
  on Mars family, 40, 42–43, 246–47, 256, 258, 280, 306, 322–23
  and military contract, 17
  and public relations, 35, 36, 47, 306
Storck GMBH, 40
Stover, Monroe, 114, 125, 140, 198, 203, 267
Strong, John, 248, 278–79, 313
Stubbe, Henry, 97–98
sugar:
  from Cuba, 137, 138
  and health scare, 249–55, 280
  in milk chocolate, 104, 109, 124
  price of, 228, 231, 239, 260–61
  wartime supplies of, 137, 152, 239
Sugar Babies, 29
Sugar Daddy, 29
Suhring, William, 193–94, 220–23, 225, 230–31, 261–62, 263
Sulka & Co., 56
Summit bar, 280
Sun-Maid chocolate-covered raisins, 321
Swiss General Chocolate Co., 101
Switzerland:
  candy makers in, 61, 63, 65
  chocolate introduced in, 94
  chocolate taste in, 63, 102
  research performed in, 12–13
Symphony chocolates, 296

T

Tancredi, Samuel, 216–17
tea, introduction of, 93
Ted Bates & Co., 172–73
Tessier, Vern, 212, 214, 217
THC (tetrahydrocannabinol), 96
theobromine, 96
3 Musketeers, 58, 59, 174, 186, 303
Tietelbaum, Leonard, 318
Tiffany, Susan, 164
tobacco, cocoa used in, 122
Tobler, Jean, 61
Toblerone, 61, 102, 110, 293
Toffifay, 40
Tootsie Roll Industries, Inc., 20, 29,
  164, 315, 321
trimethylamine, 64
Trout Brook Fruit and Nursery Farm,
  75
Twix bar, 280, 303
Twizzlers, 316, 317

U

Uhrich, Richard, 154, 216, 229–30,
  240
Uncle Ben's rice, 35, 157–58, 173,
  188
United Kingdom, see Great Britain
United States:
  candy market in, 159–60
  chocolate taste in, 113
  mature market in, 298
  wage and price controls in, 229–30
Universal Studios, 275–77

V

Valomilk, 28
Vance, Duke, 68, 193, 220, 222
Van Houten, Coenraad, 100–101,
  293
vanilla, vanillin, 64, 186
Victorian Butter Creams, 52, 54
Victory Whip, 144
Viviano, Joseph, 22, 307
Vogel, Hank, 322–23

Vogelsinger, Sue, 36
Von Moos, Roland, 287–88

W

Wadsworth, James, 94–95
Walgreen Co., 168, 321
Walt Disney Co., 303–4, 320
war:
  candy contracts in, 8–10, 294
  chocolate as necessity in, 7–8
  non-melting chocolate for, 46
  rationing in, 137, 143, 152, 204
  see also military, U.S.; specific wars
Ward, John, 321
Ward, Louis L., 30
Ward, Scott, 30
Ward, Thomas, 30
Warner-Lambert, 29
Washington Post, The, 17–18, 24, 36,
  251
Waterhouse, Andrew, 251
Waterhouse, Debra, 97
Whiskas, 35, 302
Whiteman, Arthur, 154
Whitenack, Pamela, 9, 23–24
Whitman, Arthur, 137
Whitman, Stephen F., 30
Whitman Chocolates, 30
Whitman's Sampler, 30
Whiz bar, 29
Whoppers, 31, 316
Why Women Need Chocolate (Water-
  house), 97
Williamson, George, 170
witches'-broom, 233, 234
Wolfe, Kenneth, 137, 297, 317–18, 319
World Cup, 253, 291
World War I, 8, 137, 138, 167, 169,
  239
World War II:
  Britain and, 69
  candy industry and, 171
  Hershey and, 8–10, 143–44, 152, 153,
    199, 239, 294
  Mars and, 46, 152, 156
Wrigley, William Jr., 167
Wunderbeans, 31, 316, 317

X

Xylifresh gum, 316

Y

Y&S Candies, 263
York Peppermint Patties, 25, 300

Z

Zagnut, 30
Ziegfeld Follies, 117
Zimmerman, Richard A., 223

on coating business, 182
on competition, 280, 294, 298, 301, 307
on confidentiality, 22, 27, 111, 121
on Dearden, 211
and Desert Bar, 10
on espionage, 62
and Hershey management, 261, 263, 300–301, 317
on Hershey Trust and school, 136
on manufacturing processes, 111, 112
and military contracts, 15, 18
and public relations, 23
on Staples, 198

About the Author

JOËL GLENN BRENNER began reporting on the candy business in 1989. She is the first and only journalist ever to gain access to the Mars company, and her *Washington Post Magazine* cover story on Mars won numerous prizes. She was recognized five times by the *Financial News Journalism Reporter* as one of the best financial journalists in the nation under the age of thirty. She is a 1989 graduate of the University of Missouri at Columbia. She lives in New York with her husband, Marshall Tracht, and their daughter, Danya. She can be reached at www.JoelGlennBrenner.com.

ABOUT THE TYPE

This book was set in Galliard, a typeface designed by Matthew Carter for the Mergenthaler Linotype Company in 1978. Galliard is based on the sixteenth-century typefaces of Robert Granjon, which give it classic lines yet interject a contemporary look.

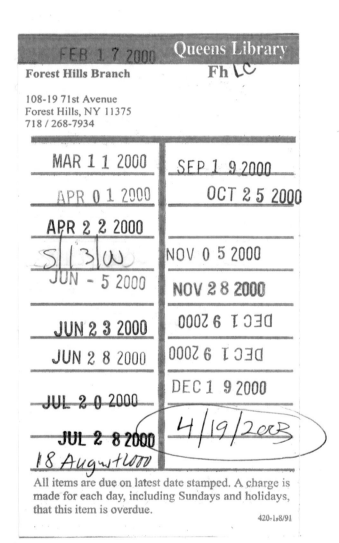